Alvin C
Christmas 2012

Joseph Smith

THE PROPHET & SEER

Joseph Smith
THE PROPHET & SEER

Edited by

RICHARD NEITZEL HOLZAPFEL
AND KENT P. JACKSON

RELIGIOUS STUDIES CENTER
BRIGHAM YOUNG UNIVERSITY

Cover illustration by Johann Schroder, painting of Nauvoo, Illinois, oil on tin, 1859, © Intellectual Reserve, Inc. Courtesy of Church History Museum.

Frontispiece by Lewis A. Ramsey, *Joseph Smith Jr.* Courtesy of Church History Museum.

Published by the Religious Studies Center, Brigham Young University, Provo, Utah
http://rsc.byu.edu

© 2010 by Brigham Young University. All rights reserved

Printed in the United States of America by Sheridan Books, Inc.

Any uses of this material beyond those allowed by the exemptions in U.S. copyright law, such as section 107, "Fair Use," and section 108, "Library Copying," require the written permission of the publisher, Religious Studies Center, 167 HGB, Brigham Young University, Provo, Utah 84602. The views expressed herein are the responsibility of the authors and do not necessarily represent the position of Brigham Young University or the Religious Studies Center.

Price: USD $29.99

Library of Congress Cataloging-in-Publication Data

Joseph Smith, the prophet & seer / edited by Richard Neitzel Holzapfel and Kent P. Jackson.
    p. cm.
  Includes bibliographical references and index.
  ISBN 978-0-8425-2753-8 (hard cover : alk. paper)
  1. Smith, Joseph, 1805-1844. 2. Church of Jesus Christ of Latter-day Saints--Doctrines. I. Holzapfel, Richard Neitzel. II. Jackson, Kent P. III. Title.

BX8695.S6J668 2009
289.3092--dc22

2009053542

10 9 8 7 6 5 4 3 2 1

Contents

Introduction VII

The Early Years, 1805–19 1
  Richard Neitzel Holzapfel

Joseph Smith and the First Principles
of the Gospel, 1820–29 23
  Richard E. Bennett

Joseph Smith's New Translation of the Bible, 1830 51
  Kent P. Jackson

A Flood of Revelations, 1831 77
  Grant Underwood

Joseph Smith and "The Vision," 1832 101
  Robert J. Woodford

Expulsion from Zion, 1833 127
  Grant Underwood

Joseph Smith and the Redemption of Zion, 1834 151
   Alexander L. Baugh

Authority, Power, and the "Government
of the Church of Christ," 1835 195
   J. Spencer Fluhman

Joseph Smith and the Kirtland Temple, 1836 233
   Steven C. Harper

Joseph Smith and the Kirtland Crisis, 1837 261
   Ronald K. Esplin

Joseph Smith in Northern Missouri, 1838 291
   Alexander L. Baugh

The Saints' Forced Exodus from Missouri, 1839 347
   William G. Hartley

Joseph Smith Goes to Washington, 1839–40 391
   Ronald O. Barney

The Nauvoo Temple, 1841 421
   Richard Neitzel Holzapfel

Joseph Smith, John C. Bennett, and the Extradition
Attempt, 1842 437
   Andrew H. Hedges

Doctrines, Covenants, and Sweet Consolation, 1843 ... 467
   Robert L. Millet

The Prophet's Final Charge to the Twelve, 1844 495
   Richard Neitzel Holzapfel

Index 525

Acknowledgments 553

RICHARD NEITZEL HOLZAPFEL
AND KENT P. JACKSON

Introduction

British author Charles Mackay published a small work in 1851, claiming that it was the first public history of "this new religion" founded in America by Joseph Smith, "one of the most remarkable persons who has appeared on the stage of the world in modern times."[1] Although Mackay was not the first to write a history of the Latter-day Saints, he was right in asserting that Joseph Smith was a most remarkable person. Since the beginning of the Restoration, many individuals have collected the Prophet's teachings and attempted to tell his story. Yet the task of reconstructing the life of Joseph Smith is fraught with difficulties, as it is with telling the story of anyone who lived in the past.

First, it is impossible to identify everything Joseph Smith said or did. Although much of what a person says or does is irrelevant to understanding who he or she is and would, if recorded, provide a rather tedious narrative, it is critical to have sufficient data in order to provide a reasonable portrait of that person. Second, there are significant gaps at critical periods in Joseph Smith's life for which there are few primary documents from which a reasonable portrait can be created.[2] For example, the contemporary sources for the years 1805–30 are sparse. As a result, some important questions from this period remain unanswered. And finally, how do historians and other observers evaluate the life of one who claimed he was a prophet? How do we interpret his motives or understand him the same way he understood himself? Even for those years where good documentation exists, how do we read the evidence?

Who Was Joseph Smith?

Joseph Smith was acutely aware of the challenge of providing a reliable account of his life and work. At the Church's April 1844 conference in Nauvoo, he said, "You never knew my heart. No man knows my hist[ory]—I can not [tell] it. I shall never undertake [it]. If I had not experienced what I have, I should not have known it myself. . . . When I am called at the trump & weighed in the balance, you will know me then."[3]

Elder Heber C. Kimball, one of the Prophet's closest associates in Nauvoo, remembered a similar statement: "Would to God, brethren, I could tell you who I am! Would to God I could tell you what I know! But you would call it blasphemy, and there are men upon this stand who would want to take my life."[4] Mary Elizabeth Lightner, one of Joseph Smith's plural wives, also recalled the Prophet making the same point in another situation: "People little know who I am when they talk to me, and they never will know until they see me weighed in the balance in the Kingdom of God. Then they will know who I am, and see me as I am. I dare not tell them and they do not know me."[5]

INTRODUCTION

What Joseph Smith meant or intended is subject to debate. Because it is impossible to interview him or any of his associates who may have had privileged information on the subject, we cannot be certain what he intended. Nevertheless, there are two reasonable possibilities, and maybe both are correct.

First, the Prophet may have been referring to his status or activities in the premortal world; the Heber C. Kimball recollection may suggest this. Through the Prophet, a flood of information about the pre-earth life was revealed, including the premortal identity of several prophets, such as Adam, who was identified as Michael, and Noah, who was identified as Gabriel.[6] It would therefore not be surprising if Joseph Smith had learned something about his own role or premortal status. One of his own statements seems to suggest as much: "Every man who has a calling to minister to the inhabitants of the world was ordained to that very purpose in the Grand Council of Heaven before this world was. I suppose that I was ordained to this very office in that Grand Council."[7]

Second, Joseph Smith's statements also seem to refer to his mortal ministry. His April 1844 conference statement highlights this point. As he said, "If I had not experienced what I have, I should not have known it myself." He must have been surprised, again and again, as his mission was unfolded to him over time—"line upon line" instead of in one singular moment. For example, young Joseph Smith did not know in 1820 that his life would end on a hot, muggy Thursday afternoon in Carthage Jail in June 1844.

After his First Vision in 1820, the Prophet quickly learned that people reacted negatively to his claim that he had seen a vision. However, opposition then was local, and the initial reaction was not the kind of physical abuse he later experienced. He was forewarned of the heavy cost of discipleship when

Moroni told him in 1823 that his name would be had for "good and evil among all nations, kindreds, and tongues" (Joseph Smith—History 1:33). His small influence would dramatically enlarge to include the entire planet, but still there was no hint of the tarring and feathering, the destroyed property or physical threats, or the abuse to himself, his family, and followers that were just beyond the horizon. Apparently the only thing he learned on that occasion was that his name "should be both good and evil spoken of among all people" (Joseph Smith—History 1:33). How puzzling it must have been to an "obscure boy," as he called himself (Joseph Smith—History 1:23), to think that he would one day be known all over the world!

Nearly six years later, in 1829, Joseph Smith's sense of what lay ahead expanded again when the Lord commanded him to remain faithful, adding, "If you do this, behold I grant unto you eternal life, *even if you should be slain*" (Doctrine and Covenants 5:22; emphasis added). The key word in this revelation was "if," not "when." Nevertheless, the possibility of martyrdom had surfaced for the first time, and it most likely caught his attention, especially in light of the recent years' increasing threats, both verbal and physical. Following the establishment of the Church in 1830, the Prophet experienced imprisonment, death threats, violence, and loss of property multiple times for the gospel cause, but he always made his way back safely to family and friends (for example, see Doctrine and Covenants 121:9).[8] By 1842 that situation changed. As he prayed in one of the early Relief Society meetings, he apparently learned for the first time that his mission would end with his martyrdom.[9] From 1842 until his death in June 1844, he repeated the prophecy more than one hundred times.[10]

The life Joseph Smith may have expected or even dreamed of when he was growing up in New Hampshire, Vermont, and

INTRODUCTION

New York was not the one he ultimately lived. He recognized that he did not always know where his life was heading. Satan opposed his work even before he himself knew what it was: "It seems as though *the adversary was aware, at a very early period of my life, that I was destined to prove a disturber and an annoyer of his kingdom*; else why should the powers of darkness combine against me? Why the opposition and persecution that arose against me, almost in my infancy?" He reflected on his lowly stature: "I soon found, however, that my telling the story had excited a great deal of prejudice against me among professors of religion, and was the cause of great persecution, which continued to increase; and *though I was an obscure boy, only between fourteen and fifteen years of age, and my circumstances in life such as to make a boy of no consequence in the world*, yet men of high standing would take notice sufficient to excite the public mind against me, and create a bitter persecution; and this was common among all the sects—all united to persecute me" (Joseph Smith—History 1:20, 22; emphasis added). In this revealing recollection, the Prophet acknowledged that he was completely and utterly surprised by the attention he received, given his humble circumstances and his own expectations about his future life, which he assumed would be "of no consequence in the world."

Joseph Smith continued to learn more about his prophetic mission as he translated the Book of Mormon. One can only imagine what he felt as he came to the section that contained the prophecies of Joseph, the beloved son of Jacob: "And his name shall be called after me; and it shall be after the name of his father. And he shall be like unto me; for the thing, which the Lord shall bring forth by his hand, by the power of the Lord shall bring my people unto salvation" (2 Nephi 3:15).

Between the revelations and the heavenly visitations, Joseph Smith was left to himself and possibly felt very much alone. There was no other human who could relate to him. Elder Dallin H. Oaks astutely observed, "In spiritual matters, Joseph Smith had no [mortal] role models from whom he could learn how to be a prophet and a leader."[11] Although his father had revealing dreams and his mother was a devout Christian, he still had no adequate mortal mentor. The Prophet's April 1844 statements, given at the end of his life, suggest that he sometimes felt isolated—alone. Even family, such as his brother William, and close friends did not always understand him. Some of his trusted colleagues, such as Oliver Cowdery, Martin Harris, David Whitmer, and William Law, abandoned him.

People living in this transitional moment in history—when the premodern world was being replaced by a world thoroughly and irreversibly influenced by the Enlightenment—may have struggled to understand Joseph Smith, given their modern expectations. There was no room in that modern scientific age for prophets, revelations, visions, and new scripture—nothing that would allow them to place his life in context. James Hannay, writing in Charles Dickens's magazine *Household Words* in 1851, criticized the Mormon message as "the absurdity of seeing visions in the age of railways."[12]

By their "modern" standards, many people living in western societies believed Joseph Smith was strange, odd, and out of place. There is no question that he was uncommon. Yet he was more than an uncommon man with a common name. Few individuals' lives and labors have been foreknown and foretold like those of this great and long-hoped-for seer. Joseph Smith's life and ministry were seen by ancient prophets "since the world began" as part of the "restitution of all things" (Acts 3:21). From the days of Adam, prophets like Enoch, Joseph,

INTRODUCTION

Moses, Isaiah, Ezekiel, Daniel, Malachi, and the Apostle Peter looked forward to his ministry and the establishment of the kingdom of God through his labors. President Brigham Young noted, "It was decreed in the councils of eternity, long before the foundations of the earth were laid, that he should be the man, in the last dispensation of this world, to bring forth the word of God to the people and receive the fullness of the keys and power of the priesthood of the Son of God. The Lord had his eye upon him, and upon his father, and upon his father's father. . . . He was foreordained in eternity to preside over this last dispensation."[13]

There may be other ancient clues about what was known about Joseph Smith in the distant past. Only recently have scholars begun to unravel the complicated history of messianic expectations that existed in ancient Israel. Although today Orthodox Jews still believe in the coming of a Messiah, their progenitors, at different times, anticipated the coming of several specially anointed servants of the Lord: (1) the Messiah ben Judah (sometimes also identified as the Messiah ben David), (2) the Messiah ben Levi (sometimes identified as the Messiah ben Aaron or Messiah the Priest), and (3) the Messiah ben Joseph (sometimes identified as the Messiah ben Ephraim). It may well be that Joseph Smith should be identified as the third anointed servant of the Lord in these traditions. Although the ancient sources are confused and in many cases even contradict one another, there are some interesting threads that weave through the sources about the Messiah ben Joseph: he would appear before the coming of the final messiah, *the* Messiah (Jesus Christ), he would restore priesthood and temple worship, he would suffer a violent death at the hands of his enemies, and he would be resurrected by the Messiah who would come at the end of time.[14]

It was not just Old Testament prophets and New Testament apostles who prophesied of his ministry. Asael Smith, Joseph Smith's own grandfather, spoke prophetically before Joseph was born: "It has been borne in upon my soul that one of my descendants will promulgate a work to revolutionize the world of religious faith."[15] Later, Asael affirmed that his grandson was the "very Prophet that he had long known would come in his family."[16]

Reconstructing the Prophet's Life

Some past efforts to tell Joseph Smith's life history have relied heavily on reminiscences recorded many years after the Prophet's death. President Joseph F. Smith recognized the limitation of such reminiscences:

> We fear that many things that are reported as coming from the Prophet Joseph Smith, and other early leaders in the church, by not being carefully recorded or told with strict regard for accuracy, have lost something of their value as historical data, and unwarranted additions have sometimes been made to the original facts, until it is difficult to determine just how far some of the traditions which have come to us may be accepted as reliable representations of what was said or what was done. Let those who feel impressed to make a record of facts, as they become acquainted with them, do so; but let them exercise the greatest care in obtaining accuracy of statement and in giving the authority for the statements they record.[17]

As a consequence of concerns like these expressed by President Smith, serious historians today shy away from secondary and reminiscent accounts of things the Prophet is purported to have said and done and focus instead on contemporary primary sources.

Some writers have attempted, with good intention, to provide a rather sanitized version of the Prophet's life, believing that such an account would serve Joseph Smith best. Much like some of our efforts at writing a personal diary or autobiography, these authors focus exclusively on the remarkable and the sensational while eliminating the Prophet's challenges, disappointments, unfulfilled aspirations, and "human foibles," as he called them. These authors forget that the scriptures themselves provide rather frank portraits of the Lord's people, including his servants, the Apostles and prophets. The greatness of Peter and Paul is the more inspiring because the scriptures also revealed their human weaknesses as they grappled with the struggles and trials so common to others.

On the other hand, downplaying the inspiration, revelation, and greatness of the Prophet's ministry would provide an incomplete portrait, and biographies that have excluded these divine connections have failed. To emphasize only the human aspects of his life is to create an exaggerated caricature in the same way that a completely sanitized version does. Neither provides the kind of history that is necessary to create a reasonable portrait. The Joseph Smith of faith-promoting rumors and sanitized stories lacks the human characteristics that endeared him to the faithful when he was known simply as "Brother Joseph." What is forgotten in the process is that the Prophet himself never claimed to be anything more than a mortal disciple of Jesus Christ, attempting to work out his own salvation with fear and trembling. We should recall that he said that a prophet was a prophet "only when he was acting as such."[18] He meant it when he said that, and those who knew him did not think the less of him because of it.

Revelations given of the Lord did not hide Joseph Smith's all-too-human struggles. He is sometimes challenged to repent in the Doctrine and Covenants (see, for example, Doctrine and Covenants 3:1–9). Additionally, in those same revelations he was reminded that the Lord is merciful and forgiving (see Doctrine and Covenants 3:10–20), something that provides hope to all disciples.

Preserving and Writing the Prophet's History

Joseph Smith realized that it would be important for the Church to have a record not only of his life but also of the communications he received from God. During his lifetime, three collections of the revelations were prepared, each one larger as new revelations came.[19] In his efforts to preserve his history, in 1838 he began an account of his life. He and his clerks compiled the record from available sources, including his memory, his journals, and the records of others. It starts with autobiographical material that the Prophet dictated to scribes and then shifts to the format of an ongoing diary, with his journals providing the framework. Although he kept intermittent journals during the 1830s, the information for that decade is not as complete as it is for the 1840s, when his clerks kept a record of his activities. Where there were gaps in the Prophet's own journals, passages from the journals of other Church members were added to supply the needed information, so none of the significant documented acts or words of Joseph Smith would be excluded. Staff members added letters, transcriptions of sermons, and other documents in their proper sequence to make the record as complete as possible.

The publication of the Prophet's history began in 1842, with installments appearing periodically in the Church's Nauvoo newspaper, the *Times and Seasons*.[20] At the time of his death,

INTRODUCTION

the history had been compiled to 1838 but was published only to 1831. But the work continued, both in Nauvoo and in Utah, where installments were published in the *Deseret News* until their completion in 1858.[21] Decades later, Elder B. H. Roberts compiled and edited the history into a six-volume book, called *History of the Church of Jesus Christ of Latter-day Saints, by Joseph Smith*.[22] It is still in print today, and it remains an important historical record.

Drawing material from the *History of the Church*, other important works have been compiled. For example, in 1938 Elder Joseph Fielding Smith of the Quorum of the Twelve Apostles published *Teachings of the Prophet Joseph Smith*, a collection of the Prophet's writings and sermons, mostly extracted from the *History of the Church*.[23] This remained the standard collection of Joseph Smith's teachings for many decades. In 2008–9, Relief Society and priesthood-meeting lessons focused on *Teachings of Presidents of the Church: Joseph Smith*.[24] Drawn mostly from the *History of the Church*, this important collection of excerpts from the Prophet's sermons and writings also includes lesser-known and previously unpublished materials. In the late twentieth century, scholars increased their efforts to locate and compile Joseph Smith's recorded words and experiences from the earliest possible primary sources.[25] The indispensable collections from those years include *The Words of Joseph Smith* (1980), *The Personal Writings of Joseph Smith* (1984, rev. ed. 2002),[26] and *The Papers of Joseph Smith* (1989, 1992).[27]

Using available documentary sources, scholars continue to study and write about the Prophet's life. The most ambitious and comprehensive recent biographical effort is *Joseph Smith: Rough Stone Rolling* (2005).[28]

In recent decades, major efforts have also been undertaken to research important scripture-based manuscripts. One such effort is the Book of Mormon Critical Text Project, under the direction of Brigham Young University professor Royal Skousen.²⁹ That project identified all known parts of the Original and Printer's Manuscripts of the Book of Mormon and provided a facsimile transcription of both manuscripts. Researchers Scott H. Faulring, Kent P. Jackson, and Robert J. Matthews prepared and published a facsimile transcription of the original Joseph Smith Translation manuscripts in 2004.³⁰ These monumental documentary projects allow us, as never before, to learn of Joseph Smith's revelatory experiences with a close-up view, and they are essential building blocks for current and future attempts to advance our understanding of his mission.

Added to these scholarly activities is the Joseph Smith Papers Project. It is the most ambitious effort to date to publish all known primary documents created by or commissioned by the Prophet. This extremely important effort, projected to take a number of years to complete, will include all of Joseph Smith's known diaries, letters, revelations, contemporary reports of his discourses, and samples of other public documents authored by him. Through this project, historians have already gained important insights to the Prophet's life and ministry and will continue to do so. This is one of the most exciting efforts to date, and it promises to provide the important sources necessary for fresh, thoughtful, careful interpretative studies on the life and ministry of Joseph Smith.

Joseph Smith Papers Project

We may never know Joseph in the same way as those who were acquainted with him personally during his life; however, we are becoming acquainted with his personal writings in a way in which many people, even his friends, could not do during his

INTRODUCTION

lifetime.³¹ In addition to having a better understanding of the times in which the Prophet lived, scholars today are gaining access to numerous documents that shed light on Joseph's life and experiences that were not available to historians a generation ago. In 2008 and 2009, the first two volumes of *The Joseph Smith Papers* were published.³² Additionally, scholars have supplementary contemporary sources, such as Wilford Woodruff's diaries, which add a wealth of primary material about the Prophet.³³ All of these sources provide an intimate view of the Prophet through the eyes of those who knew him personally.

The Joseph Smith Papers Project is not an attempt to produce narrative histories—few people will open to page 1 and then read a volume all the way through, as they would read a biography. Instead, these documents will require careful examination, as one would do when working in an archive with the original source document in front of them. However, the Joseph Smith Papers Project will provide annotations by important historians to help the reader understand the document better than if they were on their own at the Church History Library in Salt Lake City. The Papers' primary benefit to the average Latter-day Saint and to others who want to understand the Prophet will probably come as a result of the future work of scholars who will utilize the Joseph Smith Papers as a primary source in their interpretative histories. Ronald K. Esplin, the managing editor of the project, explains that the volumes contain the raw material of history—in other words, the gold of history. Like a gold mine, these volumes will contain previously unprocessed precious metal; it will be left to scholars to extract the gold to create beautiful jewelry.³⁴

The Church decided that the Joseph Smith Papers Project should be directed to scholars. Obviously if the Papers were not written for scholars, with scholarly conventions, they would not be taken seriously in the academic world. Preparing a faithful record that non–Latter-day Saint scholars will take seriously is the primary purpose for the multimillion-dollar investment and enormous effort that have been put into the project. Esplin adds, "While this scholarly emphasis is the emphasis of the project, there is a secondary purpose to make sure that Latter-day Saints are going to have access to these documents, that it is something that they can use." The two circles—the scholarly audience and the LDS audience—overlap but not completely. Esplin notes:

> This little tale about how and why we came to focus more clearly on the scholarly audience is background for the point I really want to make. When you have the opportunity, I hope you will underscore the point that our work is not designated to defend Joseph Smith so much as to understand him. Of course, we are all Latter-day Saints and the work we are doing is Latter-day Saint and Joseph Smith–centric. We are who we are. But our tone, language, approach, and intention is to understand and not defend. It is the faith and experience of everyone involved in the project that if we will do that, understand him, he will come off just fine. Since he is who he said he was his life and works can withstand scrutiny. There is no need to distort the historical record, but a great need both in order to really know Joseph and for other worthy reasons to understand it. To the degree that we do our work well, all of us will, in the future, have tools for that which we don't have now and have never had before—the material that will allow us to know Brother Joseph again.[35]

Getting to Know Brother Joseph

During the fall of 2008, we invited several scholars, including some of the editors of the Joseph Smith Papers

Project, to participate in a Brigham Young University lecture series titled "Joseph Smith's Prophetic Ministry." The lectures were released on CD, and the chapters in this book were based on their lectures. These fine scholars use fresh eyes to look at Joseph Smith, mining both old evidence and new discoveries to give us a view of who the Prophet was, what he accomplished, and why his life matters. As a result of the efforts of these and other scholars, in some ways we may know more about the Prophet than did those who lived during his lifetime, given the intimate look we have into his personal diaries and letters. But naturally his family, friends, and close associates knew him in ways in which we cannot.

The Joseph Smith emerging from this current effort is a remarkable, complex, passionate, and truly likable person. Recent research has not diminished him in the least but shows him standing taller than ever. He was truly the prophet of the Restoration, the great seer who set in place the Lord's kingdom for the latter days. He was a disciple of Jesus Christ, like those New Testament Apostles who left their nets, boats, tollbooths, and other ordinary labors to follow Jesus. One of his close associates, Wilford Woodruff, borrowing Joseph Smith's own metaphor, noted the process that refined him: "He never professed to be a dressed smooth polished stone but was rough out of the mountain & has been rolling among the rocks & trees & has not hurt him at all. But he will be as smooth & polished in the end as any other stone."[36]

We who are involved in current research on Joseph Smith do not believe that our individual efforts represent the final interpretation of his life. Certainly, historians in the future will provide fresh insights and make corrections after the discovery of new information, which, in turn, will allow them to reexamine the primary sources now available. However, we cannot wait until we know everything about Joseph Smith and the world in which he lived. We look forward to the Millennium, for only then will we "know fully" (New International Version, 1 Corinthians 13:9–12) all the things we wish we knew now. In the meantime, the current work of historians is expanding our understanding of Joseph Smith in ways that were impossible before. This effort will continue to benefit us all.

Notes

1. Charles Mackay, *The Mormons: Or Latter-day Saints* (London: Office of the National Illustrated Library, 1851), vi.

2. There are gaps in source materials used in writing Joseph Smith's history just as there are significant gaps in sources used in reconstructing the Savior's life (see F. E. D. Schleiermacher, "The Public Life of Christ to the Time of His Arrest," in *The Historical Jesus: Critical Concepts in Religious Studies*, ed. Craig A. Evans [London: Routledge, 2004], 4:34).

3. *The Words of Joseph Smith: The Contemporary Accounts of the Nauvoo Discourses of the Prophet Joseph*, ed. Andrew F. Ehat and Lyndon W. Cook, eds. (Provo, UT: Religious Studies Center, 1980), 355; capitalization and punctuation standardized.

4. Orson F. Whitney, *The Life of Heber C. Kimball* (Salt Lake City: Deseret Book, 2001), 322–23.

5. Mary Elizabeth Lightner, address to Brigham Young University, April 14, 1905, typescript, L. Tom Perry Special Collections, Harold B. Lee Library, Brigham Young University, Provo, Utah.

6. For Adam's identity, see Doctrine and Covenants 27:11; 107:54; *Words of Joseph Smith*, 8. For Noah's identity, see *Words of Joseph Smith*, 8.

7. *Words of Joseph Smith*, 367; capitalization, punctuation, and spelling standardized. Though this teaching is often applied to every man and woman, the original context focused on the calling of the

dispensation heads; see Samuel A. Richard's account of the May 12, 1844, discourse: "At the general and grand council of heaven, all those to whom a dispensation was to be committed were set apart and ordained at that time, to that calling" (*Words of Joseph Smith*, 371).

8. See Ronald K. Esplin, "Joseph Smith's Mission and Timetable: 'God Will Protect Me until My Work Is Done,'" in *The Prophet Joseph: Essays on the Life and Mission of Joseph Smith*, ed. Larry C. Porter and Susan Easton Black (Salt Lake City: Deseret Book, 1988), 280–319.

9. *Words of Joseph Smith*, 116.

10. See Richard Lloyd Anderson, "Joseph Smith's Prophecies of Martyrdom," in *The Eighth Annual Sidney B. Sperry Symposium: A Sesquicentennial Look at Church History* (Brigham Young University, Provo, UT, January 26, 1980), 1–14.

11. Dallin H. Oaks, "Joseph Smith in a Personal World," in *The Worlds of Joseph Smith: A Bicentennial Conference at the Library of Congress* (Provo, UT: Brigham Young University Press, 2006), 159.

12. James Hanney, in *Household Words: A Weekly Journal* 3 (1851): 385.

13. *Deseret News*, October 26, 1859, 266.

14. Richard Neitzel Holzapfel, "The 'Hidden' Messiah," in *A Witness of Jesus Christ: The 1989 Sperry Symposium on the Old Testament* (Salt Lake City: Deseret Book, 1990), 81.

15. Quoted in Joseph Fielding Smith, *Church History and Modern Revelation* (Salt Lake City: The Church of Jesus Christ of Latter-day Saints, 1953), 1:4; see also Richard Lloyd Anderson, *Joseph Smith's New England Heritage* (Salt Lake City: Deseret Book, 1971), 112.

16. Joseph Smith, *History of the Church of Jesus Christ of Latter-day Saints*, ed. B. H. Roberts, 2nd ed. rev. (Salt Lake City: Deseret Book, 1957), 2:443.

17. Joseph F. Smith, "Shall We Record Testimony?" *Improvement Era*, March 1898, 372.

18. Smith, *History of the Church*, 5:265.

19. 1833 Book of Commandments, 1835 and 1844 Doctrine and Covenants.

20. See "History of Joseph Smith," *Times and Seasons*, March 15, 1842, 726–28.

21. See Jessee, "The Writing of Joseph Smith's History," *BYU Studies* 11, no. 4 (Summer 1971): 439–73.

22. Joseph Smith, *History of the Church of Jesus Christ of Latter-day Saints*, ed. B. H. Roberts (Salt Lake City: Deseret News, 1902–12). A seventh volume dealing with events after the death of Joseph Smith was published in 1932.

23. Joseph Smith, *Teachings of the Prophet Joseph Smith*, comp. Joseph Fielding Smith (Salt Lake City: Deseret Book, 1938).

24. *Teachings of Presidents of the Church: Joseph Smith* (Salt Lake City: Church of Jesus Christ of Latter-day Saints, 2007).

25. See Paul H. Peterson, "Understanding Joseph: A Review of Published Documentary Sources," in *Joseph Smith: The Prophet, the Man*, ed. Susan Easton Black and Charles D. Tate Jr. (Provo, UT: Religious Studies Center, Brigham Young University, 1993), 101–16.

26. *The Personal Writings of Joseph Smith*, ed. Dean C. Jessee, rev. ed. (Salt Lake City: Deseret Book, 2002).

27. *The Papers of Joseph Smith*, vol. 1: *Autobiographical and Historical Writings*, ed. Dean C. Jessee (Salt Lake City: Deseret Book, 1989); vol. 2: *Journal, 1832–42*, ed. Dean C. Jessee (Salt Lake City: Deseret Book, 1992).

28. Richard Lyman Bushman, *Joseph Smith: Rough Stone Rolling* (New York: Knopf, 2005).

29. Royal Skousen, ed., *The Original Manuscript of the Book of Mormon: Typographical Facsimile of the Extant Text* (Provo, UT: Foundation for Ancient Research and Mormon Studies, Brigham Young University, 2001); *The Printer's Manuscript of the Book of Mormon: Typographical Facsimile of the Entire Text in Two Parts* (Provo, UT: Foundation for Ancient Research and Mormon Studies,

INTRODUCTION

Brigham Young University, 2001); M. Gerald Bradford and Alison V. P. Coutts, eds., *Uncovering the Original Text of the Book of Mormon: History and Findings of the Critical Text Project* (Provo, UT: Foundation for Ancient Research and Mormon Studies, Brigham Young University, 2002).

30. Scott H. Faulring, Kent P. Jackson, and Robert J. Matthews, eds., *Joseph Smith's New Translation of the Bible: Original Manuscripts* (Provo, UT: Religious Studies Center, Brigham Young University, 2004); Kent P. Jackson, *The Book of Moses and the Joseph Smith Translation Manuscripts* (Provo, UT: Religious Studies Center, Brigham Young University, 2005).

31. For a biographical treatment of Joseph Smith in this period, see Bushman, *Rough Stone Rolling*, 8–39.

32. Dean C. Jessee, Ronald K. Esplin, and Richard Lyman Bushman are general editors of *The Joseph Smith Papers*. The first two volumes were *Journals, Volume 1: 1832–1839*, ed. Dean C. Jessee, Mark Ashurst-McGee, and Richard L. Jensen (Salt Lake City: Church Historian's Press, 2008); and *Revelations and Translations, Volume 1: Manuscript Revelation Books*, ed. Robin Scott Jensen, Stephen C. Harper, and Robert J. Woodford (Salt Lake City: Church Historian's Press, 2009).

33. See *Wilford Woodruff's Journal, 1833–1898, Typescript*, ed. Scott G. Kenney, 9 vols. (Midvale, UT: Signature Books, 1983).

34. Ronald K. Esplin, e-mail message to author, August 27, 2008.

35. Esplin, e-mail message to author, August 27, 2008.

36. *Wilford Woodruff's Journal*, 2:297. It appears that the quote comes from a sermon by Heber C. Kimball. Richard Bushman, however, notes Brigham Young as the source of the quote (see *Rough Stone Rolling*, vii). Joseph Smith characterized himself as a "rough stone rolling down hill" ("Joseph Smith Journal," May 21, 1843; as cited in *Words of Joseph Smith*, 205; see also diary entry for June 11, 1843, in *Words of Joseph Smith*, 209).

The Prophet Joseph Smith was born in Sharon, Vermont, on December 23, 1805. The home in which he was born straddled the Royalton-Sharon township line. This monument is situated adjacent to the site where the home once stood. The monument was dedicated by Joseph F. Smith, Church President and nephew of the Prophet Joseph Smith, on December 23, 1905. (George Edward Anderson, 1907; all rights reserved.)

RICHARD NEITZEL HOLZAPFEL

1805–19
The Early Years

*H*istorians often divide human history into periods such as prehistory, antiquity, late antiquity, Middle Ages, Renaissance, and so forth. These distinctions are, of course, artificial and somewhat problematic because no one woke up one morning and said, "Great! Today is the first day of the Renaissance!" Nevertheless, such categories help scholars organize and collect data about the past in smaller units of time, facilitating very astute interpretations of the facts available. Historians also divide human history into two separate worlds: premodern and modern periods. These designations account for the tremendous technological, political, and economic advances that have been made in recent history. Referring to the premodern and modern

---

Richard Neitzel Holzapfel is a professor of Church history and doctrine at Brigham Young University.

periods also helps us deal with the significant and fundamental psychological changes humans experienced between those periods. Indeed, those living in the modern world are fundamentally and psychologically different than the people who lived in the premodern world.

The Prophet's World

Joseph Smith lived in the period of transition between the end of the premodern world and the beginning of the modern world. In some places and among some people, as in the urban centers of Europe, the premodern world had already basically ended, whereas people in other places still had a premodern worldview. In some ways Joseph Smith had one foot in the premodern world and another foot in the modern world. The premodern world can be identified as having an abundance of three commodities that are rather scarce today.

First, the premodern world had an abundance of natural darkness. Certainly there were bonfires, oil lamps, and later candles, but often people living in the premodern world experienced natural darkness in its totality. Today humans, particularly those living in a Western industrial nation, can hardly escape artificial light; for most people, traveling long distances is required to witness a natural, dark sky as it was seen in antiquity. Street lights, headlamps, TVs, and even night lights in hallways have fundamentally changed the way we see the world at night. We simply do not observe the heavens as Abraham and Sarah, Jesus, Mary, Lazarus, and Joseph and Emma saw them. Additionally, we may not appreciate the fears of natural darkness that existed for those who lived in the past. One might fall into a ditch. Wild animals might attack. It was a dark and frightening world.

The second commodity is natural sounds and silence. There was human activity in the premodern world that created sound—saws, chisels, and so on—but people often experienced the natural sounds of their environment in ways most modern people never have. Today it is difficult to escape the noise of the modern world because of the prevalence of automobile traffic, sounds from various media outlets such as the radio, sounds of electrical currents in our homes, the ubiquitous iPod, and a variety of other sources. Even in some of the quietest places in America, such as natural parks, airplanes can disturb both humans and animals.

The third commodity is personal solitude. We live in a world that frowns on someone wanting to be alone. We are generally concerned when a friend or a family member seeks solitude, wondering if we should call the suicide hotline in his or her behalf. Because the patriarchs and matriarchs, the apostles and prophets experienced natural darkness, natural silence and sounds, and personal solitude, the visions of heaven may have opened to them more readily. Today, we are often distracted by the voices, the sounds, and the lights of a busy, noisy, modern world.

The world of Joseph Smith was different from our own in other ways. For example, he did not have modern products such as shampoo or deodorant. The ability to shower and change into clean clothes every day did not exist for most people living during the premodern period. Most people living in the premodern world had no regular dental care, no orthodontics. Life expectancy was less than twenty years of age in the early nineteenth century, and the infant mortality rate was remarkably high. In a day before antibiotics, this is not surprising. Today, few parents expect to bury a child; in the past, few parents escaped this terrible duty. By the end of the nineteenth century, these numbers had shifted dramatically with the advances of technology that provided clean water, medicine, and better nutrition.

Joseph Smith's world was often open to public view. Despite moments of personal solitude, family life was rather transparent, especially for the Smith family. They lived in small, crowded homes most of their lives, and during several years of their married life, Joseph and Emma lived with other people, sharing a home with a number of people. Joseph's neighbors saw him walk to the outhouse in the backyard. Today halls, bedrooms, and locked doors create modern privacy largely unknown in the premodern world. People in Joseph Smith's time witnessed the natural rhythms of life in a way most people today have likely not experienced. They watched children being born and people dying in their homes. Friends and family of the Prophet saw him sick, tired, irritated, even angry. They also saw him happy, playful, joyful, enthusiastic, solemn, and prayerful. They saw him dressed in his Sunday best, but also sometimes in tattered clothes.[1]

Three prominent visitors—Josiah Quincy, future mayor of Boston; Charles Francis Adams, the son and grandson of two former presidents of the United States (John Quincy Adams and John Adams); and Dr. William G. Goforth, representative of the national Whig Party who had come to Nauvoo seeking votes for presidential candidate Henry Clay—stopped in Nauvoo just before the Prophet died in 1844.[2] After their visit to Nauvoo, Quincy told their story about visiting the Mormon Prophet:

> Pre-eminent among the stragglers by the door stood a man of commanding appearance, clad in the costume of a journeyman carpenter when about his work. He was a

THE EARLY YEARS

hearty, athletic fellow, with blue eyes standing prominently out upon his light complexion, a long nose, and a retreating forehead. He wore striped pantaloons, a linen jacket, which had not lately seen the washtub, and a beard of some three days' growth. This was the founder of the religion which had been preached in every quarter of the earth. As Dr. Goforth introduced us to the prophet, he mentioned the parentage of my companion. "God bless you, to begin with!" said Joseph Smith, raising his hands in the air and letting them descend upon the shoulders of Mr. Adams.[3]

Joseph did not appear as one might expect of a prophet. Some Latter-day Saints who arrived in Nauvoo were also surprised to see the young prophet dressed in rough clothes greeting them at the dock.[4] Such was the world in which Joseph Smith lived.

Also surprising to many people today is how young the Prophet was when the transcendent events of the Restoration took place; he was only fourteen years old when he saw the Father and the Son in 1820; he was only seventeen years old when Moroni visited him in 1823; he was only twenty-one years old when he received the ancient record in 1827; and he was only twenty-four years old when he became the president of the Church of Jesus Christ in 1830. It is probable that in order to accomplish the rigorous tasks ahead of him, the Lord called a young, energetic prophet.

Joseph lived during a remarkable time in U.S. history.[5] The country was expanding not only in geographic size but also in population. In 1800 there were a little over five million Americans. By 1810, there were more than seven million and within another twenty years, that number would double. Additionally, the American frontier was constantly moving westward. Joseph lived on this frontier—a rough, tough, and sometimes dangerous environment.

It is important to note that the premodern world was not a static period, though certain aspects of it had long and substantial continuity.[6]

Joseph's Early Years

Sources concerning Joseph's earliest years (1805–19) are fragmentary. The main source of information about Joseph's early years is Lucy Mack Smith's history.[7] Additionally, the Prophet prepared some brief histories that provide some personal insights.[8] Nevertheless, Lucy Mack's reminiscences remain one of the important sources to reconstructing these early years. She began to dictate her story shortly after the Prophet's death in 1844. Lucy's history provides clues to scholars, guiding them to look for tax records and other documents to expand on the hints she provides in this important reminiscence. Without Lucy Mack Smith's remarkable history of her family, we would know almost nothing about Joseph Smith's earliest years. This chapter is a review of the Prophet's early life with references to American and world history events to provide historical context.

From Lucy's history we learn that the Prophet's parents (Joseph and Lucy Smith) were married in 1796 in Tunbridge, Orange County, Vermont.[9] The Smith family moved to Randolph, Orange County, Vermont, in the wake of a failed investment that caused them to sell their farm "to avoid the embarrassment of debt" in 1802.[10] Over the next few years, they moved numerous times.[11] Nevertheless, these moves were all within a rather small geographical area, keeping them within a network of family and friends.

The Smith family moved back to Tunbridge in 1803.[12] They moved again in 1804; this time to Sharon, Windsor County, Vermont, onto the land owned by Lucy Mack Smith's parents, Lydia Gates and Solomon Mack.[13] Lucy Mack Smith recalled, "Here it was that my son Joseph was born, December 23, 1805, one who will act a more conscious part in this work than any other individual."[14] Joseph Smith was born on Monday, December 23. Named after his father, he was known as Joseph Smith Jr. until his father's death in 1840. Thereafter, the Prophet was simply known as Joseph Smith. Also during 1805, Lewis and Clark reached the Pacific Ocean.

The Smith family moved back to Tunbridge in 1807, the same year Thomas Jefferson signed the Embargo Act and Robert Fulton invented the steamboat.[15]

In 1808 the United States finally banned the importing of slaves from Africa and the Caribbean. On Sunday, March 13, Samuel Harrison Smith was born.[16] On Thursday, December 22, Beethoven premiered his newly completed Fifth Symphony. Sometime before the end of the year, the Smith family moved to Royalton, Windsor County, Vermont.[17]

Ephraim Smith was born on Monday, March 13, 1810, in Royalton. He died a few days later on Saturday, March 24. He was the second child of Lucy Mack and Joseph Smith to die in infancy.[18] Another son, William Smith, was born on Wednesday, March 13, 1811. The first steamboat to sail down the Mississippi River reached New Orleans that year.[19]

The Smith family left Vermont for the first time when they moved across the Connecticut River to Lebanon, Grafton County, New Hampshire in 1811. This move was some twenty miles away, beginning a process that would allow them to break free from their New England moorings.[20] At this time,

7

Joseph Smith Sr. had the first of seven religiously focused dreams. They continued over the next few years, revealing the spiritual struggles and challenges he was experiencing at the time.[21]

A typhoid epidemic spread through the Connecticut River Valley in 1812, killing at least 6,400 people during a five-month period.[22] Also that year, U.S. president James Madison declared war against Britain.

On Wednesday, July 23, 1813, Catherine Smith was born at Lebanon.[23] Typhoid hit the Smith family. No one died, but Joseph Smith Jr. experienced severe pain even after the fever left him. Eventually, an infection settled in his leg.[24] Dr. Nathan Smith of Dartmouth Medical School, located near the Smith home in Lebanon, operated on Joseph using a unique procedure, thereby saving the seven-year-old's leg.[25]

This episode provides an important insight into the Smith family dynamics. Joseph's parents each demonstrated different strengths during this crisis. Luck Mack, for example, was strong willed. Instead of amputating it (the standard procedure at the time), she demanded that doctors attempt to save the young boy's leg.[26] Nevertheless, before the doctors began to operate, Lucy Mack left the room, apparently unable to deal with the situation. Joseph Smith Sr. stepped in and remained in the room to hold his son during the painful procedure.[27] Both Joseph and Lucy Mack played a different but significant role in this medical crisis. After the procedure, Joseph went to stay with his uncle Jesse Smith in Salem, on the Atlantic coast of Massachusetts, in the hope that the fresh sea air would aid his recovery.[28] He gradually improved, but it took three years before he was able to walk without crutches.

THE EARLY YEARS

The British defeated Napoleon at Waterloo, and the War of 1812 ended in 1815. In mid-April of that year, Mount Tambora, a volcano in modern Indonesia, erupted and ejected some twelve cubic miles of gases and twenty-five cubic miles of debris into the atmosphere, blocking the sun and altering weather patterns across the globe for a long time afterward.

Making one final stand in New England, the family moved back across the Connecticut River and rented a farm in Norwich, Windsor County, Vermont. Don Carlos Smith was born at Norwich in 1816.[29]

According to Richard L. Bushman, during the period between 1814 and 1816, the Smith family came closer to destitution than they would at any other point in their lives.[30] In the modern technological society in which we now live, a person can live a productive and fulfilling life without owning any land. But in the premodern agricultural world, farmland ownership was necessary for family survival. For most people, there were no other safety nets such as tax-sheltered annuities, social security, and life insurance. The family farm was often the sole economic resource to sustain parents entering into the last years of life. Additionally, the family farm provided children a head start when parents gave them a section of land to begin their married life. Therefore, without farmland, the Smith family's future appeared bleak.

The year 1816 later came to be known as the "year without a summer."[31] Joseph Smith Sr. and Lucy Mack Smith most likely did not know that the eruption of Mount Tambora in 1815 was the cause of the crop failure in the region. Lucy Mack recalled, "The first year our crops failed, and we bought our bread with the proceeds of the orchard and our own industry. The second year they failed again. In the ensuing spring, Mr. Smith said that we would plant once more on this farm, and if he did not succeed better, we would go to New York."[32]

The Smiths had been in New England for five generations, but this final bad year forced them to leave.[33] Lucy Mack Smith recalled, "This was enough. My husband was altogether decided upon going to New York."[34] The reasons for their departure to western New York seemed clear: "For over a decade, weather, crop failures, creditors, illness, and business failures had battered the Smith household economy."[35] It was time to start over—a new beginning, and New York seemed the best place to do so.

Other Smith family members had already separated themselves from their New England roots by moving to New York, and as a result, the safety net of family and friends was already unraveling in Vermont.

Theologically, Latter-day Saints would not necessarily argue that God caused Mount Tambora to erupt. However, God may have used the natural consequences of the catastrophic event to bring about his divine purposes, in this case, to bring the Smith family to western New York.

New York

Joseph Smith Sr. left Vermont in the summer of 1816 for Palmyra, Ontario (modern Wayne County), New York. His family came later in the year. Joseph Smith Sr. decided not to follow his extended family to St. Lawrence on the northern edge of the state. His decision to relocate in western New York was providential.

The Lord had prepared western New York as a fertile field to bring about his divine purposes—the Restoration. Imagine a triangle consisting of three *p*'s. The first two *p*'s were the plates (Book of Mormon) and the printer (E. B. Grandin), which were in place by 1816. The final *p* was the Prophet Joseph Smith. The Lord brought the Smith family to western New York to complete the triangle.

At the same time, western New York was the location of a series of evangelical revivals, known today as the Second Great Awakening.[36] Identified as the "burned-over district" by historians because of the religious excitement that spread across the western New York landscape from 1816 through 1826.[37] These revivals sparked in young Joseph Smith a spiritual flame that could not be extinguished, leading him on a journey that lasted a lifetime.

One American historian noted, referring to the publication of the Book of Mormon and the organization of the Church at this time:

> It appeared at precisely the right moment in American history—much earlier or later and the Church might not have taken hold. The Book of Mormon would probably not have been published in the eighteenth century, in that still largely oral world of folk beliefs prior to the great democratic revolution that underlay the religious tumult of the early republic. In the eighteenth century, Mormonism might have been too easily stifled and dismissed by the dominant enlightened gentry culture as just another enthusiastic folk superstition. Yet if Mormonism had emerged later, after the consolidation of authority and the spread of science in the middle decades of the nineteenth century, it might have had problems verifying its texts and revelations. But during the early decades of the nineteenth century, the time was ideally suited for the establishment of the new faith. The democratic revolution was at its height, all traditional authorities were in disarray, and visions and prophesying still had a powerful

appeal for large numbers of people. A generation or so later, it might have been necessary for Smith and his followers to get some university professors to authenticate the characters on the golden plates. But Martin Harris's failure to get such "professional" and "scientific" verification in the 1820s did not matter. After all, ordinary plowmen had as much insight into such things as did college professors.[38]

While the move to New York was providential, it was not without its challenges. Lucy Mack had to take care of various obligations, including the payment of several debts, before leading her family to join Joseph Smith Sr. some three hundred miles away. Additionally, Joseph Smith Jr., still recovering from his leg surgery, was forced to walk much of the way by an abusive driver who had been hired to take the family to New York. The family finally arrived in Palmyra. Lucy Mack recalled: "In a short time I arrived in Palmyra with a small portion of my effects, my babes, and two cents in money, but perfectly happy in the society of my family. The joy I felt in throwing myself and my children upon the care and affection of a tender husband and father doubly paid me for all I had suffered. The children surrounded their father, clinging to his neck, covering his face with tears and kisses that were heartily reciprocated by him."[39]

The first years in New York were challenging. Joseph remembered that his father, "being in indigent circumstances [was] obliged to labor hard for the support of a large family, having nine children; and as it required the exertions of all that were able to render any assistance for the support of the family, therefore we were deprived of the benefit of an education. Suffice it to say, I was merely instructed in reading and writing and the ground rules of arithmetic, which constituted my whole literary acquirements."[40]

Eventually, by 1819, Joseph Smith Sr., Alvin (his oldest son), and Hyrum (his next oldest), had earned enough money for a down payment on a hundred-acre farm near Palmyra in Farmington Township (known today as Manchester Township).[41]

From this period we have one of the earliest word pictures of Joseph Smith by someone outside the family. A Mrs. Palmer remembered: "My father loved young Joseph Smith and often hired him to work with his boys. I was about six years old when he first came to our home. I remember going into the field on an afternoon to play in the corn rows while my brothers worked. When evening came, I was too tired to walk home and cried because my brothers refused to carry me. Joseph lifted me to his shoulder, and with his arm thrown across my feet to steady me, and my arm about his neck, he carried me to our home."[42]

This account reveals something about the Smith family: they were day laborers, not farmers. This distinction is important in any effort to reconstruct the social and economic setting of Joseph Smith's earliest years.

The Second Great Awakening

Many Americans found God during the Second Great Awakening. The series of revivals helped to create a uniquely modern religious western industrial nation in America. From about 1800, faith became more and more important in many people's lives. Joseph noted that his parents "spared no pains in instructing me in the Christian religion."[43] Contemporary illustrations and descriptions of camp meetings show that in many cases the events were large gatherings; people often assembled for long weekends to hear exhortations by circuit preachers. Naturally, these religious revivals were evangelical in nature, attempting to convict people of their sins and then convince them that only through the grace of Jesus could they be saved. It is important to note that instead of being a single event, the Second Great Awakening consisted of a series of revivals spread over time and geographical space. The Smith family was inevitably drawn into this evangelical fervor during a series of revivals during this period in western New York.[44]

Joseph's personal religious quest apparently began sometime around 1818, in the wake of the revivals of 1816 and 1817. He remembered:

> At about the age of twelve years, my mind [had] become seriously impressed with regard to the all important concerns for the welfare of my immortal Soul which led me to searching the scriptures, believing, as I was taught, that they contained the word of God—thus applying myself to them and [because of] my intimate acquaintance with those of different denominations led me to marvel exceedingly, for I discovered that they did not adorn their profession by a holy walk and Godly conversation agreeable to what I found contained in the sacred depository [of the Bible—] this was a grief to my Soul—thus from the age of twelve years to fifteen I pondered many things in my heart."[45]

A contemporary source highlights a camp meeting held in Palmyra in June 1818. Reverend Aurora Seager noted in his diary:

> I received on the 18th of June, a letter from Brother [Billy] Hibbard, informing me that I had been received the [eastern] New York Conference, and, at my request, had been transferred to the Genesee Conference. On [Friday] the 19th [of June 1919] I attended a camp-meeting at Palmyra

[nearly fourteen miles from Phelps]. The arrival of Bishop Roberts, who seems to be a man of God, and is apostolic in his appearance, gave a deeper interest to the meeting until it closed. On Monday [at the Palmyra camp meeting], the sacrament was administered, about twenty were baptized; forty united with the [Methodist] Church, and the meeting closed.[46]

No one could have predicted how these revivals would have affected Joseph Smith Jr., including members of the Smith family themselves. Neither Joseph nor Lucy Mack had any premonitions about their son's religious future. Lucy recalled that Joseph was a "remarkably quiet" and "well disposed child." Still, he was "much less inclined to the perusal of books than" the other Smith children. However, Joseph recalled that he did read the scriptures, "believing as I was taught, that they contained the word of God."[47] He was, however, "given to meditation and deep study."[48]

Fortunately, we have several brief accounts of this period. The best known is Joseph's official history, now found in the Pearl of Great Price (Joseph Smith—History). Using a traditional nineteenth-century narrative convention, Joseph conflated the events of 1816–26 when he provided this formal official history.[49] In this history, Joseph recalled that there was interdenominational strife among the various parties and sects, most likely referring to the 1816–17 and the 1824–26 revivals:[50]

> Notwithstanding the great love which the converts to these different faiths expressed at the time of their conversion, and the great zeal manifested by the respective clergy, who were active in getting up and promoting this extraordinary scene of religious feeling, in order to have everybody converted,

> as they were pleased to call it, let them join what sect they pleased; yet when the converts began to file off, some to one party and some to another, it was seen that the seemingly good feelings of both the priests and the converts were more pretended than real; for a scene of great confusion and bad feeling ensued—priest contending against priest, and convert against convert. (Joseph Smith—History 1:6)

This account reveals that people of the day were serious about salvation, though they were divided about the best means of salvation, including the interpretation of key biblical passages. The general state of division reflected to a small degree what was happening in the Smith family itself.

Milton V. Backman, for example, found that seven towns within a twenty-mile radius of the Smith farm near Palmyra reported "'unusual religious excitement' and/or increase in church membership" between 1819 and 1820 and at least two others reported "prospects of revivals."[51]

Young Joseph refrained from joining any church, although he attended several of them and was particularly inclined to the Methodist faith. Two acquaintances at the *Palmyra Register* recalled Joseph "catching the spark of Methodism in a camp meeting" and that he joined a probationary class of the Palmyra Methodist Church.[52] Joseph himself claimed some desire to be united with the Methodists. His mother and several siblings eventually joined the Presbyterian Church.[53] His father had been involved in the local Universalist association in Tunbridge, Vermont, but in New York was not attached to any denomination. He was decidedly unchurched, though religiously inclined.[54] The young children struggled for religious identity. Joseph himself recalled, that he wanted to "get Religion too wanted to feel & shout like the Rest but could feel nothing."[55]

Joseph Smith added that his mind was often called up to "serious reflection and great uneasiness" (Joseph Smith—History 1:8). First and foremost, he worried about his personal salvation, and said, "My mind became exceedingly distressed for I became convicted of my sins. . . . And I felt to mourn for my own sins and for the sins of the world. . . . Therefore I cried unto the Lord for mercy for there was none else to whom I could go and obtain mercy."[56]

At this time of religious uncertainty, the Smith family built a log home just north of Farmington (modern Manchester Township line) in Palmyra Township in 1819.[57] The family began clearing the land on their one-hundred-acre farm.

It is important to note that Joseph Smith had not attracted much notice between 1805 and 1819. He lived a rather simple life on the American frontier, an "obscure boy" as he recalled (Joseph Smith—History 1:23). However, in 1820, his world, and the religious world in which he lived, changed forever.

An Instrument in the Lord's Hands

Just before his death, Joseph Smith said that he had been foreordained "to be one of the Instruments of setting up the Kingdom of Daniel, by the word of the Lord, and I intend to lay a foundation that will revolutionize the whole world—I once offered my life to the Missouri Mob as a sacrifice for my people—and here I am—it will not be by Sword or Gun that this Kingdom will roll on—the power of truth is such that—all nations will be under the necessity of obeying the Gospel."[58]

From 1820 until his death in 1844, Joseph Smith was engaged in this religious mission. However, despite all his accomplishments as part of the Restoration, the Prophet Joseph Smith was only an instrument in the Lord's hands.

President Gordon B. Hinckley placed the Prophet's ministry in perspective for contemporary Latter-day Saints when he wrote: "I worship the God of heaven, who is my Eternal Father. I worship the Lord Jesus Christ, who is my Savior and Redeemer. I do not worship the Prophet Joseph Smith, but I reverence and love this great seer through whom the miracle of this gospel has been restored. I am now growing old, and I know that in the natural course of events, before many years, I will step across the threshold to stand before my Maker and my Lord and give an accounting of my life. And I hope that I shall have the opportunity of embracing the Prophet Joseph Smith and of thanking him and of speaking of my love for him."[59]

When we reflect on the Prophet Joseph Smith's humble beginnings in Vermont and his journey to the Sacred Grove in New York, we are filled with love and appreciation for the one "blessed to open the last dispensation," and we rejoice that "Jesus anointed that Prophet and Seer."[60]

Notes

1. See Hyrum Andrus and Helen Mae Andrus, *They Knew the Prophet* (Salt Lake City: Deseret Book, 1999); and Mark L. McConkie, *Remembering Joseph* (Salt Lake City: Deseret Book, 2003).

2. See Richard Lyman Bushman, *Joseph Smith: Rough Stone Rolling* (New York: Alfred A. Knopf, 2005), 3.

3. Josiah Quincy, *Figures of the Past from the Leaves of Old Journals* (Boston: Roberts Brothers, 1883), 380–81.

4. Andrus and Andrus, *They Knew the Prophet*, 191–92.

5. For more on the immediate context of Joseph Smith's life in the United States, see Chad M. Orton and William W. Slaughter, *Joseph Smith's America: His Life and Times* (Salt Lake City: Deseret Book, 2005).

6. For a survey history of how these various issues played out in the early nineteenth-century United States, see Daniel Walker Howe, *What Hath God Wrought: The Transformation of America, 1815–1848* (New York: Oxford University Press, 2007).

7. Lucy Mack Smith, *The Revised and Enhanced History of Joseph Smith by His Mother*, ed. Scot Facer Proctor and Maurine Jensen Proctor (Salt Lake City: Deseret Book, 1996), xxxvii; and Lavina Fielding Anderson, ed., *Lucy's Book: A Critical Edition of Lucy Mack Smith's Family Memoir* (Salt Lake City: Signature Books, 2001), 67–68.

8. See, for example, Joseph Smith's 1832 history; *Personal Writings of Joseph Smith*, ed. Dean C. Jessee (Salt Lake City: Deseret Book, 2002), 9–20.

9. Smith, *History of Joseph Smith by His Mother*, 42.

10. Smith, *History of Joseph Smith by His Mother*, 51–53.

11. Smith, *History of Joseph Smith by His Mother*, 45; and Richard Neitzel Holzapfel, "The Church on the Early 19th-Century Frontier," in *Historical Atlas of Mormonism*, ed. S. Kent Brown, Donald Q. Cannon, and Richard H. Jackson (New York: Simon and Schuster, 1994), 6–7.

12. Smith, *History of Joseph Smith by His Mother*, 53.

13. Smith, *History of Joseph Smith by His Mother*, 62.

14. Smith, *History of Joseph Smith by His Mother*, 62.

15. Smith, *History of Joseph Smith by His Mother*, 62.

16. Smith, *History of Joseph Smith by His Mother*, 62; for an overview of Samuel Harrison Smith's life see Kyle R. Walker, ed., *United by Faith: The Joseph Sr. and Lucy Mack Smith Family* (American Fork, UT: Covenant Communications, 2005), 204–307.

17. Smith, *History of Joseph Smith by His Mother*, 62.

18. Smith, *History of Joseph Smith by His Mother*, 62.

19. Smith, *History of Joseph Smith by His Mother*, 62; for an overview of William B. Smith's life, see Walker, *United by Faith*, 247–307.

20. Smith, *History of Joseph Smith by His Mother*, 64.

21. Smith, *History of Joseph Smith by His Mother*, 63–64.

22. Bushman, *Rough Stone Rolling*, 20.

23. Walker, *United by Faith*, 308–52.

24. Smith, *History of Joseph Smith by His Mother*, 69–76.

25. LeRoy S. Wirthlin, "Joseph Smith's Boyhood Operation: An 1813 Surgical Success," *BYU Studies* 21, no. 2 (Spring 1981): 131–54.

26. Smith, *History of Joseph Smith by His Mother*, 73–74.

27. Smith, *History of Joseph Smith by His Mother*, 75; see also Bushman, *Rough Stone Rolling*, 21–22.

28. Smith, *History of Joseph Smith by His Mother*, 76; for an overview of Don Carlos Smith's life, see Walker, *United by Faith*, 354–97.

29. Smith, *History of Joseph Smith by His Mother*, 76.

30. Bushman, *Rough Stone Rolling*, 27–29.

31. See Howe, *What Hath God Wrought*, 30–31; and John D. Post, *The Last Great Subsistence Crisis in the Western World* (Baltimore: Johns Hopkins University Press, 1977), 1–27.

32. Smith, *History of Joseph Smith by His Mother*, 81.

33. For more information on the history of the Smith family, refer to Richard Lloyd Anderson, *Joseph Smith's New England Heritage* (Salt Lake City and Provo, UT: Deseret Book and BYU Press, 2003).

34. Smith, *History of Joseph Smith by His Mother*, 81–82.

35. Bushman, *Rough Stone Rolling*, 28.

36. See Milton V. Backman, "Awakenings in the Burned-over District: New Light on the Historical Setting of the First Vision," *BYU Studies* 9, no. 3 (1969): 301–15.

37. See Whitney R. Cross, *The Burned-Over District: The Social and Intellectual History of Enthusiastic Religion in Western New York, 1800–1850* (Ithaca, NY: Cornell University Press, 1950).

38. Gordon S. Wood, "Evangelical America and Early Mormonism," in Dean L. May and Reid L. Neilson, *The Mormon History Association Tanner Lectures: The First Twenty Years* (Urbana: University of Illinois Press, 2006), 22.

39. Smith, *History of Joseph Smith by His Mother*, 84–86.

40. *Personal Writings of Joseph Smith*, 10; spelling, punctuation, and grammar modernized.

41. Smith, *History of Joseph Smith by His Mother*, 86.

42. Andrus, *They Knew the Prophet*, 1.

43. *Personal Writings of Joseph Smith*, 10; spelling, punctuation, and grammar modernized.

44. For an overview of the religious culture during this period, see Nathan Hatch, *The Democratization of American Christianity* (New Haven, CT: Yale University Press, 1989); and Jon Butler, *Awash in a Sea of Faith: Christianizing the American People* (Cambridge: Harvard University Press, 1990). For statistical analyses of church growth during this period, see Roger Finke and Rodney Stark, *The Churching of America, 1776–2005: Winners and Losers in Our Religious Economy* (New Brunswick, NJ: Rutgers University Press, 2005); and Edwin Gaustad and Philip Barlow, *New Historical Atlas of Religion in America* (New York: Oxford University Press, 2000).

45. *Personal Writings of Joseph Smith*, 10; spelling, punctuation, and grammar modernized.

46. E. Latimer, *Three Brothers: Sketches of the Lives of Rev. Aurora Seager, Rev. Micah Seager, Rev. Schuyler Seager, D.D.* (New York: Phillips & Hunt, 1880), 12.

47. *Personal Writings of Joseph Smith*, 10.

48. Smith, *History of Joseph Smith by His Mother*, 111.

49. *Personal Writings of Joseph Smith*, 226–39.

50. D. Michael Quinn has persuasively argued this point elsewhere ("Joseph Smith's Experience at a Methodist 'Camp-Meeting' in 1820," Expanded Version [Definitive], *Dialogue Paperless* 3 [December 2006]: 1–110, available online at http://www.dialoguejournal.com/excerpts/e3.pdf).

51. Backman, "Awakenings in the Burned-over District," 312–13.

52. Richard Lloyd Anderson, "Circumstantial Confirmation of the First Vision Through Reminiscences," *BYU Studies* 9, no. 3 (Spring 1969): 379–84.

53. See *Personal Writings of Joseph Smith*, 229.

54. Asael Smith, Joseph Smith's grandfather, organized a Universalist society in Tunbridge, Vermont, in 1797, with Joseph Smith Sr. listed among the sixteen members. His oldest sons reportedly attended meetings with him. See LaMar C. Berrett and others, eds., *Sacred Places*, vol. 1: *New England and Eastern Canada* (Salt Lake City: Bookcraft, 1999), 1:121–22.

55. Alexander Neibaur Journal, May 24, 1844, in *The Papers of Joseph Smith: Volume 1, Autobiographical and Historical Writings*, ed. Dean C. Jessee (Salt Lake City: Deseret Book, 1989), 461.

56. *Personal Writings of Joseph Smith*, 11; spelling modernized.

57. Researchers recently discovered court evidence showing Joseph as a credible witness in a legal case (evidence that the Smith family was living in Palmyra in 1819). See "A Chronology of the Life of Joseph Smith," *BYU Studies* 46, no. 4 (2007): 7.

58. *The Words of Joseph Smith: The Contemporary Accounts of the Nauvoo Discourses of the Prophet Joseph*, ed. Andrew F. Ehat and Lyndon W. Cook (Provo, UT: Religious Studies Center, Brigham Young University, 1980), 367.

59. Gordon B. Hinckley, "As One Who Loves the Prophet," in *The Prophet and His Work: Essays from General Authorities on Joseph Smith and the Restoration* (Salt Lake City: Deseret Book, 1996), 13.

60. W. W. Phelps, "Praise to the Man," *Hymns* (Salt Lake City: The Church of Jesus Christ of Latter-day Saints, 1985), no. 27.

RICHARD E. BENNETT

1820–29
Joseph Smith and the First Principles of the Gospel

So much of a biographical nature has been written lately on the life of the Prophet Joseph Smith that one may well wonder if there is anything new or important left to say about him. Dan Vogel and Richard Bushman, in their dramatically counterpoint interpretations of the Prophet—the former contending he was a "pious fraud" and the latter asserting he was a legitimate American prophet—have forced us to reconsider the earlier arguments and interpretations of Donna and Marvin Hill, Fawn Brodie, John Henry Evans, and George Q. Cannon. Yet the contrasting contributions of these latest two scholars, and the fervent, sometimes deeply emotional responses to them, have reinforced in my mind the conviction that the study of Joseph Smith's

---

Richard E. Bennett is a professor of Church history and doctrine at Brigham Young University.

life and religious contributions is a fruitful field, a field already to harvest that continually beckons new generations to careful study and reflection. Too many devotional defenders in the past have denied the value of historical documentation, while too many critics have derided the place of scriptural authority. Both are necessary for the believing Latter-day Saint.

I wish to explore Joseph Smith's life, specifically the years 1820–29, from a somewhat different perspective than some of my colleagues by suggesting a different paradigm of thought, one deeply rooted in my conviction that Joseph Smith was a man called of God. My thesis may be summarized as follows: if Joseph Smith was called to be a prophet, then God assumed the responsibility of teaching and training him in that role. Put another way, the message of the gospel would have to be lived by the messenger of the gospel. The integrity of the Restoration would require nothing less.

Our particular purpose is to explore from the pages of both Church history and holy writ how Joseph Smith was carefully and thoroughly taught the first principles of the gospel, specifically repentance, during that formative, foundational decade of the 1820s. I propose to show that during this ten-year journey of preparation from Palmyra to Fayette, Joseph Smith was taught repentance and forgiveness in a profoundly personal and convincing fashion that molded his character. Elsewhere, and in book-length form, I am addressing how he was similarly instructed in those other principles of faith in the Lord Jesus Christ, baptism for the remission of the sins, and the gift of the Holy Ghost, but in this chapter we have barely enough room to cover the second principle of the gospel. I do so not to impugn the character of the Prophet Joseph but to improve upon our understanding of his life, of Church history, and of the Restoration.

Specifically we will approach the topic of divine instruction over three different periods of time: (1) from 1820, following the First Vision, until the time Joseph Smith received the plates in September 1827 or what we might call early preparation; (2) from September 22, 1827, until early April 1829, or the Martin Harris school of hard knocks; (3) and finally, the period of translation from April 5 until July 1, 1829, during which time Joseph Smith and Oliver Cowdery were translating the Book of Mormon.

"That His Sins Were Forgiven": A Period of Preparation

If faith in the Lord Jesus Christ was the operative first principle of the First Vision, the kind of mighty faith Joseph Smith exerted to deliver him from a force that was set upon his destruction, then what was it that opened the heavens the second time? The Prophet provides us with an answer in his own account: "When, on the evening of the above-mentioned twenty-first of September, after I had retired to my bed for the night, I betook myself to prayer and supplication to Almighty God for forgiveness of all my sins and follies" (Joseph Smith—History 1:29). If the message of the gospel was to be lived by the one entrusted and foreordained to bring it forth, it only stands to reason that he would be inspired to seek help to overcome his weaknesses and have purged out of him the imperfections in his own life.

"During the space of time" between his First Vision in the spring of 1820 and September 1823, three and a half years of youthful adolescence, Joseph confesses that he mingled "with all kinds of society" and "frequently fell into many foolish errors, and displayed the weaknesses of youth" (Joseph Smith—History 1:28). He does not go into detail as to what all those problems were, but most readers will readily identify with him. It is not only our sins that condemn us but likewise our foolishness, our rash judgments, those unkind and hasty words that may cut others deeply, our irrational behaviors, and wasting of time and talent. As Nephi warned, "they sell themselves for naught; ... for the reward of their pride and foolishness they shall reap destruction" (2 Nephi 26:10). Although Joseph asserts that he was not "guilty of any great or malignant sins" (Joseph Smith—History 1:28), it appears evident that he had a magnified sense of his sins, for he "often felt condemned" for his imperfections and earnestly sought "forgiveness of all [his] sins and follies" (Joseph Smith—History 1:29).

It is a true principle that the closer one comes to God in prayer and in daily behavior, the more he will show us our weaknesses and stumbling blocks. "And if men come unto me I will show unto them their weakness," wrote the Book of Mormon prophet Moroni. "I give unto men weakness that they may be humble; and my grace is sufficient for all men that humble themselves before me; for if they humble themselves before me, and have faith in me, then will I make weak things become strong unto them" (Ether 12:27). As is often the case, while we pray for answers to what we consider to be our major problems, God in his wisdom first shows us the beam that is in our own eye. Although sin is ever destructive, the consciousness of sin can activate the conscience, which, as part of the Light of Christ, can prompt us to turn away and cause us to "forget the thing which is wrong" (Doctrine and Covenants 9:9).

So it was with young Joseph Smith. He may have had perfect faith but he was not a perfect man. Thus, what drove him to prayer that night in September 1823 in the family log cabin near Palmyra was, as Joseph later recorded, a strong desire "for forgiveness of all my sins and follies, and also for a manifestation to me, that I might know of my state and standing before him;

for I had full confidence in obtaining a divine manifestation, as I previously had one" (Joseph Smith—History 1:29).

According to the account written by the "second elder" of this dispensation, Oliver Cowdery, one of the first things Joseph remembered the angel Moroni telling him that night was "that his sins were forgiven, and that his prayers were heard."[1] Before the mission of translating the Book of Mormon could begin, the message of forgiveness first had to be communicated. Thus if faith in God opened the heavens the first time, repentance opened them the second time. This pattern of sacred instruction would be repeated in different times and places throughout the pages of early Church history.[2]

The prophet Mormon, Moroni's father, who had seen so much of sin and corruption in his life, had well taught the principle of repentance and may have even foreshadowed his own son's ongoing mission.

> Neither have angels ceased to minister unto the children of men.
>
> For behold, they are subject unto him, according to the word of his command, showing themselves unto them of strong faith and a firm mind in every form of godliness.
>
> And the office of their ministry is to call men unto repentance, and to fulfil and to do the work of the covenants of the Father, which he hath made unto the children of men, to prepare the way among the children of men, by declaring the word of Christ unto the chosen vessels of the Lord, that they may bear testimony of him. (Moroni 7:29–31)

Angels therefore come not to satisfy idle curiosity but to "call men unto repentance." And so it was that September night in 1823.

While it is entirely appropriate to study Moroni's message in the light of preparing Joseph Smith for his upcoming mission to translate "a book deposited, written upon gold plates" that contained "the fulness of the everlasting Gospel" (Joseph Smith—History 1:34), my purpose is to show how the unfolding scenes and heavenly manifestations of the Restoration taught the prophet of the Restoration the first principles of the gospel, specifically repentance. Seen from this perspective, some of what Moroni, the master prophet, began to teach his apprenticed prophet, may take on new meaning.

The very first scripture Moroni quoted—and is there not abundant irony that Moroni, a Book of Mormon prophet, was shown here to be a seasoned scholar of the Holy Bible?—was from Malachi, a warning against sinning: "For behold, the day cometh that shall burn as an oven, and all the proud, yea, and all that do wickedly shall burn as stubble" (Joseph Smith—History 1:37). Then, quoting the third chapter of Acts, Moroni spoke once again of Christ's warning that "they who would not hear his voice should be cut off from among the people" (Joseph Smith—History 1:40). He went on to quote from Joel chapter 2, verses 28 to the last, including the promise "that whosoever shall call on the name of the Lord," as Joseph himself had done, "shall be delivered," for surely "your young men shall see visions" (Joel 2:32, 28). Moroni quoted "many other passages of scripture, and offered many explanations" that are not recorded (Joseph Smith—History 1:41).

As he revisited again and again that night and the next morning, Moroni repeated everything he had said the first time, because repetition does indeed bring conviction, not only recollection. Little wonder Joseph Smith later recalled that the biblical passages he cited were either "with a little variation from the way it reads in our Bibles" (Joseph Smith—History 1:36), as was the case with the fourth chapter of Malachi, or "precisely as they stand in our New Testament" (Joseph Smith—History 1:40), as was the case of Moroni's quoting from the book of Acts. One might see here not only Joseph Smith's commission to translate the Book of Mormon but later, upon completing that work, the invitation to revise the sacred Holy Bible, not to condemn but to raise and reclaim it. Moroni, in citing the Bible, was proclaiming and redeeming it. Just as the Bible had brought Joseph to the Sacred Grove, it was here again being used to instruct him in his new mission.

In those first twenty-four hours of angelic instruction, Moroni visited Joseph five times—three presentations that took up virtually the entire night, once again the next morning while he attempted to climb the fence out of his father's field, and then again at the Hill Cumorah. Warned the night before against viewing the gold plates for their fiscal value, especially considering the indigent circumstances in which the Smith family was living, when Joseph "made an attempt to take them out," he was reprimanded and forbidden by Moroni from so doing. The angel told him that "the time for bringing them forth had not yet arrived, neither would it, until four years from that time" (Joseph Smith—History 1:53).

We see in this the beginning of a course of training and careful instruction that had everything to do with the preparation of a prophet. As a seventeen-year-old in the fall of 1823, Joseph was clearly not ready to receive the plates and with them the mission of translation, nor would he be for some time to come. Moroni informed him that on the anniversary of his first visit, he desired to meet with Joseph Smith once every year in the very same place.

The mental, emotional, and spiritual significance of an annual visit with a heavenly being can hardly be overestimated.

Latter-day Saints can identify with the current practice of an annual tithing settlement with their bishop or branch president or with regular worthiness interviews for temple recommends. There is a wonderful element of covenant accountability in such interviews. They serve as an opportunity for confessing sins, for repledging souls, and for reestablishing priorities so as to conform with the better good within us. And confession is good for the soul, not the casual mental exercise of pretending over our sins but the courageous act of admitting them to a real, listening, and sympathetic servant of God who, though not the source of forgiveness, can be the listening ear, the agent of divine reconstitution. The scripture says, "By this ye may know if a man repenteth of his sins—behold, he will confess them and forsake them" (Doctrine and Covenants 58:43).

We begin to see in Moroni's curriculum of instruction not only his role of mentor and tutor but also that of prophet and bishop. Having been told to join no existing church, where was this young man to turn for religious training and edification? His mother, Lucy Mack Smith, and some other members of the family continued to attend the Presbyterian Church, and it is likely Joseph attended with them on occasions. He obviously held several conversations with ministers during these years and may have told more than discretion called for. His father, who had been uniquely prepared to believe in his son's spiritual development through several visions and dreams of his own, believed in Moroni's visit and had replied "that it was of God" (Joseph Smith—History 1:50) and encouraged him onward. Thus young Joseph likely looked forward to this annual interview as a sacred time to commune, to confess, to explore, and to inquire. The very knowledge that such interviews were pending may have wrought enormous impact on his faith, personal behavior, and developing sense of accountability and mission.

There is ample scriptural precedent and pattern for such training. Even though Christ at the tender age of twelve confounded the master teachers of his time, his own mission would not formally begin until he too was much older. In the meantime he continued to receive instruction and preparation, "grace for grace" from his parents and from his Father in Heaven "until he received a fulness" (see Doctrine and Covenants 93:12–13). During this time, he "increased in wisdom and stature, and in favour with God and man" (Luke 2:52). The ancient Israelite prophet Samuel was similarly so instructed. The Lord had appeared to him as a trusting, believing, young boy and likewise commissioned him, saying, "Behold, I will do a thing in Israel, at which both the ears of everyone that heareth shall tingle" (1 Samuel 3:11). Yet the Lord took him under his wing, for "Samuel grew, and the Lord was with him, and did let none of his words fall to the ground. And all Israel from Daniel even to Beer-sheba knew that Samuel was established to be a prophet of the Lord" (1 Samuel 3:19–20). Nor did the Lord appear only once to Samuel, for he appeared unto him again in Shiloh, teaching and revealing much to his young prophet (see 1 Samuel 3:21). Nephi was similarly prepared by the Lord and by angels of God in his missions of obtaining the plates of Laban and of seeking a new promised land, a course of tutoring that his rebellious older brothers refused to accept. Even Paul the Apostle, after his glorious vision of Christ while on the road to Damsacus, went to be healed, anointed, baptized, and taught by the human agent of God's miracle, a man named Ananias. Though filled with his commission, Saul tarried "certain days with the disciples which were at Damascus" (Acts 10:19; see also Galatians 1:15–18), presumably not only bearing testimony and confounding the unbelieving Jews but also being instructed and guided by his fellow Christians.

Joseph Smith does not explain the confidences and confessions he may have expressed during his annual visits with Moroni. During the intervening years between 1823 and 1827, when Joseph advanced from age seventeen to twenty-one, he became involved in treasure digging with Josiah Stowell of Bainesbridge, New York. Much has been made of Joseph Smith's silver-mine diggings as a way to supplement his family's meager existence. Though treasure seeking had been a common endeavor in New England and New York for decades and involved the energies of many, Joseph grew increasingly uncomfortable with the whole process and sought to distance himself from the magic culture and folklore associated with it and the money-seeking nature of those involved, having said, at indelicate moments, more about angels and gold plates than he should have. Joseph came to regret his involvement in such activities and, as the time neared to receive the plates, tried to move on. But if he chose not to share with us the private matters covered in his interviews with Moroni, he does give us surprising clues and insights into what they discussed: "Accordingly, as I had been commanded, I went at the end of each year, and at each time I found the same messenger there, and received instruction and intelligence from him at each of our interviews, respecting what the Lord was going to do, and how and in what manner his kingdom was to be conducted in the last days" (Joseph Smith—History 1:54).

One wonders at the deliberate choice of the words "instruction" and "intelligence." The former we can all comprehend; the latter may have reference to "light and truth" that only revelation can impart, the kind of heavenly instruction, education, and refinement that sanctifies the spirit while it instructs the soul.

There was also more in Moroni's training sessions than the plates and how to obtain them. He clearly foretold impending events "respecting what the Lord was going to do," events that may have included the process of translation, the restoration of requisite authority, and further angelic instruction. Beyond the near future, Moroni also taught him "how and in what manner his kingdom was to be conducted in the last days." In these annual personal priesthood interviews, is it possible the Prophet Joseph learned how and when to organize and establish the Church of Jesus Christ, about priesthood offices, temples, and much more?

"At length," Joseph Smith received the plates, the Urim and Thummim, and the breastplate on September 22, 1827, from "the same heavenly messenger"—with this one final charge: "that I should be responsible for them; that if I should let them go carelessly, or through any neglect of mine, I should be cut off" (Joseph Smith—History 1:59), but that, if faithful, he would be protected in his work. After four years of prophetic training in the principles of truth and righteousness, he was deemed ready and worthy for the next level of instruction. Yet even after all this, he had much to learn about repentance.

Martin Harris and Preparations for Translation, 1827–29

To what extent Joseph had confided in others about his visits with the angel Moroni is unknown; however, even before he received the plates, Martin Harris, a well-known farmer and respected citizen of Palmyra, had taken an interest in the young boy's emerging mission. Joseph's senior by twenty-two years, Martin Harris had served as a road commissioner and on several local juries. A committed churchgoer, he had earned a reputation as a student of the Bible.

Much of what is known of Harris in these early years we owe to Joseph Smith's own account and to Lucy Mack Smith, Joseph's mother, whose *History of Joseph Smith by His Mother* still stands as an indispensable read, particularly for these formative years. According to her, Martin's marriage to his cousin, Lucy Harris, was less than ideal. Short-tempered and hard of hearing, Lucy Harris strenuously objected to her husband's interest in the budding Palmyra Prophet. She believed it would all lead to no good financially and insisted that she be involved in any of Martin's dealings with the Smith family.[3] Martin's anxiety to substantiate the plausibility, if not the authenticity, of Joseph Smith's work may be perfectly understandable, considering his difficult home situation. After all, it was their money that was on the line.[4]

Well before the Prophet received the plates, "rumor with her thousand tongues" was circulating all about Palmyra, tending to discredit the reputation of the Smith family (Joseph Smith—History 1:61). Resultant persecution became so intolerable that Joseph and Emma wanted to move away to her home in Harmony, Pennsylvania, some one hundred miles to the south. "In the midst of our afflictions we found a friend in a gentlemen by the name of Martin Harris," Joseph recorded, "who came to us and gave me fifty dollars to assist us on our journey" (Joseph Smith—History 1:61). By means of such timely assistance—equal to $2,500 of today's standard of exchange—the pair were enabled to leave Palmyra and immediately reach Harmony in the month of December of 1827.

Over the next few months, Joseph continued working on the translation from the large plates of Nephi, completing 116 pages of foolscap-length pages of transcription with Martin Harris apparently working as his scribe. Beset by continuing criticism at home and perhaps bothered by lingering doubts of his own, Martin pleaded for Joseph to let him take the completed pages to show his insistent wife and her doubtful family. Disregarding the Lord's warnings not to do so and his own better judgment, Joseph reluctantly agreed and surrendered the manuscript to his friend and benefactor. Regrettably, he did not make a second copy.

Martin abruptly returned to Palmyra where the worst of his intentions got the best of him. Carelessly breaking his promise to show them only to his wife and a selected few family members, he proved an unfaithful guardian of the sacred text and before long had lost them, no doubt lending them to others.

Meanwhile, hearing no news from Martin, which, as Lucy Smith recalls, "was altogether aside of the arrangement when they separated,"[5] Joseph's worries intensified that same spring of 1828 while facing another crisis at home. Emma had given birth to their first child, a son, who died in infancy. Remaining at his wife's bedside day and night for two weeks during her difficult recovery, Joseph worried not only about her health but also about the state and condition of the manuscript. Finally, at Emma's urging, Joseph returned to Palmyra for the purpose of learning the cause of Martin's absence as well as silence.

The morning of the intended rendezvous, Martin Harris was late for breakfast at the Smith home by some six hours, evidently stalling and searching, while Joseph and the rest of the family fretted within impatiently. Finally they saw him coming. With a slow, measured tread, his eyes fitted upon the ground until he reached the fence, he got upon it and drew his hat over his eyes. At length he entered the house. Lucy records what happened next:

Martin took up his knife and fork as if to use them but dropped them from his hands. Hyrum said, "Martin, why do you not eat? Are you sick?" Martin pressed his hands upon his temples and cried out in a tone of deep anguish, "Oh! I have lost my soul. I have lost my soul."

Joseph, who had smothered his fears till now, sprang from the table, exclaiming, "Oh! Martin, have you lost that manuscript? Have you broken your oath and brought down condemnation upon my head as well as your own?"

"Yes," replied Martin, "it is gone, and I know not where."

"Oh, my God, my God," said Joseph, clinching his hands together. "All is lost, is lost! What shall I do? I have sinned. It is I who tempted the wrath of God asking him for that which I had no right to ask, as I was differently instructed by the angel. . . . Then must I," said Joseph, "return to my wife with such a tale as this? I dare not do it lest I should kill her at once. And how shall I appear before the Lord? Of what rebuke am I not worthy from the angel of the Most High?"[6]

In this dramatic moment, we glimpse something of the character of Joseph Smith and the extent to which he had been taught. A lesser man would likely have turned on Martin Harris and soundly berated him for his own mistaken judgment. Human nature being what it is, we will often blame someone else for causing our problems, especially when they share so much of the fault. But in that heated moment of despair, Joseph Smith rose to his calling, taking full and complete responsibility for the entire matter: "I have sinned. It is I who tempted the wrath of God." If the first step of repentance is accepting one's own accountability, Joseph was here the teacher and Martin Harris his tormented student.

Lucy goes on to show the depths of remorse her son then showed. "I besought him not to mourn so," she wrote, hoping to offer some sort of consolation.

> For it might be that the Lord would forgive him, after a short season of humiliation and repentance. But what could I say to comfort him when he saw all the family in the same situation of mind that he was? Our sobs and groans and the most bitter lamentations filled the house. Joseph, in particular, was more distressed than the rest, for he knew definitely and by sorrowful experience the consequence of what would seem to others to be a very trifling neglect of duty. He continued walking backwards and forwards, weeping and grieving like a tender infant until about sunset, when we persuaded him to take a little nourishment.[7]

Returning home to Harmony immediately afterward, Joseph Smith continued prayerful, sensing a pending day of reckoning. Subsequently, Moroni once again appeared to him, censuring him for having delivered the manuscript into Harris's hands. The Prophet said, "As I had ventured to become responsible for this man's faithfulness, I would of necessity suffer the consequences of his indiscretion, and I must now give back the Urim and Thummim into his (the angel's) hands."[8]

Joseph then received a revelation that summer of 1828, soon after the angel had visited him, in which the young prophet was chastised in no uncertain terms:

> Behold, how oft you have transgressed the commandments and the laws of God, and have gone on in the persuasions of men.
>
> For, behold, you should not have feared man more than God. Although men set at naught the counsels of God, and despise his words—

Yet you should have been faithful; and he would have extended his arm and supported you against all the fiery darts of the adversary; and he would have been with you in every time of trouble. . . . For thou hast suffered the counsel of thy director to be trampled upon from the beginning. (Doctrine and Covenants 3:6–8, 15)

Consequently, Joseph lost his privileges of translation for a season, a time of probation during which he continued to learn humility and penitence, more aware than ever before that the Restoration of the gospel and the translation of the Book of Mormon would come to pass with or without him.

Happily, some two months later, on September 22, 1828, the fifth anniversary of Moroni's first appearance, Joseph Smith experienced the fruits of his penitence, saying, "I had the joy and satisfaction of again receiving the Urim and Thummim." His mentor, too, "was rejoiced" at the lessons Joseph had learned in repentance and "told me that the Lord was pleased with my faithfulness and humility, and loved me for my penitence and diligence in prayer."[9]

The story of Joseph Smith, Moroni, Martin Harris, and the lost manuscript has one concluding episode. Nine months later, near the end of June 1829, at the Peter Whitmer Jr. farm in Fayette, New York, the angel Moroni appeared to the Three Witnesses: Martin Harris, David Whitmer, and Oliver Cowdery. Just as Moroni had come to Joseph Smith in September 1823 to declare forgiveness and to teach Joseph repentance, so also this visit of Moroni to Harris was predicated upon that same saving principle. Said Joseph Smith beforehand when indicating to Harris the possibility of his being one of the Three Witnesses, "Martin Harris, . . . you have got to humble yourself before God this day and obtain, if possible, a forgiveness of your sins. If you will do this, it is the God's will that you . . . should look upon the plates."[10] Well known in Church history is the fact that after David, Oliver, Martin, and Joseph had retired to the woods near the Whitmer house, nothing happened until Martin excused himself, believing, "as he expressed himself, that his presence was the cause of our not obtaining what we wished for. He accordingly withdrew" while the angel appeared to the other three men. Only after Joseph rejoined Martin and accompanied him in fervent prayer, was the same vision opened to their view. "'Tis enough; 'tis enough," he said; "mine eyes have beheld; mine eyes have beheld." Then, "jumping up, he shouted, 'Hosanna,' blessing God, and otherwise rejoiced exceedingly."[11]

Joseph Smith, Oliver Cowdery, and the Process of Translation, 1829

We now come to our third and final episode, that period of translation in which Joseph Smith and his new scribe, Oliver Cowdery, completed the Book of Mormon as we now know it. Virtually the same age as Joseph, Oliver (1806–50) was also from Vermont, had been a store clerk and taught in country schools. While boarding with Joseph Smith's parents, he learned of the ancient record and the lost 116 pages. What piqued his interest in the work was the fact that he had "inquired of the Lord" on the matter. As recorded in the Doctrine and Covenants, "as often as thou hast inquired thou hast received instruction of my Spirit. If it had not been so, thou wouldst not have come to the place where thou art at this time" (Doctrine and Covenants 6:14). Joseph Smith said, "The Lord appeared unto . . . Oliver Cowdery and shewed unto him the plates in a vision and . . . what the Lord was about to do through me, his unworthy servant. Therefore he was desirous to come and write for me to translate."[12]

The two men met each other for the first time on April 5, 1829, arranged some temporal business together the following day, and began the work of translation on April 7. Partners in the translating process, the great difference between the two men was in their spiritual preparation and academic approach to the task at hand. A teacher by profession who knew how to read and write and do numbers far better than his partner, Oliver was nevertheless Joseph's pupil in the first principles.

The profound intellectual difficulties Joseph Smith faced in translating an ancient unknown language even with the aid of the Urim and Thummim are hinted at in Oliver's parallel failed experience as a translator and afford us yet another view of how repentance was once more taught during the translation process. It is noteworthy that the second elder of the Restoration began his mission by seeking the gift to translate. "Ask that you may know the mysteries of God, and that you may translate and receive knowledge from all those ancient records which have been hid up, that are sacred; and according to your faith shall it be done unto you" (Doctrine and Covenants 8:11). However, as Elder Dallin H. Oaks has indicated, Oliver soon "failed in his efforts to translate."[13] Why? "Behold, it is because that you did not continue as you commenced. . . . You have supposed that I would give it unto you, when you took no thought save it was to ask me. But behold, I say unto you that you must study it out in your mind; then you must ask me if it be right" (Doctrine and Covenants 9:5, 7–8).

At issue here was more than Oliver's attitude of teachability and humility; it was also an aptitude of intellectual application not so well developed in him as to bear results, at least not in the timely way now required. Oliver failed in the intellectually demanding work of translating because he had not thoroughly applied himself mentally to the task. As the Lord indicated,

"Behold, you have not understood; you have supposed that I would give it unto you, when you took no thought save it was to ask me. But behold, I say unto you, that you must study it out in your mind; then you must ask me if it be right, and if it is right I will cause that your bosom shall burn within you; therefore, ye shall feel that it is right" (Doctrine and Covenants 9:7–8). Joseph Smith had learned both lessons—spiritual and mental—from his previous experiences. He had been schooled in matters of character and spirit for the past nine years and from his past experience with Martin Harris and the translation of the 116 pages, clearly, in hindsight, a preparatory school of remarkable learning. Can we really expect Oliver to have learned them as well after but a few days at the task? We may wish to revise our thinking on who was the student and who was the teacher.

The intellectual demands of translating were rigorous and extremely challenging. If the experiences and Testimony of the Three Witnesses are to be taken at face value, the successful translation of the Book of Mormon was neither magical nor mythical but measured and marvelous, a careful confluence of obedience, recurring repentance, and consequent revelation on the one side, and a rigorous mental exercise of intense study, recall and recognition, and trial and error on the other. The specifics of translation remain a mystery, but it may be instructive to compare the work of Joseph Smith to that of his magnificent contemporary, the superlative translator of ancient Egyptian hieroglyphic writing, the brilliant French linguist, Jean-François Champollion. Just five years before, Champollion had finally decoded the mysterious hieroglyphs of the famed Rosetta Stone found near Alexandria by Napoleon's army in 1799. After a lifetime of studying Coptic, Arabic, Hebrew, Greek, Egyptian, and a dozen other languages, Champollion, in his famous "Lettre à Monsieur Dacier" of September 22,

1822, exactly one year before Moroni's initial visit, convinced the waiting world that he could read the ancient hieroglyphic writings of Egypt. As a result, Champollion, the man from Grenoble, is still rightfully revered as the father of modern Egyptology.

Whereas Champollion first naively believed that a thorough knowledge of Coptic would allow him to directly decipher ancient Egyptian hieroglyphs, he gradually came to the realization that such was quite dauntingly not the case. Hieroglyphic writings were not a single alphabet; they had a wide variety of spellings for the same person or place, and they had no vowels but plenty of shorthand contractions, such as in English one might write "pkg" for "parking" or "nvsty" for "university." Furthermore, the ancient Egyptian scribes assumed the reader was conversant with their combinations of right vowels and contractions, "but this knowledge had been lost, although Coptic gives clues to it."[14]

After long and painstaking effort, Champollion concluded that hieroglyphs could not be read alone but in groups or clusters. Intently comparing the Greek to the Coptic, the Coptic to the demotic (a later simplified form of ancient Egyptian writing) and, by extension, the demotic to the hieroglyphic, Champollion noted that there were three times as many hieroglyphic signs as there were Greek words. Therefore, there had to be a combination or grouping of signs to convey a single meaning—in other words, consonants and syllables, essential components to phonetic expressions. Though the hieroglyphs employed no vowels, they were a combination of phonetics and pictures. Unlike others of his scientific contemporaries, such as Thomas Young of England, Champollion was now looking not just for more clues between the hieroglyphic and the demotic, but for the ability to read the maze of what constituted hieroglyphic writing.

What finally enabled Champollion to do what neither Young nor any others were able to accomplish was applying his mastery of Coptic to the problem. As one leading scholar has written, "His knowledge of Coptic enabled him to deduce the phonetic values of many syllabic signs, and to assign correct readings to many pictorial characters, the meanings of which were made known to him by the Greek text on the Stone."[15] The system of decipherment that Champollion had been methodically developing over several years was that hieroglyphic script was mainly phonetic but not entirely so, that it also contained logograms or shorthand symbols used to write native names and common nouns from the Pharaonic period. The combination of both constituted an ancient alphabet, which he now could prove and sufficiently read or decipher. Champollion thus came to the rightful conclusion that the hieroglyphic writings were not just of the later periods of Egyptian history but of the very earliest Pharaonic era as well. He therefore decoded the entire system and showed that hieroglyphic, hieratic, and demotic all corresponded to the same language. Whereas Young may well have discovered parts of the alphabet, it was "Champollion [who] unlocked an entire language."[16]

Joseph Smith, on the other hand, could barely read or write one language, English.[17] Joseph Smith had neither the time, scholarly training, nor linguistic knowledge to decode one symbol after another; indeed his mission was not to master the linguistics required to read an ancient language but to translate or convey their meanings into English. His initial work of translation consisted of copying the various "characters," letters, phrases, or hieroglyphs found on the large plates of Nephi into some sort of working alphabet. "I copied a considerable number of them," he records, clear evidence of the strong mental exercise and careful study he too would need before translating could actually begin. Then only gradually did he begin to use what neither Champollion nor any other translator had at their command, the Interpreters. With the aid of these ancient instruments, Joseph Smith began to translate some of the characters.

It would appear that the process was less one of decoding or deciphering the precise meaning of the individual characters and inscriptions found on the plates, as Champollion had so painstakingly done with the Rosetta Stone, and more one of discerning the meanings conveyed thereon and then, in addition, struggling to transliterate such meanings into acceptable, King James Bible–vintage literary English. The translators seemed to have functioned on two levels: conveying meaning from the ancient text while simultaneously suggesting wording in biblical-sounding English far beyond the reach then in Joseph's limited grasp. Thus we might argue that Joseph Smith was not a decoder or a pure translator in the Champollion sense of the word but a transmitter/translator and writer who, with the aid of the interpreters, transposed what he saw into exquisite English prose and poetry.

For all of this, Oliver was ill prepared. The customized reprimand and gentle reproof he received in section 9 of the Doctrine and Covenants were less a rebuke and more a reminder that God had already called and prepared his prophet; what was needed now was a humble, penitent scribe and devoted supporter and trusted eyewitness to visions soon to occur. "Do not murmur my son, for it is wisdom in me that I have dealt with you after this manner; . . . it is not expedient that you should translate now. Behold it was expedient when you commenced; but you feared, and the time is past, and it is not expedient now; For, do you not behold that I have given unto my servant Joseph sufficient strength, whereby it is made up? And neither of you have I condemned. . . . Be faithful, and yield to no temptation" (Doctrine and Covenants 9:6, 10–13). It was a lesson in repentance not missed by either man.

If Joseph and Oliver learned repentance at the outset of translating, they were repeatedly reminded of its central importance as their work progressed. Well known is David Whitmer's 1882 remembrance of a time Joseph Smith could not translate, despite all the gifts he had at his command. "He could not translate unless he was humble and possessed the right feelings towards everyone," Whitmer recalled.

> To illustrate so you can see. One morning when he was getting ready to continue the translation, something went wrong about the house and he was put out about it. Something that Emma had done. Oliver and I went upstairs [obviously this was at the Whitmer home] and Joseph came up soon after to continue the translation, but he could not do anything. He could not translate a single syllable. He went downstairs, out into the orchard, and made supplication to the Lord; was gone about an hour—came back to the house, and asked Emma's forgiveness and then came up stairs where we were and then the translation went on all right. He could do nothing save he was humble and faithful.[18]

Thus, to borrow B. H. Roberts's phraseology, the translation "was not a merely mechanical process" but rather a laboratory of spiritual and mental application governed by the principles found in the very book they were now translating. Even after almost 10 years of preparation, Joseph Smith relearned the lesson that even the smallest sins or senseless hurts prevented the free flow of inspiration and revelation. By faith, faith unto repentance that led, in turn, to the guiding and revealing influence of the Spirit of the Lord, he lived his way through to the end of the translation process.

Conclusion

I suggest a new and different perspective from that offered by some of Joseph Smith's biographers. Nowhere have I argued that Joseph Smith was a perfect man or without blemish. His sins and imperfections were real, and while I have not dwelt upon them in any way to discredit his life, they surely caused him a great deal of grief and hardship. Yet our theme has been that if God called a prophet, he prepared that prophet in the first principles of the gospel. The mission of Moroni, in preparing the way for the translation of the Book of Mormon, was the charge given to angelic visitors: "to minister according to the word of his command, showing themselves unto them of strong faith and a firm mind in every form of godliness. And the office of their ministry is to call men unto repentance, and to fulfil and to do the work of the covenants of the Father" (Moroni 7:30–31). Time after time, Moroni, the master prophet, trained Joseph Smith, the apprentice prophet, in matters of the soul, of honesty and integrity, in humility and patience, in repentance and forgiveness. Joseph Smith's partners in translation, Martin Harris and Oliver Cowdery, were likewise taught the same principles and learned from hard experience that the message of the gospel had to be lived by the messengers of the gospel to have any lasting effect. Integrity, not hypocrisy, would attract the best of men and women and make for a lasting movement. This injunction was repeated all the way up to Fayette and the organization of the Church in April 1830 and indeed, for years afterward. "Preach naught but repentance:" and "the thing that will be of the most worth unto you will be to declare repentance unto this people, that you may bring souls unto me, that you may rest with them in the kingdom of my Father" (Doctrine and Covenants 19:21; 15:6; see also 16:6). Indeed, this lesson of repentance and forgiveness would be repeated numerous times throughout the pages of later Church history, including the famous vision in the Kirtland Temple in April 1836 when the Savior pronounced once again to Joseph and Oliver, "Behold, your sins are forgiven you; you are clean before me; therefore, lift up your heads and rejoice" (Doctrine and Covenants 110:5).

Notes

1. Oliver Cowdery to W. W. Phelps in *Messenger and Advocate*, February 1835, 79.

2. For instance, in the spring of 1836 at the dedication of the Kirtland Temple, when Christ himself appeared before the altars of the temple, among the very first words he proclaimed to Joseph Smith and to Oliver Cowdery were, "Behold, your sins are forgiven you; you are clean before me; . . . lift up your heads and rejoice" (Doctrine and Covenants 110:5). Just as faith precedes the miracle, repentance precedes the commission. The man must be "worthy of his hire" (Doctrine and Covenants 84:79).

3. Professors Susan Easton Black and Larry C. Porter are soon to publish a new biography of Martin Harris.

4. For more on Harris's visit to the East, see Stanley B. Kimball "The Anthon Transcript: People, Primary Sources and Problems," *BYU Studies*, vol. 10, no. 3 (Spring 1970): 325–52; see also the author's forthcoming article "'Read This I Pray Thee': Martin Harris and the Three Wise Men of the East" (accepted for publication in 2010 in the *Journal of Mormon History*).

5. Lucy Mack Smith, *The Revised and Enhanced History of Joseph Smith by His Mother*, ed. Scot Facer Proctor and Maurine Jensen Proctor (Salt Lake City: Deseret Book, 1996), 161.

6. Smith, *History of Joseph Smith by His Mother*, 164–66.

7. Smith, *History of Joseph Smith by His Mother*, 166.

8. Smith, *History of Joseph Smith by His Mother*, 174.

9. Smith, *History of Joseph Smith by His Mother*, 176.

10. Smith, *History of Joseph Smith by His Mother*, 199.

11. Joseph Smith, *History of the Church of Jesus Christ of Latter-day Saints*, ed. B. H. Roberts, 2nd ed. rev. (Salt Lake City: Deseret Book, 1957), 1:54–55.

12. *The Papers of Joseph Smith*, vol. 1, *Autobiographical and Historical Writings*, ed. Dean C. Jessee (Salt Lake City: Deseret Book, 1989), 1:10.

13. Dallin H. Oaks, "Our Strengths Can Become Our Downfall," *BYU Speeches of the Year*, June 7, 1992, 6.

14. Lesley and Roy Adkins, *The Keys of Egypt: The Obsession to Decipher Egyptian Hieroglyphs* (New York: Harper Collins, 2000), 84.

15. Ernest Alfred Wallis Budge, *The Rosetta Stone in the British Museum* (New York: AMS Press, 1976), 4.

16. Richard B. Parkinson, *Cracking Codes: The Rosetta Stone and Decipherment* (Berkeley: University of California Press, 1999), 40.

17. Emma Smith later retold the experience of the translation period to her son as follows: "I am satisfied that no man could have dictated the writing of the manuscripts unless he was inspired; For, when acting as his scribe, your father would dictate to me hour after hour; and when returning after meals or after interruptions, he could at once begin where he had left off, without seeing either the manuscript or having any portion of it read to him. This was a usual thing for him to do. It would have been improbable that a learned man could do this; and, for one so ignorant and unlearned as he was, it was simply impossible" ("Last Testimony of Sister Emma," *Saints' Herald*, October 1, 1879, 290).

18. Statement of David Whitmer to William H. Kelley and G. A. Blakeslee of Gallen, Michigan, September 15, 1882, from the Baden

and Kelley debate on the divine origin of the Book of Mormon, 186, as cited in Brigham Henry Roberts, *The Essential B. H. Roberts*, ed. Brigham D. Madsen (Salt Lake City: Signature Books, 1999), 139.

that ye may marvel; For as the Father raiseth up the dead, and quickeneth them even so the Son quickeneth whom he will; for the Father judgeth no man, but hath committed all judgment unto the Son, that all should honor the Son, even as they honor the Father. He who honoreth not the Son, honoreth not the Father who hath sent him. Verily, verily, I say unto you, he who heareth my words, and believeth on him who sent me, hath everlasting life, and shall not come into condemnation, but is passed from death into life. Verily, verily, I say unto you, the hour is coming, and now is, when the dead shall hear the voice of the Son of God, and they who hear shall live. For as the Father hath life in himself, so hath he given to the Son to have life in himself; and hath given him authority to execute judgement also, because he is the Son of man. Marvel not at this; for the hour is coming in the which all who are in their graves shall hear his voice, and shall come forth; they who have done good in the resurrection of the just; and they who have done evil, in the resurrection of the unjust and shall all be judged of the Son of man. For as I hear I judge; and my judgement is just; for I can of mine ownself do nothing; because I seek not mine own will, but the will of the Father who hath sent me. If I bear witness of myself, yet my witness is true. For I am not alone, there is another who beareth witness of me, and I know that the testimony which he giveth of me is true. Ye sent unto John, and he bare witness also unto the truth. And he received not his testimony of man, but of God. And ye yourselves say that he is a Prophet, therefore ye ought to receive his testimony. These things I say that ye might be saved. He was a burning and shining light, and ye were willing for a season to rejoice in his light. But I have a greater witness than the testimony of John; for the works which the Father hath given me to finish, the same works that I do, bear witness of me, that the Father hath sent me, And the Father himself, who sent me, hath born witness of me. And verily I testify unto you, that ye have never heard his voice at any time, nor seen his shape, For you have not his word abiding in you; for whom he hath sent, ye believe not. Search the Scriptures, for in them ye think ye have eternal; and they are they which testify of me, and ye will not come to me that ye might have life, lest ye

Manuscript page from Joseph Smith's New Translation. (Used by permission, Library-Archives, Community of Christ.)

KENT P. JACKSON

1830 Joseph Smith's New Translation of the Bible

As January dawned in the year 1830, the Prophet Joseph Smith had much on his mind. The Book of Mormon production was well under way in Egbert B. Grandin's print shop in Palmyra, New York. The previous summer, the Prophet had contracted with Grandin to publish the Book of Mormon—five thousand copies for three thousand dollars. Publishing a book was not an easy task in the days of Joseph Smith. The first edition of the Book of Mormon was an enormous undertaking of typesetting, printing, binding, and—probably—patience.[1]

Each page of the Book of Mormon required someone to insert by hand into a wooden form about twenty-five hundred tiny pieces of metal. Every comma, every space, every period, and every letter had to be inserted

---

Kent P. Jackson is a professor of ancient scripture at Brigham Young University.

The Prophet had contracted with E. B. Grandin to publish the Book of Mormon. The first edition of the Book of Mormon was an enormous undertaking of typesetting, printing, binding, and patience. Pictured is the Grandin Press building (above) and a replica of the Smith Improved Printing Press (below) that was used to print the first edition of the Book of Mormon. (Photos by Brent Nordgren.)

separately, backwards, and upside down so the text would print correctly. After the type for the first page was prepared, the workers would set the type for the next fifteen pages in sequence, for a total of sixteen pages to be printed on each side of big sheets of paper. After the sixteen pages of thousands of pieces of metal type were in place, the type was inked, a sheet of paper was placed on it, and the handle of the press was cranked to transfer the ink onto the paper. After that process was repeated twenty-five hundred times, the sheets were turned over for the printing of the same text on the other side. The text was identical on both sides of the sheets so that when they were cut in half, they produced two identical sheets containing sixteen pages of the book, eight pages on each side. Those sheets are called signatures.

After each sheet was printed, the type had to be redistributed into the cases, and then the pieces were brought out again, one by one, and reinserted into the forms to create the next group of sixteen pages, each one in order. It has been shown that to produce the first edition of the Book of Mormon, the handle on the press in Grandin's print shop had to be cranked 185,000 times to print all thirty-seven signatures in five thousand copies. When the printing for the entire book was completed, there were thirty-seven stacks of paper, each containing five thousand signatures ready to be folded, trimmed, and bound into a book.

In Joseph Smith's day, book binding was done entirely by hand. Workers laid an individual sheet of the first signature on a table and folded it by hand in such a way that the sixteen pages on it would be in the right order. Then the process was repeated with an individual sheet of the second signature and so on through all thirty-seven signatures. Workers collated the signatures in the correct sequence and then began the laborious process of binding them together. The pages of each signature had to be bound to each other with string before the thirty-seven signatures could be bound together. The workers took a needle, stitched it a few times in and out of the fold of the individual signature, looped it back to the outside, and tied it there. Thus the pages within one signature would hold together. All of the signatures were stitched that way, after which string was used to tie the thirty-seven signatures tightly together into a block of printed pages. The workers then glued together the edge of the block, put a reinforcing strip on the edge, and put the block of pages in a vice, where the folded edges on the top, bottom, and open side were shaved off with a plane. Stiff cardboard covered with leather was then added for the book's cover.

In the days of Joseph Smith, it took as much as a year or more for all the copies of an average book to be bound. Today we think of March 26, 1830, as the book's publication date, but we know that it was well over a year after that before all of the copies were completed in the bindery.

Three non–Latter-day Saints deserve our mention for assisting in bringing to pass the first edition of the Book of Mormon. Egbert B. Grandin was the owner-operator of the print shop in which the book was printed. His building, on Palmyra's Main Street, still stands and is now the Church visitors' center in the village. It houses an excellent printing museum that celebrates the publication of the Book of Mormon and the people who made it possible. Grandin's typesetter was John H. Gilbert, who not only oversaw the typesetting but also supplied most of the punctuation that we still have in the Book of Mormon today. Luther Howard was the owner of the bindery in the building. In September 1829, Howard and Grandin became partners in the publication business.[2] When the Book of Mormon was published the next spring, its publisher was the Howard and Grandin Company.

On Friday, March 26, 1830, the local newspaper, the *Wayne Sentinel*, of which Grandin was the publisher, advertised the Book of Mormon for the first time by publishing a copy of the title page. At the bottom of the advertisement are the following words, "The above work, containing about 600 pages, large Duodecimo [the term used for the size of the book], is now for sale, wholesale and retail, at the Palmyra Bookstore, by HOWARD & GRANDIN."[3] It appears that according to the Lord's timetable, it was necessary that the Book of Mormon be published before the Church was organized. Joseph Smith had received the Aaronic and Melchizedek Priesthoods the previous summer, yet it was not until the Book of Mormon came off the press that the Lord told him to organize the Church. That happened on April 6, 1830, eleven days after the publication of the Book of Mormon.

Joseph Smith's Bible Translation

The Prophet's ministry did not last very long, so the Lord did not allow him to waste time. He went from one great project to another. Very shortly after the publication of the Book of Mormon and the organization of the Church, the Lord instructed him to begin making a new translation of the Bible. At the time he began it, he was a twenty-four-year-old living in the wilderness of North America, with no academic training and no worldly background or skills, taking on the task of making changes in the Holy Bible, the cornerstone of Western civilization. It was an audacious undertaking, but it was something the Lord instructed the Prophet to do.

Joseph Smith used the term *translation* for his work, and so do we today. Yet it was not a translation in the normal sense of using ancient Hebrew or Greek texts and rendering them in a modern language. Instead, the Prophet was recasting the text into a new form by means of inspiration from the Holy Spirit. Professor Robert J. Matthews, an early scholar on the Joseph Smith Translation, offers a description of the process:

> When the Prophet Joseph Smith translated the Bible, he was not limited to what was found on the working page in front of him, whether that page was a sheet from the King James Version or a handwritten draft of his own early revision. The text seems to have been a "starting point," but the spirit of revelation was always an additional source of information. In the case of the Bible translation, the manuscript source was the King James Version. This suggested certain ideas, but the Spirit apparently suggested many enlargements, backgrounds, and additional concepts not found on the page. Thus the term "translation," when referring to Joseph Smith's translation of the Bible, differs somewhat from that

normally used when one thinks of translating languages. To a prophet, a revelation is a more vital and dependable source than a written text.[4]

Joseph Smith did not need original manuscripts. He was able to bypass them to go to the original source—the inspiration of the Holy Ghost that enlightened the original biblical writers.

The Prophet's work on the New Translation lasted roughly three years, from the summer of 1830 to the summer of 1833.[5] The final product was 446 manuscript pages, handwritten from margin to margin and from top to bottom on the page. The pages were approximately eight inches wide and thirteen inches tall. Joseph Smith had many interruptions while he worked on the translation during those three years, but it was an ongoing priority in his mind. Several of the revelations in the Doctrine and Covenants talk about the work and endorse what he was doing to bring it to pass. He made changes to about thirty-four hundred verses—about thirteen hundred Old Testament verses and twenty-one hundred New Testament verses.[6] Perhaps the immediacy of the gospel of Jesus Christ in the New Testament made it a higher priority than the Old Testament.

In Joseph Smith's day, the project was called the New Translation. That is what the Lord calls it in the Doctrine and Covenants, and that is what Joseph Smith and his contemporaries called it.[7] In the 1970s, as the Church was preparing revised editions of the English scriptures, the name Joseph Smith Translation was adopted, with the acronym JST used in the footnotes of the LDS edition of the Bible.[8] In the past, the New Translation was often called the *Inspired Version*. But we do not use that terminology now, because the term *Inspired Version* more accurately refers to the edited, printed rendering of the New Translation published by the Community of Christ (formerly the Reorganized Church of Jesus Christ of Latter Day Saints).

Why a New Translation?

Joseph Smith occasionally talked about why a new inspired translation of the Bible was needed. On one occasion he commented, "Many important points, touching the salvation of man, had been taken from the Bible, or lost before it was compiled."[9] In an editorial in the Church's newspaper in 1834, the Prophet said: "From what we can draw from the scriptures relative to the teachings of heaven we are induced to think, that much instruction has been given to man since the beginning which we have not."[10] Does that mean the instruction was never put in the Bible, or does it mean it was taken out? It probably means some of both. We have an example of such a thing in the Book of Mormon. When Jesus appeared to the children of Lehi, he found that something was left out of their record that was very important—a prophecy that Samuel the Lamanite had made. The Savior instructed that the missing text be put into the book (see 3 Nephi 23:6–13). Joseph Smith's statements may suggest that there were things that ancient prophets wrote that never were included in the book, or events that took place that no one thought to write about. On another occasion he said, "[There are] many things in the bible which do not, as they now stand, accord with the revelation of the holy Ghost to me."[11] When such discrepancies occur, we follow what has been revealed to Joseph Smith. One of the blessings of the Restoration is the fact that the Prophet was able to restore the gospel not only in its fullness but also in its purity. The restored gospel did not undergo the kinds of changes in the hands of uninspired people that the Bible experienced over the centuries.

Joseph Smith wrote, "We believe the Bible to be the word of God as far as it is translated correctly" (Articles of Faith 1:8). The word *translated* here seems to mean something other than how we normally use the word. The Prophet used the term more with the meaning of *transmitted*. "As far as it is *transmitted* correctly" would include the whole process of writing or dictating inspired words to a scribe, the making of copies, losing or damaging manuscripts, and everything else from the time of the original prophets to the present day. A final statement is descriptive: "I believe the Bible, as it ought to be, as it came from the pen of the original writers."[12] Indeed, we believe that the original authors of the Bible were inspired like the Prophet Joseph Smith and that as they taught, wrote, and recorded, they did so correctly, just as he did. But we cannot speak with certainty regarding what happened to those writings after the time of the original writing. Modern revelation, including Joseph Smith's New Translation, provides the key to understanding the Bible.[13]

Categories of Changes

The New Translation includes hundreds of changes made to existing verses in the King James Version. In those, the Prophet simply revised wording that was already in the Bible. For example, in Matthew 13:23, the King James Version reads, "But he that received seed into the good ground is he that heareth the word, and understandeth it." The New Translation revises the text simply by adding two words at the end: "But he who received seed into the good ground is he that heareth the word and understandeth *and endureth*."[14] The two words build on existing text, but they make the statement much more meaningful. Verse 30 of the same chapter in the King James translation reads: "Gather ye together first the tares and bind them in bundles to burn them but gather the wheat into my barn." The JST revision alters existing words, but in doing so it changes the order of events to make the statement more doctrinally accurate: "Gather ye together first the *wheat* into my barn, *and the tares are bound in bundles to be burned.*"[15]

This change has doctrinal implications, because in the last days, the Lord gathers his people to safety in Zion before the world is destroyed.

Those two examples show the Prophet changing existing text to provide expanded or new meanings. But there are other examples of material he added that have no counterpart in the Bible, sometimes large blocks of material. The best example is Moses 1 in the Pearl of Great Price. The Book of Moses is Genesis 1:1–6:13 of the New Translation. It is much longer than the Genesis equivalent, because much of it is material that has no counterpart in Genesis. Moses 1 is an example of entirely new text. The Old Testament starts, "In the beginning God created the heaven and the earth" (Genesis 1:1). But before we arrive at that point in the New Translation, we have forty-two verses of previously unknown visions that Moses had before God revealed to him the information about the Creation. Near the end of that record, the Lord said, "Moses, my son, I will speak unto thee concerning this earth upon which thou standest; and thou shalt write the things which I shall speak" (Moses 1:40). A few verses later, we read, "Behold, I reveal unto you concerning this heaven, and this earth; write the words which I speak. I am the Beginning and the End, the Almighty God; by mine Only Begotten I created these things; yea, in the beginning I created the heaven, and earth upon which thou standest" (Moses 2:1). And with that we begin the familiar Creation account.

Another example of a large text added to Genesis which has no counterpart in existing Bibles is the record of Enoch and his visions in Moses 6–7. The book of Genesis mentions the career of Enoch in six verses. The Joseph Smith Translation expands those six verses into 117, blessing us with much new information that is not preserved in the Bible. Was that material once in the Bible but later lost, or was it reserved by the Lord to come forth for the first time in the latter days? We do not have an exact answer to such questions, but in some cases we do have some hints.

When Joseph Smith made his New Translation, he did not annotate the changes to tell us why he made them. Likely several types of changes were made for various reasons. Some probably restore lost original text, while others probably restore teachings or events that were not ever recorded in the Bible. Some changes make the text easier to read, and some probably were made to correct errors or make the message more meaningful to modern readers.[16] An angel told Nephi that many plain and precious things would be taken from the Bible (see 1 Nephi 13:29). Near the end of the first chapter of the Book of Moses, the Lord says, "Thou shalt write the things which I shall speak. And in a day when the children of men shall esteem my words as naught and take many of them from the book which thou shalt write, behold, I will raise up another like unto thee; and they shall be had again among the children of men—among as many as shall believe" (Moses 1:41). The phrase "esteem as naught" suggests that people would disrespect or disregard the words, thus motivating them to remove them from the book. But God would later raise up someone like Moses—certainly Joseph Smith—to restore things that Moses had written but that had been taken out. Perhaps Moses 1—Moses's visions before the Creation revelation came—was one of those accounts, and perhaps the record of Enoch was as well.

We do not know the process by which all errors made their way into the scriptural text. The angel told Nephi that some would be made deliberately by those intent on changing the Bible for future generations (see 1 Nephi 13:26–28).[17] But perhaps most came by innocent means, through scribal error or through loss or damage to manuscripts. As an example,

I suspect that our current text of John 1:18 is one of these. The phrase "No man hath seen God at any time" contradicts evidence in the Bible itself, where several instances are recorded of prophets seeing God (e.g., Exodus 24:9–11; 33:11; Numbers 12:6–8; Isaiah 6:1; Amos 9:1). Joseph Smith changed it to "No man hath seen God at any time, *except he hath borne record of the Son*,"[18] which adds a new dimension to the verse and makes it historically and doctrinally correct.

Joseph Smith made many small changes in the Bible that make it more understandable for modern readers. In fact, modernization of the text is the single most common type of change he made in the New Translation. Few Latter-day Saints are aware of this, because those changes are not found in the footnotes to our Church edition of the Bible. In the years leading up to 1979, when the Church published an LDS edition of the Bible in English, the decision was made to include JST changes in the footnotes on a priority basis, because not all could be included. The significant doctrinal and historical contributions were selected to be included, but changes made to modernize grammar or make the text easier to read were not considered a high priority.[19]

Examples of this type include changing the archaic word *wot* to *know*. The Prophet instructed that *wot* be changed to *know* every time it appears.[20] The article *an* was changed to *a* before words that begin with *h*, as in the phrase *an house*. The word *saith* was often changed to *said*. This is not simply a change from an old form to a modern form, but it also revises the text from a present tense to a past tense to make the sentences read more easily. When referring to humans, the King James translation often uses the relative pronouns *that* and *which* instead of *who*: "For unto you is born this day in the city of David a Saviour, *which* is Christ the Lord" (Luke 2:11).

The Prophet generally changed those to *who*, putting them more in line with common speech. There are also places where *ye*, *thou*, and *thee* are changed to *you*, which in today's English is used in place of the three archaic forms. He also modernized verbal conjugations. In a passage from the Book of Moses, the Lord speaks to Moses of "this earth upon which *thou* stand*est*" (Moses 1:40). In his final revision of the manuscript, Joseph Smith changed it to "this earth upon which *you stand*." In the same verse, he changed "and *thou shalt* write" to "and *you shall* write," and in the next verse, "like unto *thee*" is changed to "like unto *you*."²¹ But Joseph Smith did not make changes like these with universal consistency. In Moses 6:32 we read, "all flesh is in *my* hands," but in Moses 7:36 we read, "the workmanship of *mine* hands," using the modernized form in one instance but not in the other. Inconsistencies like these are found in several places in the manuscripts, showing that modernization of the text was not the Prophet's highest priority. Even so, he made enough changes of this kind to convince me that it was his intention to modernize and simplify the text in this manner.

There are scores of places where the Prophet clarified the pronouns *he* and *she* by replacing them with the names to which those words refer. For example, "Mary abode with *her*" (Luke 1:56) is changed to "Mary abode with *Elizabeth*,"²² and "*he* went up into the ship" (Luke 8:37) is changed to "*Jesus* went up into the ship."²³ As a result of changes like these, Joseph Smith's New Translation is much more precise than traditional Bibles. Some changes may have been made as a result of cultural realities. Paul ends most of his epistles with the phrase, "Greet all the brethren with an holy kiss" (e.g., 1 Thessalonians 5:26). In the Mediterranean world, both in Paul's day and now, men openly greet male friends with a kiss on each cheek. But that was not the case in Joseph Smith's world, nor is it in Western society today. On each occasion where this phrase appears in the Bible, the Prophet replaced the word *kiss* with *salutation*.[24] I suspect that the text in the Bible accurately records Paul's original words, but Joseph Smith seems to have made a *cultural* translation here to render the passage more appropriate and useful for his own time and ours.

Dates and Scribes

Joseph Smith began Genesis in June 1830 and worked to Genesis 24 by March 1831.[25] It was during this time that the Book of Moses was revealed, which is the first chapters of Genesis from the JST. On March 7, 1831, the Lord instructed him in revelation to stop working on the Old Testament and work on the New Testament instead, because it contained things that he needed to learn (see Doctrine and Covenants 45:60–62). The next day, he began the New Testament translation, and he worked on it until July 1832. Then he went back to Genesis 24 and translated from there to the end of the Old Testament, which he finished on July 2, 1833. In addition to the initial translation, there are some parts of the work where the Prophet went through a second time to make further revisions and refinements to the translation. That work was done for the New Testament by February 1832, and it was probably done for the Old Testament by the completion date of July 2, 1833.[26]

Like most other prominent people of his day, Joseph Smith wrote little with his own hand but did most of his writing by dictating his words to scribes. For six years, I worked with a group of Brigham Young University students to decipher the JST manuscripts in preparation for their publication in a facsimile typescript. In that process, we became very familiar with the six scribes who worked on the translation with Joseph Smith. We spent much time studying their handwriting and were ultimately able to distinguish scribal hands and determine where each one began and ended. During that time, I walked into my office one day and found my research assistant Brenda Johnson practicing my signature. I thought it was odd to find her practicing her boss's signature, but I realized that I had a worker who had a gift for understanding and distinguishing handwriting. She worked on the project for several years and became an expert on the scribal hands in the New Translation manuscripts. Of the 446 handwritten pages that make up the New Translation, only a few contain Joseph Smith's handwriting. He served as his own scribe for three pages in the Old Testament, and he made small revisions in his own hand in a few other locations.

Oliver Cowdery was Joseph Smith's first scribe for the New Translation. He and the Prophet knew how to work together, having labored as seer and scribe for most of the translation of the Book of Mormon. Next, John Whitmer was called to be the scribe, probably because Cowdery was called to leave on a mission to the west in October 1830. Whitmer was the primary scribe from October to December. We have Emma Smith's handwriting on the Genesis manuscript, dated December 1. Her handwriting was not discovered until 1995. That summer, Brigham Young University researchers Robert J. Matthews and Scott H. Faulring were in Independence, Missouri, and were looking at the JST manuscripts. In the middle of the John Whitmer section, they noticed what appeared to be a different scribal hand. Professor Matthews had long suspected that Emma Smith had worked as a scribe on the New Translation, and his thoughts were confirmed when samples of her correspondence were compared with the writing on the JST manuscript.[27] In a revelation that the Prophet had received in behalf of his wife in July 1830, she was instructed, "Thou shalt . . . be unto him for a scribe, while there is no one to be a scribe for him"—that is, she was called to be the backup scribe—"that I may send my servant, Oliver Cowdery, whithersoever I will" (Doctrine and Covenants 25:6). By the time her services were needed as scribe, Cowdery had been assigned elsewhere, and John Whitmer was the primary scribe.

Sidney Rigdon was called to serve as the Prophet's scribe in December 1830 (see Doctrine and Covenants 35:20), and he served in that capacity until March 1832. His handwriting is the most common on the pages; more than half of the pages show him as the original scribe. Jesse Gause, who served as a counselor in the First Presidency with Joseph Smith and Sidney Rigdon, served also as scribe off and on in March 1832. Fredrick G. Williams replaced Gause in the First Presidency and as scribe on the New Translation. He began as scribe in July 1832 and continued until July 1833, when the translation was completed.

A look at the names of the scribes shows that Joseph Smith selected those who were closest to him in his ministry: the Second Elder and Assistant President (Oliver Cowdery), a close confidant and early Church leader (John Whitmer), counselors in the first presidency (Sidney Rigdon, Jesse Gause, and Frederick G. Williams), and his wife (Emma Hale Smith). Most of the translation was done by the First Presidency, with Joseph Smith dictating the translation and his counselors serving as scribes. That suggests that the Prophet and those he selected to help him knew this to be a sacred work.

Manuscripts and Publications

Joseph Smith and his scribes produced two Old Testament manuscripts. Old Testament Manuscript 1 is the original text for Genesis 1–24.[28] It was ended when the Prophet shifted his focus to the New Testament. While the translation of the New Testament was under way with Sidney Rigdon serving as scribe, Joseph Smith had John Whitmer make a backup copy of Old Testament 1, influenced, no doubt, by his memory of losing the manuscript of the first part of the Book of Mormon three years earlier. We call that backup copy Old Testament Manuscript 2. But when the New Testament was completed and the Prophet returned to the translation of the Old Testament, he did it not on Old Testament 1 but on Old Testament 2. It was on Old Testament 2 that he finished the translation through Malachi, and he used it when he went through Genesis again and made further revisions and refinements to what he had translated earlier. Thus the backup copy had become the manuscript on which the rest of the work was done. On the Genesis pages, one can see where the original text is and were the later refinements were added. Often the later corrections are in a darker ink, and they are almost always in a different scribal hand. Joseph Smith's pattern usually was that he would do the original translation with one scribe but make further adjustments to the text using a different scribe. He made the later refinements as he apparently studied the wording out in his mind and followed spiritual promptings to adjust it until he was satisfied that it was right.

We see the same pattern in the New Testament manuscripts. The original dictation of Matthew is on a manuscript we call New Testament Manuscript 1. The Prophet interrupted the work at Matthew 26 when he went to Missouri for much of the summer of 1831. While he was gone, John Whitmer made a backup copy, which we call New Testament 2. When the Prophet returned and resumed the New Testament translation, he did it on New Testament 2, with the backup copy again becoming the copy for the ongoing translation through the end of the New Testament. On that manuscript, he made further refinements to text already recorded until he was confident that the translation was as the Lord wanted it to be.

After the translation and later refinements were completed, probably by July 2, 1833, Joseph Smith had assistants go through the manuscripts again and add punctuation, capitalization, and chapter and verse divisions to get the translation ready for printing. Contemporary documents show that he felt an urgent desire to publish the New Translation and regularly expressed disappointment that the Saints could not raise the money to get it printed.[29] Although some excerpts were printed in newspapers during his lifetime, the work as a whole remained unpublished at the time of his death in June 1844. When he was killed, the manuscripts were in the hands of his family, and they stayed in their possession until the 1860s. During those years, Emma Smith carefully preserved them, keeping them safe and treating them as the precious documents that they are. She conveyed them to the Reorganized Church of Jesus Christ of Latter Day Saints, and they have been in the Community of Christ archival collection since that time.

In 1851, Elder Franklin D. Richards, Apostle and president of the British Mission, created a pamphlet for the benefit of his mission, containing writings that came from the Prophet Joseph Smith.[30] He called his pamphlet the *Pearl of Great Price*, drawing its name from the parable in Matthew 13. He included some excerpts from Joseph Smith's New Translation of the Bible: an early and fragmentary version of the Book of Moses that he obtained from Church newspapers and hand-copied manuscripts, and Matthew chapter 24, which he obtained from other early Latter-day Saint printings.

In 1867 the Reorganized Church of Jesus Christ of Latter Day Saints took the New Translation manuscripts and printed them in a book. The publication committee added chapter and verse divisions patterned after those in traditional Bibles (rather than following those on the manuscripts), and they standardized spelling, punctuation, and capitalization. Thus they published *The Holy Scriptures: Translated and Corrected by the Spirit of Revelation*, commonly called the *Inspired Version*.[31] It is the Community of Christ's edition of Joseph Smith's Bible revision, and it is still in print today. The work was done with great care, and for the most part it accurately reproduces what is on the manuscripts. In order to create a modern book in Bible format, the editors had to make thousands of editorial decisions, because the text contained inconsistencies in spelling, grammar, and punctuation. When they dealt with the two Old Testament manuscripts, they misunderstood the relationship between the two. As a result, they omitted from the *Inspired Version* many of the revisions the Prophet made in Genesis, and thus important changes were not passed on in later printings.

In 1878 leaders of The Church of Jesus Christ of Latter-day Saints in Utah published a Churchwide edition of Elder Richards's British Mission pamphlet. The task was placed in the hands of Elder Orson Pratt of the Quorum of the Twelve. Elder Pratt had no access to the original New Translation manuscripts, but he was aware that the Genesis material in the British Mission *Pearl of Great Price* was fragmentary and out of order. To create the Book of Moses as we have it today, he simply copied it exactly out of the 1867 RLDS *Inspired Version*, which he rightly surmised to be a more accurate and complete text than was in the British edition. This is the text that has been in all subsequent editions of the Book of Moses, with some later revising. Neither that edition nor any later edition of the Pearl of Great Price was prepared with access to the original manuscripts. At the October 1880 general conference of the Church, the Pearl of Great Price was canonized as scripture, and thus a Genesis excerpt (Book of Moses) and a Matthew excerpt (Joseph Smith—Matthew) have been part of our scriptures and standard works since then.

In 2004 the Religious Studies Center at Brigham Young University published a typographic transcription of all the original manuscript pages, complete with original spelling, punctuation, cross-outs, and insertions.[32] BYU researchers had complete access to the original manuscripts, and with the full cooperation of the Community of Christ, they transcribed them and printed them in typescript in an imposing book. Now, for the first time in history, scholars and laypeople alike can avail themselves freely of the original texts of Joseph Smith's translation of the Bible.

Blessings from the New Translation

We obtain many blessings from Joseph Smith's Bible translation. By way of direct blessings, we have the excerpts in the Pearl of Great Price and many other revised readings that strengthen the Bible's text, clarify its message, and reveal many new things that we are just beginning to learn and understand. Perhaps the best of these are found in footnotes in the English LDS Bible and in the "Guide to the Scriptures," published with the triple combination in other languages and posted on the Church's Internet site.[33] The availability of these JST readings has permanently changed gospel scholarship in the Church by bringing the translation to the place it deserves as one of the great contributions of the Prophet Joseph Smith.

But we also have many indirect blessings that derive from the Joseph Smith Translation that most Latter-day Saints have not considered before. Many of the revelations in the Doctrine and Covenants came as a result of things the Prophet was pondering and questioning as he worked on his translation of the Bible.

Seventy-seven sections of the Doctrine and Covenants, 56 percent of the total number, were revealed during the months that the Prophet was engaged in the translation. Some sections of the Doctrine and Covenants are explicitly tied to it. The vision of the three degrees of glory, section 76, came directly as a result of questions the Prophet asked while translating. He and his scribe, Sidney Rigdon, wrote, "While we were doing the work of translation, which the Lord had appointed unto us, we came to the twenty-ninth verse of the fifth chapter of John" (Doctrine and Covenants 76:15). The Lord revealed to them a revised reading of the verse, which caused them "to marvel" (Doctrine and Covenants 76:18). Then the Lord revealed the vision of the degrees of glory. Other revelations, such as sections 77, 91, and 132, can be linked to the Bible translation rather easily, and several others offer hints that they were received as a result of that work.

Another indirect blessing we enjoy because of the New Translation is the education Joseph Smith received while working on it. Robert Matthews has said, "The Lord had Joseph Smith make a translation of the Bible because of the good it would do Joseph Smith as well as the good it would also do the Church. This is the way in which the Prophet Joseph Smith learned many things about the gospel."[34] He added, "Through the experience of translating the Bible Joseph Smith was to come into possession of knowledge he did not previously have. . . . The labor was to be its own reward and would result in the spiritual education of the Prophet."[35] Indeed, Joseph Smith not only learned the Bible well from the process, but he also learned well how to understand it by the Spirit. For the rest of his life, he garnished his sermons with generous amounts of material from the Bible, usually presenting passages in a new light with expanded meanings not known by his contemporaries.[36]

The Joseph Smith Translation is a great miracle, and it is something that we have not appreciated enough over the course of the history of the Church. When I was a BYU student in the early 1970s, I had a class from Robert Matthews, who at the time was doing groundbreaking research on the Joseph Smith Translation. He quoted from it frequently in class. This worried me, because I had been taught that we should not use it because Joseph Smith did not finish it, because it was mysterious, because someone had tampered with it, because it was unreliable, and because the Church rejected it. None of those things were true, but many Latter-day Saints believed them for generations. Because of Professor Matthews's research and publications that introduced the New Translation to the Church and made it possible to have the excerpts printed in our Bible, we now know it for what it really is—a revelatory text and a witness to the divine calling of the Prophet Joseph Smith. My students today at Brigham Young University have been trained from their youth to know the New Translation and to appreciate its contributions to our understanding of the gospel. The original manuscripts themselves bear testimony to it. The Old Testament begins with these words: "A Revelation given to Joseph the Revelator."[37] Above a later Old Testament section we read, "A revelation given to the Elders of the Church of Christ." Then the New Testament starts, "A Translation of the New Testament translated by the power of God."[38] And in the Doctrine and Covenants, the Lord endorsed it in his own words when he called Sidney Rigdon to be a scribe for the translation: "And the scriptures shall be given, even as they are in mine own bosom, for the salvation of mine own elect" (Doctrine and Covenants 35:20).

Notes

1. The following discussion summarizes Kent P. Jackson, "Publishing the Book of Mormon," in *Joseph: Exploring the Life and Ministry of the Prophet*, ed. Susan Easton Black and Andrew C. Skinner (Salt Lake City: Deseret Book, 2005), 107–16.

2. See *Wayne Sentinel*, September 11, 1829.

3. *Wayne Sentinel*, March 26, 1830.

4. Robert J. Matthews, "What Is the Book of Moses?" in *Studies in Scripture*, vol. 2: *The Pearl of Great Price*, ed. Robert L. Millet and Kent P. Jackson (Salt Lake City: Randall Book, 1985), 37.

5. For the original manuscripts of the New Translation and its history, see Scott H. Faulring, Kent P. Jackson, and Robert J. Matthews, *Joseph Smith's New Translation of the Bible: Original Manuscripts* (Provo, UT: Religious Studies Center, Brigham Young University, 2004).

6. Robert J. Matthews, *"A Plainer Translation": Joseph Smith's Translation of the Bible—A History and Commentary* (Provo, UT: Brigham Young University Press, 1975), 425.

7. Doctrine and Covenants 124:89; *Times and Seasons*, July 1840, 140; Joseph Smith, *History of the Church of Jesus Christ of Latter-day Saints*, ed. B. H. Roberts, 2nd ed. rev. (Salt Lake City: Deseret Book, 1957), 1:341, 365; 4:164.

8. The title was invented because the abbreviation *NT* could not be used in the footnotes because it is commonly used for the New Testament (Robert J. Matthews, personal communication).

9. *The Papers of Joseph Smith*, vol. 1, *Autobiographical and Historical Writings*, ed. Dean C. Jessee (Salt Lake City: Deseret Book, 1989–92), 372.

10. *Evening and Morning Star*, March 1834, 143.

11. *The Words of Joseph Smith: The Contemporary Accounts of the Nauvoo Discourses of the Prophet Joseph*, ed. Andrew F. Ehat and

Lyndon W. Cook (Provo, UT: Religious Studies Center, Brigham Young University, 1980), 211.

12. *Words of Joseph Smith*, 256.

13. See Kent P. Jackson, "Asking Restoration Questions in New Testament Scholarship," in *How the New Testament Came to Be*, ed. Kent P. Jackson and Frank F. Judd Jr. (Provo, UT: Religious Studies Center, Brigham Young University; Salt Lake City: Deseret Book, 2006), 27–42.

14. New Testament Manuscript 2, Folio 1, page 25, lines 22–24, in Faulring, Jackson, and Matthews, *Joseph Smith's New Translation of the Bible*, 266–67. In some JST quotations that follow, capitalization, punctuation, and spelling are standardized. Italics are added to some passages to highlight differences between the New Translation and the King James Version.

15. New Testament Manuscript 2, Folio 1, page 25, pinned note at line 37, in Faulring, Jackson, and Matthews, *Joseph Smith's New Translation of the Bible*, 267.

16. See Faulring, Jackson, and Matthews, *Joseph Smith's New Translation*, 8–10.

17. For a possible setting for changes in the text, see Jackson, *From Apostasy to Restoration* (Salt Lake City: Deseret Book, 1996), 19–30; and "Asking Restoration Questions in New Testament Scholarship," 34–37.

18. New Testament Manuscript 2, Folio 4, pages 105–6, in Faulring, Jackson, and Matthews, *Joseph Smith's New Translation*, 443.

19. Robert J. Matthews, personal communication.

20. Old Testament Manuscript 2, page 69, line 17, in Faulring, Jackson, and Matthews, *Joseph Smith's New Translation*, 699.

21. Old Testament Manuscript 2, page 3, lines 30–34, in Faulring, Jackson, and Matthews, *Joseph Smith's New Translation*, 594. None of these changes from Moses 1:40–41 are in the current edition of the book of Moses. See Kent P. Jackson, *The Book of Moses and the Joseph*

Smith Translation Manuscripts (Provo, UT: Religious Studies Center, Brigham Young University, 2005), 66.

22. New Testament Manuscript 2, Folio 2, page 48, line 11, in Faulring, Jackson, and Matthews, *Joseph Smith's New Translation*, 362.

23. New Testament Manuscript 2, Folio 3, page 65, lines 25–26, in Faulring, Jackson, and Matthews, *Joseph Smith's New Translation*, 387.

24. For example, see New Testament Manuscript 2, Folio 4, page 135, line 26, in Faulring, Jackson, and Matthews, *Joseph Smith's New Translation*, 527.

25. A convenient timeline of the New Translation is found in Faulring, Jackson, and Matthews, *Joseph Smith's New Translation*, 57–59.

26. Evidence for the dates is presented in the introductions to the individual manuscripts in Faulring, Jackson, and Matthews, *Joseph Smith's New Translation*. See also Kent P. Jackson, "New Discoveries in the Joseph Smith Translation of the Bible," *Religious Educator* 6, no. 3 (2005): 149–60.

27. See "Emma and the Joseph Smith Translation," *Insights: An Ancient Window*, August 1996.

28. For discussions of the manuscripts individually, see the introductions to each in Faulring, Jackson, and Matthews, *Joseph Smith's New Translation*.

29. "You will see by these revelations that we have to print the new translation here at kirtland for which we will prepare as soon as possible" (Joseph Smith, Sidney Rigdon, and Frederick G. Williams to Edward Partridge, August 6, 1833, Joseph Smith Collection, Church History Library). See Robert J. Matthews, "Joseph Smith's Efforts to Publish His Bible 'Translation,'" *Ensign*, January 1983, 57–64.

30. More detailed discussions for this and the following paragraphs can be found in Jackson, *The Book of Moses and the Joseph Smith Translation Manuscripts*, 18–52.

31. *The Holy Scriptures: Translated and Corrected by the Spirit of Revelation. By Joseph Smith, Jr., the Seer* (Plano, IL: The [Reorganized] Church of Jesus Christ of Latter Day Saints, 1867).

32. Faulring, Jackson, and Matthews, *Joseph Smith's New Translation*.

33. See http://scriptures.lds.org. The two changes that I most wish had been included with the LDS edition of the Bible are an addition at the end of John 8:11 that concludes the story of the woman taken in adultery: "And the woman glorified God from that hour, and believed on his name" (New Testament Manuscript 2, Folio 4, page 116, lines 2–3, in Faulring, Jackson, and Matthews, *Joseph Smith's New Translation of the Bible*, 459); and an addition after Mark 14:28, telling that Judas betrayed Jesus because Judas was an apostate: Judas "went unto the chief priests to betray Jesus unto them, for he turned away from him and was offended because of his words" (New Testament Manuscript 2, Folio 2, page 40, lines 15–17, in Faulring, Jackson, and Matthews, *Joseph Smith's New Translation of the Bible*, 352).

34. Robert J. Matthews, "Using the Scriptures," *Brigham Young University 1981 Fireside and Devotional Speeches* (Provo, UT: Brigham Young University Publications, 1981), 123.

35. Matthews, *A Plainer Translation*, 53.

36. See Kent P. Jackson, "The Prophet's Teachings in Nauvoo," in *Joseph*, 367–79.

37. Faulring, Jackson, and Matthews, *Joseph Smith's New Translation of the Bible*, 83.

38. Faulring, Jackson, and Matthews, *Joseph Smith's New Translation of the Bible*, 159.

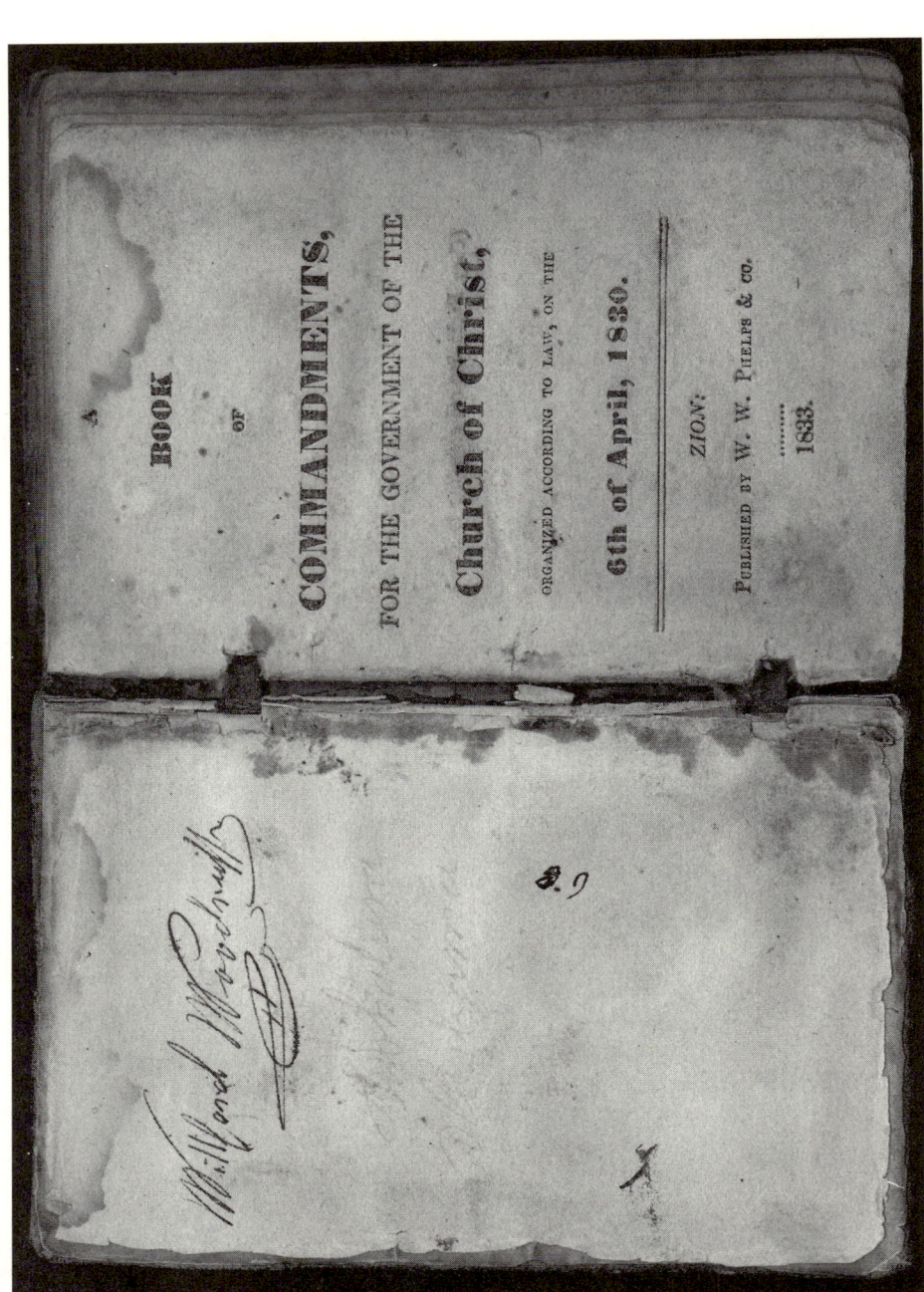

Title page, Book of Commandments. (Courtesy of Church History Library.)

GRANT UNDERWOOD

1831
A Flood of Revelations

While not all the revelations Joseph Smith dictated were canonized, it is a mistake to think his canonized revelations represent only the tip of the revelatory iceberg. There is no vast collection of unpublished, uncanonized revelations in the Church archives. The editors of the Joseph Smith Papers Project are grateful that the Church has made available every known document written or dictated by Joseph Smith. Nothing has been withheld. We have been able to look at everything that has survived, and I assure you that only a relative handful of revelations have not been canonized.[1]

Of the Prophet's 135 revelations in the Doctrine and Covenants, 38 were received in 1831. That represents

---

Grant Underwood is a professor of history at Brigham Young University and an editor of The Joseph Smith Papers.

28 percent of the canonized revelations, and a word count bumps this figure to over 30 percent. Think of that—more than a fourth of all the revealed words dictated by the Prophet Joseph Smith were received in a single year, 1831.

A few other years come close to that percentage but still fall short:

> 1829: 15 percent
> 1830: 19 percent (the second most productive year, but still significantly less than 1831)
> 1832: 18 percent
> 1833: 12 percent

Each of the other years during Joseph's life were 8 percent or less.

Revelations Received in 1831

Thus we see that 1831 produced a marvelous flood of revelations. These revelations now constitute sections 38 through 72, as well as sections 1 and 133 (the revealed preface and appendix to the Book of Commandments) and what I would call 107b. Most of the verses from 107:59 to the end of the section are actually a separate revelation received in November 1831 that the Prophet and his associates decided to append to the revealed material from March 1835 that makes up the first part of 107. Today, it is a flowing, continuous revelation.

What was it about 1831 that made this a year of such revelatory significance? First of all, at the beginning of the year, Joseph received a revelation directed to the small band of believers in New York who, in their three branches of Palmyra, Fayette, and Colesville, numbered less than one hundred. These Saints were to gather to Ohio, where the missionaries had visited Parley Pratt's old spiritual mentor, Sidney Rigdon, several months earlier. Rigdon, a number of his followers, and some others had joined the Church, and in a matter of weeks, the Church counted over a hundred converts in Ohio. So, at the beginning of 1831, a large body of recent converts was residing in northeastern Ohio, and the Lord directed Joseph Smith to bring all the Saints from New York and move to Ohio.

Always on the horizon in the early part of 1831 was the promise made in the fall of 1830 that the location of the New Jerusalem, or Zion, would be revealed. Several revelations were given regarding the New Jerusalem as the ultimate gathering place; Ohio was only the interim gathering place. A large portion of revelations in 1831, beginning in section 52 and going through section 64, in one way or another pertains to the identification of Zion and the initial efforts toward establishing it.

Several other themes stand out in the 1831 revelations. One pertains to distinguishing legitimate spiritual manifestations or spiritual gifts from counterfeit or false manifestations. Another is keen interest in the end times—a sense of the approaching return of the Lord that was stimulated by this flood of revelations and by the wording in a number of the revelations. The Saints were concerned about prophecy, and several revelations addressing that topic were received in 1831. Toward the end of the year, another important matter engaged the Prophet and his associates: the publication of Joseph's revelations. The first compilation of revelations was known as the Book of Commandments. A series of November conferences in 1831 took up the task of deciding how and under what circumstances to publish the revelations received up to that point.

Reasons for the Gathering

Before the Saints could gather to Zion, they were to gather to Ohio. A revelation given in conference on January 2, 1831, now found in the Doctrine and Covenants as section 38, gives reasons for the gathering that amount to a kind of "push-pull." Verse 31 expresses the "push" factor: "That ye might escape the power of the enemy." There had been persecution from the beginning—antagonism to the Prophet and to his work—but there had also been a particular swirl of opposition to the Saints in Colesville, the southern New York branch. Joseph had gone to Colesville the previous summer to confirm the Church members, but they faced stiff resistance from their enemies. It took a number of weeks before he could confirm the Saints; so the phrase "that you might escape the power of the enemy" was the push to leave New York.

If we want to consider the "pull" toward Ohio, it was the ideal of being "gathered unto [God] a righteous people without spot and blameless" (v. 31). Significant spiritual progress can be aided and abetted by community—by togetherness. "Wherefore," the Lord declares in verse 32, "for this cause I gave unto you the commandment that ye should go to the Ohio; and there I will give unto you my law." That happened very soon after they arrived. Then, the promise continues, "And there you shall be endowed with power from on high, and from thence whosoever I will shall go forth among all nations" (vv. 32–33). So there we see the particular promises that pulled the Saints to Ohio. Significant spiritual moments awaited them there as well as shelter from persecution.

Gathering was the major theme of 1831—at least the one addressed in most of the revelations. The previous fall, in section 29, verses 7 and 8, the Lord tells the Saints that they "are called to bring to pass the gathering of mine elect. . . . Wherefore the decree hath gone forth from the Father that they [the elect] shall be gathered in unto one place upon the face of this land." Note the rationale that follows: "to prepare their hearts and be prepared in all things against the day when tribulation and desolation are sent forth upon the wicked." The first phrase, "to prepare their hearts," suggests becoming a people without spot or blame, spiritually maturing into a united organization and group. The last phrase, to "be prepared in all things against the day when tribulation and desolation are sent forth upon the wicked," addresses a theme stated even more forcefully in the next few verses—the concept of shelter and preparation against a latter-day outpouring of divine judgment upon the wicked: "For the hour is nigh and the day soon at hand when the earth is ripe; and all the proud and they that do wickedly shall be as stubble, and I will burn them up, saith the Lord of Hosts. . . . For I will reveal myself from heaven with power and great glory, with all the hosts thereof, and dwell in righteousness with men on earth a thousand years, and the wicked shall not stand" (vv. 9, 11). Those few verses encapsulate key concepts among the early Saints. They had a powerful sense that the end was imminent and that the one place of safety, the one place of refuge, would be the gathering location: Zion, the New Jerusalem. Not surprisingly, reference to the gathering appears subsequently in many of the 1831 revelations.

Section 45, given in March 1831, directs, "And with one heart and with one mind, gather up your riches that you may purchase an inheritance which shall hereafter be appointed unto you" (v. 65). It was not for another four months, not until July, that Joseph received the revelation identifying the precise location—hence the word "hereafter." "And it shall be called the New Jerusalem, a land of peace" (v. 66). Notice the next image in that verse: "a city of refuge." Refuge from what? "From tribulation and desolation" that shall be poured out on the world, as mentioned in Doctrine and Covenants 29. In the latter days, Zion will be "a city of refuge, a place of safety for the Saints of the Most High God. And the glory of the Lord shall be there, and the terror of the Lord also shall be there, insomuch that the wicked will not come unto it, and it shall be called Zion" (vv. 66–67). Exciting concepts were revealed in these months.

Gathering to Zion

In February 1831, after gathering to Ohio, the Prophet received what we now call "the Law," a composite revelation published as section 42 of the Doctrine and Covenants. A core part of the Law pertains to what we call the "law of consecration," initially a kind of resource-sharing program outlined by the Lord. This revelation answered questions in the Saints' minds: How do we finance this growing Church? How do we utilize our limited resources to advance the work?

In March, the revelation known as section 48 came. Beginning in verse 4, the Lord again tells the Saints to get their resources ready to purchase "land for an inheritance, even the city." However, the Lord said, "The place is not yet to be revealed; but after your brethren come from the east" (v. 5). That is, after the Saints come from New York, "there are to be certain men appointed, and to them it shall be given to know the place, or to them it shall be revealed" (v. 5).

Not long thereafter, the New York Saints began to arrive, and in early June of 1831 a very important conference took place. It probably constituted the largest gathering of ordained brethren in the Church to that point. Though it would be small by our standards—perhaps fifty brethren—important things took place. In that conference the first ordinations to the office of high priest occurred. At the tail end of the conference, a revelation was given commissioning several dozen elders to take up their journey to Missouri, where, as it says in section 52, verse 2, the next conference will be held "upon the land which I will consecrate unto my people, which are a remnant of Jacob." Once there, the location of Zion would be revealed: "Wherefore, verily I say unto you, let my servants Joseph Smith, Jun., and Sidney Rigdon take their journey as soon as preparations can be made.... And inasmuch as they are faithful unto me, it shall be made known unto them what they shall do; and it shall also, inasmuch as they are faithful, be made known unto them the land of your inheritance" (vv. 3–5). This was the message they had been waiting for: go to Missouri, and there the location of Zion will be revealed.

Location of Zion

Joseph and a handful of elders arrived in Jackson County, Missouri, in mid July. There, in a small gathering, section 57 was revealed. Not all of the elders assigned had arrived, not even the majority, but those who were there heard these words: "In this land, which is the land of Missouri, which is the land which I have appointed and consecrated for the gathering of the saints. Wherefore, this is the land of promise, and the place for the city of Zion" (vv. 1–2). Then came the very specific answer, "Behold, the place which is now called Independence is the center place; and a spot for the temple is lying westward, upon a lot which is not far from the courthouse" (v. 3).[2] Sixty-three acres in a somewhat triangular shape were purchased a few months later by Bishop Edward Partridge as part of his assignment to purchase land for Zion and for the temple. Those sixty-three acres were later known as the "temple lot."[3]

Section 57 mentions only one temple. Two years later, in 1833, Joseph expanded his plans to build twenty-four temples. At this point in time, temples did not have the same meaning they do today. A temple was usually understood as a meetinghouse. It was not a site where members needed a temple recommend to enter and where special, sacred ceremonies were performed. The temple endowment, as it is known today among the Saints, was not revealed until May 1842. Thus, temples in the 1830s are better understood as meetinghouses or facilities for administrative purposes. In 1833, when Joseph had the city plan for Zion drawn up, he anticipated a future population of ten to fifteen thousand. In such circumstances twenty-four temples, or meetinghouses, would be needed to accommodate the Saints in their Sunday worship.

Sabbath Observance

While in Missouri, the Prophet received the revelation we now know as section 59, which deals with Sabbath observance. Missouri in the 1830s was a rough place. A missionary from another church described Missourians as a very uncivilized people—untrained, uncouth; indulging in gambling, horseracing, and cockfighting. "Christian Sabbath observance here appears to be unknown," he wrote. "When the Santa Fe wagon trains return here, or pass through on their way eastward, there is a multiplication of sin beyond the usual amount. There appears to be an overabundance of females here practicing the world's oldest profession. . . . Gouging and more serious forms of violence are common."[4] Concerns about these behaviors elicited this revelation, which was actually published very early as a broadside by the Latter-day Saints to affirm their vision of the Christian Sabbath. I believe today Sabbath behavior among the Latter-day Saints sets us apart from many other Christians who take Sabbath observance a little more lightly than we do.

Foundation of Zion

"On the second day of August," while still in Missouri, the Prophet "assisted the Colesville branch of the Church to lay the first log, for a house, as a foundation of Zion in Kaw township, twelve miles west of Independence. The log was carried and placed by twelve men, in honor of the twelve tribes of Israel. At the same time, through prayer, the land of Zion was consecrated and dedicated by Elder Sidney Rigdon for the gathering of the Saints. It was a season of joy to those present, and afforded a glimpse of the future, which time will yet unfold to the satisfaction of the faithful."[5]

Several sections in the 50s pertain to the Colesville Branch, the first branch to arrive in Missouri. Section 51 is about previously settling them on a piece of Ohio property that a particular individual had supposedly made available. When that individual withdrew his goodwill, the question arose: what happens now? Section 54 answers that question by saying, in essence: "You get to be the first branch to gather to Missouri—the first group of people other than those ordained elders commissioned in section 52 to go to Missouri as a group." Section 56 has a few more things to say about that.

A point of interest in terms of understanding the emerging Church can be found in a couple of verses sometimes overlooked in section 57—verses 15 and 16. The verses are directed to Bishop Edward Partridge and Sidney Gilbert. Gilbert was designated as the "agent," which essentially amounted to a real estate or business agent. He and Bishop Partridge were to work together to acquire the land for the beginning of Zion. The Lord says, "And now concerning the gathering—let the bishop and the agent make preparations for those families which have been commanded to come to this land" (v. 15). At this point in time, the only families aside from the Colesville Branch that had been commanded to come were the families of several of the leaders—Edward Partridge, Sidney Gilbert, and W. W. Phelps—addressed earlier in section 57. The leaders families were back in Ohio nearly a thousand miles away and now were commanded "to come to this land, as soon as possible," after which the bishop and agent were to "plant them in their inheritance" (v.15). The revelation then concluded with these words: "And unto the residue of both elders and members further directions shall be given hereafter" (v. 16). This set the stage for subsequent revelations that told the general membership that they were not intended to immediately race off to Zion. One imagines that many of the early Saints were hoping for just that, but by reason and revelation Joseph cooled their spirits a bit.

In section 58, received a few days later, more is said about bringing out the aforementioned families: "Now, as I spake concerning my servant Edward Partridge, this is the land of his residence, and those whom he has appointed for his counselors; and also the land of the residence of him whom I have appointed to keep my storehouse [Sidney Gilbert]; wherefore, let them bring their families to this land, as they shall counsel between themselves and me. For behold, it is not meet that I should command in all things" (vv. 24–26). Remember that the word "command" had a richer meaning then. What was the first collection of revelations called? Not the Book of Revelations, but the Book of Commandments. Commandments, in Joseph's usage, meant something far more than simply, "Thou shalt" or "thou shalt not." It was any instruction, insight, or direction from God, so commandments served as a synonym for revelations. Thus, when the Lord says, "It is not meet that I should command in all things" (v. 26), it meant "it is not meet that I reveal or direct in all things." Now, this was a wonderfully pragmatic statement. The Lord had to wean the Saints from constant dependence on the Prophet for revelation on every matter. Such a dependence would not work when Edward Partridge and Sidney Gilbert were a thousand miles from the Prophet, and the Lord apparently used this occasion to teach the brethren that "the power [was] in them wherein they [were] agents unto themselves" (v. 28).

The Law of Consecration

To build Zion, of course, would require money to purchase land and section 58 counseled the Saints to consecrate their money for the gathering: "And now I give unto you further directions concerning this land. It is wisdom in me that my servant Martin Harris should be an example unto the church, in laying his moneys before the bishop of the church" (vv. 34–35). It is in the Law (D&C 42) where the provision for resource sharing, for what we call "consecration," is found, and Martin Harris, the great financial patron of the Restoration, was here once again being asked to lay his monies before the bishop of the Church. "And also, this is a law unto every man that cometh unto this land to receive an inheritance; and he [the bishop] shall do with his moneys according as the law directs" (v. 36).

Zion was not just a nice place to live; it was a consecrated community. In fact, the next year, after a number of Latter-day Saints had gathered there, not all of whom had done it the right way—by consecration—the Lord said in a letter later canonized as section 85: "A general church record is to be kept of all things that transpire in Zion and of all those who consecrate properties, and receive inheritances" (v. 1). Inheritance was the religious term for the plot of land members would receive in Zion once they had consecrated their property. All those who received inheritances were to receive them legally from the bishop. The Lord continued directing the Saints in verse 3: "It is contrary to the will and commandment of God that those who receive not their inheritance by consecration, agreeable to his law which he has given, that he may tithe his people, to prepare them against the day of vengeance and burning, should have their names enrolled with the people of God." This verse uses strong language to say that it was against God's will for the Saints to gather to Zion without authorization and without consecrating their property.

Counsel to Early Missionaries

Section 58 also mentions the elders not specifically addressed: "Concerning the residue of the elders, the time has not yet come for many years for them to receive their inheritance in this land, except they desire it through the prayer of faith, only as it shall be appointed unto them of the Lord" (v. 44). If they were not to gather to Zion in the near future, what were the elders supposed to do? The Lord commands them to "push the people together from the ends of the earth" (v. 43).

As for the Saints generally, the divine word was, "Let the work of the gathering be not in haste, nor by flight; but let it be done as it shall be counseled by the elders of the church at the conferences, according to the knowledge which they receive from time to time" (v. 56). The knowledge needed would come from Zion: "Let the privileges of the lands be made known from time to time, by the bishop or the agent" (v. 55). The gathering was to take place in a regulated, sensible fashion. Sadly, not everyone paid attention to this, and a fair number of less-than-wise Saints gathered to Zion on their own initiative and without consecrating.

Now, I would like to turn to section 60 and draw your attention to a couple of smaller items. This revelation is directed toward the elders who had traveled to Missouri and were now told to go home, preaching the gospel along the way. In verse 15, a New Testament idea is invoked: "And shake off the dust of thy feet against those who receive thee not, not in their presence, lest thou provoke them, but in secret; and wash thy feet, as a testimony against them in the day of judgment." At times certain expressions take on a life of their own that is beyond the original meaning of the text. "Dusting off" the feet is one such example. Many sensational stories have been generated among the Latter-day Saints about how God punishes the unresponsive after the missionaries have dusted off their feet against them. In reality, this practice is an acknowledgment that the elders have discharged their duty to proclaim the gospel and have turned matters over to the Lord to handle this situation on Judgment Day. Joseph Smith later wrote, "If a man forbid his wife, or his children . . . to receive the Gospel, then it should be the duty of the Elder to go his way, and use no influence against him, and let the responsibility be upon his head; shake off the dust of thy feet as a testimony against him."[6] The missionary is no longer responsible for their salvation. We do not dust our feet in hope that some disaster will befall those who reject the Lord's servants. Feet dusting is not Mormon voodoo. The Prophet says, "Use no influence against him." We leave judgment to the Lord, but, oh, how at a popular level the idea of feet dusting has been sensationalized over the years!

Caution about Gathering to Zion

Next comes section 61. While the elders were on their way home, they were canoeing down the Missouri River, which occasionally had floating on its edges logs and trees that had fallen over. At one point, the elders crashed into such a floating tree and capsized the canoe. In a day when many people did not know how to swim, that was a very frightening and unsettling experience. The elders managed to pull themselves to land, but the whole experience shook them. There had also been some squabbling among the brethren earlier in the journey. The Lord used this occasion to give them some interesting counsel: "What I say unto one I say unto all, that you shall forewarn your brethren concerning these waters, that they [shall not come] in journeying upon them, lest their faith fail and they are caught in snares; I, the Lord, have decreed, and the destroyer rideth upon the face thereof, and I revoke not the decree. I, the Lord, was angry with you yesterday, but today mine anger is turned away" (vv. 18–20).

It is important to look at revelations in context and understand that certain passages may have had a particular meaning at that time. Here is an example. We can look at this and wonder, how did the Saints understand these words? Within a matter of months, a cholera pandemic broke out in the United States. It was one of the great pandemics in United States history, and the Lord here is giving them a forewarning. *The Evening and the Morning Star* offers a glimpse at how this revelation was understood at the time: "Besides the saving of time and money, [as you travel by land rather than by boat to Zion], you save risks and many dangers: Firstly, of disasters upon the waters." There were many steamboat disasters in those days, and the explosions burned and killed numbers of people. "And secondly, in some degree, the fear and trouble of the Cholera, which the Lord has sent into the world, and which may, without repentance, ravage the large towns near the waters, many years, or, at least, till other judgments come."[7] Thus perhaps the early understanding of this text was, "The destroyer that rides upon the water is particularly the cholera. It's much safer for us to travel by land."

A FLOOD OF REVELATIONS

Some years ago at the Missionary Training Center, Elder Rex D. Pinegar responded to the question, "Why can't missionaries swim?" Many missionaries probably thought he was going to quote section 61, "The destroyer rideth upon the waters." But instead he quoted a statistic. He said that in the age-group of young adults eighteen to twenty-five there are about eight or nine deaths per ten thousand (I can't remember the exact number) from water accidents each year. He basically went on to say, "With thirty thousand missionaries, we don't want to defy those odds. We can't just assume that the Lord is going to protect us when we haven't done all we can to protect ourselves." That was a fine down-to-earth explanation. Let us never forget, as Elder John A. Widtsoe titled his book nearly a hundred years ago, that we have a "rational theology."

Interestingly, the proscription against missionaries swimming has not always existed. Earlier in the twentieth century, missionaries sometimes went swimming. I particularly like a little quote I found in the *Improvement Era*, where mission president Samuel O. Bennion of the Central States Mission met with the South and West Texas Conference in the 1920s: "Three spirited, well attended meetings were held. Reports of the elders showed good work accomplished. Twenty-one baptisms reported for the past three months. On May 24 we enjoyed an excursion to Galveston and a swim in the Gulf of Mexico."[8] Some missionaries today may wish they were back in the 1920s! But again, as with dusting off the feet, folklore proliferates like that little weed, morning glory, which we all deal with in our gardens. Many young people today just assume that water is the devil's domain and that is why missionaries cannot go swimming. That is not our doctrine, however.

It Mattereth Not

On the topic of weaning members from dependency on the Prophet for all answers, there is an interesting phrase that appears in four successive revelations just following section 58, where the Lord said: "It is not meet that I should command in all things." In section 60 verse 5, the elders wanted to know, "Should we buy or make a watercraft?" The Lord said, "It mattereth not unto me." In 61:22, he said, "It mattereth not unto me . . . whether they go by water or by land" on their way home; "let this be as it is made known unto them according to their judgments"—in other words, using human reason and judgment. In 62:5, to the question, "Shall we go home as one big group or two by two?" the answer is, "As seemeth you good, it mattereth not unto me." Finally, in 63:40, the Lord commands that "all the moneys which can be spared" should be sent to Zion, although he says the amount "mattereth not unto me."

In these verses, the Lord is not saying he does not care about us, but he does want us to know we have the power within ourselves to make sound decisions. As he said in section 58, "Do many things of [your] own free will" (v. 27). In many decisions we make in life, the answer may well be "as seemeth you good; it mattereth not unto me." The Lord actually shows he cares about us by allowing us to exercise our agency. It is interesting that the Lord taught this principle just at the time some of the Saints were moving to Missouri, hundreds of miles away from Ohio, where they no longer had convenient access to the Prophet to discuss their concerns or questions.

Warning about Gathering in Haste

After the Prophet returned to Ohio, he received a revelation in which the Lord reiterates to an expectant group of Saints that the gathering to Zion should not be made "in haste" (D&C 63:24). Verse 41 says that Joseph Smith will discern by the Spirit who is to go up to Zion and who shall tarry in the east. An interesting twist on this was revealed several weeks later in section 64. Frederick G. Williams was told in verse 21 to keep his farm: "For I, the Lord, will retain a stronghold in the land of Kirtland, for the space of five years." That time frame must have been disappointing to some folks who thought the gathering and Second Coming would take place in the very near future. In one article, *Evening and Morning Star* editor William W. Phelps recalculated biblical numbers and reasoned that as of 1832, the beginning of the seventh thousand years and the Millennium may only have been nine years away.[9] And compared to others at the time, Phelps's view was conservative! Some were probably hoping it was only nine months away. Even Joseph himself can be read to have believed that the end was nigh. In his first published proclamation to the general American public, he declared: "The hour of his Judgement is come, repent ye repent ye and embrace the everlasting covenant and flee to zion before the overflowing scourge overtake you for there are those now living upon the earth whose eyes shall not be closed in death until they see all these things which I have spoken fulfilled."[10]

The Voice of Warning

The sense of an imminent end imparted urgency to the "warning voice" the Saints were to raise. Look in section 63, verse 33. Here the Lord says that in his wrath he has decreed wars on the face of the earth in which the wicked would slay the wicked. Verse 34 adds that the Saints will "hardly escape," and that the Lord "will come down in heaven from the presence of my Father and consume the wicked." Again, we see this apocalyptic scenario. However, he notes, "This is not yet, but by and by" (v. 35).

In verse 37, the Lord instructs the elders: "That every man should take righteousness in his hands and faithfulness upon his loins, and lift a warning voice unto the inhabitants of the earth; and declare both by word and by flight that desolation shall come upon the wicked." The message of the elders in that day was a warning voice, warning all to repent or suffer the consequences. This was very biblical. We remember the prophet Jeremiah who was always warning of imminent judgments on Israel, which is how we got the English word *jeremiad*. We do not use it much today, but when someone is taking people to task, warning them of consequences, that is a jeremiad. And missionaries delivered more than a few jeremiads in the early years. In the emerging Church, we see a sense of urgency. Those early Saints felt it, saying, "We have got to get out and spread the word and share the gospel because of the judgments of God that will soon come upon those who do not respond to the Lord's message."

Book of Commandments

Let's shift to November 1831, when a series of important elders' conferences were held. They took place in the John Johnson home in Hiram, Ohio, in a very small room and involved just a handful of individuals. Let us just summarize what happened quickly. On the first day, they decided how many copies of the Book of Commandments to publish. The Lord gave a preface to the book by revelation; we have it now as section 1 of the Doctrine and Covenants. Later the same day, the Lord gave them a revelation with the particular testimony of the book he wanted them to affirm. Just as the witnesses signed a testimonial to the Book of Mormon, there were also to be witnesses who endorsed the Book of Commandments. But something apparently happened overnight—a few of the elders seemed to have become convinced that they could not in good conscience sign that revealed testimony. And so sometime that morning, the Lord gave another revelation to them, section 67. In verse 3 he says: "Ye endeavored to believe that ye should receive the blessing which was offered unto you; but behold, verily I say unto you there were fears in your hearts, and verily this is the reason that ye did not receive." Apparently, a few of the brethren did not receive the confirming witness they were hoping to receive, and the Lord explains in verse 3 that it was so because "there were fears in your hearts." But there was more than fear. In verse 5, the Lord says: "Your eyes have been upon my servant Joseph Smith Jun., and his language you have known, and his imperfections you have known; and you have sought in your hearts knowledge that you might express beyond his language; this you also know."

A few of the brethren apparently were having some qualms about some of the wording of the revelations. So the Lord essentially said, "We are going to do a little experiment here." Verses 6–8 give instructions for the experiment: Pick out any one of the revelations in the Book of Commandments, and then appoint someone who is educated and wise, and if he can make one comparable, then you can say they are not true. But if he fails, then you are under condemnation if you do not bear testimony of the book.

William McLellin tried and failed, but seven or eight years later when this story was recorded in Joseph Smith's history, McLellin was criticized for making the attempt. By that time, he had turned against the Prophet and was considered a bit of a traitor. So it was said of him, probably reflecting his later behavior more than his 1831 attitude, that McLellin was "the wisest man in his own estimation, having more learning than sense."[11] That's a strong statement and a real barb that McLellin actually may not have deserved in 1831.

McLellin had arrived in Ohio just days before these conference meetings, and he was overwhelmed by the impressiveness of the brethren, including Joseph Smith. On Sunday, October 30, two days before this experience, he was called on to preach. He recorded in his diary: "It seemed to me as if I could not. Here was the Church who had been instructed by the first Elders in the church. Here was Brothers John, Sidney, Oliver, and Joseph and it did not seem to me as if I could instruct them or even entertain the Congregation."[12] Does this sound like a man who was full of himself, the "wisest man" in his own estimation? Perhaps it might be good to consider McLellin, who was a schoolteacher and well educated, as being invited or asked to write a revelation. Then, when he could not produce one, the elders would be reassured that the Lord was inspiring the Prophet. So McLellin did it—perhaps not out of arrogance, but by assignment.

The Literary Firm

With the revelations for the Book of Commandments ready to go, Section 69 says, in essence, "I want John Whitmer to accompany Oliver Cowdery in carrying them to Missouri to get them published." In so many words, section 70 says, "I want a group of men to take charge of the publishing of Church literature, beginning with the Book of Commandments." This group was called the "Literary Firm," and in section 70, verse 5, they were told, "This is their business, . . . to manage [Church publications] and the concerns thereof, yea, the benefits thereof." They were to be supported or aided financially by the anticipated profits from the sale of Church literature.

"Nevertheless," verse 7 says, "inasmuch as they receive more than is needful for their necessities and their wants, it shall be given into my storehouse." This was the same procedure all stewards were to follow.

Section 107

Embedded in the 1835 revelation now known as section 107 is another, which had been given in 1831. The revelation in question is mentioned at the end of verse 58 and begins in verse 59: "To the Church of Christ in the land of Zion in addition to the Church laws, respecting Church business." Then it goes forward. When we look at D&C 107:59 carefully, it contains the 1831 name of the Church, and mention of the Church "in the land of Zion" makes sense for 1831, whereas by 1835 the Saints had been expelled from Zion. Most of the verses from 59 onward were given in November 1831. A few, however, like 70, 73, 76, and 77, reflect later understandings that were inserted in the revelation, and verses 90 through 98 refer to the office of Seventy, which had only been constituted in 1835. This composite revelation illustrates that the Prophet seemed impressed to make the Doctrine and Covenant as comprehensive and up-to-date as possible. Elsewhere, he made a number of revisions to the revelations to update them or to clarify meaning. Literally hundreds of words in the earliest versions of the revelations were deleted and hundreds more were added to bring greater clarity, to make them consistent with current Church procedures, or to provide additional light and knowledge. It is a fascinating study. All of that took place sometime between the initial dictation and the final preparation for publication in the 1835 Doctrine and Covenants. Most Latter-day Saints have heard that there were little changes, commas here, a word there, changes in verb tense; but prior to 1835 there were a number of significant revisions. Since 1835, changes have been largely inconsequential and have had little effect on meaning. The earlier revisions, however, offer a wonderful window on how the Prophet worked under inspiration to refine and polish the revelations.

Dealing with Apostasy

Section 71 was received in December 1831. Ezra Booth, one of the elders assigned to travel the previous summer to Missouri, lost faith during that time, came home, and reverted to his former religion. He published a series of letters describing his dissatisfaction with the Saints. They appeared in a newspaper called the *Ohio Star* and were published serially for a number of weeks in late 1831.

Section 71 invites Joseph and Sidney to call upon their "enemies" to meet them "in public and in private." We do not instruct missionaries to do that today. This was a special circumstance, and these were special individuals. They did as the Lord instructed them. Sidney Rigdon ran an ad in the *Ohio Star* in which he said, "The Lord willing, I will deliver a lecture on the Christian Religion in the village of Ravenna on Sunday, the 25th inst. at the brick school house, or at the school house owned by Dr. DeWolf. I give notice to Ezra Booth, that his attendance is desired, as I shall review the letters written by him and published in the Ohio Star, headed Mormonism, as those letters are an unfair and false representation of the subjects on which they treat."[13] In the same ad, he challenged Symonds Ryder, a prominent citizen of nearby Hiram, Ohio, who had also apostatized, to a debate. In the end, neither one showed up, and the case was closed.

Conclusion

The year 1831 was a wonderfully rich year, one in which a flood of revelations poured forth to guide the Saints in a variety of matters. The revelations instructed them to gather first to Ohio, then to Zion. They offered guidance on numerous temporal concerns and activities. At the same time, the revelations dealt with signs of the last days, explained how missionary work was to be done, and gave guidance on having the revelations printed—all this in thirty-eight glorious revelations in the year 1831. We thank the Lord that we have them.

Notes

1. These few revelations were not canonized for good reasons. Most are short and deal with administrative matters, such as how to obtain paper to publish the Book of Commandments or how particular individuals should complete their missionary labors.

2. As it turns out, "not far" really is not very far. Were you today to be able to go to downtown Independence, visit the old courthouse site, and walk for ten minutes or so, you would be to the location of the original temple property.

3. Today, on that original acreage can be found the Community of Christ (formerly RLDS) auditorium, the Community of Christ temple across the street, and the headquarters of the Church of Christ (Temple Lot), so known because it actually owns that tiny portion of the sixty-three acres where Joseph subsequently designated the first temple should be built.

4. Quoted in T. Edgar Lyon, "Independence, Missouri, and the Mormons, 1827–1833," *BYU Studies* 13 [Autumn 1972]: 15–16.

5. Joseph Smith, *History of the Church of Jesus Christ of Latter-day Saints*, ed. B. H. Roberts, 2nd ed. rev. (Salt Lake City: Deseret Book, 1957), 1:196.

6. Joseph Smith, *Messenger and Advocate*, November 1835, 211.

7. "The Way of Journeying for the Saints of the Church of Christ," *Evening and Morning Star*, December 1832, 53.

8. "Messages from the Missions," *Improvement Era*, February 1924, 973.

9. "Present Age of the World," *Evening and Morning Star*, August 1832, 21–22.

10. *Personal Writings of Joseph Smith*, ed. Dean C. Jessee, rev. ed. (Salt Lake City: Deseret Book; Provo, UT: Brigham Young University Press, 2002), 298.

11. *The Papers of Joseph Smith*, vol. 1, *Autobiographical and Historical Writings*, ed. Dean C. Jessee (Salt Lake City: Deseret Book, 1989), 367.

12. *The Journals of William E. McLellin, 1831–1836*, ed. Jan Shipps and John W. Welch (Provo, UT: BYU Studies; Urbana: University of Illinois Press, 1994), 46.

13. Sidney Rigdon, advertisement, *Ohio Star*, December 15, 1831.

ROBERT J. WOODFORD

1832 Joseph Smith and "The Vision"

The first significant event recorded in the historical accounts of Joseph Smith's life during 1832 is a conference he attended at Amherst, Ohio, on January 25. Two important developments occurred at that conference. The previous November, Joseph had received a revelation, now part of section 107 of the Doctrine and Covenants, wherein the Lord told him there should be a president for the high priesthood (see vv. 64–66). At the conference, Joseph was sustained by common consent of the members and was then ordained president of the high priesthood by Sidney Rigdon. The other important development was the reception of section 75 of the Doctrine and Covenants, which called numerous men

---

Robert J. Woodford is a retired seminary and institute instructor and an editor of The Joseph Smith Papers.

to serve missions, principally in the eastern part of the United States. These men, who were mostly farmers, served with great sacrifice. They left just before the planting season and were gone during the entire growing season. When they returned in September, Joseph Smith received section 84, an important revelation about the priesthood and missionary work.

The most notable event during February occurred on the sixteenth. Joseph Smith received section 76 of the Doctrine and Covenants, which is discussed following this review.

In March, several important events took place. Joseph received section 78 of the Doctrine and Covenants, which commands a business organization of the Church. The organization was called the United Firm and was formed to manage the temporal affairs of the Church. It was headed by the leaders of the Church under the law of consecration. On March 8, Joseph Smith chose two counselors to serve with him in the presidency of the high priesthood: Jesse Gause and Sidney Rigdon. On March 15, Joseph received section 81 of the Doctrine and Covenants, which outlined Gause's duties. After Jesse Gause apostatized later in the year, his name was removed from the revelation, and the name of the man who replaced him—Frederick G. Williams—was added. The substitution is appropriate because the section outlines the duties of a counselor in the presidency; Jesse Gause's name is now included in the introduction to section 81, though it never appeared there until the 1981 edition. In a sense, the names of the current counselors in the First Presidency could just as easily be substituted into the revelation. On March 24, a tragic event happened to the Prophet Joseph Smith: he and Sidney Rigdon were tarred and feathered at Hiram, Ohio, by a mob led by disgruntled former members of the Church. Five days later, his adopted son Joseph Murdock Smith died as a result of the exposure he suffered during that mobbing.

Part of section 78, received on the first of March, instructed Joseph Smith to travel to Missouri to complete the organization of the United Firm. On the first day of April, he left Hiram, Ohio, for Missouri, and he took with him Newel K. Whitney, who would soon become the second bishop of the Church; Peter Whitmer, who is one of the eight witnesses; and Sidney Rigdon and Jesse Gause, his counselors in the presidency of the high priesthood. They arrived in Independence, Missouri, on April 24. Two days later, in a meeting there with the brethren, Joseph was acknowledged, or sustained, as president of the high priesthood. (In 1833, this presidency became what we now know as the First Presidency.) Section 82 was also received at that meeting, further setting up the United Firm.

In May, Joseph Smith left Independence to return to the Kirtland area. On the way, there was an accident. The horses on the stage were spooked. While trying to jump from the stage, Newel K. Whitney got a foot caught in the spokes of the wheel and broke his leg and foot quite badly. He was laid up for about four weeks in Greenville, Indiana, and Joseph Smith stayed with him. An impassioned letter from Joseph to Emma indicates that this was a very frustrating time in the life of the Prophet.

Joseph returned sometime in mid- to late June to Kirtland, Ohio. He immediately recommenced his translation of the Bible, which occupied him for the rest of the summer. He finished his work on the New Testament near the end of July and began again on the Old Testament. At that same time, he began a short history of his life, with Fredrick G. Williams acting as scribe for part of it. Included in this history was the Prophet's first known attempt to relate the First Vision in writing.

In August, Jesse Gause and Zebedee Coltrin began a mission journey to the eastern part of the United States together. On August 19, Elder Coltrin returned to Kirtland because, as his journal records, he had a terrible headache, probably a migraine, for nineteen days. Zebedee Coltrin wrote in his journal on the nineteenth that he and Jesse had been "praying with and for each other,"[1] and that is the last we hear of Jesse Gause; he evidently apostatized.

In September, the missionaries who were called in section 75 began to return. In response to their return, Joseph Smith received section 84 of the Doctrine and Covenants. The first 102 verses were received on the twenty-second, and the remainder the following day. Sometime in late September or early October, Joseph Smith and Newel K. Whitney traveled to Albany, Boston, and New York City. One purpose for going to New York was to buy supplies for the bishops' storehouse in Kirtland. But there was a second reason: the Lord had commanded Whitney in section 84, verses 112 to 116, to go there and to the other two cities to preach and to warn the people.

On November 6, Joseph Smith returned from this journey to the East hours after his son Joseph Smith III was born. Joseph III was the first child of Emma and Joseph Smith to survive more than a few hours. (He later became the first president of the Reorganized Church of Jesus Christ of Latter Day Saints.) Two days after the birth of Joseph III, Brigham Young, Brigham's younger brother Joseph Young, and Heber C. Kimball arrived in Kirtland. This was shortly after their baptism, and it was the first time that Joseph Smith had ever met them. After meeting Brigham Young and knowing him for only a matter of hours, Joseph prophesied that Brigham Young would someday lead the Church. Levi Hancock recalled:

I was living with Joseph Smith Jr. and had completed the translating room and had seen many new brethren, and had heard Joseph speak many things concerning them, but no observation sunk with such weight on my mind as the one that he made about Brigham Young and Joseph Young. Sometime in the month of Nov. 1832, these men came to Joseph Smith in the evening and sung and prayed with us. After they had gone from there Joseph Smith said to me, "how do you like the men?" or something near it. After he had got my answer he said, "these are good men," and "there is Brigham Young, [he] is a great man and one day the whole kingdom will rest upon him; and there is the smaller one, he is a great man, but his brother [Brigham] is greater."[2]

On December 6, Joseph Smith received section 86, which includes a commentary on the parable of the wheat and the tares. When this section was first put into the Doctrine and Covenants, the title was "On Priesthood." It is a priesthood revelation, not just an explanation of a parable, and it tells us who has rights to the priesthood. On December 25, as the brethren were discussing the slave question, a voice whispered to the Prophet Joseph Smith, delivering section 87, the prophecy on war. Then on December 27 and 28 and on January 3, 1833, Joseph received section 88, which he described in a letter to Missouri as "an olive leaf... plucked from the tree of Paradise, the Lord's message of peace to us."[3]

There are two additional events that continued through all of 1832. One was the hard feelings and disagreements between the leaders of the Church in Kirtland and in Missouri, which was difficult to reconcile because of distance and lack of communication. This strife began the previous year, when the first group went to Missouri, and it continued throughout 1832. When Joseph Smith met with the brethren in Missouri in April

1832, he thought he had the whole thing settled. He was upset to find, when he stayed with Newell K. Whitney in Greenville, Indiana, that he had not resolved the conflict and that there were still hard feelings. Some letters confirm that this animosity remained throughout the year. Section 88, sent to Missouri with an accompanying letter, seems to have ameliorated the feelings of Church leaders in Missouri from that point on.

The other major event that took place that year was a worldwide outbreak of cholera. Thousands upon thousands died. Joseph Smith mentions in his letter from Greenville, Indiana, that he had gone to the cemetery and found many new graves of people who had passed away from it. When he went to New York, the outbreak was essentially over, and he lamented that people had already forgotten how terrible it was. Surviving correspondence, newspapers, and discourses show that Latter-day Saints viewed the outbreak as one of the judgments to come upon the earth in the last days.

Doctrine and Covenants Section 76

Among the major events in Joseph's life in 1832 was his reception of the vision of the three degrees of glory (section 76). Joseph Smith recorded:

> While we were doing the work of translation, which the Lord had appointed unto us, we came to the twenty-ninth verse of the fifth chapter of John, which was given unto us as follows—
>
> Speaking of the resurrection of the dead, concerning those who shall hear the voice of the Son of Man:
>
> And shall come forth; they who have done good, in the resurrection of the just; and they who have done evil, in the resurrection of the unjust.

Now this caused us to marvel, for it was given unto us of the Spirit.

And while we meditated upon these things, the Lord touched the eyes of our understandings and they were opened, and the glory of the Lord shone round about. (vv. 15–19)[4]

In his history, Joseph made this statement before recording the revelation:

"Upon my return from Amherst conference, I resumed the translation of the Scriptures. From sundry revelations which had been received, it was apparent that many important points touching the salvation of man, had been taken from the Bible, or lost before it was compiled. It appeared self-evident from what truths were left, that if God rewarded every one according to the deeds done in the body, the term 'Heaven,' as intended for the Saints' eternal home, must include more kingdoms than one. Accordingly, on the 16th of February, 1832, while translating St. John's Gospel, myself and Elder Rigdon saw the following vision."[5]

After recording the vision, he wrote some thoughts about it:

Nothing could be more pleasing to the Saints upon the order of the Kingdom of the Lord, than the light which burst upon the world through the foregoing vision. Every law, every commandment, every promise, every truth, and every point touching the destiny of man, from Genesis to Revelation, where the purity of the Scriptures remains unsullied by the folly of men, go to show the perfection of the theory [of different degrees of glory in the future life] and witnesses the fact that that document is a transcript from the records of the eternal world. The sublimity of the ideas; the purity of the language; the scope for action; the continued duration for completion, in order that the heirs of salvation may confess the Lord and bow the knee; the rewards for faithfulness, and the punishments for sins, are so much beyond the narrow-mindedness of men, that every honest man is constrained to exclaim: "It came from God."[6]

According to Philo Dibble, Joseph Smith did not receive section 76 in a closed room with just Sidney Rigdon; there were at least a dozen other people viewing what was taking place. Such was the case with many of the revelations Joseph Smith received. Philo Dibble gave this familiar recollection about section 76:

> The vision which is recorded in the Book of Doctrine and Covenants [D&C 76] was given at the house of "Father Johnson," in Hiram, Ohio, and during the time that Joseph and Sidney were in the spirit and saw the heavens open, there were other men in the room, perhaps twelve, among whom I was one during a part of the time—probably two-thirds of the time,—I saw the glory and felt the power, but did not see the vision.
>
> The events and conversation, while they were seeing what is written (and many things were seen and related that are not written,) I will relate as minutely as is necessary.
>
> Joseph would, at intervals, say: "What do I see?" as one might say while looking out the window and beholding what all in the room could not see. Then he would relate what he had seen or what he was looking at. Then Sidney replied, "I see the same." Presently Sidney would say "what do I see?" and would repeat what he had seen or was seeing, and Joseph would reply, "I see the same."

This manner of conversation was reported at short intervals to the end of the vision, and during the whole time not a word was spoken by any other person. Not a sound nor motion made by anyone but Joseph and Sidney, and it seemed to me that they never moved a joint or limb during the time I was there, which I think was over an hour, and to the end of the vision.

Joseph sat firmly and calmly all the time in the midst of a magnificent glory, but Sidney sat limp and pale, apparently as limber as a rag, observing which, Joseph remarked, smilingly, "Sidney is not used to it as I am."[7]

Later, in Nauvoo, Joseph Smith made this statement about section 76:

Paul ascended into the third heavens, and he could understand the three principal rounds of Jacob's ladder—the telestial, the terrestrial, and the celestial glories or kingdoms, where Paul saw and heard things which were not lawful for him to utter. I could explain a hundred fold more than I ever have of the glories of the kingdoms manifested to me in the vision, were I permitted, and were the people prepared to receive them.

The Lord deals with this people as a tender parent with a child, communicating light and intelligence and the knowledge of his ways as they can bear it.[8]

Later revelations may reflect some of what Joseph Smith learned when he received section 76. For instance, section 88 tells of the laws one must live to enter the celestial kingdom, the terrestrial kingdom, and the telestial kingdom. It also outlines the order of the resurrection: those worthy of the celestial kingdom are resurrected first, the terrestrial second, and so on. Section 93 discusses the pre-earth life. Section 130 discusses the planets God created. Section 131, which asserts there are three degrees within the celestial kingdom, also conveys a doctrine about life after death. Section 137 tells about Joseph's vision of the celestial kingdom, in which he saw his own brother Alvin.

Though we do not have the dictation copy of section 76, we assume that it was in the handwriting of Sidney Rigdon because he was there, and he and the Prophet were told to write it. The earliest surviving manuscript was recorded within a matter of days by Frederick G. Williams in a book called the Kirtland Revelation Book. Others also made copies for their own use.

Two missionaries, the Prophet Joseph's brother Samuel H. Smith and his companion, Orson Hyde, left Kirtland on February 1, sixteen days before this revelation was received. They were traveling in the state of Maine on March 21, when Samuel H. Smith recorded this experience in his journal: "Went on again. Came across a man by the name of Haskins. He told us that he had been to Kirtland and to [Hiram] (for he was a brother) and that he had been ordained an elder of the Church, and he told us that he had seen Joseph and Sidney and that they had had a vision and that they had seen great and marvilous things, and that they had got along wonderfully well in translating. Haskins was strong in the faith. Left him and went on to Portland. Tarried all night."[9] Six days later, on the twenty-seventh, he wrote: "This day Brother Seth and Joel Johnson came from Amherst and they told us that they staid all night at my father's [Joseph Smith Sr.'s] in Kirtland. We rejoiced to hear from our brethren to the west. They had the vision with them which Joseph and Sidney had seen and we had the privilidge of reading it."[10]

On August 13, after the vision had been printed in the Church newspaper, *The Evening and the Morning Star*, Samuel

Smith recorded, "The papers [meaning *The Evening and the Morning Star*] had come and we read them and the Vision was in them. This evening the sisters came together and we read the Vision to them and explained it unto them."[11] Samuel did not reference the vision in his journal again, but his missionary companion, Orson Hyde, mentioned it. On September 9, he wrote, "Came up to New Rowley met the Brethren and a large no. of people from all quarters had the vision and explained it."[12]

Some of the revelations to be published in the Book of Commandments were first printed in *The Evening and the Morning Star*. Since this vision was included in the July 1832 issue, it is assumed that it was also to be published in the Book of Commandments, but antagonists caused the publication of that book to be halted before it was finished.

Many members of the Church found the doctrine of the three degrees of glory in section 76 hard to accept, even though the Bible says, "In my Father's house are many mansions" (John 14:2), and Paul had talked about a celestial glory, a terrestrial glory, and other glories (see 1 Corinthians 15:40–42). Mainstream Protestant thought allowed only for a heaven and a hell. Because all of the adult members of the Church in 1832 were converts, and most of them came from a Protestant background, the idea of multiple heavenly kingdoms was new to them. Grant Underwood wrote the following about Protestant theology:

> After surveying the religious landscape in America in 1844, the eminent German churchman Philipp Schaff remarked that "the reigning theology of the country... is the theology of the Westminster Confession." The Westminster Confession, a creedal delineation of faith formulated two hundred years earlier by Reformed divines from England

and Scotland, declared that upon death the souls of the "righteous" were received into heaven while the "wicked" were cast into hell. "Besides these two places for souls separated from their bodies," concluded the Confession, "the Scripture acknowledgeth none."[13]

Until section 76, the kingdoms of glory seem only to separate the good and the bad, the righteous and the wicked, those on God's right hand and those on his left hand, the sheep and the goats. Even section 29, verses 27 through 30, says,

> And the righteous shall be gathered on my right hand unto eternal life; and the wicked on my left hand will I be ashamed to own before the Father;
> Wherefore I will say unto them—Depart from me, ye cursed, into everlasting fire, prepared for the devil and his angels.
> And now, behold, I say unto you, never at any time have I declared from mine own mouth that they should return, for where I am they cannot come, for they have no power.
> But remember that all my judgments are not given unto men; and as the words have gone forth out of my mouth even so shall they be fulfilled, that the first shall be last, and that the last shall be first in all things whatsoever I have created by the word of my power, which is the power of my Spirit.

There were some denominations that divided life after death into more than just heaven and hell. The Catholics, of course, had limbo and purgatory. One who is sometimes mentioned as having parallel beliefs is Emanuel Swedenborg, who described heaven as consisting of three divisions, though he did not call them telestial, terrestrial, and celestial. Though members of the Church today are accustomed to section 76, the early members of the Church, most of them former Protestants, did not know how to respond to it. President Brigham Young said:

> After all, my traditions were such, that when the Vision came first to me, it was directly contrary and opposed to my former education. I said, Wait a little. I did not reject it; but I could not understand it. I then could feel what incorrect tradition had done for me. Suppose all that I have ever heard from my priest and parents—the way they taught me to read the Bible—had been true, my understanding would be diametrically opposed to the doctrine revealed in the Vision. I used to think and pray, to read and think, until I knew and fully understood it for myself, by the visions of the Holy Spirit. At first it actually came in contact with my own feelings, though I never could believe like the mass of the Christian world around me; but I did not know how nigh I believed, as they did. I found, however, that I was so nigh, I could shake hands with them any time I wished.[14]

Joseph Smith's instructions to the first missionaries in England were, "To adhere closely to the first principles of the Gospel, and remain silent concerning the gathering, the vision, and the Book of Doctrine and Covenants, until such time as the work was fully established, and it should be clearly made manifest by the Spirit to do otherwise."[15] One of those early missionaries to England was Joseph Fielding, who had been born in England. He approached a relative, Timothy Matthews, who was the minister of a church. When Joseph explained to him that he was now a missionary from America with a gospel to preach, Timothy Matthews was excited to hear it, so he invited the missionaries to preach in his church after regular Sabbath services and during the week. Joseph Smith's history records: "The Elders at Bedford continued to lecture in the basement of Mr. Matthews' chapel from evening to evening, with the most flattering prospects until this evening, when Elder [John] Goodson, contrary to the most positive instructions of President Kimball [Heber C. Kimball], and without advising with any one, read publicly the vision from the Doctrine and Covenants, which turned the current of feeling generally, and nearly closed the door in all that region."[16]

The vision overwhelmed the people in that congregation. Joseph Smith had said earlier that he could reveal a hundred times more if the people were prepared and if the Lord permitted it. These people were not prepared, so Timothy Matthews would not let the missionaries preach in his church any longer.

Mysteries

Having related the background of section 76, I will expound on two important doctrines therein. Section 76 reads:

> For thus saith the Lord—I, the Lord, am merciful and gracious unto those who fear me, and delight to honor those who serve me in righteousness and in truth unto the end.
>
> Great shall be their reward and eternal shall be their glory.
>
> And to them will I reveal all mysteries, yea, all the hidden mysteries of my kingdom from days of old, and for ages to come, will I make known unto them the good pleasure of my will concerning all things pertaining to my kingdom.
>
> Yea, even the wonders of eternity shall they know, and things to come will I show them, even the things of many generations.
>
> And their wisdom shall be great, and their understanding reach to heaven; and before them the wisdom of the wise

shall perish, and the understanding of the prudent shall come to naught.

For by my Spirit will I enlighten them, and by my power will I make known unto them the secrets of my will—yea, even those things which eye has not seen, nor ear heard, nor yet entered into the heart of man. (vv. 5–10)

Therefore, the Lord is willing to reveal eternal truths to the obedient. The word *mystery* in the New Testament comes from the Greek *mysterion*, a derivative of *muō*, which means "to shut the mouth." Many mysteries of the Church are taught in the temple, where we are instructed to not speak about them; they are only for the initiated. Verses five through ten allow us to also receive mysteries via personal revelation if we are faithful. This definition of mystery also fits the Book of Mormon. Alma 12 reads, "It is given unto many to know the mysteries of God; nevertheless they are laid under a strict command that they shall not impart only according to the portion of his word which he doth grant unto the children of men" (v. 9).

Section 76 expounds upon the degree of revelation the Lord is willing to grant. Though Joseph Smith said he could give the Saints a hundred times more, the Lord would not allow it because we could not bear it. Alma 12 continues, commanding men that they should "not impart only according to the portion of his word which he doth grant unto the children of men, according to the heed and diligence which they give unto him. And therefore, he that will harden his heart, the same receiveth the lesser portion of the word; and he that will not harden his heart, to him is given the greater portion of the word, until it is given unto him to know the mysteries of God until he know them in full" (vv. 9–10).

In other words, it is given him to know everything that the Lord is willing to reveal in this day and age. Verse 11 continues,

"And they that will harden their hearts, to them is given the lesser portion of the word until they know nothing concerning his mysteries [in other words, they no longer understand what they once understood]; and then they are taken captive by the devil, and led by his will down to destruction. Now this is what is meant by the chains of hell."

Section 76 teaches more about the mysteries of God. Verses 113–15 say, "This is the end of the vision which we saw, which we were commanded to write while we were yet in the Spirit. But great and marvelous are the works of the Lord, and the mysteries of his kingdom which he showed unto us, which surpass all understanding in glory, and in might, and in dominion; which he commanded us we should not write while we were yet in the Spirit, and are not lawful for man to utter."

Thus, these verses teach us to keep sacred the mysteries that God reveals to us. Verses 116–18 continue, "Neither is man capable to make them known, for they are only to be seen and understood by the power of the Holy Spirit, which God bestows on those who love him, and purify themselves before him; to whom he grants this privilege of seeing and knowing for themselves; that through the power and manifestation of the Spirit, while in the flesh, they may be able to bear his presence in the world of glory."

Because of the brevity of section 76, we now have a whole new series of questions about life after death. But the Lord has revealed all that he is willing to reveal at this time, except to those to whom he would reveal it personally, and then he commands them to say nothing about it. Four statements from Church leaders develop the idea of mysteries.

Joseph Smith said: "Let us be faithful and silent, brethren, and if God gives you a manifestation, keep it to yourselves; be watchful and prayerful, and you shall have a prelude of those joys that God will pour out on that day."[17]

His brother Hyrum said: "Therefore beware what you teach! for the mysteries of God are not given to all men; and unto those to whom they are given they are placed under restrictions to impart only such as God will command them; and the residue is to be kept in a faithful breast, otherwise he will be brought under condemnation. By this God will prove his faithful servants, who will be called and numbered with the chosen."[18]

Deciding to keep our sacred experiences to ourselves saves our audience from having to judge whether the experience really happened and if it is appropriate to share. If the Lord wanted to spread an important revelation beyond one person, he would give it to the prophet, who could then share it with the Church. If the Lord sends to one person an angel or an important revelation, that is for that one person, and that person alone.

President Brigham Young gave two important statements about sharing revelation:

> There is one principle that I wish the people would understand and lay to heart. Just as fast as you will prove before your God that you are worthy to receive the mysteries, if you please to call them so, of the Kingdom of heaven—that you are full of confidence in God—that you will never betray a thing that God tells you—that you will never reveal to your neighbour that which ought not to be revealed, as quick as you prepare to be entrusted with the things of God, there is an eternity of them to bestow upon you. Instead of pleading with the Lord to bestow more upon you, plead with yourselves to have confidence in yourselves, to have integrity in yourselves, and know when to speak and what to speak,

> what to reveal, and how to carry yourselves and walk before the Lord. And just as fast as you prove to Him that you will preserve everything secret that ought to be—that you will deal out to your neighbours all which you ought, and no more, and learn how to dispense your knowledge to your families, friends, neighbours, and brethren, the Lord will bestow upon you, and give to you, and bestow upon you, until finally he will say to you, "You shall never fall; your salvation is sealed unto you; you are sealed up unto eternal life and salvation, through your integrity."[19]

Thus, we are to dispense that which the Lord has given to all mankind—the scriptures and teachings of the brethren. Personal revelation is exactly that, *personal*, and should be kept within the person who received it. The second statement by Brigham Young was given just a few weeks before the first:

> Now I want to tell you that which, perhaps, many of you do not know. Should you receive a vision of revelation from the Almighty, one that the Lord gave you concerning yourselves, or this people, but which you are not to reveal on account of your not being the proper person, or because it ought not to be known by the people at present, you should shut it up and seal it as close, and lock it as tight as heaven is to you, and make it as secret as the grave. The Lord has no confidence in those who reveal secrets, for He cannot safely reveal Himself to such persons. It is as much as He can do to get a particle of sense into some of the best and most influential men in the Church, in regard to real confidence in themselves. They cannot keep things within their own bosoms.[20]

Based on this principle, the Lord might reveal something such as the name of a new stake president to a member of the

Church. He would do that so that when the name is presented, that member can say, "Yes. I know that he is supposed to be the stake president." Through that revelation, the Lord gives that member a special witness that he has chosen that man. Personal revelation is important in this Church, but so is keeping confidences within ourselves. Verses 5–10 of section 76 teach a tremendous lesson: The Lord is willing to reveal many things to those who prove faithful and obedient and who will keep their confidences.

The Testimony of Jesus

A second important doctrine section 76 teaches is the testimony of Joseph Smith concerning the Father and the Son. Verse 19 begins this testimony:

> And while we meditated upon these things, the Lord touched the eyes of our understandings and they were opened, and the glory of the Lord shone round about.
>
> And we beheld the glory of the Son, on the right hand of the Father [two separate beings], and received of his fulness;
>
> And saw the holy angels, and them who are sanctified before his throne, worshiping God, and the Lamb, who worship him forever and ever.
>
> And now, after the many testimonies which have been given of him, this is the testimony, last of all, which we give of him: That he lives!
>
> For we saw him, even on the right hand of God; and we heard the voice bearing record that he is the Only Begotten of the Father—
>
> That by him, and through him, and of him, the worlds are and were created, and the inhabitants thereof are begotten sons and daughters unto God. (vv. 19–24)

Joseph said, "This is the testimony, last of all, which we give of him." Joseph had the First Vision in the spring of 1820. In February of 1832, twelve years later, he received the vision of the three degrees of glory, in which he also saw the Father and the Son. In July of 1832, a few months later, section 76 was published in *The Evening and the Morning Star*. The members of the Church now had the Prophet Joseph Smith's testimony of the truth that God and the Savior are separate beings and of the role of the Savior as Creator. The very next month, August 1832, Joseph Smith wrote the First Vision down for the first time of which we have any record. He would write it again in 1838 in the form that now appears in the Pearl of Great Price, but that account was not published until 1842, when it was printed in *Times and Seasons*. Interestingly, the First Vision was not published until ten years after this vision of the Father and Son that is recorded in section 76. So, playing on words, the "last" testimony was the first one published, and the *First Vision* was the last one of the two published. Few members of the Church knew about the First Vision prior to section 76. Numerous journal entries reveal that it was not the First Vision but the Book of Mormon that aided in the conversion of the Saints in Joseph's day. The vision of section 76 was thus the first of Joseph's testimonies of the Savior to which the Saints had access.

The importance of a testimony of the Savior is revealed in verse 51, which describes the people in the celestial kingdom as those who received the testimony of Jesus, believed on his name, were baptized, etc. Thus, the testimony of Jesus is a qualification to enter the celestial kingdom. Verse 74 discusses the terrestrial kingdom: those entering the terrestrial kingdom are they who received not the testimony of Jesus in the flesh but received it afterwards. Verse 79 also says of those in the terrestrial world:

"These are they who are not valiant in the testimony of Jesus; wherefore, they obtain not the crown over the kingdom of our God." So the testimony of Jesus is also taken into consideration for those who enter the terrestrial kingdom. Verse 82 mentions those in the telestial kingdom: "These are they who received not the gospel of Christ, neither the testimony of Jesus." The Lord repeats himself in verse 101, saying that those in the telestial kingdom "received not the gospel, neither the testimony of Jesus, neither the prophets, neither the everlasting covenant." But verse 110 says of these souls, "These all shall bow the knee, and every tongue shall confess to him who sits upon the throne forever and ever." Those in outer darkness are excluded because they fight against the testimony of Jesus, against the Savior. Verse 35 describes those in outer darkness: "Having denied the Holy Spirit after having received it, and having denied the Only Begotten Son of the Father, having crucified him unto themselves and put him to an open shame." Thus, what an individual does with the testimony of Jesus becomes an important consideration at the time of judgment.

Two latter-day Church authorities further emphasize the importance of the testimony of Jesus Christ. First, President Ezra Taft Benson said, "A most priceless blessing available to every member of the Church is a testimony of the divinity of Jesus Christ and His Church. A testimony is one of the few possessions we may take with us when we leave this life." He then defines a testimony of Jesus:

> To have a testimony of Jesus is to possess knowledge through the Holy Ghost of the divine mission of Jesus Christ.
>
> A testimony of Jesus is to know the divine nature of our Lord's birth—that He is indeed the Only Begotten Son in the flesh.

A testimony of Jesus is to know that He was the promised Messiah and that while He sojourned among men He accomplished many mighty miracles.

A testimony of Jesus is to know that the laws which He prescribed as His doctrine are true and then to abide by these laws and ordinances.

To possess a testimony of Jesus is to know that He voluntarily took upon Himself the sins of all mankind in the Garden of Gethsemane, which caused Him to suffer in both body and spirit and to bleed from every pore. All this He did so that we would not have to suffer if we would repent.

To possess a testimony of Jesus is to know that He came forth triumphantly from the grave with a physical, resurrected body. And because He lives, so shall all mankind.

Thus, part of having a testimony of Jesus is to know that one will be resurrected as he was. President Benson continues:

To possess a testimony of Jesus is to know that God the Father and Jesus Christ did indeed appear to the Prophet Joseph Smith to establish a new dispensation of His gospel so that salvation may be preached to all nations before He comes.

To possess a testimony of Jesus is to know that the Church, which He established in the meridian of time and restored in modern times is, as the Lord has declared, "the only true and living church upon the face of the whole earth" (D&C 1:30).

Having such a testimony is vital. But of even greater importance is being valiant in our testimony.

To be valiant in a testimony of Jesus means that we accept the divine mission of Jesus Christ, embrace His gospel, and do His works. It also means we accept the prophetic mission of Joseph Smith and his successors and follow their counsel. As Jesus said, "Whether by mine own voice or by the voice of my servants, it is the same."[21]

This talk by President Benson offers a fairly comprehensive list of the various components of the testimony of Jesus. But it is not enough simply to have a testimony of Jesus; one must also be valiant in that testimony. Elder Bruce R. McConkie teaches what it means to be valiant in the testimony of Jesus:

> Now, what does it mean to be valiant in the testimony of Jesus?
>
> It is to be courageous and bold; to use all our strength, energy, and ability in the warfare with the world: to fight the good fight of faith. "Be strong and of a good courage," the Lord commanded Joshua, and then specified that this strength and courage consisted of meditating upon and observing to do all that is written in the law of the Lord. (See Josh. 1:6–9.) The great cornerstone of valiance in the cause of righteousness is obedience to the whole law of the whole gospel.
>
> To be valiant in the testimony of Jesus is to "come unto Christ, and be perfected in him"; it is to deny ourselves "of all ungodliness," and "love God" with all our "might, mind and strength" (Moro. 10:32).
>
> To be valiant in the testimony of Jesus is to believe in Christ and his gospel with unshakable conviction. It is to know of the verity and divinity of the Lord's work on earth.
>
> But this is not all. It is more than believing and knowing. We must be doers of the word and not hearers only (James 1:22). It is more than lip service; it is not simply confessing

with the mouth the divine sonship of the Savior. It is obedience and conformity and personal righteousness. "Not every one that saith unto me, Lord, Lord, shall enter into the kingdom of heaven; but he that doeth the will of my Father which is in heaven" (Matt. 7:21).

To be valiant in the testimony of Jesus is to "press forward with a steadfastness in Christ, having a perfect brightness of hope, and a love of God and of all men." It is to "endure to the end" (2 Ne. 31:20). It is to live our religion, to practice what we preach, to keep the commandments. It is the manifestation of "pure religion" in the lives of men; it is visiting "the fatherless and widows in their affliction" and keeping ourselves "unspotted from the world" (James 1:27).

To be valiant in the testimony of Jesus is to bridle our passions, control our appetites, and rise above carnal and evil things. It is to overcome the world as did he who is our prototype and who himself was the most valiant of all our Father's children. It is to be morally clean, to pay our tithes and offerings, to honor the Sabbath day, to pray with full purpose of heart, to lay our all upon the altar if called upon to do so.[22]

Elder McConkie then summarized: "To be valiant in the testimony of Jesus is to take the Lord's side on every issue. It is to vote as he would vote. It is to think what he thinks, to believe what he believes, to say what he would say and do what he would do in the same situation. It is to have the mind of Christ and be one with him as he is one with his Father."

That is a marvelous statement. Then, because we do not see all things clearly, he adds:

Our doctrine is clear; its application sometimes seems to be more difficult. Perhaps some personal introspection might be helpful. For instance:

Am I valiant in the testimony of Jesus if my chief interest and concern in life is laying up in store the treasures of the earth, rather than the building up of the kingdom?

Am I valiant if I have more of this world's goods than my just needs and wants require and I do not draw from my surplus to support missionary work, build temples, and care for the needy?

Am I valiant if my approach to the Church and its doctrines is intellectual only, if I am more concerned with having a religious dialogue on this or that point than I am on gaining a personal spiritual experience?[23]

I have taught from the Doctrine and Covenants for many years, and if I did not have a testimony of Joseph Smith and of these revelations, I would have abandoned the institute of religion classroom and taught math and physics, which I was originally trained to do. However, I know the revelations in the Doctrines and Covenants are from the Lord, and that section 76 privileges Latter-day Saints with a new perspective on life after death. However, there is more revelation for us to receive, and we need to live worthily so we can obtain it and be worthy to stand in the presence of the Lord at the last day.

Notes

1. Zebedee Coltrin Journal, August 19, 1832, Church History Library, The Church of Jesus Christ of Latter-day Saints, Salt Lake City.

2. Handwritten Statement by Levi Ward Hancock (1803–1882), Church History Library; some grammar and spelling modernized.

3. Introduction to Doctrine and Covenants section 88.

4. Joseph Smith, *History of the Church of Jesus Christ of Latter-day Saints*, ed. B. H. Roberts, 2nd ed. rev. (Salt Lake City: Deseret Book, 1957), 1:245.

5. Smith, *History of the Church*, 1:252–53.

6. "Joseph Smith, the Prophet," *Historical Record*, January 1888, 402.

7. Philo Dibble, in *Juvenile Instructor*, May 1892, 303–4.

8. Smith, *History of the Church*, 5:402.

9. Samuel H. Smith Journal, March 21, 1832, Church History Library.

10. Smith Journal, March 27, 1832.

11. Smith Journal, August 13, 1832.

12. Orson Hyde Journal, September 9, 1832, Church History Library.

13. Grant Underwood, *The Millenarian World of Early Mormonism* (Urbana: University of Illinois Press, 1999), 54.

14. Brigham Young, in *Journal of Discourses* (London: Latter-day Saints' Book Depot, 1858), 6:281.

15. Smith, *History of the Church*, 2:492.

16. Smith, *History of the Church*, 2:505.

17. Smith, *History of the Church*, 2:309.

18. Hyrum Smith, "Our City, and the Present Aspect of Affairs," *Times and Seasons*, March 15, 1844, 471.

19. Brigham Young, in *Journal of Discourses*, 4:371.

20. Brigham Young, in *Journal of Discourses*, 4:288.

21. Ezra Taft Benson, "Valiant in the Testimony of Jesus," *Ensign*, February 1987, 2.

22. Bruce R. McConkie, "Valiant in the Fight of Faith," *Ensign*, November 1974, 33.

23. McConkie, "Valiant in the Fight of Faith," 33.

GRANT UNDERWOOD

1833 Expulsion from Zion

This chapter focuses on three moments in 1833 that make the year a milestone in the Prophet's life and in Church history. First we will turn to February of 1833 and examine the Word of Wisdom, a revelation that has been as influential as any in this dispensation. Next we will briefly consider the commencement of the building of the first temple. Then we will conclude with a traumatic episode: the expulsion from Zion, or Jackson County, Missouri.

The Word of Wisdom

Regarding the historical background of the Word of Wisdom, most of us have heard the Brigham Young

---

Grant Underwood is a professor of history at Brigham Young University and an editor of The Joseph Smith Papers.

account of Emma Smith being tired of chewing-tobacco stains, and that was indeed part of what prompted the Word of Wisdom. I would like to enrich that background a little bit. Much less known is that the temperance movement—the movement to curb the excessive consumption of alcohol—and health reform in general were strong contributing factors. Just days before the first Latter-day Saint missionaries arrived in Ohio, the Kirtland Temperance Society was founded, and among its members were individuals with names like Morley and Lyman, who would become Latter-day Saints. Later, just weeks before what we know as the Word of Wisdom was received, the Kirtland Temperance Society succeeded in shutting down the Kirtland distillery. Add to that another interesting element: Joseph Smith subscribed to a non-Mormon periodical known as the *American Revivalist and Rochester Observer*, that regularly covered the temperance movement, particularly the relationship between temperance and the cholera epidemic that was under way. All of this then raises a question for us: Can we not broaden the background of the Word of Wisdom to include the temperance and health reform sentiment that was abroad in the land?[1]

What we have today as the first three verses of section 89 was initially an introductory statement, and it was not until the 1870s that Elder Orson Pratt, on assignment from the First Presidency, put that beginning paragraph into verse form. Verse 4 talks about the "evils and designs which do and will exist in the hearts of conspiring men." One of the fascinating aspects of historical investigation is that we come to understand how the early Saints read those words and understood them. Hyrum Smith, for instance, targets the fact that there were enemy forces involved in producing many of these goods, and one could not be confident that they would not be adulterated or poisoned or contaminated in some way. That may be what many early Saints saw behind the phrase the "evils and designs which do and will exist in the hearts of conspiring men."

As we move forward through the revelation, verses 5 and 6 say, "Inasmuch as any man drinketh wine or strong drink among you, behold it is not good, neither meet in the sight of your Father, only in assembling yourselves together to offer up your sacraments before him. And, behold, this should be wine, yea, pure wine of the grape of the vine, of your own make." From the beginning, the Latter-day Saints had no trouble with wine as part of the sacrament. For dietary consumption at a meal it was not acceptable, but for use in the sacrament it was. Indeed, many early journals give a glimpse of its common use. John Murdock, an ordinary elder, included this notation in his diary: "By my advice the sisters gathered currants and made wine for our communion."[2] At this very early period, the Saints naturally used some of the terminology from their former faiths. They had not yet restricted themselves to the word *sacrament*; sometimes they would use the word *communion* or the phrase "Lord's Supper," and occasionally the word *Eucharist*. Elizabeth Ann Whitney wrote, "We had a very fine orchard and garden, all planned and arranged according to our own taste and skill, among other fruits we had a very great quantity of the red currants, from which we had ourselves manufactured wine of a very superior flavor and quality, although purely domestic, or homemade, this wine we had appropriated for the sacrament, and was the first wine used by our people for that purpose."[3]

Years later Brigham Young said, "I anticipate the day when we can have the privilege of using, at our sacraments pure wine, produced within our borders. I do not know that it would injure us to drink wine of our own make, although we would be better without it than to drink it to excess."[4] True to Brother Brigham's comment, Latter-day Saints attempted where and when they could to grow grapes and produce wine primarily for use in the sacrament. There was even the "Dixie Wine Mission" in southern Utah throughout the latter half of the 1800s. The First Presidency and Quorum of the Twelve did not stop using wine in their weekly temple sacrament meetings until 1906.

In the early years, Bishop Newel K. Whitney once noted in his account book, "Received of the church for wine, $13.12. The church had two quarts wine, fourth proof."[5] This purchase was consistent with what was acceptable then. Bishop Whitney purchased wine and noted the price, quantity, and proof. The word *proof* means twice the percentage of alcohol; thus at "fourth proof," this wine had only 2 percent alcohol, a very mild drink. Back then, before Louis Pasteur devised his system, it was not possible to prevent fermentation, and thus pasteurized grape juice was not an option.

What did the term *pure wine* mean? When Newel and Polly Knight visited Joseph Smith in the summer of 1830 and the occasion to partake the sacrament arose, the revelation we know as section 27 directed them, "Wherefore, a commandment I give unto you, that you shall not purchase wine neither strong drink of your enemies; wherefore, you shall partake of none except it is made new among you" (vv. 3–4). The Saints were focusing on contamination. They made it themselves so they could be sure that it did not have improper ingredients.

Let's consider the historical use of the term *sacrament*. It was not uncommon in that day to consider marriage a sacrament, and part of the marriage custom of the time was to toast with a glass of wine. Indeed, the Saints partook of this custom, as did Joseph Smith. We have an account from his diary when he performed a wedding in January 1836 and afterward wrote, "We then partook of some refreshments, and our hearts were made glad with the fruit of the vine. This is according to the pattern set by our Savior Himself, and we feel disposed to patronize all the institutions of heaven."[6] The Savior himself graced the marriage in Cana of Galilee and turned the water into wine.

So when did water become part of the sacrament? People assume that the early members used water from the time section 27 was revealed onward. Not at all. The revelation merely *allows* but does not *command* the use of a beverage other than wine. Where wine had historically been customary, the Lord now said it did not matter what they used. Both water and wine were used for many years. However, when the Saints arrived in the Great Basin and the Dixie wine mission could not supply more than the local population, water became dominant in the sacrament service.

The Word of Wisdom says, "Inasmuch as any man drinketh wine or strong drink among you, behold it is not good" (Doctrine and Covenants 89:5). At that point there were different types of alcoholic drinks: wine, often with a higher alcoholic content than the liquid that Bishop Whitney purchased; hard cider, a little less alcoholic; and beer, with the lowest alcohol content of all (not like today's beers). At that time, "strong drinks" were in a category by themselves. They were distilled liquors—whiskey, rum, gin, and brandy. Most of them had 40 percent or more alcohol content.

The Word of Wisdom mentions that strong drinks are for washing the body. The people did not have denatured alcohol then; we use denatured alcohol today to clean wounds or to get an especially good cleanse. We read of a meeting in 1836 in which Oliver Cowdery records, "Met in the evening with bro. Joseph Smith, jr. at his house, in company with bro. John Corrill, and after pure water was prepared, called upon the Lord and proceeded to wash each other's bodies, and bathe the same with whiskey, perfumed with cinnamon. This we did that we might be clean before the Lord for the Sabbath, confessing our sins and covenanting to be faithful to God. While performing this washing unto the Lord with solemnity, our minds were filled with many reflections upon the propriety of the same, and how the priests anciently used to wash always before ministering before the Lord."[7] Because they did not have denatured alcohol, they added cinnamon to whiskey to change the smell. When one understands the context, this is a beautiful and spiritual experience and shows that the Saints used what was available to them at that time.

The Word of Wisdom next mentions the term *hot drinks*. Hyrum Smith made the famous statement some years later, "And again, 'hot drinks are not for the body, or belly;' there are many who wonder what this can mean; whether it refers to tea, or coffee, or not. I say it does refer to tea, and coffee."[8] That statement from the *Times and Seasons* has become the official interpretation of verse 9. Of course, there was then widespread agreement that drinks taken at an elevated temperature were harmful. That was a common idea from the time. And of growing concern to health reformers was the fact that tea and coffee, in particular, were not beneficial to the body. Tea and coffee had not been a prominent topic in temperance campaigns because the American drink of choice at this time was whiskey, which was the most readily available. When the temperance people got Congress to remove the tariff on tea and coffee, it could compete with whiskey, a distilled liquor. An objective of the temperance movement was to remove whiskey from society, so they proposed tea and coffee as a milder replacement. Later, with passage of time, people began to see problems with tea and coffee as well.[9]

The Word of Wisdom talks about the benefit of herbs, saying, "All wholesome herbs God hath ordained for the constitution, nature, and use of man" (Doctrine and Covenants 89:10). What did the term *herbs* mean? Back then it included more than the grasses and numerous plants used for culinary purposes. Herbs were also widely used medicinally, and there were a number of "herb doctors" in the Church, including Dr. Frederick G. Williams and Dr. Willard Richards. They were not medical doctors but botanic physicians. This same type of practice is found in the Book of Mormon where a brief passage mentions "the excellent qualities of the many plants and roots which God had prepared to remove the cause of diseases, to which men were subject by the nature of the climate" (Alma 46:40). The early Saints were very in tune with the idea of using herbs.

What about animal flesh and its consumption? The Word of Wisdom affirms it, as had several other revelations previously. "Flesh also of beasts and of the fowls of the air, I, the Lord, have ordained for the use of man with thanksgiving; nevertheless they are to be used sparingly" (Doctrine and Covenants 89:12). Section 49 earlier said, "Whoso forbiddeth to abstain from meats, that man should not eat the same, is not ordained of God" (v. 18). And a few months later, another revelation said, "All things which come of the earth . . . are made for the benefit and the use of man, both to please the eye and to gladden the heart; yea, for food and for raiment, for taste and for smell, to strengthen the body and to enliven the soul. And it pleaseth God that he hath given all these things unto man; for unto this end were they made to be used, with judgment, not to excess" (Doctrine and Covenants 59:18–20).

The Word of Wisdom cautions against excessive use of meat: "Nevertheless, they are to be used sparingly" (Doctrine and Covenants 89:12). Putting this idea into historical context, what do we know about meat consumption in the 1830s? One study said the early American diet had the highest percent of meat consumption in the world: the average American probably consumed a full pound of meat every day.[10] Therefore, maybe "sparingly" means to go from a pound to a half or a quarter or even to use it occasionally. The phrase "And it is pleasing unto me that they should not be used, only in times of winter, or of cold, or famine" reflected the conventional realities of the day, given the technologies of preservation available at the time (v. 13). This practice would have been seen as wisdom by all who read it.

What about the use of grains? The Word of Wisdom says, "All grain is ordained for the use of man and of beasts, to be the staff of life" (Doctrine and Covenants 89:14). Latter-day Saints, particularly in the twentieth century, took a fancy to wheat. There was a period in the last half century where wheat consumption was especially common in Latter-day Saint households.

Also among the grains, the revelation talks about barley and its uses for "mild drinks" (v. 17). Let us understand something about liquid consumption at the time. We have wonderful, clean, and pure water today, but many have served missions around the world and know that the Church advises the missionaries not to drink the water but to drink a soft drink instead. Americans in the 1830s did not drink much water. That was not the wisdom or the practice in Joseph Smith's day. Given that fact, what were the alternatives? One alternative was a mildly alcoholic beverage, and one of the best candidates was beer, which at the time had a low alcoholic content. This may have been envisioned in the phrase "mild drinks." For instance, Joseph Smith in his diary in March 1843 had his clerk record, "I told Theodore Turley that I had no objection to his building a brewery."[11] When you think of how different beer was back then and the mild content and what the alternatives were, it was actually a service for Brother Turley to build his brewery.

What can we say in summary? It took time for such practices as the Word of Wisdom to catch on. President Joseph F. Smith made a statement that the Word of Wisdom "was not given, at that time, by way of commandment or restraint but by revelation."[12] It was not really until the 1920s and 1930s that the Word of Wisdom became a commandment.[13] One can canvass the nineteenth century and find many great Saints who either had a broader interpretation of the Word of Wisdom than we do today or who neglected some aspect of it.

The Kirtland Temple

In December 1832, in that great revelation that we know as section 88, the Lord first instructed the Saints to build a house to his name. The revelation also includes a command to institute a school of the prophets. The house of the Lord in Kirtland was not intended to be a temple like those we have today. It was essentially a meetinghouse and a schoolhouse. Although months went by after the command to build the temple without any activity, beginning in May of 1833 there was some movement: a committee was appointed to gather funds. By early June they had prepared a circular, introducing themselves to the Saints as the individuals in charge of collecting funds. In this circular they wrote, "Unless we fulfill this command, viz.: establish an house, and prepare all things necessary whereby the Elders may gather into a school, called the School of the Prophets, and receive that instruction which the Lord designs they should receive, we may all despair of obtaining the great blessing that God has promised to the faithful of the Church of Christ."[14] Shortly thereafter, Joseph received section 95, in which the Saints were chastened for letting the better part of six months go by without doing much. The revelation can also be seen as reinforcing the recent surge of interest and activity.

Section 95 discusses the endowment in a way that shows how the early Saints understood it. The Lord said, "I gave unto you a commandment that you should build a house"—six months ago I gave you that commandment—"in the which house I design to endow those whom I have chosen with power from on high; for this is the promise of the Father unto you; therefore I command you to tarry, even as mine apostles at Jerusalem" (vv. 8–9). In the last chapter in Luke, the Lord tells the Apostles to tarry in Jerusalem until they are endowed with power from on high (see Luke 24:49). Luke, who is generally considered the author of Acts, continues the story at the beginning of Acts, indicating that the Apostles who had tarried in Jerusalem were gathered together to celebrate Pentecost. On that occasion there was a great outpouring of the Spirit that enabled the Apostles to powerfully preach the gospel and that included a dramatic display of the gift of tongues (see Acts 2:4).

This echo from Luke helps us understand what the endowment was for the earliest Saints. It was a repetition of that Pentecostal moment, of that special empowerment for the ministry. Many have discerned in the book of Acts a narrative pattern. An initial Pentecostal outpouring and empowerment is followed in subsequent chapters by the description of missionaries going out empowered with the Spirit and generating remarkable conversions. Thus early Latter-day Saints heard in the word *endowment* a promise of spiritual power, rather than a separate ceremony or a new sacred liturgy—not at this time, at least. The endowment was a spiritual empowerment enabling them to go out and preach.

This very vision is captured in the words of the house's dedicatory prayer. The Prophet prays, "Let the anointing of thy ministers be sealed upon them with power from on high. Let it be fulfilled upon them, as upon those on the day of Pentecost; let the gift of tongues be poured out upon thy people, even cloven tongues as of fire, and the interpretation thereof. And let thy house be filled, as with a rushing mighty wind, with thy glory" (D&C 109:35–37)—again a clear echo of Acts chapter 2 and its vision of the endowment as an empowering outpouring of the Spirit.

With the Mormon population in Missouri nearing a thousand, the Prophet had Fredrick G. Williams draw up plans for what the Zion temple was to look like and sent them to Missouri. Interestingly, the temples in Missouri and Kirtland were basically the same design. The temple in Missouri was to be a bit larger, but the plans that have survived from the temple in Zion depict a structure very much like the Kirtland Temple. The irony here is that although none of the plans for the Kirtland Temple have survived, it was actually built; whereas the plans for the first temple in Zion have survived, but it never was built. Now, section 95 mentions a revealed "pattern" for the temple. This the First Presidency saw in vision, but we also know that what they saw was apparently a general pattern for how the temple was to be built. Architectural historians have found that minor construction details such as the molding were worked out by individual craftsman using commonly available carpentry manuals and were not laid out in the plans developed by Joseph Smith, Sidney Rigdon, and Frederick G. Williams. The First Presidency defined the major elements of the Kirtland Temple design, but individual builders worked out structural and ornamental details to the best of their abilities. That is consistent with the Prophet's declaration, "I teach them correct principles, and they govern themselves."[15] In other words, I give the general guiding vision and allow my fellow servants to work out the details.

Expulsion from Zion

By the summer of 1833, there were more Saints in Zion than in northeastern Ohio. Still the whole Church was barely the size of a typical stake today. Having gathered to Zion, there were over a thousand Saints in Jackson County, Missouri. What were some of the tensions that led to difficulties? Why did this great dream unravel in the latter half of 1833? Let's look first at internal factors and then comment briefly on external factors.

Internally, there had been a history of tensions between Church leaders in Zion and in Kirtland. Today's Church leaders do not go on record criticizing each other, but the early brethren were young and inexperienced. Joseph was in his late twenties. Many of the other Church leaders were in their early thirties. Petty arguments had occurred off and on from the fall of 1831 to the summer of 1833. Surviving letters show they were trying to work through their disagreements, but a lack of full harmony among the leadership seemed to persist. This is reflected in a January 1833 letter—in fact, the letter that accompanied that great revelation known as the "Olive Leaf" (section 88) when it was sent to Missouri. Joseph writes, "If Zion will not purify herself, so as to be approved of in all things, in His sight, He will seek another people." He then tells the leaders, "Seek to purify yourselves, and also all the inhabitants of Zion, lest the Lord's anger be kindled to fierceness. Repent, repent, is the voice of God to Zion; and strange as it may appear, yet it is true, mankind will persist in self-justification until all their iniquity is exposed, and their character past being redeemed, and that which is treasured up in their hearts be exposed to the gaze of mankind. I say to you (and what I say to you I say to all,) hear the warning voice of God, lest Zion fall, and the Lord sware in His wrath the inhabitants of Zion shall not enter into His rest. ... This from your brother who trembles for Zion, and for the wrath of heaven, which awaits her if she repent not."[16]

That was said in January—six months before trouble broke out in Jackson County—and that was not the only warning. Joseph had pleaded repeatedly with the leadership to reconcile themselves and to promote harmony throughout the Church.

There were external factors as well. The Saints came from the North, and under the Missouri Compromise, Missouri had been admitted to the Union as a slave state just a decade earlier. An article appeared in *The Evening and the Morning Star* in July that proved to be the spark that lit the powder keg. It advised immigrating Saints to be careful about including free blacks among their companies because there were restrictions in Missouri. What actually appeared in print was distorted by the Missourians, and the rumors spread that the Mormons were inviting free blacks into Missouri and that it would play havoc with their slaves.[17] The reality was that relatively few Jackson County citizens owned slaves, but this article riled them up anyway. Days before trouble broke out, the Church issued an "extra," trying to assuage the angry feelings and clarify the situation. They were unable to do so, and a riot occurred a few days later. It resulted in the destruction of the printing press operation. Printer Phelps and family were turned out of the building, and the press and shop were vandalized. Bishop Partridge was tarred and feathered, and an ultimatum was given to the Saints to leave within a matter of months.

Sadly, this kind of violence was not uncommon in antebellum America. Abraham Lincoln in 1837 decried "the increasing disregard for law which pervades the country; the growing disposition to substitute the wild and furious passions, in lieu of the sober judgement of Courts; and the worse than savage mobs, for the executive ministers of justice.... Whenever the vicious portion of population shall be permitted to gather in bands of hundreds and thousands, and burn churches, ravage and rob provision stores, throw printing presses into rivers, shoot editors, and hang and burn obnoxious persons at pleasure, and with impunity; depend on it, this government cannot last."[18] By this quote, we learn that such vigilantism was business as usual in violent frontier America.

A couple of days after all this chaos in Independence, John Whitmer, one of the leaders in Zion, sat down and wrote a letter to report the disaster to Joseph. Missouri Church leaders dispatched Oliver Cowdery with the letter, and he hand carried it to Kirtland. But Whitmer included a silver lining to the dark cloud: "Marvelous to tell in the midst of all the rage of persecution God is pouring out his Spirit upon his people so that most all on last thursday at the school [of the prophets] received the gift of tongues & spake & prophesied. The next day David [Whitmer, John's brother] called his branch together and most of them received the gift." "Many old things are coming to light," continued Whitmer, "that had it not been for this gift would have remained in the dark & brought the wrath of God upon the inhabitants of Zion." What a fascinating little glimpse at the emotionally charged and spiritually heightened environment of that time. He then concludes, "Our daily cry to God is to deliver thy people from the hand of our enemies send thy destroying angels, O God in the behalf of thy people that Zion may be built up."[19]

A few days after Joseph Smith received Whitmer's letter and heard additional firsthand reports from Oliver, he sat down and wrote a letter. It is a rare gem—in part because it is in the

Prophet's own hand. Joseph did very little writing in his own hand. The vast majority of his record, 95 percent plus, is in the hand of scribes. But on August 18, 1833, after hearing about the disaster that had befallen his beloved Saints in Missouri, Joseph took pen in hand and wrote one of the longest letters in his own hand that we have. As part of it, echoing what John Whitmer had said, he petitioned the Lord with reference to "all those ungodly men who have committed those ungodly deeds . . . let thine anger <is> be enkindled against them and <let> them <and they shall> be consumed before thy face and be far removed from Zion."[20] That is strong Old Testament–like rhetoric, but it was part of the background and mindset that early Saints grew up with and brought with them into the Church. They were not saying, "Let me take vengeance, Lord," but, "Please do it, Lord. It's time to settle accounts. Let the wicked have their due. We know you can do it."

Joseph expressed himself quite emotionally in this letter, and remember, we are not getting him filtered through a clerk here. This is right out of his mind, unedited, onto the paper: "Dear Brotheren in fellowship and <love> towards you and with a broken heart and a contrite spirit I take the pen to address you but I know not what to say to you and the thought <that> this <of> letter will be so long coming to you my heart faints within me I feel to exclaim O Lord let the desire of my heart be felt and realized this moment <upon you[r] hearts> and teach you all things thy servent would communicate to would you my Brotheren."[21] We sense Joseph's frustration when he writes about his letter taking a long time to arrive. Two to three weeks was typical. Oliver raced to Ohio as fast as he could, but it took him ten days to get there. Joseph knew that this riot in Missouri broke out in late July. He wrote on August 18, and the Saints were not going to see it before the first of September, almost six weeks after the tragedy. Think how much pain and suffering they endured before hearing the first consoling word from their prophet. Think about that in contrast to our quick response to disasters today and our nearly instantaneous systems of communication.

Hear a bit more from his letter: "Now what shall I say to cumfort your hearts well I will tell you that you have my whole confidence yea there is not one doubt in <my heart> not one place in me but what is filld with perfect confidince and love for you." Imagine what such words would have meant to the Saints when they finally arrived. "And this affliction is sent upon us not for your sins but for the sins of the chirch."[22] Here was a gentle prophet, spreading around responsibility. He could have accused them. He had written them numerous letters before warning them in no uncertain terms to repent and shape up, telling them that God would have a new people if they did not rise to the occasion. But in this case he shares ownership of the problem. We all contributed to it, he says. We all had our pettiness. We here in Kirtland did not respond to the Lord's pleas to gather money to buy all the property we should have. We did not work through our own shortcomings. Then he adds, "God has suffered it not for your sins but that he might <pre>prare you for a grateer work that you might be prepared for the endowment from on high we cast no reflections upon you." Notice how he takes a positive view of what their afflictions will lead to—an endowment from on high. The Saints are improved through the refiner's fire. "We have had the word of the Lord that you shall [be] deliverd from you[r] dainger and <shall> again flurish in spite of hell."[23]

He reiterates this later in his letter: "I verily know that he will spedily deliver Zion for I have his immutible covenant that this shall be the case but god is pleased to keep it hid from mine

EXPULSION FROM ZION

eyes the means how exactly the thing will be done."[24] Is that not beautiful? Joseph Smith has felt the whispering of the Spirit that all will be well, but he cannot yet discern how it will happen. "The chirch in Kirtland," he continued, "concluded with one accord to die with you or redeem you and never at any time have I felt as I now feel that pure love and for you my Brotheren the wormth and Zeal for you[r] safty that we can scarcely hold our spirits but wisdom I trust will keep us from madness and desperation and the power of the Go[s]pel will enable us to stand."[25] Don't you love Joseph Smith? I love his passion, his feeling, his pathos. What a glimpse! Do you not sense a wonderful, loving, frustrated prophet here? It is like what you would probably write to your loved ones, to your family, were they taken hostage in some foreign country or caught in some disaster in another land. You too would be driven to "madness and desperation" to be here and unable to bail them out. Those Missouri Saints were not just so many membership statistics for Joseph Smith—they were his brothers and sisters.

He finishes the letter with a few equally wonderful lines: "Now I conclude by telling you that we wait the Comand of God to do whatever he plese and if <he> shall say go up to Zion and defend thy Brotheren by <the sword> we fly and we count not ~~dear~~ our live[s] dear to us I am your Brother in Christ. Joseph Smith Jr."[26] A passionate prophet was ready to lay down his life for his beloved Saints. It brings to my mind a couple of statements in the revelation given on the day the Church was organized, section 21. The Savior says of the Prophet, "His prayers I have heard. Yea, his weeping for Zion I have seen" (vv. 7–8). Do we feel this way about the people around us? Do we have that kind of love and devotion? When was the last time we shed a tear for some of our flock? Brother Joseph sets a great example.

Another aspect of this turmoil in Missouri is that it takes place in the context of millennial, end-time expectation. Here is the setting. When the Saints, rather than simply starting to pack their bags, begin to seek legal redress, the Missourians are riled. By late October they take up arms and drive the Saints from their homes, across the Missouri River into Clay County. The expulsion is essentially complete by the end of the first week in November. Then just a few days after that event, but before Joseph knows they have been driven out, on November 13, a remarkable Leonid meteor shower occurred, one that is well known in all books on astronomical history, a phenomenon seen all across the United States. Many contemporary sketches and paintings were made of this famous meteor shower that coincides with this crisis moment. Given their scriptural background, the tension of the times, and their pronounced millennialism, we are not surprised that Joseph writes as follows, again in his own hand, "Nothing of note transpired from the 4th of Nove[m]ber u[n]til this day in the morning at 4 Oh clock I was awoke by Brother Davis knocking at <my> door saying Brother Joseph come git <up> and see the signs in the heavens and I arrose and beheld to my great Joy the stars fall from heaven yea they fell like hail stones a litteral fullfillment of the word of God as recorded in the holy scriptures and a sure sign that the coming of Christ is clost at hand Oh how marvellous are thy works Oh Lord and I thank thee for thy me[r]cy u<n>to me thy servent Oh Lord save me in thy kingdom for Christ sake Amen."[27] What a wonderful, intimate peek at the Prophet! One sees here his natural and understandable private reflections and expectations. Remember this was not a canonized revelation nor a carefully deliberated policy statement; this was Joseph Smith the man, reacting as any of us might under the circumstances of those difficult days. It is a perfectly understandable expression from a devout, impassioned twenty-eight-year-old.

Because the Prophet had faith that Zion would be restored, that August letter reminded the Saints it was "the will of the Lord" that "not one foot of land ~~the~~ perchased should <be> given to the enimies of god or sold to them but if any is sold let it be sold to the chirch."[28] The idea of holding on to the Jackson County property occurs in several other letters the Prophet wrote later on. For instance, on December 5 he wrote, "Retain your lands, even unto the uttermost."[29] An August 1834 "Appeal" published in *The Evening and the Morning Star* put it this way: for the Saints to sell their land "would amount to a denial of their faith, as that land is the place where the Zion of God shall stand."[30]

In early December 1833, after finally hearing of the expulsion, the Prophet wrote, "It is your privilege to use every lawful means in your power to seek redress for your grievances, but," he adds poignantly, "it will be impossible for us to render you any temporal assistance, as our means are already exhausted, and we are deeply in debt, and know of no means whereby we shall be able to extricate ourselves." The Church in Ohio was also in quite a predicament. "The inhabitants of this country threaten our destruction, and we know not how soon they may be permitted to follow the example of the Missourians."[31] Days later and just a week before receiving what is now Doctrine and Covenants 101, Joseph wrote as follows to his brethren in Missouri:

> I cannot learn from any communication by the spirit to me that Zion has forfeited her claim to a celestial crown notwithstanding the Lord has caused her to be thus afflicted; except it may ~~it may~~ be some individuals who have walked in disobedience and forsaken the new covenants; all such will

be made manifest by their works in due time. I have always expected that Zion would suffer sore affliction from what I could learn from the commandments which have been given. but I would remind you of a certain clause in one which says that after much tribulation cometh the blessing. by this and also others, and also one received of late, I know that Zion, in the own due time of the Lord will be redeemed, but how many will be the days of her purification, tribulation and affliction, the Lord has kept hid from my eyes; and when I enquire concerning this subject the voice of the Lord is, Be still, and know that I am God! all those who suffer for my name shall reign with me, and he that layeth down his life for my sake shall find it again.[32]

This expression sets the stage for a fascinating glimpse at how revelations sometimes came together in the mind of the Prophet. "Now there are two things of which I am ignorant," Joseph writes in this same letter, "and the Lord will not show me—perhaps for a wise purpose in himself. I mean in some respects, and they are these, Why God hath suffered so great calamity to come upon Zion; or what the great moving cause of this great affliction is. These two things and again by what means he will return her back to her inheritance. . . . These two things brethren, are in part kept back they are not plainly [shown unto me]."[33] Why God had "suffered so great calamity to come upon Zion" is the question, the distress of soul, that had been on the Prophet's mind since August. One week later, it is finally answered in what becomes Doctrine and Covenants 101, verses 2 and 7: "I, the Lord, have suffered the affliction to come upon them, wherewith they have been afflicted, in consequence of their transgressions; . . . They were slow to hearken unto the voice of the Lord their God; therefore, the Lord their God is slow to hearken unto their prayers, to answer them in the day of their trouble."

Toward the end of section 101 is a description about importuning the government authorities. It provides a good example of how thoughts in the Prophet's mind build toward revelation. In his letter to the Saints in Missouri the week before, recording Doctrine and Covenants 101, Joseph had written: "Pray to God day and night to return you in peace and in safety to the Lands of your inheritance and, when the Judge fails you, appeal unto the Executive, and when the Executive fails you, appeal unto the President, and when the President fails you, and all laws fail you and the humanity of the people fails you, and all things else fails you but God alone, and you continue to weary him with your importunings, as the poor woman the unjust Judge, he will not fail to exicute Judgment upon your enemies and to avenge his own elect that cry unto him day and night."[34]

Then, seven days later, he dictated these words in Doctrine and Covenants 101: "Let [the Saints] importune at the feet of the judge; and if he heed them not, let them importune at the feet of the governor; and if the governor heed them not, let them importune at the feet of the president; and if the president heed them not, then will the Lord arise and come forth out of his hiding place, and in his fury vex the nation; and in his hot displeasure, and in his fierce anger, in his time, will cut off those wicked, unfaithful, and unjust stewards, and appoint them their portion among hypocrites and unbelievers, even in outer darkness" (vv. 86–90). Isn't that interesting? You see that same image from Luke—the parable of the importuning widow—and similar verbiage from the letter included in the revelation.

The Saints continued to seek redress, though ultimately to no avail, and they continued to reflect on the meaning of the expulsion from Zion. A few years later, these words appeared in the Church's newspaper:

> Many are ready to cry out against the Saints, and murmur against the dealings of God with his people. But from only once reading of those paragraphs, it will be seen, that in scarcely a single instance has the commands of God been heeded. The Saints have neglected the necessary preparation beforehand; they have not sent up their wise men with money to purchase land, but the rich have generally staid back and with held their money, while the poor have gone first and without money. Under these circumstances what could be expected but the appalling scene that now presents itself? The Lord always chastises his people, the people to whom he gives immediate revelation, more quickly, and apparently more severely for their transgressions, than he does those who disregard all revelation. We do hope the saints here and elsewhere; will learn humility, wisdom and obedience by the things which their brethren in the West now have to suffer.[35]

That is a worthy invitation for all of us to embrace as we conclude our discussion of important events in 1833. May we draw inspiration from the example of how the Prophet dealt with these very challenging moments, and may we, too, grow in humility, wisdom, and obedience.

Notes

1. On temperance, see Ian Tyrell, *Sobering Up: From Temperance to Prohibition in Antebellum America* (Westport, CT: Greenwood Press, 1979). For health reform, see Stephen Wissenbaum, *Sex, Diet, and Debility in Jacksonian America: Sylvester Graham and Health Reform* (Westport, CT: Greenwood Press, 1980).

2. John Murdock, Journal, August 11, 1833, Church History Library, The Church of Jesus Christ of Latter-day Saints, Salt Lake City.

3. Elizabeth Ann Whitney, "A Leaf from an Autobiography," *Woman's Exponent*, October 1, 1878, 71.

4. Brigham Young, in *Journal of Discourses* (Liverpool: F. D. Richards, 1854–86), 10:300.

5. Newel K. Whitney, Account Book, August 2, 1835, L. Tom Perry Special Collections, Harold B. Lee Library, Brigham Young University, Provo, Utah.

6. Joseph Smith, *History of the Church of Jesus Christ of Latter-day Saints*, ed. B. H. Roberts, 2nd ed. rev. (Salt Lake City: Deseret Book, 1957), 2:369.

7. Quoted in Leonard J. Arrington, "Oliver Cowdery's Kirtland, Ohio, 'Sketch Book,'" *BYU Studies* 12, no. 4 (Summer 1972): 416.

8. Hyrum Smith, "The Word of Wisdom," *Times and Seasons*, June 1, 1842, 800.

9. See William J. Rorabaugh, *The Alcoholic Republic* (New York: Oxford University Press, 1979). A contemporaneous publication warning about tea and coffee was William A. Alcott, *Tea and Coffee: Their Physical, Intellectual Effects on the Human System* (New York, 1839).

10. Rorabaugh, *The Alcoholic Republic*, 113.

11. Smith, *History of the Church*, 5:300.

12. Joseph F. Smith, in Conference Report, October 4, 1908, 4.

13. See Thomas G. Alexander, *Mormonism in Transition* (Urbana: University of Illinois Press, 1986), 250–71.

14. Joseph Fielding Smith, *Life of Joseph F. Smith* (Salt Lake City: Deseret Book, 1938), 48–49.

15. Quoted by John Taylor, in *Millennial Star*, November 15, 1851, 339.

16. Smith, *History of the Church*, 1:316–17.

17. See Newel G. Bringhurst and Darron T. Smith, *Black and Mormon* (Urbana: University of Illinois, 2004), 14.

18. Quoted in Christopher Waldrep, *Lynching in America: A History in Documents* (New York: NYU, 2006), 58, 66.

19. John Whitmer to Joseph Smith and Oliver Cowdery, July 29, 1833, Church History Library.

20. *Personal Writings of Joseph Smith*, ed. Dean C. Jessee, rev. ed. (Salt Lake City: Deseret Book; Provo, UT: Brigham Young University Press, 2002), 308.

21. *Personal Writings of Joseph Smith*, 308.

22. *Personal Writings of Joseph Smith*, 310.

23. *Personal Writings of Joseph Smith*, 310–11.

24. *Personal Writings of Joseph Smith*, 308–9.

25. *Personal Writings of Joseph Smith*, 309.

26. *Personal Writings of Joseph Smith*, 311–12.

27. *Personal Writings of Joseph Smith*, 7–8.

28. *Personal Writings of Joseph Smith*, 311.

29. Smith, *History of the Church*, 1:455.

30. *Millennial Star*, August 1834, 183.

31. Smith, *History of the Church*, 1:450.

32. *Personal Writings of Joseph Smith*, 329.

33. *Personal Writings of Joseph Smith*, 329.

34. *Personal Writings of Joseph Smith*, 330–31.

35. *Messenger and Advocate*, September 1836, 379.

ALEXANDER L. BAUGH

1834
Joseph Smith and the Redemption of Zion

*I*n 1834, the Church was still young—less than four years old. Membership was probably between 2,000 and 2,500, with approximately 1,200 Saints living in Missouri and another six to eight hundred living in Kirtland and northeastern Ohio. The remaining three to four hundred resided in scattered branches primarily in Pennsylvania, New York, Michigan, and Ontario, Canada.

Joseph Smith himself was young—a youthful twenty-eight; his wife Emma, twenty-nine. Their children were young. Julia Murdock Smith, their adopted daughter, was almost three. Joseph III, his namesake, was just over a year.

When I began to write this sketch of Joseph Smith's life in 1834, I tried to put myself in the place of Joseph

---

Alexander L. Baugh is an associate professor of Church history and doctrine at Brigham Young University and an editor of The Joseph Smith Papers.

Smith. What would he think were the highlights or major events of his life during that year? Based on the available historical records, I have sincerely tried to piece together a one-year narrative of his life that would be representative of the Prophet of the Restoration. I did the best I could. I hope Joseph would approve.

Kirtland Stake High Council Organized

With the growth of the Church and other advances came the need to expand Church organization and widen its leadership. During the first three years of the Church (1830–33), Church councils composed of elders, bishops, and high priests had been attending to problems in the Church. But a higher governing body was needed to resolve "important difficulties . . . which could not be settled by the church or the bishop's council" (Doctrine and Covenants 102:2). Such responsibilities included the formulation of rules and policies and the disciplining of errant members.

On February 17, 1834, Joseph Smith told a body of priesthood brethren and others who were assembled that he "would show the order of councils in ancient days as shown to him by vision."[1] He then proceeded to organize a new council, known as the stake high council, or in more familiar terms, the Kirtland Stake. The creation of the Kirtland Stake marked the first time a formal ecclesiastical subunit of the Church was established. The council was to comprise a presidency of three high priests with twelve additional high priests selected as councilors with responsibilities to govern in local administrative and judicial matters. Significantly, Joseph Smith, Sidney Rigdon, and Frederick G. Williams, who were serving at the time as the Church's First Presidency, were also chosen to serve as the presidency of Kirtland Stake.[2] The minutes of the first meeting of the Kirtland stake presidency and high council were recorded in the Kirtland Council Minute Book and later canonized as section 5 in the 1835 edition of the Doctrine and Covenants. Today, the minutes make up Doctrine and Covenants section 102.

The Zion's Camp Revelation, Recruitment, and Preparation

With a governing body in place in Kirtland, Joseph turned his attention to a far weightier matter. On November 25, 1833, Orson Hyde and John Gould arrived in Kirtland, Ohio, after having traveled from Missouri, bringing word of the forced removal of some 1,200 Latter-day Saints from Jackson County during the first week of November.[3] Meanwhile, Missouri Church leaders informed state officials of the events surrounding their expulsion and requested assistance. R. W. Wells, Missouri's attorney general, was the first to respond and was sympathetic. Two weeks after the expulsion, he wrote to David Rice Atchison and Alexander W. Doniphan, two Liberty lawyers who had been secured as legal counsel by the Church, informing them that if the Mormons "desire to be replaced in possession of their property . . . an adequate force will be sent forthwith to effect that object." Furthermore, he believed the Mormons had the legal right to "organize themselves into regular companies, or a regular company of militia, either volunteers or otherwise."[4] Based upon Wells's conjecture, on December 6, the leading Missouri elders petitioned Missouri governor Daniel Dunklin directly, requesting they be restored to their "lands, houses, and property, and protected in them by the militia of the state, if legal, or by a detachment of the United States Rangers."[5] Writing to Oliver Cowdery in December 1833, John Corrill expressed hope that the governor would take action in their behalf. "The Governor had manifested a willingness to restore us back, and will if we request it," he wrote, "but this will be of but little use unless he could leave a force there to help protect us."⁶ Later, Dunklin reiterated this position in a formal reply. He fully acknowledged the Mormons had a right to organize a military body; "indeed it is [your] duty to do so," he wrote. However, "as to the request for keeping up a military force to protect your people, and prevent the commission of crimes and injuries," he believed such a request did not warrant the use of state troops since in his opinion it was not, under militia law, an "emergency."⁷ Based upon what they were told by Missouri officials, Mormon leaders in Missouri believed the following would transpire. First, the state would render assistance by mustering a militia force which would help reinstate the displaced Saints back in Jackson County. Second, the Latter-day Saints were authorized to organize their own independent military unit, which body would join forces with the state militia in helping restore the Saints to their lands. And third, after the Jackson Saints were reinstated, the Mormon contingent would remain for a time to provide protection and maintain order until peace was restored.

A revelation given to the Prophet Joseph Smith the previous December (1833) intimated the Church would respond to the Missouri difficulties with an organized military body. The revelation summoned "all the strength of mine house, which are my warriors, my young men, and they that are of middle age also among all my servants, who are the strength of mine house ... [to go] straightway unto the land of my vineyard, and redeem my vineyard; for it is mine" (Doctrine and Covenants 101:55–56). When Elders Parley P. Pratt and Lyman Wight arrived in Kirtland on February 22, 1834, following a lengthy midwinter journey from Missouri, the two men informed Joseph Smith of the latest developments in connection with the exiled members. The two men delivered a letter written by William W. Phelps informing the Prophet that "the Governor is willing to restore us, but . . . the constitution gives him no power to guard us when back."[8] Clearly the Missouri Saints were asking for the Kirtland members to come to their assistance. On February 24, two days after the arrival of Pratt and Wight, Joseph Smith received a revelation reiterating the previous one (see Doctrine and Covenants 101), calling for five hundred men but settling for no less than one hundred recruits to make up the company (see Doctrine and Covenants 103:32–34). The revelation instructed the Saints to organize companies of tens, twenties, fifties, and hundreds (see Doctrine and Covenants 103:30) and called for Joseph Smith to take command of the entire operation (see Doctrine and Covenants 103:21–22, 35). Seven additional men—Parley P. Pratt, Lyman Wight, Sidney Rigdon, Hyrum Smith, Frederick G. Williams, Orson Hyde, and Orson Pratt—were instructed to obtain supplies and money, recruit volunteers, and organize the companies (see Doctrine and Covenants 103:29–34, 37–40). Later that same day the Prophet met with the Kirtland high council and told them he was going to Missouri and asked for volunteers to head up the expedition later known as Zion's Camp.[9] May 1, 1834, was set as the departure date for the company.[10] For eight months Zion's Camp occupied the Prophet's attention, and it was the primary focus of his activity during the months preceding the journey (January–April), during the expedition (May–July), and ending with his return to Kirtland (August).

One can only imagine the weight of responsibility Joseph Smith felt. The task must have been formidable and daunting. He was young, only twenty-eight years old, and inexperienced in military activities and affairs. Furthermore, the expedition would entail traveling over nine hundred miles (one way) through four states over rough roads and sometimes uncharted terrain. In addition, two months of food, provisions, and supplies would be needed for more than two hundred individuals. Perhaps most significant, however, was the fact that he would ultimately be responsible for the overall day-to-day operations and activities and the physical safety and well-being of the participants. For Joseph Smith, Zion's Camp tested his leadership skills at an early stage in his prophetic ministry.

Joseph Smith wasted no time in moving forward with his plans to organize Zion's Camp. On February 26, only two days after the receipt of Doctrine and Covenants section 103, he left Kirtland in company with Parley P. Pratt to recruit volunteers. The two leaders traveled east, visiting Church branches and recruiting men and means primarily in northeastern Ohio and western New York. The Prophet was absent from Kirtland for over a month, returning on March 28.[11] On that date, his journal includes the following entry written in his own hand: "Came home found my Family all well and the Lord be praised for this blessing."[12] Orson Hyde and Orson Pratt made rounds in Pennsylvania; Lyman Wight and Sidney Rigdon visited congregations in Ohio, Pennsylvania, and New York; and Frederick G. Williams and Hyrum Smith labored in the East for a period of time. In late April, Hyrum Smith and Lyman Wight went to Michigan to recruit volunteers.

Recruiting men for Zion's Camp proved to be difficult. Many expected there would be armed conflict and that their safety could be in jeopardy. To Brigham Young and his older brother Joseph, the Prophet promised: "If you will go with me in the camp to Missouri and keep my counsel, I promise you, in the name of the Almighty, that I will lead you there and back again, and not a hair of your heads shall be harmed."[13] Family and work responsibilities caused others to be reluctant or to not heed the call altogether. On the other hand, the prospects of participating in an extended overland adventure to western Missouri proved exciting for the more adventuresome type, such as sixteen-year-old George A. Smith, younger cousin of the Prophet. Although underage, he was permitted to go and was placed under the care and keeping of the Prophet. His responsibilities included taking care of Joseph's arms and assisting Zebedee Coltrin, one of the camp's cooks.[14] Other Smith family members also enlisted, including Joseph's younger brother William Smith (age twenty-three); Wilkins Jenkins Salisbury (age twenty-three), the Prophet's brother-in-law; and Jesse J. Smith (age twenty-five), another younger cousin.

Joseph Smith v. Philastus Hurlbut

April 1834 was an extremely busy time for Joseph Smith as he was putting final plans in place for the departure of Zion's Camp. However, during the first week of April the Mormon leader was also involved in a highly publicized court hearing involving Philastus Hurlbut (his first given name was actually "Doctor"), a disgruntled ex-Mormon. Hurlbut had joined the Church in Kirtland in March 1833, but his membership in the Church was short lived when he was excommunicated the following June on the charge of adultery. Following his dismissal, Hurlbut traveled to Palmyra, New York, where he collected sixteen affidavits from individuals in the community who claimed to have associated with the Smith family. The subjectively gathered affidavits contained negative and derogatory reports about Joseph Smith and the entire Smith family. Hurlbut's affidavits and a series of nine letters written by Ezra Booth, also an ex-Mormon, were used as the basis for the first anti-Mormon book, *Mormonism Unvailed*, published later in 1834 in Painesville, Ohio, by Eber D. Howe, editor of the *Painesville Telegraph*.[15] But Hurlbut had also personally threatened Joseph Smith's life, resulting in the charges that culminated in a court hearing. The hearing convened in Geauga County, Court of Common Pleas in Chardon, Ohio, on April 2 and concluded on April 7. At the conclusion of the hearing, Hurlbut was found guilty and ordered to pay a two-hundred-dollar bond and to keep the peace for six months. He was also ordered to pay the court cost, which amounted to $112.59. In his journal dated April 7, Joseph notes that Hurlbut's conviction "was in answer to our prayer for which I thank my heavenly father."[16]

Medina Conference—Vision of Adam and Eve

On April 18 the Prophet, accompanied by Sidney Rigdon, Oliver Cowdery, and Zebedee Coltrin, left Kirtland to attend a conference in Medina County, situated fifty miles south of Kirtland, near present-day Akron, Ohio. The Kirtland Council Minute Book contains a summary of the Prophet's remarks on the occasion of the first day of the conference, April 21. Among other subjects, he recounted how he obtained and translated the Book of Mormon, the occasion when he and Oliver Cowdery received the Aaronic and Melchizedek Priesthoods, and the events associated with the organization of the Church. Returning to the significance of the Book of Mormon and modern revelation, he told his hearers, "Take away the book of Mormon, and the revelations, and where is our religion? We have none."[17]

During the course of the two-day conference, Joseph, Oliver, and Zebedee experienced a most unusual vision. The Prophet asked Oliver and Zebedee to walk with him "to a place where there was some beautiful grass, and grapevines," Coltrin later recounted. The Prophet then requested they each pray in turn. After praying, Joseph said, "'Now breth[r]en . . . we will see some visions.'" Joseph laid on the ground, and Oliver and Zebedee rested their heads on his outstretched arms. "The heavens gradually opened," Coltrin recalled, and the brethren "saw a golden throne, on a circular foundation, something like a light house, and on the throne were two aged personages, having white hair, and clothed in white garments." These personages were "the two most beautiful and perfect specimens of mankind" Coltrin had ever seen. Joseph called them "our first parents, Adam and Eve." Coltrin remembered Adam as a "large broadshouldered man, and Eve as a woman . . . large in proportion."[18]

Dissolution of the United Firm—Doctrine and Covenants 104

On April 23, 1834, two days after returning from Medina County, Joseph was directed by revelation to dissolve the Church's business-holding company, called the United Firm, and to distribute its assets to the directors of the firm. The United Firm had been established in 1832 to assist the poor in the Church (see Doctrine and Covenants 78), but because of the firm's heavy debt, its dissolution was advisable. The revelation, which makes up what is today Doctrine and Covenants 104, is often ignored simply because its detailed directives primarily discuss the distribution of the assets of the firm.[19] Interestingly, on April 28, 1834, five days after the receipt of Doctrine and Covenants 104, the Prophet received another revelation concerning the United Firm. It is not well known, primarily because it was never canonized. It comprises only three sentences, consisting of a total of eighty-eight words.[20]

Prophecy regarding the Future Size of the Church

One of those who responded to the call-up of Zion's Camp was none other than twenty-seven-year-old Wilford Woodruff. On December 29, 1833, while living at Richland, Onondaga County, New York, Wilford and his older brother Azmon first heard the restored gospel preached by Zera Pulsipher and Elijah Cheney. Two days after being introduced to Mormonism (December 31), the two brothers were baptized and became part of the newly formed Richland Branch. In early April 1834, Parley P. Pratt visited Richland recruiting volunteers for Zion's Camp. Azmon, who was married, declined the invitation, but Wilford, who was single, signed on, and on April 11, he left Richland to journey to Kirtland, where he arrived two weeks later on April 25.[21] Shortly after his arrival, he met Joseph Smith for the first time. Wilford's recollections of that meeting were as follows:

> I first met Joseph Smith in the streets of Kirtland. He had on an old hat, and a pistol in his hand. Said he, "Brother Woodruff, I've been shooting at a mark, and I wanted to see if I could hit anything." And, said he, "Have you any objection to it?" "Not at all," said I. "There is no law against a man shooting at a mark, that I know of." He invited me to his house. He had a wolf skin, which he wanted me to help to tan; he wanted it to sit on while driving his wagon team. Now, many might have said. "You are a pretty [interesting] prophet; shooting a pistol and tanning a wolf skin." Well, we tanned it, and used it while making a journey of a thousand miles. This was my first acquaintance with the Prophet Joseph.[22]

On April 27, three days before the scheduled departure of Zion's Camp, Wilford heard Joseph Smith preach for the first time. The meeting took place in a small log schoolhouse in Kirtland. The Prophet's remarks left a profound impression on Wilford, especially a prophecy made by the Mormon leader at the close of the meeting about the future size of the Church. Wilford wrote:

> On Sunday the 27 of April the saints met togather and held a testamony meeting, and many of the elders spoke and bore their testamony; among the number was... Joseph Smith the Prophet who closed by saying "Brothering [brethren] we are laying the foundation of a great work and you know it not, you comprehend it not. The work we are engaged in will grow, spread, and increas[e] untill it will fill the land: it will go from sea to sea it will fill the Rocky Mountains: all nations will hear it: it will fill its destiny; It is the work of Almighty God, and he will maintain and defend it."[23]

Speaking in general conference in April 1898, Woodruff reflected upon the April 1834 meeting and remarked:

> On Sunday night the Prophet called on all who held the Priesthood to gather into the little log school house they had there. It was a small house, perhaps 14 feet square. But it held the whole of the Priesthood of The Church of Jesus Christ of Latter-day Saints who were then in the town of Kirtland, and who had gathered together to go off in Zion's camp.... When we got together the Prophet called upon the Elders of Israel with him to bear testimony of this work. When they got through the Prophet said, "Brethren, I have been very much edified and instructed in your testimonies here tonight, but I want to say to you before the Lord, that you know no more concerning the destinies of this Church

and kingdom than a babe upon its mother's lap. You don't comprehend it." I was rather surprised. He said, "It is only a little handful of Priesthood you see here tonight, but this Church will fill North and South America—it will fill the world." Among other things he said, "It will fill the Rocky Mountains. There will be tens of thousands of Latter-day Saints who will be gathered in the Rocky Mountains, and there they will open the door for the establishing of the Gospel among the Lamanites, who will receive the Gospel and their endowments and the blessings of God. This people will go into the Rocky Mountains; they will there build temples to the Most High. They will raise up a posterity there, and the Latter-day Saints who dwell in these mountains will stand in the flesh until the coming of the Son of Man. The Son of Man will come to them while in the Rocky Mountains."[24]

New Name for the Church

On May 1, the scheduled date of departure of Zion's Camp, the first group consisting of twenty men left Kirtland.[25] Joseph Smith may have purposely delayed his departure to preside at a conference scheduled for May 3. It appears that the main purpose for this conference was to discuss and adopt a new name for the Church. The conference minutes read:

> MINUTES of a Conference of the Elders of the church of Christ, which church was organized in the township of Fayette, Seneca county, New-York, on the 6th of April, A.D. 1830. The Conference came to order, and JOSEPH SMITH JR. was chosen Moderator, and FREDERICK G. WILLIAMS and OLIVER COWDERY, were appointed clerks.
> After prayer the Conference proceeded to discuss the subject of names and appelations, when a motion was made

by SIDNEY RIGDON, and seconded by NEWEL K. WHITNEY, that this church be known hereafter by the name of THE CHURCH OF THE LATTER DAY SAINTS. Appropriate remarks were delivered by some of the members, after which the motion was put by the Moderator, and passed by unanimous voice.[26]

At the time of the organizational meeting in April 1830 the Church was simply called the Church of Christ (see Doctrine and Covenants 20:1). However, to distinguish themselves from other Christian denominations having similar titles, particularly Alexander Campbell's Disciples of Christ, and because members believed the establishment of the Church was a restoration of the ancient order of the New Testament Christian Church under the leadership of Jesus Christ and his Apostles, members began identifying themselves as "Saints" living in the days preceding the second coming, or the Saints in the latter days. The adoption of the name The Church of the Latter Day Saints therefore marks the second of three names by which the Church has officially been known. The name remained in place for nearly four years (May 1834–July 1838). By revelation (see Doctrine and Covenants 115:4), on April 26, 1838, the former and latter names of the Church were essentially merged into one to form the current name of the Church—The Church of Jesus Christ of Latter-day Saints (albeit a hyphen has been added between "Latter" and "Day," and "Day" is no longer capitalized).

Joseph Marches at the Head of Zion's Camp

On Sunday, May 4, the day previous to the departure of Joseph Smith and the main company of Zion's Camp from

Kirtland, the Prophet gave some remarks and counsel. George A. Smith reported Joseph Smith's words on the occasion:

> He impressed upon them the necessity of being humble, exercising faith and patience and living in obedience to the commands of the Almighty, and not murmur at the dispensations of Providence. He bore testimony of the truth of the work which God had revealed through him, and promised the brethren that if they all would live as they should before the Lord, keeping his commandments, and not like the children of Israel murmur against the Lord and his servants, they should all safely return, and not one of them should fall upon the mission they were about to undertake; for if they were united and exercised faith, God would deliver them out of the hands of their enemies; but should they, like the children of Israel, forget God and his promises, and treat lightly his commandments, He would visit them in his wrath, and vex them in his sore displeasure.[27]

On Monday, May 5, the main company of Zion's Camp, consisting of eighty-five men under the leadership of the Prophet, pulled out of Kirtland. Wagons were loaded with supplies, provisions, armaments, munitions, and "clothing and other necessaries to carry to [those] who had been robbed and plundered of nearly all their effects."[28] Coincidentally, the same day the Prophet's company left Kirtland, a smaller group consisting of seventeen persons left Pontiac, Michigan, under the direction of Hyrum Smith and Lyman Wight, with intentions of joining with the main body en route.[29] Significantly, at least twelve women and nine children are known to have traveled with the two divisions.[30]

For over a month, additional men and volunteers fell in with the company, increasing their ranks and numbers. Parley P.

Pratt was the main recruiter. "I was chiefly engaged as a recruiting officer," he wrote, "and, not being much with the camp, can give but little of its history. I visited branches of the Church in Ohio, Indiana, Illinois and Missouri, and obtaining what men and means I could, fell in with the camp from time to time with additional men, arms, stores, and money."[31]

On Sunday, May 18, less than two weeks into the journey, near Richmond, Indiana, Joseph Smith wrote a heartfelt letter to his wife, Emma. The letter, written by his own hand, reflects his love of family, his concern for others, and his optimism:

> My Dear Wife
>
> meeting being over I sit down in my tent to write a few lines to you to let you know that you are on my mind and that I am sensible of the dut[i]es of a Husband and Father and that I am well and I pray God to let his blessings to rest upon you and the children and all that are a round you untill I return to your society the few lines you roa wrote and sent by the ha[n]d of Brother Lyman [E. Johnson] gave me satisfaction and comfort and I hope you will continue to communicate to me by your own hand for this is a consolation to me that to convirse <with> you in this way in my lonely moments which is not easily discribed I will indeavour to write every Su[n]day if I can and let you know how I am <and> Brother Fredrick [G. Williams] will write to Oliver [Cowdery] and give him the names of the places we pass through and a history of our jou[rn]ey from time to time so that it <will> not be nessary for me to endevou[r] to write it but feel a satisfaction to write a few lines with my own hand in this way I can have the privelege to communicate some of my feelings that I should not dare to reveal as you know that <my> situation is a very critacal one Brother Jinkins [Salisbury] and William [Smith] Jese [J. Smith] and Jeorge

[A. Smith] are all well and are humble are detirmined to be faithful and finally all the Kirtland Broth[r]en are well and cannot fail I must close for I cannot write on my knees sitting on the ground to edification O may the blessings of God rest upon you is the prayre of your Husband until death

[Joseph Smith, Jr.][32]

Zion's Camp was a long-distance march, and most company members walked the entire distance from Ohio to Missouri and back. Most days the expedition covered between twenty and thirty miles; however, on occasion they traveled as many as forty. Hot, humid days, torrential rains, mud, uncomfortable sleeping conditions, broken equipment, and food shortages, in addition to unhealthy food, added to their suffering. Surviving records clearly reveal that physical fatigue, discomfort, sickness, hunger, and thirst proved to be the most trying of their ordeals.

One might expect that Joseph Smith, being the officer in charge, would have fared better than the others. However, he took few, if any, privileges. "The Prophet Joseph took a full share of the fatigues of the entire journey," George A. Smith reported. "In addition to the care of providing for the Camp and presiding over it, he walked most of the time and had a full proportion of blistered, bloody, and sore feet."[33] Heber C. Kimball wrote, "I frequently invited the Prophet to ride, seeing him lame and footsore. On such occasions he would bless me and my team with a hearty good will."[34] George A. further recalled that the Prophet maintained a constant sense of optimism, never expressing the slightest dissatisfaction. "During the entire trip he never uttered a murmur or complaint, while most of the men in the Camp complained to him of sore toes, blistered feet, long drives, scanty supply of provisions, poor quality of bread, bad corn dodger, frouzy butter, strong honey, maggoty bacon and cheese, . . . even a dog could not bark at some men without their murmuring at Joseph."[35]

Sadly, the hardships generated hard feelings, quarrels, and frequent contention among the company. Sylvester Smith was particularly outspoken and contentious, and his influence spread to other camp members. On Tuesday, June 3, after nearly a month's travel, during their noon halt, Joseph stood on the back of a wagon and issued a condemnation and warning. George A. Smith reported him as having said, "The Lord was displeased with us; that our murmuring and fault-finding and want of humility had kindled the anger of the Lord against us; and that a severe scourge would come upon the Camp and many would die like sheep with the rot. He said, 'I cannot stop it; it must come; but by repentance and humility and the prayer of faith, the chastisement may be alleviated but cannot be entirely turned away, for as the Lord lives this Camp must suffer a severe scourge for their wickedness and rebellion. I say it in the name of the Lord.'"[36] In spite of the pronouncement, some continued to display a contentious spirit.

On June 4, following nearly a month's journey, Joseph dictated a letter to Emma wherein he notes some of his own ailments yet voices no disparagement:

> My Dear Companion,
>
> I now embrace a few moments to dictate a few words that you may know how it is with us up to this date.
>
> We arrived this morning on the banks of the Mississippi, and were detained from crossing the river, as there was no boat that we could cross in, but expect a new one to be put into the river this evening, so that we are in hopes, to be able to cross to morrow, and proceed on our journey. A tolerable degree of union has prevailed among the brethren or camp up to the present moment, and we are all in better circumstances

of health apparently than when we started from Kirtland. . . . I have been able to endur[e] the fatigue of the journey far beyond my most sanguine expectations, except have been troubled some with lameness, have had my feet blistered, but are now well, and have also had a little touch of my side complaint. . . . The whole of our journey, in the midst of so large a company of social honest and sincere men, wandering over the plains of the Nephites, recounting occasionaly the history of the Book of Mormon, roving over the mounds of that once beloved people of the Lord, picking up their skulls & their bones, as a proof of its divine authenticity, and gazing upon a country the fertility, the splendour and the goodness so indescribable, all serves to pass away time unnoticed, and in short were it not at every now and then our thoughts linger with inexpressible anxiety for our wives and our children our kindred according to the flesh who are entwined around our hearts; And also our brethren and friends; our whole journey would be as a dream, and this would be the happiest period of all our lives. We learn this journey how to travel, and we look with pleasing anticipation for the time to come, when we shall retrace our steps, and take this journey again in the enjoyment and embrace of that society we so much love. . . . Tell Father Smith [Joseph Smith Sr.] and all the family, and brother Oliver [Cowdery] to be comforted and look forward to the day when the trials and tribulations of this life will be at an end, and we all enjoy the fruits of our labour if we hold out faithful to the end which I pray may be the happy lot of us all.

From your's in the bonds of affliction.
Joseph Smith Jr.[37]

In spite of their physical hardships, Zion's Camp was also a spiritual time. Group prayers were conducted morning and evening. Sundays were usually reserved for rest for sabbath worship, including partaking of the sacrament, singing, preaching, and bearing testimony. The company experienced several miraculous healings, divine intervention, and at times demonstrated powerful expressions of faith. Experiences and encounters along the way provided the Prophet with opportunities to teach gospel principles and practical lessons about living a more Christlike life. The camp was also the object of his stern reproofs when he observed sin and error. He was known to have prophesied from time to time, and on at least two occasions he related visionary experiences he received while with the company.[38]

On June 5–6, following a month of travel through Ohio, Indiana, and Illinois, picking up recruits along the way, the Mormon army crossed the Mississippi near Louisiana, Missouri. On June 7 the troops arrived at a small branch of the Church known as the Salt River or Allred Settlement (named after James Allred, an early convert), situated in present-day Monroe County, where they waited for Lyman Wight and Hyrum Smith's small company from Michigan. With the arrival of this last contingent on June 8, Zion's Camp consisted of a force of just over two hundred men. Here, final preparations were made for the push to western Missouri. On June 12 the army of Israel broke camp and commenced the trek across northern Missouri.[39]

While camped on the Salt River, the Prophet sent Parley P. Pratt and Orson Hyde to Jefferson City, the state capital, to meet with Governor Dunklin, expecting to receive orders concerning the role Zion's Camp would play in conjunction with the troops called out by the state. According to Elder Pratt, the governor backed down, refusing to intervene militarily, stating that "he dare not attempt the execution of the laws in that respect, for fear of deluging the whole country in civil war and bloodshed," but he believed the Saints should continue their efforts through the courts.[40] Dunkin's position was devastating news because without the immediate support of state troops, the reinstatement of the displaced Missouri Saints in Jackson County—the primary object of Zion's Camp—could not take place.

Immediately following their meeting with the governor, Elders Pratt and Hyde hurried to catch up with the company and to report Dunklin's position to Joseph Smith. On June 15 the two men arrived in camp. Upon learning of the governor's decision not to intervene, Joseph was extremely disappointed. What could they do now? How were they to proceed? In spite of the news, the decision was made to move on to at least meet and confer with the Church leaders and members living in Clay County and hope that a revelation would be received giving some direction.

Meanwhile, their movements had not gone unnoticed, particularly while passing through Ray and into Clay County. On June 19 a large band of some two hundred men from Jackson crossed the Missouri River and collected near the Mormon encampment on Fishing River ford in eastern Clay County, intending to terminate the Mormon advance. A fierce confrontation would have likely occurred had not a violent storm intervened, causing the belligerents to disperse.[41]

On June 22, while camped on a branch of the Fishing River just over the line in Clay County, the hoped-for revelation was received. In the revelation, sometimes called the "Fishing River revelation," the Lord informed Zion's Camp that because of present circumstances, the redemption of Zion would yet be in the future (see Doctrine and Covenants 105:9). Furthermore, they were assured that their journey and sacrifice was not performed in vain. "I have heard their prayers, and will accept of their offering," the Lord declared, then indicated that it was expedient that the journey was undertaken "for a trial of their faith" (Doctrine and Covenants 105:19). Meanwhile, the majority of the men were instructed to return to Ohio, where they were assured that they would receive "a great endowment and blessing to be poured out upon them"—a promise later fulfilled in connection with the blessings associated with the Kirtland Temple (Doctrine and Covenants 105:12). To the Missouri Saints who had lost their homes and property in Jackson County, the Lord promised they would find "peace and safety" living among the citizens of Clay (Doctrine and Covenants 105:25).

The following day, June 23, Zion's Camp advanced about two miles east of Liberty and arrived at the property owned by Algernon Sidney Gilbert and George Burkett, both Mormons. Gilbert operated the Church storehouse in Independence and also acted as agent for the Church and Bishop Edward Partridge while in Jackson County. Here, Joseph Smith and the Kirtland brethren experienced a joyful reunion with a number of Missouri Church members, including Bishop Partridge, William W. Phelps, Isaac Morley, John Corrill, Thomas B. Marsh, Lyman Wight, and a number of Whitmer family members. However, their rejoicing was short-lived. The next day, June 24, cholera struck the camp. Cholera is caused by a bacterial infection in the intestine. In the case of the Zion's Camp members, it was probably contracted from bad drinking water (it is not contagious) and is characterized by diarrhea, vomiting, and leg cramps. Individuals with severe cholera experience a rapid loss of fluid, causing dehydration and shock, which can result in death in a matter of a few hours. For several days the disease ravaged the camp in fulfillment of the "scourge" Joseph Smith predicted would come upon them because of their unruly and contentious behavior. Sixty-eight members suffered in varying degrees from the effects of the disease. When the outbreak first occurred, even Joseph and Hyrum were taken ill for a short time. While the brothers were praying for relief, Hyrum sprang to his feet, exclaiming, "I have had an open vision, in which I saw mother kneeling . . . and she is now asking God, in tears, to spare our lives. . . . The Spirit testifies that her prayers, united with ours, will be answered."[42] Although they subsequently recovered, others were not as fortunate. Tragically, by week's end, fifteen Latter-day Saints had died, thirteen of whom were camp members, including one woman, Betsy Parrish. Two others from the area, Algernon Sidney Gilbert and nine-year-old Phoebe Murdock (Phoebe was the daughter of John Murdock and Julia Clapp Murdock and was probably living with the Gilberts), also died.[43] The dead were wrapped in blankets and buried in makeshift graves near Rush Creek.[44]

One can sense the depth of the sorrow experienced by Joseph Smith over the deaths of his associates and fellow Church members. After all, they had made the entire trek without the loss of life, only to have death overtake them at journey's end. Upon returning to Kirtland, he would bear the responsibility and burden of informing the families of the deaths of their loved ones. Perhaps the most painful death for him to bear was that of his cousin Jesse J. Smith. Jesse was the last victim to die from the disease.[45] In February of the following year, the Prophet received some solace regarding the deaths of the cholera victims. "I have seen those men who died of the cholera in our camp," said Joseph Smith to Brigham and Joseph Young, "and the Lord knows, if I get a mansion as bright as theirs, I ask no more."⁴⁶

On July 3 a general meeting was held for the Saints then living in Missouri and the members of Zion's Camp. The meeting was held on the property owned by Michael Arthur, situated about three miles south of Liberty. Arthur, a non–Latter-day Saint, had befriended the Saints and employed a number of them. During the meeting, Joseph Smith officially disbanded Zion's Camp and instructed them that they were free to return to their homes. Significantly, however, during this same meeting the Prophet organized the Missouri Stake, along similar lines to that of the Kirtland Stake, appointing twelve high councilors and designating David Whitmer as president, with William W. Phelps and John Whitmer as assistant presidents or counselors.⁴⁷

Zion's Camp members did not return to Ohio together in one large body but made their way home in smaller groups. Joseph Smith spent a few more days in Clay County counseling and instructing the leaders before beginning the return trip. He left on July 9, arriving back in Kirtland around August 1 after a nearly three-month absence.⁴⁸

Regrettably, some members of Zion's Camp subsequently apostatized because they fully expected they would fight, while others lost faith because the Missouri Saints were not restored to their homes and property, believing "Zion was not redeemed." In short, there were some then and there are some today who may view the march to western Missouri in 1834 as a failure. But for those who see through the eye of faith, Zion's Camp was successful in many ways. By responding to the call, the Saints in Ohio, Michigan, Pennsylvania, and New York demonstrated their love and loyalty for the members of the Church living in Missouri. Church members in the East also provided the exiled Saints with needed money, provisions, and supplies. Furthermore, while in Missouri, Joseph Smith organized the Missouri Stake and high council, thus further strengthening and solidifying the organizational structure of the Church. However, most important of all, for those who demonstrated their steadfastness and loyalty, this trial of faith solidified their faith and commitment, further preparing them for their future leadership roles.

For men such as Wilford Woodruff and Brigham Young, Zion's Camp provided them with their first opportunity to be with Joseph Smith for an extended period of time, and in spite of their trials, they rejoiced in that which they learned from him. Elder Woodruff wrote, "We gained an experience that we never could have gained in any other way. We had the privilege ... of travelling a thousand miles with [the Prophet], and seeing the workings of the Spirit of God with him, and the revelations of Jesus Christ unto him."[49]

Brigham Young was even more explicit. "I have travelled with Joseph a thousand miles, as he led the Camp of Israel. I have watched him and observed every thing he said or did ... and for the town of Kirtland I would not give the knowledge I got from Joseph from this Journey; and then you may take the State of Ohio and the United States, and I would not give that knowledge for them.... This was the starting point of my knowing how to lead Israel."[50] On another occasion he reported, "When I returned ... to Kirtland, a brother said to me, 'Brother Brigham, what have you gained by this journey?' I replied, 'Just what we went for; but I would not exchange that knowledge I have received this season for the whole of Geauga County.'"[51]

In 1835, soon after organizing the first Quorum of the Twelve and the first Quorum of Seventy, Joseph commented,

"Brethren, some of you [were] angry with me, because you did not fight in Missouri; but let me tell you, God did not want you to fight. He could not organize His kingdom with twelve men to open the Gospel door to the nations of the earth, and with seventy men under their direction to follow . . . unless He took them from a body of men who had offered their lives, and who had made as great a sacrifice as Abraham."[52] Significantly, nine of the original Twelve and all of the original Seventy had marched to Missouri.[53]

Lastly, we should not overlook Joseph Smith. How did Zion's Camp affect him? What influence did it have on his life? As the commander, he may have gained and learned more from the experience than anyone else.

The Sylvester Smith Church Hearings

No sooner had Joseph Smith and the majority of the members of Zion's Camp returned to Kirtland, than the cantankerous Sylvester Smith, who had generated so much contention while on the expedition, began circulating negative statements about Joseph Smith's conduct while journeying to and from Missouri. Sylvester claimed the Prophet prophesied lies, distributed camp funds and supplies unfairly, and abused his (Sylvester's) character. Sylvester's reports and accusations must have caused a considerable stir in the community because Church leaders were eventually compelled to call a meeting to investigate Sylvester's claims.

The August 11 hearing was moderated by Kirtland bishop Newel K. Whitney. Also present were a number of high priests and elders. During the meeting Joseph spoke in defense of himself, explaining the circumstances regarding his "rebukes and chastisements" toward Sylvester, calling upon others present who had participated in Zion's Camp to attest to the same, which they did. All seventeen men present spoke in his defense, while the report shows no one sided with Sylvester. Following considerable discussion, the council concluded that the Prophet had "acted in every respect in an honorable and proper manner." Bishop Whitney then proposed that a statement be published in *The Evening and the Morning Star* indicating that the council had investigated the Prophet's conduct and concluded that he was innocent of any wrongdoing. The minutes indicate that Sylvester Smith made a partial confession and that Whitney directed him to issue a public confession, which was also to be published in *The Evening and the Morning Star*, which he agreed to do.[54]

It is important to note that the minutes of the meeting clearly show that this was not a formal hearing against Joseph Smith. I mention this only because some have erroneously concluded that the August 11 meeting was actually a formal court or disciplinary council against Joseph Smith as the defendant. If this were so, the hearing would be, in essence, conducted against the Prophet to try him for his membership in the Church. But this was not the case. The meeting was merely called to investigate Sylvester Smith's accusations.

Sylvester Smith's repentance was apparently short-lived, because on August 27 he was issued a summons to appear in a formal hearing before the Kirtland high council for failing to submit his public confession in the *Star* and for continuing to charge Joseph Smith with improper conduct. The hearing, which began on August 28, lasted the better part of two days and did not adjourn until three a.m. on the morning of August 30. During the deliberations, the twelve high councilors spoke freely and openly. A number of Zion's Camp participants also testified as witnesses, each of whom spoke favorably in defense of the Prophet. At the conclusion of the meeting, the council issued a statement that if he would publicly acknowledge that he had failed to act upon the previous requirements issued by the previous council (i.e., to issue a public confession in the *Star*) and that he had maliciously told falsehoods against the character of Joseph Smith, he would be permitted to remain a member of the Church. Sylvester complied by writing the following statement: "I hereby certify that the foregoing charges or complaint[s] are just and true, and hereby acknowledge the same, as set forth in the decisions of this council, but signing my own proper name to their minutes with my own hand. [Signed] Sylvester Smith."[55] Sylvester made good on his word, and in the first issue of the *Latter Day Saints Messenger and Advocate*, the editors included his lengthy apology:

> It is true, that some difficulties arouse between bro. J. Smith Jr. and myself, in our travels the past summer to Missouri.... But I am now perfectly satisfied that the errors of which I accused [Joseph Smith] before the council . . . were never committed by him; and my contrition has been and still continues to be deep, because I admitted thoughts into my heart which were not right concerning him, and because that I have been the means of giving rise to reports which have gone abroad, censuring the conduct, of bro. J.S. jr. which reports are without foundation. And I hope, that this disclosure of the truth, written by my own hand, and sent abroad into the world, through the medium of the Messenger and Advocate, will put a final end to all evil reports and censurings, which have sprung out of any thing that I have said or done."[56]

An interesting postscript to the Sylvester Smith affair was played out just a few months later when the First Quorum of the Seventy was organized by Joseph Smith on February 28, 1835.

Significantly, on that occasion the Prophet called Sylvester to be one of the seven presidents of the quorum, an action that reveals Joseph's remarkable and extraordinary ability to exercise forgiveness toward one who had demonstrated such personal public animosity against him.[57] Sadly, during the economic crisis in 1837, Sylvester turned against the Prophet once again and was one of nearly a dozen of the leading elders who became disenchanted with Joseph's leadership and was excommunicated from the Church.[58]

A Second Zion's Camp

In mid-August, just over two weeks after his return to Kirtland following Zion's Camp, and during the height of the Sylvester Smith controversy, Joseph Smith dictated a letter to several of the Church leaders in Missouri. One of the most significant aspects of the document is that the Prophet fully expected that during the months ahead, Mormons would continue to gather to western Missouri (particularly Clay County), such that there would come a time when there would be a sufficient number of Saints assembled there that they could return to Jackson County and reclaim their lands. Joseph even set a date. Note his words in the letter: "Use every effort to prevail on the churches to gather to those regions and situate themselves to be in readiness to move into Jackson Co. in two years from the Eleventh of September next which is the appointed time for the redemption of Zion." In other words, the Prophet anticipated that on September 11, 1836, the Church would make another attempt—a second Zion's Camp—to return to Jackson County. He counseled them further to keep quiet. "Let not this be noised abroad let every heart beat in silence and every mouth be shut."[59]

During the next two years, Mormon emigration to western Missouri continued and expectations that the Saints would make another attempt to return to Jackson continued. However, by the summer of 1836, some of Clay's citizens became concerned with the ever-increasing number of Mormons in the region resulting in isolated outbreaks of violence. These hostilities led Missouri Church leaders to search out other places for Mormon settlement. In August, W. W. Phelps and John Whitmer purchased land, one mile square, in a relatively uninhabited portion of Ray County and there established Far West as the new place of gathering. In short, in spite of the Prophet's expectation to return to Jackson County in September 1836, conditions at the time necessitated that the Saints relocate rather than reoccupy, and the Jackson plan or second Zion's Camp was abandoned.

Construction Continues on the Kirtland "House of the Lord"

The June 1834 Fishing River revelation ending Zion's Camp redirected Joseph's attention. The revelation explained that Zion's future success depended on completion of the Kirtland Temple and the need for the elders to purify their lives to be able to commune with God in the House of the Lord, where they would receive an endowment of his power in anticipation of impending eschatological events and the millennial reign of Christ (see Doctrine and Covenants 105:9–13). Pursuant to these objectives, upon returning from Zion's Camp, Joseph Smith's primary goal was to move forward with the construction of the temple and to prepare selected men to receive a spiritual endowment. Construction on the Kirtland Temple, which had begun in June 1833, resumed in September 1834 under the direction of Artemus Millet, a Mormon convert from Canada. Meanwhile, in December 1834, the Church completed construction on a two-story frame printing house and school behind the temple to be used also as a meetinghouse awaiting the completion of the temple.[60]

Recognizing the need to prepare the priesthood holders for missionary service and the anticipated outpouring of spiritual blessings associated with the Kirtland Temple, beginning in November 1834 and continuing through March 1835, the School of the Elders (formerly known in 1833 as the School of the Prophets) was reorganized and reconstituted under the direction of Joseph Smith. Members of the school came primarily from the ranks of the elders and high priests from Kirtland. However, several Missouri Church leaders spending the winter of 1834–35 in Kirtland also attended the school. The Prophet and Sidney Rigdon presided over the school and were the main teachers and instructors, although a number of other men were invited to speak and teach the men. Beginning in December 1834 and continuing through January 1835, a series of formal theological lectures (later titled the Lectures on Faith) were prepared and presented to the participants. Classes were held periodically throughout the winter in a room below the printing office situated immediately west of the Kirtland Temple which, as noted, was under construction.[61]

Joseph Smith as Publisher

The 1830s witnessed an eruption of print media throughout the United States and almost everyone with a cause used the press to promote his or her position and opinions. Joseph Smith understood the power of the printed word and the need to disseminate and defend the views, policies, and doctrines of the Church to both Church members and the general public. Thus, beginning in 1834, the Mormon leader began to plan a more active role in the printing efforts and operations of the Church.

Following the July 1833 destruction of the Church's printing house and *The Evening and the Morning Star* press in Independence, Missouri, printing operations were suspended until Church leaders in Ohio were able to acquire another press and build a printing office in Kirtland. After obtaining a new press in Kirtland in December 1833, ten more issues of the *Star* were published, the final number in September 1834. That same month, a publication committee was formed, composed of Joseph Smith, Oliver Cowdery, Sidney Rigdon, and Frederick G. Williams, whose main objective was to publish a second time a book containing the Prophet's revelatory documents. To complete this task, W. W. Phelps, who had edited the *Star* and a second Mormon newspaper, the *Upper Missouri Advertiser*, was recruited and moved from Missouri to Kirtland to assist in the project.

In October 1834, the first issue of the *Latter Day Saints' Messenger and Advocate* appeared, succeeding the *Star* as the official organ of the Church. During the newspaper's three-year run, Oliver and Warren Cowdery, W. W. Phelps, and John Whitmer served as editors, while the names of Joseph Smith, Sidney Rigdon, and William Marks appear as publishers.[62] Articles, letters, and statements by Joseph Smith appear prominently throughout the pages of the paper, illustrating his desire to promulgate his views and prophetic voice. Furthermore, during this period, Church leaders, including Joseph Smith, often spoke freely and openly about government, politics, and the social issues of the day.

Revelation to Warren Cowdery

In late November 1834, Warren Cowdery, Oliver's older brother (by eight years), visited Kirtland. At the time, Warren was living in Freedom, New York, situated in the extreme western part of the state. In 1831 he and his family were baptized into the Church. In early March 1834, while recruiting men for Zion's Camp, Joseph Smith and Parley P. Pratt spent three days (March 9–11) in the Cowdery home in Freedom.[63] During Warren Cowdery's 1834 visit to Kirtland, he requested the Prophet pronounce a blessing or revelation in his behalf. In the revelation he was called to be the presiding high priest over the Freedom Branch with the charge to "devote his whole time to this high and holy calling." "I will have mercy on him," the revelation continued, "notwithstanding the vanity of his heart. . . . And I will give him grace and assurance wherewith he may stand; and if he continue to be a faithful witness and a light unto the church I have prepared a crown for him in the mansions of my Father." The revelation was recorded in the Kirtland Revelation Book and was later canonized as section 99 of the 1835 Doctrine and Covenants. Today, the revelation is part of Doctrine and Covenants section 106.

Appointment of Oliver Cowdery as Assistant President

On December 5, 1834, an important organizational change was made in the Church. On this date, Joseph Smith presided over the appointment and ordination of Oliver Cowdery as "assistant President of the High and Holy Priesthood." The minutes of the meeting read as follows:

> According to the direction of the Holy Spirit, Presidents Smith, assistant Presidents, Rigdon and Williams, assembled for the purpose of ordaining first High Counsellor Cowdery

to the office of assistant President of the High and Holy Priesthood in the Church of the Latter-Day Saints.

It is necessary, for the special benefit of the reader, that he be instructed into or concerning the power and authority of the above named Priesthood.

First. The office of the President is to preside over the Whole Church; to be considered as at the head; to receive revelations for the Church; to be a Seer,—~~and~~ Revelator and Prophet having all the gifts of God:—taking Moses as an example. Which is ~~Second~~ the office and station of the above President Smith, according to the calling of God, and the ordination which he has received.

Second. The office of Assistant President is to assist in presiding over the whole Church, and to officiate in the absence of the President, according to ~~their~~ his work and appointment, viz: President Cowdery, first; President Rigdon Second, and President Williams Third, as they ~~are~~ were generally called. The office of this Priesthood is also to act as Spokesman—taking Aaron for an ensample

The virtue of this above Priesthood is to hold the keys of the Kingdom of heaven, or the Church militant.

The reader may further understand, that ~~Presidents~~ the reason why High Counsellor ~~President~~ Cowdery was not previously ordained to the Presidency, was in consequence of his necessary attendance in Zion, to assist Wm W. Phelps in conducting the printing business; but that this promise was made by the Angel while in company with President Smith, at the time they received the office of the lesser priesthood. And further: The circumstances and situation of the Church requiring Presidents Rigdon and Williams were previously ordained, to assist President Smith.[64]

In this capacity, Cowdery was elevated in authority above that of Sidney Rigdon and Frederick G. Williams, the two counselors in the First Presidency. His priesthood authority and responsibilities were second only to those of Joseph Smith. This appointment was also consistent with Cowdery's earlier designation as "second elder" on the day of the Church's organization (April 6, 1830). Cowdery continued in the office of Assistant President until his excommunication on April 12, 1838.

On January 19, 1841, Hyrum Smith was appointed to fill the office vacated by Cowdery. Note the following words: "And from this time forth I appoint unto him [Hyrum] that he may be a prophet, and a seer, and a revelator unto my church, as well as my servant Joseph; that he may act in concert also with my servant Joseph . . . and be crowned with the same blessing, and glory, and honor, and priesthood, and gifts of the priesthood, that once were put upon him that was my servant Oliver Cowdery" (Doctrine and Covenants 124:94–95). Following Hyrum's death on June 27, 1844, the office of Assistant President was discontinued.

Joseph Smith's Patriarchal Blessing

Perhaps the culminating event of the year 1834 for Joseph was the privilege he had to receive his patriarchal blessing under the hand of his sixty-three-year-old father. On December 18, 1833, Joseph Smith ordained his father to the office of patriarch, but perhaps because of his desire to be worthy of such a sacred office and the responsibility it carried to declare a prophetic voice, for nearly a year after his ordination Joseph Sr. did not officiate in his office and no patriarchal blessings were conferred. However, on December 9, 1834, Joseph Sr. pronounced the first patriarchal blessings upon his children and their spouses at the home of the Prophet. Oliver Cowdery was present and acted as recorder. The order of the blessings was from the eldest to the youngest, Hyrum being first, followed by his wife Jerusha. Calvin W. Stoddard, husband of Sophronia was blessed third, followed by Sophronia. Joseph's blessing was fifth. While the entire blessing will not be given here, a few selected passages can be highlighted:

> The Lord thy God has called thee by name out of the heavens: thou hast heard his voice from on high from time to time, even in thy youth....
>
> Thou hast sought to know his ways and from thy childhood thou hast meditated much upon the great things of his law....
>
> Thou hast been an obedient son: the commands of thy father and the reproofs of thy mother, thou hast respected and obeyed—for all these things the Lord my God will bless thee....
>
> Thou hast been called, even in thy youth to the great work of the Lord: to do a work in this generation which no other man would do as thyself....
>
> I bless thee with the blessings of thy fathers Abraham, Isaac and Jacob; and even the blessings of thy father Joseph, the son of Jacob. Behold, he looked after his posterity in the last days, when they should be scattered and driven by the Gentiles, and wept before the Lord: he sought diligently to know from whence the son should come who should bring forth the word of the Lord, by which they might be enlightened, and brought back to the true fold, and his eyes beheld thee, my son: his heart rejoiced and his soul was satisfied....
>
> Thou shalt live to do the work which the Lord shall command thee: thou shalt hold the keys of this ministry,

even the presidency of this Church, both in time and in eternity....

Thousands and tens of thousands shall come to a knowledge of the truth through thy ministry, and thou shalt rejoice with them in the Celestial Kingdom.[65]

Such promises provide a fitting tribute to Joseph Smith.

Summary

To summarize, 1834 was a busy year for Joseph Smith. He was absent from home some four months. For over a month he traveled through northeastern Ohio, Pennsylvania, and western New York recruiting for Zion's Camp. In mid-April he traveled to Medina County to conduct a conference, and that same month he spent several days in Chardon, Ohio, to attend the court hearing against the ex-Mormon Philastus Hurlbut. And for nearly three months he was on the road with Zion's Camp.

Ecclesiastically, he organized the Kirtland Stake high council in February and the Missouri stake high council in July, with the minutes of the Kirtland council later being included as section 5 in the 1835 edition of the Doctrine and Covenants (now Doctrine and Covenants 102). In addition, Oliver Cowdery received his appointment as Assistant President in December. Finally, the Church adopted a new name—The Church of the Latter Day Saints.

In his role as a visionary or a seer, he continued to experience visions—at least four—including the pattern and organization of Church councils (February), a vision of Adam (April), and two visions while on Zion's Camp (May–June). He also received at least five revelations, four which have been canonized (Doctrine and Covenants sections 103, 104, 105, and 106), and one noncanonized revelation received on April 28, 1834. In his prophetic role he predicted that the Church would experience large numerical growth throughout the world, but particularly in North and South America.

It is impossible to measure the leadership experience or the Christlike attributes Joseph Smith gained or further developed from his Zion's Camp experience, the Philastus Hurbut trial, or the Sylvester Smith hearings—all trials of his personal faith. These are spiritual intangibles. However, in 1839, while incarcerated in Liberty Jail, the Lord revealed to him the principle that all of the events or happenings that make up our lives, whether positive or negative, "shall give thee experience, and shall be for thy good" (Doctrine and Covenants 122:7). Surely all that Joseph Smith experienced in 1834 was for his good. Surely, he learned valuable gospel lessons—lessons regarding "faith, virtue, knowledge, temperance, patience, brotherly kindness, godliness, charity, humility, [and] diligence" (Doctrine and Covenants 4:6). In short, the year 1834 was an important chapter in the life of Joseph Smith that further defined and refined him as a prophet-leader to the Latter-day Saints.

Notes

1. Kirtland Council Minute Book, 29–30, Church History Library, The Church of Jesus Christ of Latter-day Saints, Salt Lake City.

2. On February 18, the day after the first council meeting, Joseph Smith made corrections to the minutes. Then, on February 19, a larger body of priesthood members met and by "unanimous voice" accepted the rewritten minutes as the "constitution of the high council of the Church of Christ" (Kirtland Council Minute Book, 36; see also Doctrine and Covenants 102:3, 10, 12).

3. Joseph Smith Jr., *History of The Church of Jesus Christ of Latter-day Saints*, ed. B. H. Roberts, 2nd ed. rev. (Salt Lake City: Deseret Book 1971), 1:446; hereafter cited as *History of the Church*.

4. R. W. Wells to Alexander W. Doniphan and David R. Atchison, November 21, 1833, in Smith, *History of the Church*, 1:444–45.

5. "To His Excellency, Daniel Dunklin, Governor of the State of Missouri," in Smith, *History of the Church*, 1:451–52.

6. John Corrill to Oliver Cowdery, December 1833, in *The Evening and the Morning Star*, January 1834, 126.

7. "Governor Dunklin to the Brethren in Missouri," February 4, 1834, in Smith, *History of the Church*, 1:476–78.

8. W. W. Phelps to Joseph Smith, December 15, 1833, in Smith, *History of the Church*, 1:457.

9. "Minutes," in Smith, *History of the Church*, 2:39.

10. See Milton V. Backman Jr., *The Heavens Resound: A History of the Latter-day Saints in Ohio, 1831–1838* (Salt Lake City: Deseret Book, 1983), 173–74; Roger D. Launius, *Zion's Camp: Expedition to Missouri, 1834* (Independence: Herald House, 1984), 33–39; and *Autobiography of Parley P. Pratt*, ed. Parley P. Pratt Jr. (Salt Lake City: Deseret Book, 1985), 87–92.

11. *The Papers of Joseph Smith*, vol. 2, *Journal, 1832–1842*, ed. Dean C. Jessee (Salt Lake City: Deseret Book, 1989–1992), 21–27.

12. *Papers of Joseph Smith*, 2:27.

13. Brigham Young, *Manuscript History of Brigham Young, 1801–1844*, ed. Elden J. Watson (Salt Lake City: Smith Secretarial Service, 1968), 8.

14. See George A. Smith, "My Journal," *Instructor*, February 1946, 78; and Smith, "My Journal," *Instructor*, April 1946, 195.

15. See Eber D. Howe, *Mormonism Unvailed: or, A Faithful Account of That Singular Imposition and Delusion, from Its Rise to the Present Time* (Painesville, OH: By the author, 1834).

16. *Papers of Joseph Smith*, 2:29. Joseph Smith reported that Hurlbut was charged nearly three hundred dollars in court costs (*History of the Church*, 2:49). However, the actual amount was $112.59 (*Papers of Joseph Smith*, 2:29 n. 1).

17. Kirtland Council Minute Book, 44; see also Smith, *History of the Church*, 2:52.

18. Salt Lake City School of the Prophets Minute Book, 1883, October 11, 1883, 67, Church History Library. Joseph Smith's journal is the source for the date of the conference which took place on April 20–21, 1834 (*Papers of Joseph Smith*, 2:30–32; Smith, *History of the Church*, 2:52–54).

19. The most commonly cited verses in the revelation are Doctrine and Covenants 104:14–18. For a detailed discussion of the United Firm in the context of Doctrine and Covenants section 104, see Max H. Parkin, "Joseph Smith and the United Firm," *BYU Studies* 46, no. 3 (2007): 5–66.

20. The revelation reads: "Verily thus saith the Lord concerning the division and settlement of the United Firm. Let there be reserved three thousand Dollars for the right and claim of the Firm in Kirtland for inheritances in due time, even when the Lord will; and with this claim, to be had in remembrance when the Lord shall reveal it for a right of inheritance, ye are made free from the Firm of Zion; and the Firm in Zion is made free from the Firm in Kirtland: Thus saith the Lord. Amen" (Kirtland Revelation Book, 111).

21. Thomas G. Alexander, *Things in Heaven and Earth: The Life and Times of Wilford Woodruff, a Mormon Prophet* (Salt Lake City: Signature Books, 1993), 21, 28.

22. Wilford Woodruff, "Discourse by Wilford Woodruff," *Millennial Star*, October 5, 1891, 627–28.

23. Wilford Woodruff, Diary, April 27, 1834, Church History Library; published in *Wilford Woodruff's Journal, 1833–1898, Typescript*, ed. Scott G. Kenney (Midvale, UT: Signature Books, 1983–84), 1:9.

Woodruff noted further in his journal: "It appeared to me there was more light made manifest in that meeting pertaining to the gospel and kingdom of God than I had ever receieved from the whole Sectarian world. The Prophet called the men togather who were going up to Zion before leaving Kirtland [p. 4] [and] seal[ed] them up to eternal life."

24. Wilford Woodruff, in *Annual Conference of The Church of Jesus Christ of Latter-day Saints* (Salt Lake City: The Church of Jesus Christ of Latter-day Saints, 1898), 57. It is interesting to note that the April 1898 general conference would be Wilford Woodruff's last (he died the following September) and that he would feel inclined on this occasion to share his recollections surrounding the first time he heard Joseph Smith preach.

25. Smith, *History of the Church*, 2:61.

26. *The Evening and the Morning Star*, May 1834, 160. David Whitmer recalled that Rigdon was primarily responsible for changing the name from the Church of Christ to The Church of the Latter Day Saints (David Whitmer, *An Address to all Believers in Christ*, [Richmond, MO: By the Author: 1887], 73). Whitmer also said he objected to the name because it did not contain the name of Christ (Whitmer, *An Address to All Believers in Christ*, 62, 74).

27. George A. Smith, Autobiography, 18, Church History Library.

28. "History of Joseph Smith," *Times and Seasons*, January 1, 1846, 1074; also Launius, *Zion's Camp*, 51–52.

29. See Craig K. Manscill, "'Journal of the Branch of the Church in Pontiac, 1834': Hyrum Smith's Division of Zion's Camp," *BYU Studies* 39, no. 1 (2000): 167–88. In Illinois, Charles C. Rich joined the Michigan group, bringing the total to eighteen.

30. See Andrea G. Radke, "We Also Marched: The Women and Children of Zion's Camp," *BYU Studies* 39, no. 1 (2000): 147–65.

31. *Autobiography of Parley P. Pratt*, 93.

32. Joseph Smith to Emma Hale Smith, Community of Christ Library-Archives, Independence, Missouri; in *The Personal Writings of Joseph Smith*, ed. Dean C. Jessee, rev. ed. (Salt Lake City: Deseret Book; Provo, UT: Brigham Young University Press, 2002), 340–41.

33. George A. Smith, "My Journal," *Improvement Era*, May 1946, 217.

34. Orson F. Whitney, *Life of Heber C. Kimball* (Salt Lake City: Bookcraft, 1979), 42.

35. Smith, "My Journal," *Improvement Era*, May 1946, 217.

36. George A. Smith, "My Journal," *Instructor*, April 1946, 184; Smith, *History of the Church*, 2:80.

37. Joseph Smith to Emma Hale Smith, July 4, 1834, Joseph Smith Letterbook 2, 56–58, Church History Library, published in *Personal Writings of Joseph Smith*, 344–46.

38. The best-known vision Joseph Smith received while on Zion's Camp was the vision of Zelph ("History of Joseph Smith," *Times and Seasons*, January 1, 1846, 1076; and *History of the Church*, 2:79–80). For a scholarly examination of the Zelph incident, see Kenneth W. Godfrey, "The Zelph Story," *BYU Studies* 29, no. 2 (1989): 31–56; and Kenneth W. Godfrey, "What Is the Significance of Zelph in the Study of Book of Mormon Geography?" *Journal of Book of Mormon Studies* 8, no. 2 (1999): 71–79. Nathan Tanner reported another vision received by the Prophet while traveling with Zion's Camp. He recorded: "I had the pleasure of seeing him [Joseph] in a vision when he saw the country over which we had traveled in a high state of cultivation. This was while he was riding, and when he camped, he had a wagon run out in the middle of the corral of wagons, and got up into it, and told the camp what he had seen while in the Spirit. It was glorious and grand to hear" (Nathan Tanner, Reminiscences, in George S. Tanner, *John Tanner and His Family* [Salt Lake City: Publishers Press, 1974], 382–83).

39. *History of the Church*, 2:87–88. The figure for the total number of males who made up Zion's Camp at the time the two companies merged at the Allred settlement varies. *History of the Church* states there were 205. Launius gives the figure of 208 (*Zion's Camp*, 103). Milton V. Backman Jr. states there were 207 (*The Heavens Resound: A History of the Latter-day Saints in Ohio, 1830–1838* [Salt Lake City: Deseret Book, 1983], 185, see also Appendix A, 377).

40. *Autobiography of Parley P. Pratt*, 94; see also *History of the Church*, 2:24.

41. See Smith, *History of the Church*, 2:102–5.

42. Lucy Mack Smith, *Biographical Sketches of Joseph Smith, the Prophet, and His Progenitors for Many Generations* (London: S. W. Richards, 1853), 201.

43. See Smith, *History of the Church*, 2:114–20. The total number of cholera deaths given in most histories about Zion's Camp is fourteen, and includes Gilbert, although as noted in the text, he was not a camp member. Phoebe Murdock's death brought the total number of cholera victims to fifteen.

44. In 1958, Boyd Park, owner of some farm property on Rush Creek, found three human skeletons that had been kicked up by his cattle. Anatomical reports by the University of Missouri later confirmed the remains to have been those of members of Zion's Camp. On March 25, 1976, the skeletons were reinterred in the Mound Grove Cemetery in Independence, Missouri (LaMar C. Berrett and others, eds., *Sacred Places*, vol. 4: *Missouri* [Salt Lake City: Deseret Book, 2004], 200–201).

45. Smith, *History of the Church*, 2:120.

46. Joseph Young, "History of the Organization of the Seventies," as cited in Smith, *History of the Church*, 2:181 n.

47. See Smith, *History of the Church*, 2:122–24.

48. Smith, *History of the Church*, 2:139.

49. In *Journal of Discourses* (London: Latter-day Saints' Book Depot, 1854–86), 13:158.

50. Salt Lake High Council Record, 1869–1872, 83–84, Church History Library, as cited in Leonard J. Arrington, *Brigham Young: American Moses* (New York: Alfred A. Knopf, 1985), 45–46.

51. In *Journal of Discourses*, 2:10.

52. Young, "History of the Organization of the Seventies," as cited in Smith, *History of the Church*, 2:182 n.

53. The three who were not members of Zion's Camp were Thomas B. Marsh, David W. Patten, and John F. Boynton. Marsh and Patten were living in Clay County, which explains why they were not participants. Boynton was on a mission in Maine at the time Zion's Camp left.

54. "Minutes of a Council Held at Kirtland, August 11, 1834," Smith, *History of the Church*, 2:142–43. The statement or report issued by the council was subsequently published as "Conference Minutes" in *The Evening and the Morning Star*, August 1834, 182; see also Smith, *History of the Church*, 2:147–49.

55. The minutes of the August 28 hearing are published in Smith, *History of the Church*, 2:151–59.

56. Sylvester Smith to Oliver Cowdery, October 28, 1834, in *Latter-day Saints' Messenger and Advocate*, October 1834, 10–11.

57. Smith, *History of the Church*, 2:203. For a discussion of Joseph Smith's relationship with Sylvester Smith, see Arnold K. Garr, "Joseph Smith: Man of Forgiveness," in *Joseph Smith: The Prophet, the Man*, ed. Susan Easton Black and Charles D. Tate Jr. (Provo, UT: Religious Studies Center, Brigham Young University, 1993), 127–32.

58. Backman, *Heavens Resound*, 328.

59. Joseph Smith to Lyman Wight, Edward Partridge, John Corrill, Isaac Morley, and others, August 16, 1834, Joseph Smith Letter Book 1, 85, Church History Library; Smith, *History of the Church*, 2:145.

60. Backman, *Heavens Resound*, 156.

61. Backman, *Heavens Resound*, 268–70.

62. See Peter Crawley, *A Descriptive Bibliography of the Mormon Church* (Provo, UT: Religious Studies Center, Brigham Young University, 1997, 2005), 1:32–34, 47–49.

63. For a brief discussion of Joseph Smith's and Parley P. Pratt's visit to Freedom, New York, in March 1834, see Mark A. Steele, "Finding Saints: Mormon Conversions in Freedom, New York," *Mormon Historical Studies* 8, nos. 1–2 (Spring/Fall 2007): 42–43.

64. Manuscript History of the Church, A-1, 17, Church History Library. The document is in the handwriting of Oliver Cowdery; see also *Papers of Joseph Smith*, 1:20–22; 2:36; and Smith, *History of the Church*, 2:176.

65. Blessing, Joseph Smith Sr. to Joseph Smith Jr., Patriarchal Blessing Book 1, 3–4, Church History Library.

J. SPENCER FLUHMAN

1835
Authority, Power, and the "Government of the Church of Christ"

This chapter will first review the events of 1835 in the life of Joseph Smith. There were no uneventful years in his life, and 1835 was as bewilderingly busy and meaningful as any. Second, it will focus on the establishment of two additional presiding Church quorums—the Twelve and the Seventy—and situate those key moments in the larger story of the Church's ecclesiastical development. Most Saints today know something of the beginnings of priesthood and Church government, but the story is more interesting and inspiring than most of us realize.[1]

J. Spencer Fluhman is an assistant professor of Church history and doctrine at Brigham Young University.

1835: The Year in Review

In January 1835, Joseph Smith worked on a set of theological lectures, the "Lectures on Faith," which were eventually published in the Doctrine and Covenants. The Prophet's involvement is still debated by historians. While tradition has designated Joseph Smith as the lectures' lone author, most historians agree that they were likely not the product of a single person. Various analyses, in fact, have suggested that Sidney Rigdon likely played a lead role in the writing of many of the lectures. In any case, Joseph Smith presided over the preparation of the lectures, and their inclusion with Joseph's revelations prompted a name change for the final collection. The first compilation of revelations had been called Book of Commandments (1833), but the new version was named Doctrine and Covenants (1835). The lectures, according to the subheadings in the new volume, were to be the "doctrine" section, and the revelations served as the "covenants" section. The lectures remained in the volume in its various editions throughout the nineteenth century but were removed in 1921.[2]

In early February, Joseph Smith received a vision not described in any section of the Doctrine and Covenants (though it is noted in *History of the Church*).[3] Joseph Young remembered the Prophet bringing him and his brother Brigham to his residence in Kirtland and explaining that he had seen a vision of the men who died on Zion's Camp: "Brethren, I have seen those men who died of the cholera in our camp; and the Lord knows, if I get a mansion as bright as theirs, I ask no more." After that, Joseph Smith "wept, and for some time could not speak." When he had composed himself, the Prophet explained that a Church conference should be convened where brethren would be called as Apostles and Seventies.[4]

According to these instructions, Joseph Smith presided over the meetings on February 14 when new Apostles were called and ordained. After a reading of John 15 and a prayer, Joseph Smith announced to the group that "God had commanded [the meeting] and it was made known to him by vision and by the Holy Spirit."[5] The Prophet would repeat that the priesthood organization was according to "vision" on several occasions.[6] In accordance with an earlier revelation (Doctrine and Covenants 18), the Book of Mormon witnesses selected and helped ordain men to serve as members of the Quorum of the Twelve. Some were ordained the following day and others later in the week.[7] A few days after the February 14 meeting, the First Presidency approved the publication of the 1835 Doctrine and Covenants.

On February 27, the Prophet invited nine of the new Apostles and several others to his home, where he taught them of their duties and bemoaned the fact that the brethren had kept inadequate records of their priesthood meetings. "It is a fact (said President Smith) that if I now had in my possession every decision which has been had upon important items of doctrine and duties which have been given since the commencement of this work, I would not part with it for any sum of money. But we have neglected to take minutes of such things, thinking, perhaps, that they would never benefit us afterwards, which, had we now, would decide almost any point of doctrine."[8]

The following day, February 28, Joseph Smith presided over the calls of the Seventy, some of whom were ordained that day, others the next.

On March 28, Joseph Smith received the final portions of Doctrine and Covenants 107, the grand revelation on priesthood and Church government. As with many of the revelations, the final document as we now read it in the Doctrine and

Covenants was given in stages, in a process more drawn out than we sometimes imagine it.

In early May, Joseph Smith was forced to respond to charges brought by Dennis Lake that the Prophet owed him eight hundred dollars. Joseph Smith denied owing Lake the money.

On June 2, Joseph Smith wrote a few lines to a cousin at the end of a letter that W. W. Phelps intended for loved ones in Liberty, Missouri. Many of the Saints forced from their Jackson County homes had ended up in Clay County, and Joseph's letter to Almira Scobey communicated his heartache at what the Missouri Saints had suffered. The lines are poignant:

> Cousin Almyra, Scoby ... Brother W W phelps has left a little space for me to occupy and I gladly improve it, I would be glad to see the Children of Zion and del[i]ver the <word> of Eternal life to them from my own mauth but cannot this year nevertheless the day will come that I shall injoy this privilege I trust. and we all shall receive an inheritance in the land of refuge which is so much to be desired seeing it is under the direction of the Allmighty therefore let us live faithful before the Lord and it shall be well with us I feel for all the Chilldren of Zion and pray for them in all my prayers peace be multiplied unto their redeemtion and favor from God Amen Joseph Smith Jr.[9]

On June 15, Joseph Smith wrote to the Missouri brethren to inform them of plans to publish his New Translation of the Bible, now commonly called the Joseph Smith Translation. Despite these intentions, the Saints did not publish the work in the Prophet's lifetime. He had pronounced the work complete as early as 1833. That same day, the suit brought against the Prophet by Dennis Lake was dismissed; the court ruled that

Lake had failed to provide sufficient evidence. A few days later, Joseph Smith pledged five hundred dollars to the building of the Kirtland Temple.

During the first days of July, Joseph Smith examined several Egyptian mummies and papyrus scrolls from antiquities dealer Michael Chandler. Joseph Smith's translation of some of the hieroglyphs became the Book of Abraham, now in our Pearl of Great Price. Throughout the month, the Prophet "was continually engaged in translating an alphabet to the Book of Abraham, and arranging a grammar of the Egyptian language as practiced by the ancients."[10] Joseph Smith worked on the translation throughout the fall.

In August, Joseph Smith traveled to Michigan. In his absence, the Brethren approved the new Doctrine and Covenants as scripture and voted to accept a statement on government now appearing as section 134.

In early September, the Prophet began writing a long treatise "to the elders of the church" instructing them "in the way of their duty" and providing them a statement of "religious principles" to help correct false impressions about the Church.[11] Portions of the treatise were published serially in the *Latter Day Saints' Messenger and Advocate*, the Church paper in Kirtland.

Joseph Smith spent September 22 dictating blessings for some of the Church's leading brethren, though he and Oliver Cowdery found it difficult to complete the work because of "a multitude of visitors."[12]

On October 4, Joseph Smith's journal noted that on a trip with John Corrill to Perry, Ohio, "about a mile from home we saw two Dears playing in the field which diverted our minds by giving an impatus to our thoughts upon the subject of the creation of God."[13]

The Prophet's journal entry for October 11 reads, "visited my Father <again> who was verry sick <in secret prayer in the morning the Lord said my servant thy father shall live> I waited on him all this day with my heart raised to god in the name of Jesus Christ that he would restore him to health again."[14] He and David Whitmer administered to Joseph Smith Sr.; he regained his health in a few days.

On October 17, the Prophet's journal reported, somewhat tersely, that he "called my family together and aranged my domestick concerns and domestic dismissed my boarders."[15]

On October 29, a dispute with his younger brother William became so heated, according to Joseph's journal, that "I told him he was out of place & asked him to set down he refused I repeated my request he become enraged I finally ordered him to set down he said he would not unless I knocked him down I was agitated in my feeling at on the account of his stubournness and was about to call leave the house, but my Father requsted me not to <do so> I complied."[16]

On November 3, Joseph Smith dedicated the "Elders School," spoke to the gathered brethren, attended a meeting of his brother Samuel's parents-in-law's patriarchal blessings (Samuel's daughter was blessed and named in the same meeting) and preached that evening to a crowded congregation at the Kirtland schoolhouse.[17]

A few days later, Joseph Smith entertained a visitor at Kirtland who identified himself as "Joshua the Jewish Minister." After hearing the stranger explain his religious views, Joseph Smith discovered that the visitor was in fact Robert Matthews, the infamous "prophet Matthias" from New York, who had recently stood trial for the suspicious death of a follower. Joseph was ultimately unimpressed with Matthews: "I told him, that my God told me that his God is the Devil, and I could not keep him any longer, and he must depart." The visit was not a total loss, however, because Joseph Smith had recounted the First Vision for Matthias before discovering his identity. A scribe recorded the Prophet's recital of the vision: "I called on the Lord in mighty prayer, a pillar of fire appeared above my head, it presently rested down upon my <me> head, and filled me with joy unspeakable, a personage appeared in the midst, of this pillar of flame which was spread all around, and yet nothing consumed, another personage soon appeared like unto the first, he said unto me thy sins are forgiven thee, he testifyed unto me that Jesus Christ is the Son of God; <and I saw many angels in this vision>."[18]

On November 19, Joseph Smith inspected the finish coat of plaster on the Kirtland Temple. On the way home, he chatted with a couple of disaffected Latter-day Saints.

The following day, November 20, was spent translating the Egyptian papyri. Oliver Cowdery, having recently returned from a trip to New York, delivered a Hebrew Bible, Hebrew and Greek lexicons, and a Webster's dictionary.

On November 24, Joseph Smith performed a marriage ceremony for Newel and Lydia Knight.

On December 2, Joseph Smith took a sleigh ride with his family to a neighboring town, and, while passing another sleigh, the other travelers "bawled out, do you get any revelation lately[?]" Joseph wrote that he was not surprised with that kind of treatment from folks from *that* side of town.[19]

The following day, December 3, Joseph performed a marriage ceremony for Warren and Martha Parrish.

On December 10, the Prophet helped put out a fire at the Kirtland lumber kiln. The loss of wood delayed the completion of the temple.

On the evening of December 12, the Prophet attended a debate at the home of his brother, William. Various speakers debated on the question "was it necessary for God to reveal himself to man, in order for their happiness[?]" Joseph Smith's journal records, simply, "I was on the affirmative and the last One to speak on that side of the question."[20] He left early to administer to a sick sister.

On December 16, the debate from a few days earlier was continued at William Smith's. The affirmative position won, but, to quote the Prophet's journal, "some altercation took place" when it was suggested that the debates would come to no good and should be discontinued. William Smith opposed the measure and "at length become much enraged particularly at me and used violence upon my person . . . for which I am grieved beyond expression, and can only pray God to forgive him inasmuch as he repents."[21] Two days later, Joseph Smith replied by letter to a repentant William. The letter concluded with these lines: "And now may God have mercy upon my fathers house, may God take away enmity, from betwe[e]n me and thee, and may all blessings be restored, and the past be forgotten forever, may humble repentance bring us both to thee <O God> and to thy power and protection, and a crown, to enjoy the society of father mother Alvin Hyrum Sophron[i]a Samuel Catharine [Katharine] Carloss [Don Carlos] Lucy the Saints and all the sanctify[ie]d in peace forever<, is the prayer of> ~~This from~~ Your brother Joseph Smith Jun."[22]

Things calmed down in time for Christmas. The Prophet spent Christmas day at home with family. On the day after Christmas in 1835, Joseph Smith studied Hebrew and received the revelation now appearing as section 108.

"GOVERNMENT OF THE CHURCH OF CHRIST"

December 29 was spent preaching for over three hours, this time at the Kirtland schoolhouse to a large gathering that included many of the town's Presbyterians.

New Year's Eve 1835 was spent "attending to the duties of my family," in the printing office studying, and in a meeting with the "council of the 12."[23]

In no way can 1835 be described as leisurely. Even so, Joseph could note at the outset of 1836 that "my heart is filled with gratitude to God, that he has preserved my life and the life <lives> of my family while another year has rolled away, we have been, sustained and upheld in the midst of a wicked and perverse generation, and exposed to all, the afflictions temptations and misery that are incident to human life, for which I feel to humble myself in dust and ashes, as it were before the Lord."[24] I turn now to focus in on a theme that dominated that momentous year: the development of Church government.

"Government of the Church of Christ"[25]

As some of the earliest Latter-day Saint missionaries traveled through Ohio in the fall of 1830, they made some startling claims. In an effort to circumvent any influence the Mormon elders might have in the area, local newspaper editor Eber Howe summarized their message by writing that "[Oliver] Cowdry claims that he and his associates are the only persons on earth who are qualified to administer in [Christ's] name."[26] Howe guessed right, but only in part, that his readers would take offense at such religious audacity. Then, as now, American Protestants bristled at Latter-day Saint claims that Christian ordinances are essential for salvation and that the Latter-day Saint priesthood is uniquely authorized to perform those rites. Predictably, Howe was dumbfounded when hundreds of Ohio

Protestants flocked to the missionaries for baptism. By early 1831, four branches of the infant Church dotted the Ohio landscape.[27] Looking back on his conversion to Mormonism, Edward Partridge remembered having concluded prior to the missionaries' arrival that God would surely "again reveal himself to man and confer authority upon some one, or more, before his church could be built up in the last days." Convinced that the Christian pastors of his day ministered "without authority from God," Partridge wholeheartedly embraced the Latter-day Saint missionaries' message and joined the Church of Christ, as the Church was initially called.[28]

The contradictory reactions of Howe and Partridge illustrate the divisiveness of the early Saints' message and the puzzle their church presented to conventional Christians. Based on what the Saints regarded as scriptural precedents, the Church in the 1830s was at once recognizably Christian and something quite new. Joseph Smith's revelations unfolded a complex and highly successful institution, and the Prophet and the Saints alike worked to implement the revelations as best they could. Indeed, the early history of Latter-day Saint Church government makes clear that while the revelations drove the development, Church leaders constantly grappled with questions, complications, and a good deal of trial and error. In retrospect, modern Saints see an orderly procession of events leading to a finished product. This, however, is apparent only in retrospect. For the Saints of the 1830s and '40s, the story was thrilling but not nearly so neat. At times, they seemed to feel their way, hardly conceiving what the finished product might look like. It often took years for important terms or concepts—"apostle," "Melchizedek Priesthood," "sealing," and just about every other key word for Church government—to take on their modern meanings. This terminological instability with regards to priesthood and

Church government has led to years of historians' debates about what happened and when. Where some modern Saints might assume that the full-blown Church of today was more or less an understood given, one modern Church leader has cautioned that such a perspective obscures the challenges facing nineteenth-century Saints:

> Some suppose that the organization [of the Church] was handed to the Prophet Joseph Smith like a set of plans and specifications for a building, with all of the details known at the beginning. But it did not come that way. Rather, it came a piece at a time as the Brethren were ready and as they inquired of God. . . . It took a generation of asking and receiving before the order of things as we know it today was firmly in place. Each move to perfect that order has come about in response to a need and in answer to prayer. And that process continues in our day.[29]

The revelations, in other words, did not force themselves on the early Saints. Rather, only as early Church leaders were ready and asking did they move into new periods of ecclesiastical development and understanding.

So looking back, we should expect the processes that brought us the modern Church to be more dynamic, more rooted in human agency, and more drawn out than we sometimes imagine. And while it is tempting to get lost in the details of the early Church's governmental particularities, I hope to call attention to just how complex and effective early Church government became. Noting the complexities and successes in the same sentence is intentional: the perplexities of establishing a new church *ex nihilo* illustrates the kind of human striving that cheers modern hearts. If history is any guide, Latter-day Saints will succeed as their predecessors did, namely, by looking to the revelations for direction, leaning on experience, staying open to change, and seeking for heaven's help in meeting new and confounding challenges.

Christian Authority in Joseph Smith's America

Joseph Smith's revelations sought several critical balances in erecting an ecclesiastical structure for the Church of Christ. Questions pressed themselves on Joseph Smith early and often. How does a church serve the many without missing the one? What was the relationship between Joseph Smith's revelatory experiences and those of ordinary Saints? Was the Bible or Book of Mormon (or both) to be taken as a guide for building a modern church? Would it be up to Joseph Smith himself to decide every ecclesiastical question? Over the first dozen years of Church history, these questions about the Church and its governance occupied a prominent place in the revelations; but again, the early Saints were often left to wrestle with their implications and implement them as best they could. Clearly, the expectations of former Protestants—as nearly all the early Saints were—were at times validated in the revelations; at other times, the Saints were nudged into new understandings of authority and church power.

While a tiny smattering of Roman Catholics joined the Church in its early years, the overwhelming majority of converts came from Protestant churches. While Protestantism had taken myriad forms by 1830, most of the newly minted Saints shared some general assumptions about church polity and the place of ordinances. Protestantism had for centuries honed a critique of Roman Catholicism's reliance on religious rituals—"sacraments" in Catholic and Protestant parlance—as the "usual vehicles" of God's saving grace. For Catholics, the church and its priesthood thus functioned as critical mediators of God's power. God's saving power was potentially available to all, but the church, as the lone authorized dispenser of the sacraments, became the critical intermediary between heaven and earth. An elaborate hierarchy oversaw the church's ordinances and, at the local level, priests administered the sacraments to lay Catholics. For Catholics, the notion of salvation apart from the church and its sacraments was unthinkable.

The place of the sacraments in Catholic theology was no small problem for Martin Luther, the Catholic monk who is sometimes credited with touching off the sixteenth-century Protestant Reformation. For Luther, the book of Romans in the New Testament sparked a spiritual crisis that culminated in a new understanding of sacraments, priestly power, and salvation. His reading of Romans 1:17, especially the phrase "the just shall live by faith," came to describe Luther's critique of Catholicism. Rather than believing that the church and its sacraments somehow mechanically dispensed salvation to humanity, Luther argued that salvation sprang from saving faith alone. No human striving, no human achievement could merit salvation. Rather, one was declared righteous, or justified, by faith in Christ's saving gift, which was itself a gift of God for Luther. The church, in Luther's reckoning, did not dispense salvation but rather was to be a loving body of believers only.

Priesthood was redefined too. Rather than a body of uniquely authorized men vested with power needed for salvation, Luther called for a "priesthood of all believers." Authority rested in the Bible and in Christ, not in a special priesthood. Luther reduced the sacraments from seven to two—he kept only baptism and communion (which, ironically, Latter-day Saints call the "sacrament")—and redefined them in the process. Luther refused to view any sacrament as essential for salvation, instead believing they functioned as important symbols or moments along the Christian path. They would call to mind important truths and unite the faithful in sacred settings, but Luther, like other Protestants generally, removed intermediaries and demanded that Christians look to Jesus Christ alone for salvation.

Other reformers added an array of emphases to Luther's main teachings, but most agreed with salvation by grace through faith and were similarly leery of Catholic-looking emphasis on churches, priests, or rituals. John Calvin, for instance, retained the two sacraments Luther had (baptism and communion) but became even more anti-ritualistic. He discarded formalized, structured worship and insisted that preaching alone would be the centerpiece of true Christian churches. Calvin's emphasis on the Bible, predestination, and the "irresistible Grace" of God wielded no small influence in the English Reformation, as generations of Puritans worked to nudge the Church of England further and further from its Catholic past.[30]

In terms of sheer numbers and influence, in fact, Calvin cast a larger shadow on early America than Luther did, as the British colonies in North America were, of course, British. With Calvinistic Puritans and Calvinistic Presbyterians predominating before the American Revolution (they ranked first and second in terms of church membership), especially in New England and the middle colonies, historians have described the Christianity of the early American republic as generally anti-ritualistic, largely suspicious of Catholic-looking church hierarchies, and insistent that faith alone—not ordinances—offered salvation to the human family.[31] Waves of Irish immigration brought Catholics in large numbers to both the colonies and new nation, putting Protestants on notice that "true religion" was under siege and that Catholics had to be controlled lest the nation be imperiled by what critics saw as Catholicism's ultra-authoritarianism, its superstitious attachment to ordinances, and its theologically dangerous obsession with priestly power.

Enter Oliver Cowdery and his missionary companions, declaring sole authorization for essential Christian ordinances. As one might expect, American Protestants typically met these claims with alarm. Some saw in the Latter-day Saint message an affront to the very core of Protestantism. Even so, Americans like Joseph Smith and Edward Partridge found in the Restoration a satisfying and compelling alternative to the dizzying array of Protestant denominations. Though the message seemed unavoidably controversial given its historical context, Americans by the dozens, then hundreds, then thousands found a spiritually steadying bulwark in the Restoration's claims to certainty, authority, and power.

Priesthood Authority in the Early Church

This detour through Christian and early American history reminds us of how new and old the revelations might have looked to Christians of Joseph Smith's day, not to mention the early Saints themselves. Some elements of the revelations were recognizable to early Saints as reflecting Protestant understandings. Others appeared to outsiders to be theological throwbacks to Catholic practices or beliefs. Some elements of the revelations seem altogether foreign when viewed against the backdrop of Joseph Smith's religious environment. No wonder the early Saints struggled to come to grips with, much less implement, some of the revelations.[32] As just one example, when the revelations now appearing as section 20 called for quarterly conferences, early Saints instinctively called them "general conferences." Quarterly general conferences, as it turns out, had been a staple of early Methodist church government, and Joseph Smith, Brigham Young, and other Latter-day Saint converts with experience in Methodist churches relied on the models they had grown up with. When the Lord declared in Doctrine and Covenants section 1 that "I am God . . . these commandments are of me, and were given unto my servants in their weakness, after the manner of their language, that they might come to understanding" (v. 24), he apparently meant what he said. I am inclined to see the phrase "after the manner of their language" broadly. These early Latter-day Saint converts were heirs to an ecclesiastical language inherited from the Christian tradition that the revelations routinely assumed, appealed to, and utilized to both reinforce old ideas and communicate new ones.

It appears that the translation of the Book of Mormon provided Joseph Smith and his earliest associates with the first forum in which to work out questions of priesthood and Church governance. While the Book of Mormon was not exactly a handbook for organizing the Church, the text provided important principles and hinted at future developments. The text named several positions of significance in the ancient Church: priest, teacher, elder, apostle, and high priest.[33] The relationship and duties of each was only partially clear in the text, though, and it is evident that early Church leaders initially lacked a clear sense of how they would work together. Even so, two points in 3 Nephi came through loud and clear: first, one needed authority from Christ to baptize; and, second, there was a distinction between those who could baptize and those who could also give the gift of the Holy Ghost. Joseph Smith and the early brethren were certain of this much. Their prayer about the former—the power to baptize—was answered with an angelic visitation. With the lesser authority in place, Joseph Smith and Oliver Cowdery baptized each other and eventually others.

"GOVERNMENT OF THE CHURCH OF CHRIST"

The higher office or power was a different story, though. That Joseph Smith received additional authority from other angelic beings is clear enough, but exactly when and what he made of those experiences at the time are still questions for Church historians. There is no recorded date, for instance, for the visit of Peter, James, and John, like there is for the visit of John the Baptist.[34] Furthermore, Joseph Smith and the other brethren early on used the terms "elder," "high priesthood," "high priest," and "Melchizedek Priesthood" in sometimes confusing ways. While even young Latter-day Saints now rattle off that Peter, James, and John restored the Melchizedek Priesthood, it is curious that Joseph Smith did not use this kind of language until 1835. I am suggesting that the Prophet came to an understanding of things more slowly than we have imagined. There are clues as to how some understandings apparently came together. In the Book of Mormon text, for instance, the terms "elder" and "disciple" seem to have been used interchangeably. Drawing as they did on the language of both the Bible and Book of Mormon, Joseph Smith and Oliver Cowdery instinctively used "apostle," "disciple" and "elder" synonymously in the earliest documents. Note, for instance, the now-curious language of Doctrine and Covenants 20:38: "An apostle is an elder, and it is his calling to baptize." It is surprising, too, to find John Whitmer's preaching license naming him an "apostle"—unless, that is, we have this earliest usage in mind. Similarly, Oliver Cowdery and David Whitmer were referred to "apostles" in a revelation from 1829 (section 18), though they are hardly remembered these days as being among the Church's first Apostles. In the Church's first months, though, with the understanding apparently then in place, this made perfect sense.

Even so, this apostolic language invests Peter, James, and John's visit with special significance for modern Saints. When Joseph Smith set about to prepare the revelations for the 1835 Doctrine and Covenants, he unapologetically added some significant lines to the revelation now appearing as section 27. When elaborating on the idea of the Lord visiting the earth for a kind of millennial sacrament meeting, the revelation listed several additional figures who would participate, including "Peter, James, and John, whom I have sent unto you, by whom I have ordained you and confirmed you to be apostles, and especial witnesses of my name" (v. 12). So while the earliest documents use "apostle" somewhat more generally than would be the case later, in 1835 Joseph Smith's revelation narrated the visit of Peter, James, and John in an unmistakably powerful way. The point was not lost on the first generation of Church leadership. Brigham Young, speaking in 1852, reminded his audience that "Joseph Smith, Oliver Cowdery, and David Whitmer were the first Apostles of this dispensation."[35] A few years later, Heber C. Kimball agreed, stressing that "the moment that the Almighty sent Peter, James, and John, and ordained Joseph Smith an Apostle, the seed of [the] Priesthood and Church was planted."[36] If Young or Kimball were writing this essay, in other words, they would no doubt report that modern Saints have rather dramatically undervalued the visit of Peter, James, and John by thinking it restored only the Melchizedek Priesthood.

The fact that Joseph Smith continued to describe higher authority in perplexing ways might hint at the fact that he viewed this higher authority, as one historian has described it, as a succession of keys.[37] Joseph Smith learned the hard way that as soon as he said something like "We now have all the authority or power God intends for his people," some other authority, power, or deep insight came and rearranged the ecclesiastical furniture. In 1831, a conference conferred "high priesthood" on several elders, a circumstance that is confusing to modern readers because they were already ordained elders. Within months, the office of "high priest," named in the Book of Mormon but not yet a part of Church governance, was applied to several brethren, leaving some modern commentators to conclude that "high priesthood" simply meant "high priests." Eventually, the distinction between office and priesthood itself became clearer in Latter-day Saint minds.[38]

By 1835, the offices of the modern Church were more or less in place. Those offices named in the Book of Mormon were introduced first chronologically, a testament to the importance of the translation experience.[39] Priests and teachers, described almost synonymously in the Book of Mormon, appeared at the beginning. Elders and Apostles, though indistinguishable in the Church's first months, were eventually separated into distinct offices. The office of bishop did not appear in the Book of Mormon, though it does in the Bible (see 1 Timothy 3:1–7) and was introduced in 1831. Originally, the bishops had responsibilities administering the law of consecration and stewardship and functioning as the first rung in a system of Church courts. The pastoral duties of the office were not added until the early Utah period, when the first congregational wards were introduced. The office of deacon, like that of bishop, had a New Testament precedent (see 1 Timothy 3:8–13) but none in the Book of Mormon. The office also appeared in 1831. High priests, as mentioned above, were noted in the Book of Mormon but did not appear until 1831 or 1832 (depending on one's interpretation of the events of the 1831 conference where "high priesthood" was introduced).[40] A "president of the high priesthood" working in tandem with counselors was appointed by revelation in 1831, though it took some time for the presidency to function as a unit.[41] The office of patriarch, introduced in 1833, related to an Old Testament rather than a New Testament or Book of Mormon model. In the case of the presiding patriarch, the office passed from father to son, making it unlike any other calling in church government. Other patriarchs were called starting in 1837; their offices did not pass to sons.[42] An early Church leader described practice with regards to patriarchs: "It also was a rule in the church to have one in each stake (most generally the oldest, if suitable) appointed and ordained a patriarch, whose duty it was to be a sort of father to the church, and bless such children as had no natural father to bless them."[43] As this account underscores, initially fathers gave their children patriarchal blessings; the Church patriarch and stake patriarch gave blessings to those who did not have a living Latter-day Saint father to bless them. The first high council was appointed in 1834; the minutes of its first meeting were eventually canonized and now appear as Doctrine and Covenants 102. "Apostle," the word applied to Joseph Smith and a select few others in the months just before and after the organization of the Church, roared back in 1835 with added emphasis. An apostolic Quorum of Twelve was called in 1835, with a president designated on the basis of seniority (originally based on age). The Seventy came just days later in 1835. Most of the members of these two quorums were chosen from the Zion's Camp ranks.

With this list in place, we can consider the significance of the early revelations relating to priesthood. Doctrine and Covenants 20, the Church's founding "articles and covenants," had listed the duties of the several offices and described select Church ordinances, but sections 84 and 107 fit both into a theological and ecclesiastical framework. The revelation we know as Doctrine and Covenants 84, given in 1832, drew several distinctions between the lesser and higher priesthoods and connected both to the temple and covenants. Following an introductory section relating to the building of a latter-day temple, verses 6–31 added a parenthetical note on priesthood history. The verses traced priesthood backward from Moses to Adam, stating in each case that a recipient received priesthood "under the hand" of another. This account itself is interesting, as the language underscored a lineal decent of authority that shared little with many Protestant conceptualizations of church authority. Divine authority descending through the years with a physical ordinance in an apparent top-down direction would have struck many Protestants as a Catholic practice. Even those with more hierarchical church structures like the Episcopalians and Methodists were forced, in the press of early American democratization, to demonstrate how church authority ultimately ran bottom up.[44] The Church of Jesus Christ of Latter-day Saints would retain the principle of common consent in its government but, when viewed in conjunction with prophets, apostles, keys, and priesthood, it remains true that no other church in early American history cared so little for democratic church government.[45]

Section 84 also detailed how the higher priesthood was taken from Israel, along with Moses, because Israel's tribes "hardened their hearts" and could not endure the presence of God. A lesser priesthood was "confirmed" on Aaron and his seed, and it predominated among the Israelites until the time of Jesus Christ (see vv. 18–28). Embedded in the account was this important phrase: "Therefore, in the ordinances thereof, the power of godliness is manifest" (v. 20). While no Saint of the 1830s took special notice of that verse, so far as we can tell, when viewed in retrospect, it reads like a sign of things to come.

More to the point, where most of Joseph Smith's contemporaries tended to see ordinances in strictly symbolic terms, the thrust of Joseph Smith's ministry was to call greater and greater attention to what other Christians would call sacramentalism.

Indeed, the trajectory of Latter-day Saint theology and practice in the early years led away from the standard Protestant position on the sacraments. What lingering Protestant attachments the early Saints might have held were systemically undone by the revelations. Added to the early insight from the Book of Mormon that special divine authorization was needed to baptize, some early converts were no doubt surprised to learn that their Protestant baptisms "didn't count," as it were, for entrance into the Church of Christ. The revelation on the subject was less than diplomatic: one could be baptized "an hundred times," but it would avail nothing; "you cannot enter in at the strait gate . . . by your dead works" (Doctrine and Covenants 22:2). Leaving little room for doubt about the place of authorized baptism in Latter-day Saint doctrine, section 76 listed baptism by immersion as a qualification for those inheriting celestial glory. That Joseph Smith took passages like these literally is clear enough: in an 1836 vision of celestial glory (now appearing as section 137), Joseph Smith was confused at seeing his own brother Alvin, who had died in 1823, in the celestial kingdom. As the Prophet explained, he "marveled" at Alvin's presence there because "he had departed this life before the Lord had set his hand to gather Israel the second time, and had not been baptized for the remission of sins" (v. 6).

So, viewed against the backdrop of Latter-day Saint thinking about ordinances, section 84 sounded an important chord. With the power of godliness manifest in the ordinances of higher priesthood alone, it is unsurprising that the revelation went on to call all men to the priesthood. Even while power in the restored Church remained top-down in its orientation, the net of priesthood was cast wide. How is that for a paradox? A prominent historian has recently written this about what I described above as a thoroughly anti-democratic church: "In a democratic time, the Mormons emerged as the most democratic of the churches, rivaled only by the Quakers."[46] The revelation went on to link priesthood with exaltation itself, noting that those who received and magnified the priesthood would receive "all that my Father hath" (vv. 33, 38). It even cautioned those who would try to avoid priesthood responsibility. "And wo unto all those who come not unto this priesthood which ye have received," the revelation warned, making clear that God intended all men to receive it.

Section 107 elaborated on these themes. It stressed the distinction between lesser and higher priesthoods, described the various offices of the Church, and outlined the relationship between the various quorums. Importantly, it also made clear the concept of presidency. "Of necessity," verse 21 reads, "there are presidents, or presiding officers growing out of, or appointed of or from among those who are ordained to the several offices in these two priesthoods." The *necessity* was evident enough in the early years of the Church. With its democratic male priesthood, some kind of ordering mechanism was needed to prevent disunity, confusion, and factionalism. That mechanism was presidency, which was most often articulated in the language of *keys*. Though the word was used in at least three distinct ways in the early Church, for our purposes the critical function of keys was to designate presiding officers.[47] While faithful men could receive priesthood, only presidents would receive keys, giving them the right to preside in a jurisdiction. Ultimately, the revelation stipulated, a quorum of presidents presided over the whole Church: "Of the Melchizedek Priesthood, three

Presiding High Priests, chosen by the body, appointed and ordained to that office, and upheld by the confidence, faith, and prayer of the church, form a quorum of the Presidency of the Church" (v. 22). There was not a quorum, in fact, without a president, though a couple of the presidencies were unique. The apostolic quorum would have a single president without counselors, and the Seventy's presidency would feature seven presidents without counselors. In every other case, a president with two counselors oversaw quorums in the Church.

The revelation related the Church's presiding quorums in an interesting way. The First Presidency, the Quorum of Twelve Apostles, and the Seventy were described as "equal in authority and power" in verses 23–24, giving the impression to casual readers that the quorums perhaps shared presiding power. Verse 33 corrects that impression, though, stating that "the Twelve are a Traveling Presiding High Council, to officiate in the name of the Lord, *under the direction of the Presidency* of the Church" (emphasis added). Whatever "equal" meant in the earlier verses, then, it did not place the Twelve and Seventy on par with the First Presidency. (The stake high councils, moreover, were accounted as "equal" with the Presidency and Twelve in verses 36–37.) While the Saints were left to sort through the equality language in those verses, it should be noted that the Twelve's being described as a "Traveling Presiding High Council" points to the position early Apostles found themselves in during the 1830s and '40s. Whereas local stake councils in Kirtland or Missouri had responsibility to act under their presidencies in administering the needs of the Church, the Twelve were originally given authority only where there were no organized stakes. The modern apostolic quorum still scatters across the earth in fulfillment of its original directive—to act as "special witnesses of the name of Christ in all the world" (v.

23)—but they play a role at Church headquarters today that their 1830s counterparts never did.

The Seventy, according to the revelation, were organized "according to the vision showing [their] order" (v. 93). The seven presidents, with one presiding over the six, were to oversee the work of a potentially large number of seventies. The revelation empowered Church leaders to call not just a single quorum of seventies, but perhaps many more "if the labor in the vineyard of necessity requires it" (v. 96). This flexibility is an important aspect of early Church government. While ideal membership numbers were set for the various quorums, the sizes were not set in stone. The First Presidency, for instance, had its number set at three, but Joseph Smith felt free to expand the quorum as needed. He not only added Oliver Cowdery as "Assistant" or "Associate" President for a few years in the 1830s—a position that Cowdery described as above the counselors but beneath the president—but also added additional counselors in Nauvoo.[48] Ecclesiastical adjustment and modification, in other words, should not trouble the Latter-day Saints. The Seventy, in fact, have undergone as much adjustment as any office in the Church.[49]

Priesthood Power, the House of the Lord, and the Grace of Jesus Christ

With all the structuring, ordaining, and organizing, one thing became clear to Joseph Smith: the Brethren would amount to little without power in their priesthood work. Modern Latter-day Saint missionaries learn that priesthood authority comes by ordination, but real power depends on their faithfulness.[50] This distinction between authority and power was not always explicit in the revelations or in the Prophet's speaking and writing, but it runs through early Church history in unmistakable ways (see Doctrine and Covenants 121:34–46). In short, neither Joseph Smith nor the revelations sought a cohesive organization or efficient institution only. Rather, since the salvation of the human family was the end of all the ecclesiastical means, the Saints sought nothing less than divine power to bless lives.[51] I will limit my illustration of early priesthood power to two examples, each a key term in the development of Latter-day Saint understanding of priesthood: endowment and sealing. Unsurprisingly, each in turn leads to *temple*, a word and place that serves as something of a crown jewel in the ministry of Joseph Smith. With the thought in mind, then, that all ecclesiastical paths lead to the temple, we can situate endowment, sealing, and temple together under heading of "power in the priesthood."

The Lord's instructions to his ancient Apostles that they should tarry at Jerusalem until they were "endued with power from on high" (Luke 24:49) probably framed Joseph Smith's early understanding of the priesthood's potential. That word *endue* would enter Joseph Smith's vocabulary with particular force. He used it interchangeably with the word *endow*. He expected an outpouring of divine power, in fact, that would rival the ancient Apostles' experience at Pentecost as recorded in the New Testament. The spiritual gifts experienced by the early Saints, he taught, would signal God's working in an unmistakable way to empower the newly ordained brethren. A dramatic experience of this sort of divine manifestation accompanied the ordinations to the "high priesthood" in 1831. Shortly after gathering to Ohio, in fact, a revelation (section 43) had promised an endowment to Saints: "Sanctify yourselves and ye shall be endowed with power" (v. 16). In the June conferences of 1831, several of the brethren assembled there left accounts of a variety of dramatic spiritual experiences—healings, visions, speaking in tongues, and so on—that some expected would constitute the promised endowment of power.[52] Others were unconvinced that the promised endowment had come, and questions persisted.

One question related to *sealing*, a term perhaps unsurpassed in the transformation it underwent in the Church's early years. After the November 1831 high priesthood conference, Joseph Smith instructed the elders on their appointments by linking high priesthood with the power to assure eternal life for faithful Saints. Speaking at a conference four months after the ordinations to high priesthood, Joseph Smith, according to the conference minutes, said that "the order of the High-priesthood is that they have power given them to seal up the Saints unto eternal life."[53] Some early missionaries, acting on what understanding of the concept they had, began "sealing up" entire congregations to eternal life! Leaders later sometimes used this same "sealing" language in their patriarchal blessings, in their descriptions of initiation into the School of the Prophets, and in conjunction with the first temple ordinances practiced in Ohio.[54] Even so, Joseph Smith would eventually come to understand sealing in still different terms.

A revelation in 1833 (section 95) coupled "endowment" with "temple." Intended for the Saints in Jackson County, Missouri, it related a "commandment that you should build a house, in the which house I design to endow those whom I have chosen with power from on high" (v. 8). This would dramatically redirect the Saints' energies with regard to the endowment of power. Oliver Cowdery took the new directions to heart. "We want you to understand that the Lord has not promised to endow his servants from on high," he wrote to a fellow priesthood leader in 1834, "only on the condition that they build him a house; and if the house is not built the Elders will not be endowed with power, and if they are not they can never go to the nations with the everlasting gospel."[55]

After the 1833 Missouri mobbings made a temple there impossible and the 1834 Zion's Camp recall made an immediate return unlikely, the Saints, armed with the knowledge that an endowment would not come without a temple, eventually built one in Ohio. The Pentecostal experiences before and after the dedication of the Kirtland Temple struck Joseph Smith as an endowment of power. After recording the visions, tongues, and angelic visitations of March 30, 1836, Joseph Smith's journal records the following: "It was a penticost and enduement indeed, long to be remembered for the sound shall go forth from this place into all the world, and the occurrences of this day shall be handed down upon the pages of sacred history to all generations, as the day of Pentecost, so shall this day be numbered and celebrated as a year of Jubilee and time of rejoicing to the saints of the most high God."[56] It was in Nauvoo, of course, that the term *endowment* took its final form in the Restoration. Predisposed to see endowment in terms of divine power and temple, the Saints experienced endowment as a distinct ordinance beginning in 1842. In a public sermon in early May of that year, Joseph Smith discoursed on the coming endowment and the difference between it and the preliminary ordinances revealed in Kirtland: "The keys are certain signs and words by which false spirits and personages may be detected from true, which cannot be revealed to the Elders till the Temple is completed—The rich can only get them in the Temple—the poor may get them on the Mountain top as did Moses."[57]

Sealing, too, found its final forms in Nauvoo. The "sealing up unto eternal life" that the early Saints had spoken of since 1831, like *endowment*, was at last associated with the ordinances of the temple.[58] Just as important, the Prophet used sealing in new and consequential ways in Illinois. Whereas sealing had essentially linked individuals to God in the 1830s, the Nauvoo Saints learned that it could also link husbands and wives and parents and children together in eternal, covenantal relationships. In a conversation with William Clayton and Benjamin Johnson in May 1843, the Prophet explained that "except a man and his wife enter into an everlasting covenant and be married for eternity while in this probation by the power and authority of the Holy priesthood they will cease to increase when they die (i.e. they will not have any children in the resurrection) but those who are married by the power & authority of the priesthood in this life . . . will continue to increase and have children in the celestial glory."[59]

That same teaching was reinforced two months later when Joseph Smith dictated the revelation on celestial marriage (section 132). Sealing, importantly, seems to have functioned three ways in this last canonized revelation of Joseph Smith. The long-discussed "sealing up unto eternal life" appears in verse 49, where Joseph Smith was told, "For verily I seal upon you your exaltation, and prepare a throne for you in the kingdom of my Father." The seventh verse speaks of ordinances themselves being sealed by the Holy Spirit in order to be valid, and, lastly, the net effect of the revelation was to assure that those worthily married for eternity were sealed to each other.[60] In section 132, the promised blessings related to sealing were supernal: "They shall pass by the angels, and the gods, which are set there, to their exaltation and glory in all things, as hath been sealed upon their heads, which glory shall be a fulness and a continuation of the seeds forever and ever. Then shall they be gods, because they have no end; therefore shall they be from everlasting to everlasting, because they continue; then shall they be above all, because all things are subject unto them. Then shall they be gods, because they have all power, and the angels are subject unto them" (vv. 19–20).

A month later, in August of 1843, Joseph Smith preached a sermon in which he explained that the sealing of husbands and wives would extend to their children: "When a seal is put upon the father and mother it secures their posterity so that they cannot be lost but will be saved by virtue of the covenant of their father."[61] Just months before his death in 1844, the Prophet put the finishing touch on the doctrine of sealing, explaining that it would be possible to "seal those who dwell on earth to those which dwell in heaven."[62] Is there a doctrine taught by Joseph Smith that gives more comfort and purpose to modern Latter-day Saint families?

In conclusion, I hope that this brief review will deepen our appreciation for these early Saints on several counts. First, while most modern Latter-day Saints know that the revelations came "precept upon precept; line upon line" (Isaiah 28:10), getting into the details of the beginnings of priesthood and Church government might convince us that we have underestimated how demanding and drawn out the process can be. Those of us who struggle with our own limited understanding might find some comfort in this. To grapple with what light and truth we have, and to yearn for more, is to stand in good company. Joseph Smith, Brigham Young, John Taylor, and the rest came to know these processes well. Second, we might perhaps see in the temple the culminating contribution of Joseph Smith's ministry. This chapter wound up at the temple because Joseph Smith's prophetic work did; in one way or another, each of the doctrines, organizations, and practices found its ultimate expression in the house of the Lord. The trajectory of the Prophet's teaching on priesthood and Church government pointed to ordinances and the covenants they offered. The

Church in 1830, in the rear-view mirror, seems considerably less sacramental than it would in 1844. The Saints came a long way, both theologically and ecclesiastically, in less than two decades.

One question remains unanswered. What of that great question dividing Catholics and Protestants? What of the relationship between the sacraments and saving grace? That question animated the theologies of Luther, Calvin, and the other early Protestants and framed a major disagreement between the two Christian communities. Interestingly, in early Latter-day Saint scripture one finds ample support for *both* sides of that particular Christian divide. With all that I have presented here, there can be little doubt that ordinances came to occupy a prominent—and seemingly non-Protestant—place in the Restoration.[63] Baptism for the dead made unmistakably clear that ordinances were something well beyond symbols for the early Saints. Even so, Luther and Calvin would have approved of the early Church's statement of faith given at its founding, as recorded in that unforgettable section 20. Here is its article on justification: "And we know that justification through the grace of our Lord and Savior Jesus Christ is just and true" (v. 30). That simple statement of Jesus Christ's place in the Restoration should warm Latter-day Saint hearts—and Protestant hearts, too!

How, though, do these sacramental and grace sides of Latter-day Saint scripture come together? How should they fit in Latter-day Saint lives? I propose that the answer might lie in Doctrine and Covenants 84, the revelation on the priesthood's oath and covenant discussed above. After the history lesson in verses 6–31, but before the overwhelming promise of "all that my Father hath" in verse 38, the revelation briefly but powerfully pulls together the ordinances of the priesthood and the Atoning

One: "And also all they who receive this priesthood receive me, saith the Lord; for he that receiveth my servants receiveth me; and he that receiveth me receiveth my Father" (vv. 35–37). For me, that word *receive* is the grand key. Every ritual act in the Church is in fact an act of reception or acceptance. In my mind, participation in the ordinances of the Church does not *earn* salvation for the Saints. I am not convinced that ordinances can *qualify* us for exaltation, either. No decision, no earthly work, no human striving could possibly *merit* "all that my Father hath." Does any Latter-day Saint think that the accumulated righteousness of a lifetime could deserve *that*? Theologically speaking, it just does not add up. No, Latter-day Saints stand with the rest of Christendom, "all amazed . . . [and] confused at the grace that so fully he proffers" us.[64] Rather, as section 84 reminds us, by being baptized, confirmed, or endowed, we receive Jesus. His unmatched gifts are just that: gifts. And no one earns gifts. But for gifts to matter, for gifts to be enjoyed, they must be received. In the final tally, the Restoration's revelations on priesthood underscore the fact that to "come unto Christ," as the revelations so often put it, is to receive his goodness and grace.

Notes

1. Chronology items are drawn from "A Chronology of the Life of Joseph Smith," *BYU Studies* 46, no. 4 (2007), 67–78. I gratefully acknowledge two extensive studies of early Church government that inform this essay: Richard L. Bushman, *Joseph Smith: Rough Stone Rolling* (New York: Alfred A. Knopf, 2005), especially chapter 13; and Gregory A. Prince, *Power from On High: The Development of Mormon Priesthood* (Salt Lake City: Signature Books, 1995).

2. Larry E. Dahl and Charles D. Tate Jr., eds., *The Lectures on Faith in Historical Perspective* (Provo, UT: Religious Studies Center, Brigham Young University, 1990), 1–10.

3. Joseph Smith, *History of the Church of Jesus Christ of Latter-day Saints*, ed. B. H. Roberts, 2nd ed. rev. (Salt Lake City: Deseret Book, 1957), 2:221.

4. Joseph Young, *History of the Organization of the Seventies: Names of the First and Second Quorums, Items in Relation to the First Presidency of the Seventies, also a Brief Glance at Enoch and His City* (Salt Lake City: Deseret News, 1878), 1–2.

5. Fred C. Collier and William S. Harwell, eds., *Kirtland Council Minute Book* (Salt Lake City: Collier's Publishing Company, 1996), 70.

6. See, for instance, Doctrine and Covenants 107:93: "And it is according to the vision showing the order of the Seventy."

7. Collier and Harwell, *Kirtland Council*, 72–80.

8. Collier and Harwell, *Kirtland Council*, 85.

9. *Personal Writings of Joseph Smith*, ed. Dean C. Jessee, 2nd ed. rev. (Salt Lake City: Deseret Book; Provo, UT: Brigham Young University Press, 2002), 358.

10. Smith, *History of the Church*, 2:238.

11. Smith, *Personal Writings*, 368–88.

12. Dean C. Jessee, Mark Ashurst-McGee, and Richard L. Jensen, eds., *Journals, Volume 1: 1832–1839*, vol. 1 of the Journals series of *The Joseph Smith Papers*, ed. Dean C. Jessee, Ronald K. Esplin, and Richard Lyman Bushman (Salt Lake City: The Church Historian's Press, 2008), 62.

13. Jessee, Ashurst-McGee, and Jensen, *Journals*, 1:68.

14. Jessee, Ashurst-McGee, and Jensen, *Journals*, 1:71.

15. Jessee, Ashurst-McGee, and Jensen, *Journals*, 1:72.

16. Jessee, Ashurst-McGee, and Jensen, *Journals*, 1:77, 79.

17. Jessee, Ashurst-McGee, and Jensen, *Journals*, 1:83–84.

18. Jessee, Ashurst-McGee, and Jensen, *Journals*, 1:88, 95.

19. Jessee, Ashurst-McGee, and Jensen, *Journals*, 1:113.

20. Jessee, Ashurst-McGee, and Jensen, *Journals*, 1:120–21.

21. Jessee, Ashurst-McGee, and Jensen, *Journals*, 1:124.

22. Jessee, Ashurst-McGee, and Jensen, *Journals*, 1:134.

23. Jessee, Ashurst-McGee, and Jensen, *Journals*, 1:140.

24. Jessee, Ashurst-McGee, and Jensen, *Journals*, 1:140.

25. "Government of the Church of Christ" appears on the title page of the Book of Commandments (Zion [Independence, MO]: W. W. Phelps and Co., 1833).

26. *Painesville [OH] Telegraph*, December 7, 1830.

27. Milton V. Backman Jr., *The Heavens Resound: A History of the Latter-day Saints in Ohio, 1830–1838* (Salt Lake City: Deseret Book, 1983), 42.

28. Edward Partridge Papers, 1839, as quoted in Backman, *Heavens Resound*, 16.

29. Boyd K. Packer, "The Twelve Apostles," *Ensign*, November 1996, 6.

30. For an accessible review of Catholic and Protestant perspectives, see Peter W. Williams, *America's Religions: From Their Origins to the Twenty-first Century* (Urbana: University of Illinois Press, 2002), 64–99.

31. For early American churches and their theologies, see Edwin S. Gaustad and Philip L. Barlow, *New Historical Atlas of Religion in America* (New York: Oxford University Press, 2001); E. Brooks Holifield, *Theology in America: Christian Thought from the Age of the Puritans to the Civil War* (New Haven, CT: Yale University Press, 2003).

32. For a prominent example, see Grant Underwood, "'Saved or Damned': Tracing a Persistent Protestantism in Early Mormon Thought," *BYU Studies* 25, no. 3 (Summer 1985): 85–103.

33. See Prince, *Power from On High*, 47–78.

34. See Brian Q. Cannon, "Priesthood Restoration Documents," *BYU Studies* 35, no. 4 (1996): 162–73.

35. Brigham Young, in *Journal of Discourses* (London: Latter-day Saints' Book Depot, 1854–86), 6:320.

36. Heber C. Kimball, in *Journal of Discourses*, 7:231.

37. Bushman, *Rough Stone Rolling*, 251–69.

38. See Bushman, *Rough Stone Rolling*, 156–60; Prince, *Power from On High*, 15–21.

39. When they were making preparations for the organization of the Church, in fact, Oliver Cowdery received a revelation never included in the Doctrine and Covenants (probably because it functioned as something of a forerunner to Doctrine and Covenants 20). In it, various Book of Mormon passages describing Church offices were emphasized. Oliver had earlier been instructed to "rely on that which is written" in his efforts to "build up my church" (Doctrine and Covenants 18:3). See Scott H. Faulring, "An Examination of the 1829 'Articles of the Church of Christ' in Relation to Section 20 of the Doctrine and Covenants," in John W. Welch and Larry Morris, eds., *Oliver Cowdery: Scribe, Elder, Witness* (Provo, UT: Neal A. Maxwell Institute for Religious Scholarship, Brigham Young University, 2006), 155–93.

40. See Mosiah 23:16–17, Alma 13.

41. Prince, *Power from On High*, 22; Doctrine and Covenants 81, 107.

42. See Irene M. Bates and E. Gary Smith, *Lost Legacy: The Mormon Office of Presiding Patriarch* (Urbana: University of Illinois Press, 1996).

43. John Corrill, *A Brief History of the Church of Christ of Latter Day Saints, (Commonly Called Mormons)* (St. Louis: Printed for the Author, 1839), 47.

44. See Kathleen Flake, "From Conferences to Councils: The Development of LDS Church Organization, 1830–1835," in *Archive*

of Restoration Culture: Summer Fellows' Papers, 1997–1999 (Provo, UT: Joseph Fielding Smith Institute of Latter-day Saint History, 2000), 1–8; David Holland, "Priest, Pastor, and Power: Joseph Smith and the Question of Priesthood," in *Archive of Restoration Culture: Summer Fellows' Papers, 1997–1999* (Provo, UT: Joseph Fielding Smith Institute of Latter-day Saint History, 2000), 9–16.

45. Flake, "From Conferences to Councils," 2.

46. Bushman, *Rough Stone Rolling*, 153. See also Richard L. Bushman, *Mormonism: A Very Short Introduction* (New York: Oxford University Press, 2008), 49–63.

47. See Jason Lindquist, "'Unlocking the Door of the Gospel': The Concept of 'Keys' in Mormonism and Early American Culture," in *Archive of Restoration Culture: Summer Fellows' Papers, 1997–1999* (Provo, UT: Joseph Fielding Smith Institute of Latter-day Saint History, 2000), 29–41.

48. D. Michael Quinn, *The Mormon Heirarchy: Origins of Power* (Salt Lake City: Signature Books, in association with Smith Research Associates, 1994), 44–45.

49. See Alan K. Parrish, "Seventy: Overview," and Richard G. Roberts, "First Council of the Seventy," *Encyclopedia of Mormonism*, ed. Daniel H. Ludlow (New York: Macmillan, 1992), 3:1300–3.

50. *Preach My Gospel: A Guide to Missionary Service* (Salt Lake City: The Church of Jesus Christ of Latter-day Saints, 2004), 83; see also Boyd K. Packer, "The Aaronic Priesthood," *Ensign*, November 1981, 30: "Your authority comes through your ordination; your power comes through obedience and worthiness."

51. Bushman, *Rough Stone Rolling*, 203.

52. Bushman, *Rough Stone Rolling*, 156–60.

53. Donald Q. Cannon and Lyndon W. Cook, eds., *Far West Record: Minutes of The Church of Jesus Christ of Latter-day Saints, 1830–1844* (Salt Lake City: Deseret Book, 1983), 20–21.

54. See Prince, *Power from On High*, 20, 155–65.

55. Oliver Cowdery to John F. Boynton, May 6, 1834, in Oliver Cowdery letterbook, Huntington Library, 45–46, as quoted in Prince, *Power from On High*, 32.

56. Jessee, Ashurst-McGee, and Jensen, *Journals*, 1:216.

57. *The Words of Joseph Smith: The Contemporary Accounts of the Nauvoo Discourses of the Prophet Joseph*, ed. Andrew F. Ehat and Lyndon W. Cook (Provo, UT: Religious Studies Center, Brigham Young University, 1980), 119–20.

58. See Prince, *Power from On High*, 166, 187–91.

59. *An Intimate Chronicle: The Journals of William Clayton*, ed. George D. Smith (Salt Lake City: Signature Books and Smith Research Associates, 1995), 102.

60. This last sense of sealing (that is, the sealing of husbands to wives) appeared for the first time explicitly in January 1844 in the journal of Wilford Woodruff (Prince, *Power from On High*, 167–68).

61. *An Intimate Chronicle*, 115–16.

62. Wilford Woodruff Journal, March 10, 1844, as cited in Prince, *Power from On High*, 170.

63. Bushman writes, "The priesthood doctrines opened a ritual world that Protestantism, with its emphasis on preaching, had closed off" (*Rough Stone Rolling*, 205).

64. Charles H. Gabriel, "I Stand All Amazed," *Hymns* (Salt Lake City: The Church of Jesus Christ of Latter-day Saints, 1985), no. 193.

Kirtland Temple, Kirtland, Ohio. In one sense, Moroni enlisted the seventeen-year-old seer to save the world when he told young Joseph that he had a role in fulfilling ancient prophecy, adding that "if it were not so, the whole earth would be utterly wasted." (George Edward Anderson, August 1907, Church History Library, image digitally enhanced.)

STEVEN C. HARPER

1836
Joseph Smith and the Kirtland Temple

The story of the Kirtland Temple began in Joseph Smith's bedroom. "When I was about 17 years," Joseph said, "I had another vision of angels; in the night season, after I had retired to bed; I had not been asleep, but was meditating on my past life and experience. I was well aware I had not kept the commandments, and I repented heartily for all my sins and transgressions, and humbled myself before him, whose eye surveys all things at a glance. All at once the room was illuminated above the brightness of the sun; An angel appeared before me."

"I am a Messenger sent from God," he told Joseph, introducing himself as Moroni. He said that God had vital work for Joseph to do. There was a sacred book written

---

Steven C. Harper is an associate professor of Church history and doctrine at Brigham Young University and an editor of The Joseph Smith Papers.

on golden plates and buried in a nearby hillside. "He explained many of the prophecies to me," Joseph said, including "Malachi 4th chapter." Moroni appeared three times that night and twice the next day, emphasizing and expounding the same message. There was something vital in that prophecy—something Joseph needed to know.[1]

When Joseph wrote his history beginning in 1838, he captured the words Moroni spoke, noting the "little variation from the way it reads in our Bibles." Moroni "quoted the fifth verse [of Malachi 4] thus, 'Behold I will reveal unto you the Priesthood by the hand of Elijah the prophet before the coming of the great and dreadful day of the Lord.' He also quoted the next verse differently. 'And he shall plant in the hearts of the children the promises made to their fathers, and the hearts of the children shall turn to their fathers, if it were not so the whole earth would be utterly wasted at his coming.'"[2]

The angel's words obviously made a deep impression on the teenage seer. Whether he understood all the words that night is not clear, but they remained in his mind and heart until he witnessed their fulfillment and comprehended them well. Malachi foretold that Elijah, the Old Testament prophet, would return to the earth on a mission to turn the hearts of the first Israelites with whom God made covenants to the hearts of their descendants, to whom Malachi wrote. The prophecy was vague. All a Bible reader could tell is that the Lord would send Elijah sometime before the Second Coming—but to do what? Moroni made the prophecy directly relevant to Joseph, specifying that Elijah would reveal priesthood that would plant the same promises God made to the patriarchs deep in the hearts of their covenant-keeping descendants.

Young Joseph had only sought forgiveness of personal sins, but here was an angel telling him that he had a role in fulfilling ancient prophecy, adding that "if it were not so, the whole earth would be utterly wasted" (Doctrine and Covenants 2:3). Nearly thirteen years passed before Elijah fulfilled the prophecy by bringing Joseph the priesthood keys needed to seal families. Meanwhile, Moroni prepared Joseph to receive and use those keys. Joseph's role was to use them—and enable others to use them—to give every willing soul, living and dead, full access to the Atonement of Jesus Christ. He was to assist the Savior in offering eternal life. Elder Russell M. Nelson taught that "eternal life, made possible by the Atonement, is the supreme purpose of Creation. To phrase that statement in its negative form, if families were not sealed in holy temples, the whole earth would be utterly wasted."[3] So, in one sense, Moroni enlisted the seventeen-year-old seer to save the world.

The Temple Revelation

Joseph subsequently translated the Book of Mormon, received the holy priesthood, restored the Church of Jesus Christ, and obeyed a revealed command to gather all who were willing to Ohio. There, in December 1832, he assembled nine high priests in his translating room and taught them that "to receive revelation and the blessing of Heaven, it was necessary to have our minds on God and exercise faith and become of one heart and one mind." He asked them each to pray in turn that the Lord would "reveal His will to us concerning the upbuilding of Zion and for the benefit of the saints and for the duty ... of the elders." Each man "bowed down before the Lord, after which each one arose and spoke in his turn his feelings and determination to keep the commandments of God."[4]

The revelation known as Doctrine and Covenants section 88 began to flow, and by nine o'clock that night it had not ended. The brethren retired but returned the next morning and received more revelation.[5] Samuel Smith, Joseph's younger brother and one of those present, wrote briefly about the experience. He did not like to write, and what he chose to put down tells us what he thought was important about the revelation. Like Joseph, he focused on what the Lord told him to do. "Some of the elders assembled together," Samuel wrote, "& the word of the Lord was given through Joseph & the Lord declared that those Elders who were the first labourers in this last vineyard should assemble themselves together that they should call a solemn assembly & evry man call upon the name of the Lord & continue in Prayre that they should Sanctify themselves & wash their hands and feet for a testimony that their garments were clean from the Blood of all men & the Lord commanded we the first Elders to Establish a School & appoint a teacher among them & get learning by study & by faith."[6]

Section 88 is a thoroughly temple-oriented revelation. Beginning with a promise of eternal life through Jesus Christ to the faithful, the revelation describes the purposeful creation of the earth and then tells how to obey divine law to advance by degrees of light or glory through a perfect resurrection and into the presence of God.[7]

Section 88 is expansive. It maps the universe. Its concepts stretch the mind, inviting inquiry and awe. "Truth shineth," it says, introducing a string of related if not synonymous concepts that include *truth, light, power, life, spirit,* and even *law* (see vv. 7–15). The concepts in section 88 pervade other temple texts. Methodist scholar Margaret Barker wrote that in such texts, "light and life ... are linked and set in opposition to darkness and death. The presence of God is light; coming into the presence of God transforms whatever is dead and gives it life."[8]

The word "therefore" in verse 117 marks the beginning of the Lord's final point in the initial two-day revelation (see

vv. 117–26). This concluding segment reviews the revelation's instructions in what one might call the "therefore what?" It is a temple preparation text. The "therefore what" of the whole revelation is "therefore, sanctify yourselves that your minds become single to God, and the days will come that you shall see him" (Doctrine and Covenants 88:68).

In response to section 88's command for the Saints to build a house of God, call a solemn assembly in it, and present themselves there sanctified in order to enter the Lord's presence, the Saints were obedient. They built the Kirtland Temple, the first in this last dispensation, and entered, both symbolically and literally, into the presence of the Lord.

Preparing to Enter the Lord's Presence

But the process was not easy or cheap; ultimate blessings never are. Joseph struggled to help the Saints understand what section 88 called the great and last promise. It was a promise of entering the Lord's presence based on the conditions that they would build a temple, convene a solemn assembly in it, and sanctify their lives in the process. A few days after section 88 was completed, Joseph sent a copy of it with a rebuke to Church leaders in Missouri. Hard feelings continued to fester there, and the Missouri Saints had not acted on section 84's earlier command to build a temple in Zion. "I send you the . . . Lord's message of peace to us," Joseph wrote, "for though our Brethren in Zion, indulge in feelings towards us, which are not according to the requirements of the new covenant yet we have the satisfaction of knowing that the Lord approves of us & has accepted us, & established his name in kirtland for the salvation of the nations, for the Lord will have a place from whence his word will go forth in these last days in purity, for if Zion, will not purify herself so as to be approved of in all things in his sight he will seek another people for his work will go on untill Isreal is gathered & they who will not hear his voice must expect to feel his wrath."⁹

Joseph drew on section 84 to remind the Missouri Saints that, like the children of Israel, they were in danger of losing their temple blessings. "Seek to purefy yourselves, & also all the inhabitants of Zion," he wrote, "lest the Lords anger be kindled to fierceness, repent, repent, is the voice of God, to Zion, & yet strange as it may appear, yet it is true mankind will presist in self Justification until all their eniquity is exposed & their character past being redeemed, & that which is treasured up in their hearts be exposed to the gaze of mankind, I say to you (& what I say to you, I say to all) hear the <warning> voice of God lest Zion fall, & the Lord swear in his wrath the inhabitants of Zion shall not enter into my rest."¹⁰

Joseph assured the Saints in Zion that "the Brethren in Kirtland pray for you unceasingly, for knowing the terrors of the Lord, they greatly fear for you." Referring to the copy of section 88 he had sent, Joseph suggested that the Lord, frustrated with disobedience in Zion, had also commanded the Saints in Kirtland to build a temple. "You will see," Joseph wrote, "that the Lord commanded us in Kirtland to build an house of God, & establish a school for the Prophets, this is the word of the Lord to us, & we must yea the Lord helping us we will obey, as on conditions of our obedience, he has promised <us> great things, yea <even> a visit from the heavens to honor us with his own presence."¹¹

Joseph had learned from section 84 that the only way into the presence of God was through the temple. Nothing should therefore be more important. Yet, like Moses, he worried that Latter-day Saints would harden their hearts and provoke the Lord's wrath (see Doctrine and Covenants 84:24). "We greatly fear before the Lord lest we should fail of this great honor which our master proposes to confer on us," Joseph said. "We are seeking for humility & great faith lest we be ashamed in his presence." He concluded his letter to the Missouri Saints by saying that "if the fountain of our tears are not dried up we will <still> weep for Zion, this from your brother who trembles greatly for Zion, and for the wrath of heaven which awaits her if she repent not."[12]

Joseph worked hard to get the Saints to see the importance of the momentous revelation and to understand the temple and ultimate blessings. Like Moses, he wanted to usher his sometimes shortsighted people into the presence of the Lord (see Doctrine and Covenants 84). The temple revelations preoccupied Joseph's attention. He wanted their promised blessings, and he worked to explain them to the Saints. Joseph was driven by section 88's command to build a temple and by the promise that the Lord would honor them with his presence (see Doctrine and Covenants 88:68). He urged the Saints forward, at enormous sacrifice, to build the house of the Lord in Kirtland. Joseph established schools and convened priesthood meetings to train and motivate the brethren because the promise that the Savior would "visit from the heavens" was predicated not only on building the temple but on his command to "sanctify yourselves" (Doctrine and Covenants 88:68).[13]

The Saints in Kirtland began building the house of the Lord in the summer of 1833 and, after some interruptions and a rebuke (see section 95), they dedicated it in 1836. Joseph, meanwhile, instructed the Saints to purify and prepare themselves for an outpouring of the Lord's power—an endowment. In November 1835 he met with the newly called Apostles. He confessed his own shortcomings and then taught them section 88, or, as he called it, "how to prepare your selves for the great things that God is about to bring to pass."[14]

Joseph told them he had assumed the Church was fully organized, but then the Lord had taught him more, including "the ordinance of the washing of feet" mentioned in section 88:139. "This we have not done as yet," Joseph taught the Apostles, "but it is necessary now as much as it was in the days of the Saviour, and we must have a place prepared, that we may attend to this ordinance, aside from the world." He continued to emphasize the need for the temple:

> We must have all things prepared and call our solem assembly as the Lord has commanded us [see Doctrine and Covenants 88:70], that we may be able to accomplish his great work: and it mu[s]t be done in Gods own way, the house of the Lord must be prepared, and the solem assembly called and organized in it according to the order of the house of God and in it we must attend to the ordinance of washing of feet; it was never intended for any but official members, it is calculated to unite our hearts, that we may be one in feeling and sentiment and that our faith may be strong, so that satan cannot over throw us, nor have any power over us,—the endowment you are so anxious about you cannot comprehend now, nor could Gabriel explain it to the understanding of your dark minds, but strive to be prepared in your hearts, be faithful in all things that when we meet in the solem assembly that is such as God shall name out of all the official members, will meet, and we must be clean evry whit.[15]

Echoing section 88:123–26, Joseph urged the brethren:

Do not watch for iniquity in each other if you do you will not get an endowment for God will not bestow it on such; but if we are faithful and live by every word that procedes forth from the mouth of God I will venture to prophesy that we shall get a blessing that will be worth remembering if we should live as long as John the Revelator, our blessings will be such as we have not realized before, nor in this generation. The order of the house of God has and ever will be the same, even after Christ comes, and after the termination of the thousand years it will be the same, and we shall finally roll into the celestial Kingdom of God and enjoy it forever [see Doctrine and Covenants 88:96–117]:—you need an endowment brethren in order that you may be prepared and able to over come all things.[16]

Joseph helped them understand the relationship between the power with which God intended to endow them and their calling to preach the gospel (see Doctrine and Covenants 88:80–82). Then he concluded his teaching by reaffirming what section 88 twice calls the "great and last promise": "I feel disposed to speak a few words more to you, my brethren, concerning the endowment. All who are prepared and are sufficiently pure to abide the presence of the Savior will see Him in the solemn assembly" (Doctrine and Covenants 88:69, 75).[17] William Phelps wrote to his wife in Missouri about what he was learning from Joseph. "Our meeting[s] will grow more and more solemn, and will continue till the great solemn assembly when the house is finished! We are preparing to make ourselves clean, by first cleansing our hearts, forsaking our sins, forgiving every body; putting on clean decent clothes, by anointing our heads and by keeping all the commandments. As we come nearer to God we see our imperfections and nothingness plainer and plainer."[18] Oliver Cowdery gave even more detail about one of these temple preparation meetings, noting how the Latter-day Saints followed Old Testament patterns in washing and anointing priests for temple service. Oliver wrote that he met with Joseph and others at the Prophet's house. "And after pure water was prepared, called upon the Lord and proceeded to wash each other's bodies, and bathe the same with whiskey, perfumed with cinnamon. This we did that we might be clean before the Lord for the Sabbath, confessing our sins and covenanting to be faithful to God. While performing this washing with solemnity, our minds were filled with many reflections upon the propriety of the same, and how the priests anciently used to wash always before ministering before the Lord."[19]

Redemption of the Dead

When the house of the Lord (as the early Saints called the Kirtland Temple) was nearing completion Joseph convened the preparation meetings in the rooms of its third-floor garret on the evening of January 21, 1836. There, in the westernmost room, Joseph met with his secretary, other members of the First Presidency, his father (the Church's patriarch), and the bishoprics from Missouri and Ohio. The brethren came to the meeting freshly bathed, symbolizing their efforts to repent and present themselves sanctified before the Lord. The First Presidency consecrated oil, then anointed and blessed Father Smith, who in turn anointed and blessed Joseph. Then the heavens opened. Oliver Cowdery wrote that "the glorious scene is too great to be described.... I only say, that the heavens were opened to many, and great and marvelous things were shown." Bishop Edward Partridge affirmed that some of the brethren "saw visions & others were blessed with the outpouring of the Holy Ghost."[20] Joseph was the only one present who described in detail some of what he experienced.

Doctrine and Covenants section 137 derives from his journal, where Joseph described his vision of the future celestial kingdom. There he saw his oldest brother, Alvin, who had died painfully in 1823, shortly after Moroni appeared to Joseph and taught him of the Book of Mormon plates. Nearly twenty years later, Joseph dictated an entry in the Book of the Law of the Lord, the blessing and record book he kept near the end of his life. "I remember well the pangs of sorrow that swelled my youthful bosom and almost burst my tender heart, when he died," Joseph said of Alvin. "He was the oldest, and the noblest of my fathers family. He was one of the noblest of the sons of men."[21] Even so, at Alvin's funeral his mother's minister, Reverend Benjamin Stockton, "intimated very strongly that he had gone to hell, for Alvin was not a Church member." Joseph's father "did not like it."[22] Father Smith recognized what theologians call the "soteriological problem of evil," meaning a dilemma between doctrines of salvation.[23] The problem seems to arise from three truths, any two of which can work together but not all three:

1. God desires the salvation of his children.
2. Salvation comes only through one's acceptance of Christ's Atonement.
3. Many, many of God's children have lived and died without an opportunity to accept Christ's Atonement.

The Book of Mormon clarified that unaccountable infants would not be damned, but it said nothing of accountable adults who died before accepting the gospel. Joseph received the priesthood, restored the Church, worked to establish Zion, and built the house of the Lord. But for all Joseph knew, Reverend Stockton had been right. Not until the temple was nearly finished did the Lord refute the reverend's doctrine. Then he did so beautifully in the vision recorded for us in Doctrine and

Covenants section 137. The point of that revelation is to resolve the soteriological problem of evil, which it does in verses 7–10. But before revealing the answer, the Lord showed Joseph a vision that begged the question. Joseph envisioned the flaming gate to the celestial world, the golden streets, and the Father and the Son on their blazing throne. He saw Adam and Abraham. And he saw Alvin and his parents there, too. He "marveled" at Alvin's appearance, since he had not been baptized before his death (Doctrine and Covenants 137:6).

The Lord spoke the answer not just for Alvin but for "all who have died without a knowledge of this gospel, who would have received it if they had been permitted to tarry" (v. 7). They will inherit celestial glory. Indeed, anyone who dies without knowing the gospel but who would have received it otherwise, will receive it. The emphatic point is that death is not a deadline that determines salvation, "for I, the Lord, will judge all men according to their works, according to the desire of their hearts" (v. 9). Desire—not the timing of one's death—is the determinant of salvation through Christ.

Some of the greatest theological minds have wrestled with the soteriological problem of evil. Early Christians believed that the Lord had planned a "rescue for the dead," as one scholar called it.[24] Put simply, early Christians baptized each other for their kindred dead, as the Apostle Paul noted at 1 Corinthians 15:29 and Hugh Nibley demonstrated.[25] Later Christian philosophers recognized the problem and believed that Christ would somehow save all the righteous, but already they had lost the significance of truths Peter and Paul taught, leaving no certain answer to the question, "Shall those be wholly deprived of the kingdom of heaven who died before Christ's coming?"[26] Then later, largely influenced by Augustine, Christianity apostatized generally from the doctrine of redemption for the dead, giving rise to the soteriological problem.

By the eighteenth century, the Puritan theologian Jonathan Edwards longed to find a solution. One contemporary Evangelical scholar finds in Edwards the seeds of a "dispositional soteriology," or a doctrine of salvation that only requires one's disposition to be redeemed by God through Christ. It does not require one to knowingly accept the Savior.[27] But such a solution negates agency and Bible passages to the contrary. The question persists, what about those who never heard? The revealed answer is not to subtract from the three known truths but to add one that makes them all compatible and whole rather than problematic. That truth is found in verses 8–9 of section 137: all who have died or will die without knowledge of the gospel who would otherwise have received it, will receive it according to their desires and thus inherit the celestial kingdom. "Thank God for Joseph Smith!" wrote Latter-day Saint philosopher David L. Paulsen, who knows full well the problem and therefore appreciates the profound solution. His gratitude for Joseph is "not merely for being God's conduit in resolving one more thorny problem of evil, but for being the instrument through whom God restored the knowledge and priesthood powers that make the redemption of the dead possible."[28]

Later, in Nauvoo, Joseph revealed the ordinance of baptism for the dead that enables all humankind to make and keep gospel covenants (see sections 127–28). Joseph taught the doctrine to his father on his deathbed. In contrast to his reaction to Reverend Stockton's sermon, Father Smith "was delighted to hear" the truth and asked Joseph to attend to the ordinance. Joseph and Hyrum fulfilled their father's dying wish. "I see Alvin," Father Smith said just a few minutes before his passing.²⁹ Prophetically, section 137 solved a persistent problem faced by Joseph's family and many, many others.

The Temple Dedication

Meanwhile, in March 1836 the Saints put finishing touches on the house of the Lord in Kirtland and prepared to assemble in it solemnly as section 88 had commanded them more than three years earlier (see Doctrine and Covenants 88:70, 117). Joseph spent the day before the solemn assembly making final arrangements with his counselors and secretaries.³⁰ Oliver Cowdery's diary tells us that he assisted Joseph "in writing a prayer for the dedication of the house."³¹ The next morning the house of the Lord filled to capacity with nearly a thousand Saints. An overflow meeting convened next door. The solemn assembly began at nine with scripture readings, choir singing, prayer, a sermon, and the sustaining of Joseph Smith as prophet and seer. In the afternoon session the sustaining continued, with each quorum and the general body of the Church sustaining, in turn, the leaders of the Church.³² Another hymn followed, "after which," Joseph's journal says, "I offered to God the . . . dedication prayer."³³

That prayer is preserved for us in Doctrine and Covenants section 109. It is an inspired prayer. It begins with thanks to God, then makes requests of him in the name of Jesus Christ. It is based heavily on section 88's temple instructions as well as other temple-related scriptural texts. It "sums up the Church's concerns in 1836, bringing before God each major project."³⁴ It is a temple prayer.

What does one pray for in such settings? Joseph began by asking God to accept the temple on the terms he had given in section 88 and the Saints had tried to fulfill in order to obtain the promised blessing of entering the Lord's presence (see

Doctrine and Covenants 88:68; 109:4–12). Joseph prayed that all who worshipped in the temple would be endowed with God's power, that they would be taught by God "that they may grow up in thee, and receive a fulness of the Holy Ghost, and be organized according to thy laws, and be prepared to obtain every needful thing" (Doctrine and Covenants 109:15). Joseph prayed, in other words, a temple prayer that the Saints would become like their Heavenly Father by degrees of glory as they obeyed his laws and prepared to enter his presence. He prayed for what section 88 taught him to pray for.

Joseph prayed that the Saints, "armed" or endowed with priesthood power from the temple, could go to "the ends of the earth" with the "exceedingly great and glorious tidings" of the gospel to fulfill prophecies (vv. 22–23). He asked Heavenly Father to protect the Saints from their enemies (see vv. 24–33). He asked for mercy upon the Saints and to seal the anointing ordinances that many of the priesthood brethren had received in the weeks leading up to the solemn assembly. He asked for the gifts of the Spirit to be poured out as on the biblical day of Pentecost (see Acts 2:2–3). He asked the Lord to protect and empower the missionaries and postpone judgment until they had gathered the righteous. He prayed that God's will would be done "and not ours" (Doctrine and Covenants 109:44).

Joseph prayed that the Saints would be delivered from the prophesied calamities. He asked Heavenly Father to remember the Saints who had been oppressed and driven from Jackson County, Missouri, and he prayed for their deliverance. He asked how long their afflictions would continue until avenged (see v. 49). He asked for mercy "upon the wicked mob, who have driven thy people, that they may cease to spoil, that they may repent of their sins if repentance is to be found" (v. 50). Joseph prayed for Zion.

Joseph prayed for mercy on all nations and political leaders, so that the principles of individual agency captured in the United States Constitution would be established forever. He prayed for "all the poor, the needy, and afflicted ones of the earth" (v. 55). He prayed for an end to prejudices so that the missionaries "may gather out the righteous to build a holy city to thy name, as thou hast commanded them" (v. 58). He asked for more stakes to facilitate the gathering and growth of Zion. He asked for mercy for the scattered remnants of Jacob and for the Jews. Indeed, he prayed for "all the scattered remnants of Israel, who have been driven to the ends of the earth, [to] come to a knowledge of the truth, believe in the Messiah, and be redeemed from oppression" (v. 67).

Joseph prayed for himself, reminding the Lord of his sincere effort to keep his covenants. He asked for mercy upon his family, praying that Emma and the children "may be exalted in thy presence" (v. 69). This is the first usage of "exalted" in Joseph's revelations to refer to the fulness of salvation through temple blessings.[35] Joseph prayed for his in-laws to be converted. He prayed for the others in the First Presidency and their families. He prayed for all the Saints and their families and their sick and afflicted. He prayed, again, for "all the poor and meek of the earth," and for the glorious kingdom of God to fill the earth as prophesied (see vv. 68–74).

Joseph prayed that the Saints would rise in the First Resurrection with pure garments, "robes of righteousness," and "crowns of glory upon our heads" to "reap eternal joy" (v. 76). Thrice repeating his petition, Joseph asked the Lord to "hear us" and accept the prayers and petitions and offerings of the Saints in building the house to his name (v. 78). He prayed for grace to enable the Saints to join the choirs surrounding God's throne in the heavenly temple "singing Hosanna to God and the Lamb" (v. 79). Joseph concluded the prayer, "And let these, thine anointed ones, be clothed with salvation, and thy saints shout aloud for joy. Amen, and Amen" (v. 80).

Joseph's prayer dedicated the first house of the Lord in the last dispensation and set the pattern for all subsequent solemn assemblies met for the same holy purposes. It teaches the Saints how to pray, including what to pray for, and to ask according to the will of God. It teaches the doctrine and evokes the imagery of the temple, perhaps most poignantly in the idea that temple worshippers can "grow up" by degrees of glory until they become like their Heavenly Father (compare section 93). This is what it means to be exalted in God's presence. The temple revelations call this "fulness," including fulness of joy. The prayer continues the expansive work of the temple revelations in sections 76, 84, 88, and 93 and points us forward to the culminating revelation on exaltation, section 132:1–20. Joseph's temple prayer invites mortals, who occupy a polluted telestial planet where they cannot think of more than one thing at a time and generally only in finite terms, to receive power that will enable them to journey to the real world where God lives "enthroned, with glory, honor, power, majesty, might, dominion, truth, justice, judgment, mercy, and an infinity of fulness, from everlasting to everlasting" (v. 77).[36]

Keys

A week after he dedicated the house of the Lord in Kirtland, Joseph attended meetings there, including an afternoon sacrament meeting. For Christians it was Easter Sunday, while Jews were celebrating the Passover season.[37] After sacrament, Joseph and Oliver Cowdery retreated behind the heavy curtains used to divide the room. They bowed in what Joseph's journal describes as "solemn, but silent prayer to the Most High," noting that "after rising from prayer [a] vision was opened to both of them."[38]

The Lord unveiled the minds of his seers, who envisioned and heard the Lord standing before them. Three times, in a voice like rushing water, he declared, "I am," evoking Old Testament revelations in which he repeatedly identified himself saying, "I am the Lord your God" (see Exodus 20 and Leviticus 19). This is a play on the related words of the Hebrew verb for *to be* and the name transliterated in English as *Jehovah*. It is the Lord Jesus Christ declaring that he is the God who told Moses to tell the Israelites that "I AM hath sent me unto you" (Exodus 3:14). It is Jesus of Nazareth testifying that he is the God of Israel, the promised Messiah, and proclaiming it in this dispensation in a building that still exists.

In a powerful juxtaposition of present and past verb tenses, the Savior declared himself the crucified Christ who conquered death: "I am he who liveth. I am he who was slain; I am your advocate with the Father" (Doctrine and Covenants 110:4). He forgave Joseph and Oliver, pronounced them clean, and commanded them and those who had built the temple to rejoice. He accepted the temple and made conditional promises to manifest himself to his people there, prophesying that tens of thousands would rejoice in the endowment poured out on his servants in the house of the Lord as its fame spread to foreign lands.

The Lord disappeared, and Moses appeared and committed keys for gathering Israel from all the earth, the permission to lead the lost tribes of Israel from their scattered locations. Next Elias appeared and dispensed the gospel of Abraham, "saying that in us and our seed all generations after us should be blessed" (v. 12). Another glorious vision followed as Elijah, who went to heaven without tasting death, appeared and said that it was time to fulfill Malachi's prophecy that Elijah would turn the hearts of the fathers to their children and vice versa before the dreadful day of the Lord. The vision closed with a heavenly announcement that Joseph now held the keys of the last dispensation. He had received the priesthood several years earlier. What he had now was permission to put it to work in new ways—including sealing families, officiating in temple ordinances, and sending missionaries globally.

The glorious vision, recorded for us in Doctrine and Covenants section 110, fulfilled the Lord's conditional promise to the Saints in section 38 that if they would move to Ohio and build him a holy house, he would endow them with power in it (see sections 38, 88, 95). It fulfilled section 88's great and last promise that the sanctified would come into the presence of the Lord.[39] Finally, it fulfilled Malachi's multilayered prophecy. Through Malachi the Lord prophesied, "I will send you Elijah the prophet before the coming of the great and dreadful day of the Lord" (Malachi 4:5). Moroni reiterated that prophecy to Joseph Smith in 1823 (see Doctrine and Covenants 2). Elijah fulfilled it less than thirteen years later. Jews had long awaited Elijah's prophesied return and still invite him into their homes during the Passover Seder. During the very season that some Jews were celebrating the sacred meal with the hope that Elijah would return, he came to the house of the Lord.[40]

Moses's appearance is just as significant. "His appearance in company with Elijah offers another striking parallel between Mormon teachings and Jewish tradition, according to which Moses and Elijah would arrive together at the 'end of time.'"[41] Joseph and Oliver's vision reenacts the endowment received in the biblical account of the Mount of Transfiguration (see Matthew 17:1–9).

Few texts weld dispensations as thoroughly as this revelation. Given on Easter and during the Passover season, the revelation links Israel's Old Testament deliverance with Christ's New Testament resurrection and affirms that Joseph Smith and the temple-building Latter-day Saints are the heirs of God's promises to the Israelite patriarchs. Christ is the Passover lamb who "was slain" and then resurrected and now appears to Joseph in Kirtland to approve of the latter-day work and commission the Prophet to fulfill the work of Moses (the gathering of Israel), Elias (the gospel of Abraham), and Elijah (the sealing of families).

Joseph put these priesthood keys to use against great opposition. Not long after receiving the keys to gather Israel from Moses, Joseph found Heber C. Kimball in the temple and whispered in his ear a mission call to Great Britain. Joseph had previously sent missionaries on short local or regional missions. Heber and his companions began the ongoing process of gathering Israel from the ends of the earth. Though oppressed by what seems like a concerted opposition that included financial collapse, widespread apostasy, an executive order driving the Saints from Missouri, and then unjust imprisonment in Liberty, Missouri, Joseph began to teach and administer the ordinances of the temple. In sum, the endowment of priesthood keys he received authorized him to begin performing temple ordinances.

The vision recorded in section 110 communicated temple knowledge and power. It came in the temple behind a veil, was recorded but not preached, and was acted on but not publicly explained.[42] After the revelation, Joseph used the keys to gather, endow, and seal in anticipation of the Savior's Second Coming. Section 110 marks the restoration of temple-related power and knowledge that Moses possessed and "plainly taught," but which had been forfeited by the children of Israel (see Doctrine and Covenants 84:19–25).

"So Great a Cause"

Imagine for a moment being Joseph Smith. Imagine that you are a seventeen-year-old seer. You know that God lives and Jesus is the very Christ, that they love you and have promised to provide you further knowledge in due time. But you don't have any idea about temples, salvation for the dead, or the prophecies of Isaiah, Joel, and Malachi. You do not have the first hint that Malachi's prophecy of Elijah's return will intimately involve you. You're worried about simple, sincere things: your own teenage sins, the religious divisions in your family, and your uncertain future. You pray for personal forgiveness, and an angel greets you with a staggering learning curve and a call to assist in saving the world.

Now you are twenty-seven years old. You have just received one of the most sublime revelations on record, including a command to build a house for the Lord and assemble your followers in it, solemn and sanctified (see Doctrine and Covenants 88). You have your own weaknesses and sins to wrestle with in addition to the shortcomings of a sincere but fallen body of Latter-day Saints. You do everything in your power to explain the imperative need they have for the power that only flows through the temple and the Savior's promise to reveal himself if you will build him a house and sanctify your lives. Try as you might, the Saints are slow to grasp the magnitude of what you alone seem to sense. You keep trying. You quarry rock. You get the Saints to see as you see, to sacrifice as you sacrifice, and to be sanctified as you are sanctified through service. You rebuke them. You receive rebukes. You wash, anoint, and bless them. You wash their feet. You have an indomitable will. You raise the house of the Lord upward until it is finished. And then you call the solemn assembly as you were commanded. You do exactly as you were commanded to do, and then you report on your mission. You kneel in solemn prayer and anticipate the promised blessings. You expect the Lord to unveil himself, to appear in his holy house. And he does. He forgives your sins. Perhaps you remember your prayer for just such a blessing as a seventeen-year-old.

You are thirty years old. Moses, Elias, and Elijah have committed into your hands the keys of the last dispensation. You now have all the power and permission you need to gather Israel, endow them with power, and seal them together before the Lord's imminent coming. All hell seems to break loose. Intense opposition stalks you. The "envy and wrath of man" are your lot all the days of your life (Doctrine and Covenants 127:2). Your best efforts to deliver your people financially result in bankruptcy. You receive a revelation warning you and your faithful friends to flee Kirtland and the house of the Lord. You arrive in Missouri only to have an extermination order issued against you. You are captured, charged with treason, and imprisoned on a capital offense in a state where there is no due process of law for Latter-day Saints. You are imprisoned in a tiny, stinking, depressing cellar, powerless to support your refugee wife and children. If God had not called you to the work, you would back out. "But I cannot back out," you say, for "I have no doubt of the truth."[43] And so you work and watch and fight and pray with all your might and zeal.[44] Eventually, the Lord delivers you from your enemies so you can exercise the keys of the holy priesthood. You reunite with your family and call for the Apostles.

Five years to the day before you will be killed, you begin the process of endowing the Apostles with power.[45] You teach, endow, and ordain them as quickly as you can. Three months before your death, you finish. "I roll the burthen and responsibility of leading this church off from my shoulders on to yours," you tell the Apostles. "Now, round up your shoulders and stand under it like men; for the Lord is going to let me rest a while."[46] You are thirty-eight years old. The commission you received at age seventeen from an angel sent from the presence of God specifically to you is now fulfilled. Your work on earth is done. You are no longer safe. You publicly declare, "I dont blame you for not believing my history had I not experienced it [I] could not believe it myself."[47] It has been remarkable—not because you were flawless or immortal, but because you were not. You were an imperfect, sincere seventeen-year-old seeking the salvation of your soul. Little did you know that your own salvation would be so wrapped up in God's vast, eternal plan for the salvation of the human family. But as you began to grasp the glad tidings, as you began to piece together line by line and precept by precept, with the help of ministering angels, how the keys, powers, and privileges of the holy priesthood would be restored to everyone who wants them, you rejoiced and resolved to push the work forward. "Forward and not backward," you said to the Saints. "Courage, brethren; and on, on to the victory! Let your hearts rejoice, and be exceedingly glad. Let the earth break forth into anthems of eternal praise to the King Immanuel, who hath ordained, before the world was, that which would enable us to redeem them out of their prison; for the prisoners shall go free" (Doctrine and Covenants 128:22).

Indeed, they shall. Because of what occurred in the house of the Lord in Kirtland, the prisoners shall go free. Oh, how well Joseph knew what it meant for the prisoners to be free! His heart rejoiced and was exceedingly glad. I fervently pray that Joseph's rhetorical question will ever ring in our ears—"Shall we not go on in so great a cause?" (Doctrine and Covenants 128:22). We are the heirs of Joseph's legacy. Let us spend our lives gathering, endowing, and sealing the living and the dead. Let us present ourselves sanctified in the house of the Lord against great opposition. Let us "as Latter-day Saints, offer unto the Lord an offering in righteousness; and let us present in his holy temple . . . the records of our dead, which shall be worthy of all acceptation" (Doctrine and Covenants 128:24).

Notes

1. *The Papers of Joseph Smith*, vol. 1, *Autobiographical and Historical Writings*, ed. Dean C. Jessee (Salt Lake City: Deseret Book, 1989–92), 127.

2. *Papers of Joseph Smith*, 1:278.

3. Russell M. Nelson, in Conference Report, October 1996, 97.

4. Kirtland Minute Book, December 27, 1832, Church History Library, The Church of Jesus Christ of Latter-day Saints, Salt Lake City.

5. Kirtland Minute Book, December 27, 1832; Kirtland Revelation Book, 47–48, 166, Church History Library.

6. Samuel H. Smith Journal, Church History Library.

7. Richard Lyman Bushman, *Joseph Smith: Rough Stone Rolling* (New York: Alfred A. Knopf, 2005), 206.

8. Margaret Barker, *On Heaven as It Is in Earth: Temple Symbolism in the New Testament* (Edinburgh: T&T Clark, 1995), 13.

9. Joseph Smith, Kirtland, Ohio, to William W. Phelps, Independence, Missouri, January 11, 1833, in Joseph Smith Letterbook 1, 18–20, in hand of Frederick G. Williams, Joseph Smith Collection, Church History Library.

10. Joseph Smith, Kirtland, Ohio, to William W. Phelps, Independence, Missouri, January 11, 1833, in Joseph Smith Letterbook 1, 18–20. Compare with Doctrine and Covenants 84:23–25.

11. Joseph Smith, Kirtland, Ohio, to William W. Phelps, Independence, Missouri, January 11, 1833, in Joseph Smith Letterbook 1, 18–20.

12. Joseph Smith, Kirtland, Ohio, to William W. Phelps, Independence, Missouri, January 11, 1833, in Joseph Smith Letterbook 1, 18–20.

13. Joseph Smith, Kirtland, Ohio, to William W. Phelps, Independence, Missouri, January 11, 1833, in Joseph Smith Letterbook 1, 18–20.

14. Joseph Smith discourse, Kirtland, Ohio, November 12, 1835, Joseph Smith Journal, in *The Papers of Joseph Smith*, vol. 2, *Journal, 1832–1842*, 76; see also 75–78.

15. Joseph Smith, Discourse, Kirtland, Ohio, November 12, 1835, Joseph Smith Journal, in *Papers of Joseph Smith*, 2:76–77.

16. Joseph Smith discourse, Kirtland, Ohio, November 12, 1835, Joseph Smith Journal, in *Papers of Joseph Smith*, 2:77.

17. Joseph Smith, *History of the Church of Jesus Christ of Latter-day Saints*, ed. B. H. Roberts, 2nd ed. rev. (Salt Lake City: Deseret Book, 1957), 2:308; fulfillments of this prophecy are documented in Steven C. Harper, "'A Pentecost and Endowment Indeed': Six Eyewitness Accounts of the Kirtland Temple Experience," in *Opening the Heavens: Accounts of Divine Manifestations, 1820–1844*, ed. John W. Welch and Erick B. Carlson (Provo, UT: Brigham Young University Press; Salt Lake City: Deseret Book, 2005): 327–71.

18. William W. Phelps to Sally Waterman Phelps, January 1836, L. Tom Perry Special Collections, Harold B. Lee Library, Brigham Young University, Provo, UT.

19. Oliver Cowdery Sketch Book, January 16, 1836, Church History Library.

20. Harper, "'A Pentecost and Endowment Indeed,'" 338, 344; see Joseph's description on 354.

21. *Papers of Joseph Smith*, 2:440.

22. According to Joseph's brother, William Smith, cited in *Deseret News*, January 20, 1894, cited in Bushman, *Rough Stone Rolling* (New York: Knopf, 2005), 110.

23. David L. Paulsen, "Joseph Smith and the Problem of Evil," *BYU Studies* 39, no. 1 (2000): 61.

24. See Jeffrey A. Trumbower, *Rescue for the Dead: The Posthumous Salvation of Non-Christians in Early Christianity* (New York: Oxford University Press, 2001).

25. See Hugh Nibley, "Baptism for the Dead in Ancient Times," in *Mormonism and Early Christianity* (Salt Lake City: Deseret Book; Provo, UT: FARMS, 1987), 148–49.

26. Hugh Nibley, *Mormonism and Early Christianity* (Salt Lake City: Deseret Book, 1987), 103.

27. Gerald R. McDermott, *Jonathan Edwards Confronts the Gods* (New York: Oxford University Press, 2000).

28. Paulsen, "Joseph Smith and the Problem of Evil," 62.

29. Lucy [Mack] Smith, Biographical Sketches, 265–66, 270. Richard E. Turley Jr., "The Latter-Day Saint Doctrine of Baptism for the Dead," BYU family history fireside, Joseph Smith Building, November 9, 2001, copy in author's possession. Nauvoo baptismal records show that Alvin was baptized at the instance of his brother Hyrum (Nauvoo Temple, Baptisms for the Dead 1840–45, Book A, 145, 149, Church History Library).

30. *Papers of Joseph Smith*, 2:191.

31. Oliver Cowdery, Sketch Book, March 26, 1836, Church History Library.

32. Harper, "'A Pentecost and Endowment Indeed,'" 327–71.

33. *Papers of Joseph Smith*, 2:195.

34. Bushman, *Rough Stone Rolling*, 317.

35. See section 49:10, 23 for earlier usages in a different context.

36. Hugh Nibley, *"A House of Glory"* (Provo, UT: FARMS, 1993).

37. John P. Pratt, "The Restoration of Priesthood Keys on Easter 1836, Part 2: Symbolism of Passover and of Elijah's Return," *Ensign*, July 1985, 55.

38. *Papers of Joseph Smith*, 2:209.

39. Joseph Smith, Kirtland, Ohio, to William W. Phelps, Independence, Missouri, January 11, 1833, in Joseph Smith Letterbook 1, 18–20.

40. Stephen D. Ricks, "The Appearance of Elijah and Moses in the Kirtland Temple and the Jewish Passover," *BYU Studies* 23, no. 4 (1983): 483–86.

41. Ricks, "Appearance of Elijah and Moses," 485.

42. Bushman, *Rough Stone Rolling*, 320–21.

43. Discourse, April 6, 1843, Nauvoo, Illinois, Joseph Smith, Papers, Journals, Church History Library; also in Faulring, *An American Prophet's Record*, 347–50; *The Words of Joseph Smith*, ed. Andrew F. Ehat and Lyndon W. Cook (Provo, UT: Religious Studies Center, Brigham Young University, 1980), 177–80; and Smith, *History of the Church*, 5:333–37.

44. Will L. Thompson, "Put Your Shoulder to the Wheel," *Hymns* (Salt Lake City: The Church of Jesus Christ of Latter-day Saints), no. 252.

45. Wilford Woodruff Journal, June 27, 1839, Church History Library.

46. Declaration of the Twelve, circa 1844, Church History Library.

47. Discourse, April 7, 1844, Nauvoo, Illinois, Joseph Smith, Papers, Journals, Church History Library; also in Smith, *History of the Church*, 6:302–17; *Words of Joseph Smith*, 340–43; and Faulring, *An American Prophet's Record*, 465–76.

Two of the toughest years in Joseph Smith's life and ministry were 1837 and 1838, yet he believed in his calling and in the revelations. He rose time and again from his most challenging difficulties and demonstrated remarkable resilience. (Portrait by unknown artist, 1840s; Community of Christ.).

RONALD K. ESPLIN

1837
Joseph Smith and the Kirtland Crisis

*E*ighteen thirty-seven was a tough year. In fact, 1837 and 1838 were probably the two toughest years of Joseph Smith's life and ministry. Eighteen thirty-seven was emotionally disastrous and ended in apostasy and division. Eighteen thirty-eight in Missouri was militarily disastrous and ended in pain and suffering.[1] Together these two years comprised a very trying period. One of the things that I have been impressed with as we have worked on *The Joseph Smith Papers* is how resilient Joseph Smith was. He believed in his calling. He believed in the revelations. And partly because of this faith, and maybe also because of the constitution and will he was born with, he could rise, time and again, from the ashes of defeat and do something even better. He did so after

Ronald K. Esplin is managing director of the Joseph Smith Papers Project.

1837, and 1838 in Missouri started out promising. After the military and physical disaster there, the Saints straggled into Nauvoo and built the greatest city of Joseph's administration in a short five years.

Lessons from 1837

Even though 1837 was a difficult, sometimes discouraging year, it is one we need to understand. Exploring it helps us to understand Joseph Smith, but there are also lessons we can learn. One is that we are all susceptible to what may be called the cycle of prosperity, also known as the Nephite disease. President Brigham Young, a year after Joseph Smith's death, gave an interesting sermon in Nauvoo, one of his best before he went west, in which he said essentially that for twelve years under Joseph Smith the Saints had suffered through adversity and were still fine spiritually. Despite setbacks, they had made it through; they had done what they needed to do. Not so in prosperity, he concluded—one year of prosperity had almost killed them. Since Joseph's death, they had had some peace, some good times, and it had been too much. Adversity is a better environment for making Saints, perhaps. Another thing we can learn is how adversity tries men and women, revealing character as they make decisions in difficult circumstances. The 1837 Kirtland crisis, or Kirtland apostasy as it is sometimes known, cost us perhaps a third of the leadership—not a third of the members, but some of the elite, some of the well-educated, some of the more prosperous. And it happened so suddenly that it is a lesson for all of us.

Another lesson of 1837 is the importance of having our loyalties in the right place. There was a cultural war going on in the Church in 1837 over what Joseph Smith was trying to introduce: a new way of thinking about society and religion based on ancient scripture models and modern revelation. This was the model of Enoch leading his people or Moses at the head of the children of Israel, where a religious leader had a great deal to say about everyday life and about how society was organized. This model was not the American way, nor is it today. People had to look into their hearts and decide what they were willing to do at the behest of a religious leader. Some liked the American civil religion, as it has sometimes been called. They liked the idea that they were free as Americans to do their business six days a week and on the seventh day go to church where a preacher would teach them morals and maybe a little doctrine. But they did not expect this preacher to interject himself into their politics, their property, or their economic organization. This was the Protestant model, the model most early Latter-day Saints grew up with. Yet little by little, Joseph Smith was trying to teach them the model of Enoch and of Moses, of organizing society around religious principles and around religious leaders. So one of the lessons we learn is that if we are in a situation where much is demanded, ultimately we will have to decide where our loyalties are. Very good people, including some leaders who left for a while and came back, had difficulty with that. For a while they thought their real loyalty was what they had done as "Sons of '76." They wanted to live life as Americans and not as Latter-day Saints or as children of Israel. Think of these lessons as we see how 1837 unfolds.

Contemporary Accounts of Kirtland in 1837

It has been difficult to understand 1837, and it is interesting why we have this trouble. Joseph Smith kept a wonderful diary from the fall of 1835 into the spring of 1836. It ended on April 3, 1836, with the coming of Elijah, Elias, and Moses to the Kirtland Temple. That closed his best diary of the 1830s, although we have a pretty decent one for part of 1838 in Missouri. But from early April 1836 through all of 1837 and well into 1838, we have no Joseph Smith diary. Not until March 13, 1838, when he arrived in Far West, Missouri, did the Prophet begin a new diary.

Not only do we not have any diary from Joseph Smith, we do not have any from his closest associates. So we have had difficulty understanding the story of how things came apart in the fall of 1836 and throughout 1837. We have many accounts and considerable information, but almost all are reminiscent accounts written much later. Eliza R. Snow and Lorenzo Snow later wrote of this pivotal period, and there are many reminiscences in the *Journal of Discourses* about these days. But they were written decades after the fact, and it is not possible to sort out from those accounts how all the events unfolded. These later accounts leave an impression that all the key events of this crisis year occurred in the summer of 1837, which was not the case. One result of this misconception is that apostasy has been connected almost exclusively to the failure of the bank and the economic difficulties, or to the economic Panic of 1837, as it was called. The bank failure and its aftermath played an important role, but the reality was more complex—and also more interesting and instructive.

In a broad sense, one might find some of the roots of this apostasy as far back as the aftermath of Zion's Camp in 1834. But the immediate roots can be seen in the late summer and fall of 1836, during Kirtland's brief prosperity. Before economic troubles had even started, there was an effort to depose Joseph Smith, hardly the scenario one would expect from reading the reminiscent accounts alone. Gratefully we are not left with only those. We can sort this out more clearly thanks to two contemporaneous sources. One is the diary of Wilford

Woodruff, who returned to Kirtland after thirty months on missions in various places. A great diary keeper, he kept a very important record from the fall of 1836 until the end of May of 1837, when he departed Kirtland for yet another mission. At the very time he left, Mary Fielding, who had come to Kirtland with her brother Joseph and her sister Mercy, started a series of letters to Mercy, who had returned to Canada. These letters overlap a few days with Woodruff's diary and continue recording her firsthand observations of Kirtland through much of the summer, weeks after Woodruff's diary falls silent.

With these two sources and a few corroborating evidences such as lawsuits, we can create a chronology that helps us put the reminiscences into context so that we can better understand not only how this unfolded but why. When we do that, we discover that what was at issue was not simply prosperity or economic decline or the failure of the bank, although all of those were important. The central issue for many was their understanding of prophetic leadership: What was the role of a prophet? Was a prophet, like the Protestant minister in American tradition, expected to preach to us on Sunday out of the Book of Mormon or modern revelation, but not lead the community? Or was a prophet to lead a community of gathered Saints into a new way of organizing themselves, where all of their labors worked together to build the kingdom of God on earth? This second model was what Nauvoo became. This was what Joseph was beginning to teach and trying to implement to some degree in Kirtland. And this—the role of prophetic leadership—was what people divided over.

A Bit of 1836

To understand 1837, we must mention a few events of 1836. The temple dedication was in late March of 1836, and

Joseph's diary closes on the third of April, a few days later. This is the diary that provides the best contemporary evidence of all the great spiritual experiences connected with the completion of the Kirtland Temple. But we know from other accounts that the great spiritual highlights of 1836 did not just stop when the diary stopped. Reading the diary conveys a sense that now that Christ and Moses and Elijah had come, what more was there to say? That was the climax of the season of spiritual experiences and the diary ended with that account. But the temple and the community of Saints who had participated in these great events still enjoyed a lingering aura that stayed for months. On April 6 the temple provided the setting for a great jubilee marking the sixth anniversary of the organization of the Church. The spiritual experiences and the warm feelings of gathering in the house of the Lord continued into the summer.

It was in this atmosphere that members of the Quorum of the Twelve left Kirtland on their summer mission. Since their call in 1835, the Apostles had begun a pattern of being at home in the winter, when each took care of farm and family, and spending the summers preaching. When they returned to Kirtland in the fall of 1836, just a few months later, the scene had changed dramatically. Heber C. Kimball's reaction demonstrates what it meant to them to see this shocking change: "We were much grieved ... on our arrival in Kirtland, to see the spirit of speculation that was prevailing in the Church. Trade and traffic seemed to engross the time and attention of the Saints.... Some men, who, when I left, could hardly get food to eat, I found on my arrival to be men of supposed great wealth; in fact everything in the place seemed to be moving in great prosperity, and all seemed to be engaged to become rich."[2]

Warren A. Cowdery, editor of the *Messenger and Advocate*, also commented on the changes. He wrote in the *Messenger and Advocate* a few months later that many of the Saints were "guilty of wild speculation and visionary dreams of wealth and worldly grandeur, as if gold and silver were their gods, and houses, farms and merchandize their only bliss or their passport to it."³ That was quite a change from the early spring of 1836 when members of the Quorum of the Twelve—Brigham Young, Heber C. Kimball, and others—left. Interestingly, when the Saints had nothing, they felt more comfortable with the idea that Joseph Smith would guide them in their economic development. But when prosperity hit them briefly and they had dreams of gaining prosperity on their own power, and some had actual prospects of doing so, the situation looked very different to many.

The Cowdery Brothers against "Tyranny"

I will use the Cowdery brothers, Warren and Oliver, to demonstrate how this worked. By the middle of 1837, Warren Cowdery, still writing in the Church's newspaper, was really writing against what Joseph Smith was trying to do. Warren Cowdery argued against allowing religious leaders to cross traditional American boundaries: "If we thus barter away our liberties, we are unworthy of them."⁴ In another place he said that ecclesiastical tyranny was tyranny just the same, as if he were accusing Joseph Smith of this. "Whenever a people have unlimited confidence in a civil or ecclesiastical ruler or rulers, who are but men like themselves, and begin to think they can do no wrong, they increase their tyranny, and oppression, establish a principle that man, poor frail lump of mortality like themselves, is infallible. Who does not see a principle of popery?"⁵ Today it is difficult to understand how demeaning that criticism was meant to be. Popery, the Catholic system of priests presiding among the people, was viewed as the opposite of the religious model in America. It was viewed as priestcraft, as privileged religious leaders lording over the people. "Who does not see a principle of popery and religious tyranny involved in such an order of things? Who is worthy the name of a freeman, who thus tamely surrenders, the rights the privileges, and immunities of an independent citizen? . . . Intelligence of the people is the only guarantee against encroachments upon their liberties, whether those encroachments are from the civil or eclesiastical power."[6]

In 1838, Oliver Cowdery was excommunicated. He was charged, among other things, with virtually denying the faith by declaring that he would not be governed by any ecclesiastical authority nor revelation whatever in his temporal affairs. He was essentially asked, "If your church organization and ecclesiastical leaders offered guidance to help organize your temporal life, would you submit to their guidance?" Oliver Cowdery said he would not. He answered by paraphrasing in writing a central charge against him: "I will not be influenced, governed, or controlled, in my temporal interests by any ecclesiastical authority or pretended revelation whatever, contrary to my own judgment." He said, "Such being still my opinion [I] shall only remark that the three great principles of English liberty, as laid down in the books, are 'the right of personal security, the right of personal liberty, and the right of private property.'" He continued: "My venerable ancestor was among the little band, who landed on the rocks of Plymouth in 1620. . . . I am wholly unwilling to exchange [his American principles] for anything less liberal, less benevolent, or less free."[7]

Others agreed that this was a central issue but saw it from a very different perspective. During the height of the 1837 crisis, new convert Mary Fielding expressed the opposite view—that the crisis was not because Joseph Smith or the presidency attempted to exert too much influence but because some leaders and members did not submit enough. She wrote to her sister Mercy, "I know not what the Lord will have to do with his Church before it will submit to be governed by the Head but I fully believe we shall have no prosperity till this is the case."[8] Wilford Woodruff and Brigham Young, among others, would share Mary's view, not Oliver's.

We may be grateful that we are not generally asked to make the same kind of choice that Oliver Cowdery was asked to make in 1837 and 1838 between what he saw as his rights as a free man and his responsibility as a Latter-day Saint. Perhaps this is useful food for thought about where our loyalties would lie if one day we organize around communities of Saints where ecclesiastical leaders will help to organize temporal as well as spiritual affairs, as was the emerging situation in Kirtland in 1837.

Wilford Woodruff's Views of Unfolding Events

Wilford Woodruff's diary helps us establish a chronology that sheds light on how events unfolded. We also gain insight from the power of his personal reaction to all of this and from what he conveyed of Joseph Smith's own experience as he viewed Joseph Smith combating the great vortex of disaffection, dissention, and difficulty. His Kirtland account opens in November 1836 with excitement and optimism. "We soon entered the village [of Kirtland] & I spent one of the happiest days of my life at this time in visiting Kirtland & the House of the Lord & the Presidents & Elders of the Church. I was truly edified to again strike hands with President Joseph Smith Jr. & many other beloved saints of God who are rolling on the mighty work of God & of Israel."[9] He described how he was filled with joy at doing this and how he had longed to see with his own eyes the house of the Lord. Construction had barely begun when he left, and now finally it was real: "After Spending a short time in Conversing With my friends A more important scene was now to open to my view than Kings ever saw or Princes ever Knew in this generation."[10] This scene was the temple. He described in his diary his feelings at going inside and seeing the pulpits and the fine workmanship of the interior, at visiting the top story to see the mummies and the Book of Abraham, and then going outside and seeing the printing shop and the bank—the Kirtland Bank, which still was a thing of hope and promise for the Saints.

All of this caused him to ponder the wonderful progress that had occurred in the "two & a half years since I left Kirtland with my Brethren in their Poverty to go fourth and to visit our brethren in tribulation in Zion. Then our Brethren in Kirtland were poor, despised, & even looked upon . . . with Disdain & disgrace."[11] And now, he said, "How Changed the scene now I behold cheerfulness beaming upon every countenance that indicates Prosperity & the noise of the ax & the hammer & the sight of their walls & dwellings newly erected & their Bank & markets & esspecially house of God."[12] He went on to say that the community had been transformed in the thirty months he had been gone. He could not have known, as Heber C. Kimball and his fellow Apostles did that same fall, that except for the completion of the temple, much of this remarkable transformation had occurred in only a few months.

Two days later, Wilford Woodruff had his first experience meeting with the Saints in the house of the Lord, a moving, wondrous experience that he described in some detail. Elders Parley P. Pratt and Orson Pratt of the Quorum of the Twelve were seated in the pulpits, but so was Warren Parrish, the scribe for Joseph Smith's Kirtland journal and Wilford's close friend with whom he was lodging. "I truly felt to thank God that his promises had been verifyed unto me by giving me a seat & a name within his house."[13] He also wrote about Joseph Smith addressing the Saints and how marvelous everything was.

That was in late November 1836. Two weeks later, on another Sunday, the tone of Wilford's account had changed. He now knew that not all was well in Zion. "I went up to the house of God to worship & O what a meeting. May it be Printed upon my heart as a memorial forever. For on this day the God of Israel Sharply reproved this stake of Zion (Kirtland) through the Prophets & Apostles for all our sins & backslidings & also a timely warning that we may escape the Judgments of God that otherwise will fall upon us."[14] Wilford did not mention what the failings were, but he did record that Joseph Smith and other Church leaders pointedly chastised the Saints and warned them to repent and mend their ways or face the consequences.

It was Wilford Woodruff's habit, as a year ended, to write a summary of his year: whom he baptized, what blessings he had given, how many miles he had walked, how many times he had preached. To this he might add an assessment. This year he wrote: "1836 is gone. It cannot be recalled. . . . The endowment of the Latter Day Saints hath b[e]spake a God in Israel, & is sufficient to show that though the heavens & earth pass away the word of God spake through the Prophets must all be fulfilled."[15] As he began 1837, he wrote of the things he hoped for the year, especially that by the end of the year he could say that great things had happened in Kirtland and in the Kingdom. Unfortunately, what 1837 had in store was not happy for the Saints or for Joseph Smith.

January and February 1837: A Warning and a Mutiny

The year started out well for Wilford Woodruff. On January 3 he was made a member of the first Quorum of the Seventy. On his first missions he had been a priest, on later missions an elder, and now he became a member of the Seventy, organized about the time he left Kirtland in 1835. His return to Kirtland also gave him the opportunity to attend the high school as well as prayer meetings and other worship services in the Kirtland Temple and listen to Joseph Smith and others talk optimistically about the Kirtland Safety Society. All this he appreciated and enjoyed. But despite a very hopeful beginning, by January 10 Wilford's diary took on a much more somber tone, and by the end of January, there was nothing but difficulty on the horizon.

On Tuesday, January 10, Woodruff wrote, "I met in the House of the Lord with the quorum of the Seventies. . . . We had a spiritual meeting. Elder Brigham Young one of the twelve gave us an interesting exhortation & warned us not to murmer against Moses (or) Joseph or the heads of the Church."[16] Very early, Brigham Young used this terminology for Joseph Smith. Joseph was the Moses whom the Lord had given them. If the Saints wanted a Moses at the head, then Joseph was that man. If they, like Brigham Young and Wilford Woodruff, wanted him to do what Moses did, then they were going to be fine with what Joseph Smith was trying to do. But for Church members like Oliver Cowdery who wanted to be Americans first and Saints second, then there was a problem. This undercurrent of murmuring emerged early in the year while there was still a feeling of prosperity. Before the bank failed, before the severe economic downturn, the murmuring had already begun.

On Sunday, January 15, Woodruff "attended a meeting in the House of the Lord. President Rigdon preached in the Spirit & exhorted the Church to union that they might be prepared to meet every trial & difficulty that awates them."[17] There was an impending sense that something bad was coming—that they needed to be united or they would be destroyed as a people. On the seventeenth, Wilford "met at Candle light With the quorums of the Seventies & was favored with a lecture [a rebuke, not instructions] from President David Whitmer."[18] David Whitmer, president of the Church in Missouri, had not yet left Kirtland following the temple experiences he had come to participate in. "He warned us to humble ourselves before God lest his hand rest upon us in anger for our pride & many sins that we were runing into in our days of prosperity as the ancient Nephites did & it does now appear evident that a scourge awates this stake of Zion even Kirtland if their is not great repentance immediately." Woodruff concluded that "almost every Countenance" of the heads of the Church indicated their agreement and approval of this point of view. "May the Lord in mercy enable us to Meet every event with resignation," he wrote.[19]

Though the Saints held more meetings in the temple, the sense of foreboding was not dispelled. By January 29, "the latter part of the day was spent in communion & addresses from Presidents O Cowdery & J Smith Jr. JOSEPH blessed us in the name of the Lord & Said if we would be faithful we should rise above our imbarressments & be delivered from the hands of our enemies." The inverse, of course, was that if they were not faithful, they would not escape impending difficulties. On January 31, they "herd an address from President's J. Smith jr and S Rigdon on the temporal business of the Church."[20] The brethren were still hoping to have a great blessing out of the bank, hoping to get out of their financial troubles, and still saying that in unity they could and would get through this.

Despite these concerns, things were going along well enough at this point that Joseph Smith decided that he could leave on business. His business probably had to do with the Bank of Monroe, a chartered bank in Michigan that the Church had purchased to help support their unchartered bank in Ohio. He had been gone less than three weeks when on Sunday, February 19, he returned and addressed the Saints. Wilford Woodruff did not detail what had occurred to lead Joseph Smith to rise up "in the power of God" to defend himself and denounce those who betrayed him, but we know from reminiscences what happened. While Joseph Smith was gone, dissenters who did not accept the direction the Church was going tried to depose Joseph Smith and place David Whitmer in his stead.

In his diary entry for February 19, Woodruff wrote: "I beheld President JOSEPH SMITH Jr. arise in the stand & for several hours addressed the Saints in the power of God. Joseph had been absent from Kirtland on business for the Church, though not half as long as Moses was in the mount, & many were stir'd up in their hearts & some were against him as the Israelites were against Moses. But when he arose in the power of God in their midst, as Moses did anciently, they were put to silence for the complainers saw that he stood in the power of a Prophet"[21] in defense of himself. A week later on Sunday, Joseph Smith again addressed the congregation of the Saints "in the power and spirit of God." The problems continued, and he continued to stand forward and defend the point of view of the presidency of the Church, trying to help his people become a community, a people of God.

April and May 1837: Friends and Enemies

Following the problems of winter, tensions within the Church at Kirtland eased for a time, and by April the Saints briefly enjoyed better times. On the anniversary of the Kirtland Temple dedication, they had a number of affirming temple experiences. Joseph presided over another solemn assembly for the elders who had been abroad so that they could receive their endowments of power, and Woodruff and other Kirtland residents enjoyed other great experiences as well. Woodruff's diary contains a moving account of his feelings as he saw Joseph Smith and, for a time at least, the Saints united in these temple experiences. He gloried in what he saw and heard "out of the heart & mouth of the prophet JOSEPH whose Soul like Enochs swell'd wide as eternity. I say such evidences presented in such a forcible manner ought to drive into oblivion every particle of unbelief & dubiety from the minds of the hearers."[22] The plans that Joseph Smith was unfolding did not resonate with all the Saints, however. Some began to distance themselves from his purposes.

On April 9 there was a powerful but also painful set of meetings regarding the ailing bank. With economic problems looming, President Rigdon addressed the Saints and told them to be united and they would get through this yet. "Sidney Closed and Joseph arose & like the lion of the tribe of JUDAH poured out his Soul in the midst of the Congregation of the Saints. . . . Yea in the name of God he proclaimed that Severe Judgment awaited those Characters that had professed to be his friends . . . But had turned tritors & opposed the Currency [of the the bank] & its friends which has given power into the hands of the enemy. . . . Joseph uttered the feelings of his Soul in pain while viewing the poverty & afflictions of . . . the Saints in Kirtland."[23]

As a single young man, Wilford Woodruff had served many missions; now he planned to settle down with the love of his life, Phoebe Carter, and Joseph Smith agreed to perform their marriage ceremony. But when the appointed day came, Joseph had left Kirtland, fearing for his life because of threats from dissenters and enemies outside of the Church. The marriage, however, proceeded in Joseph Smith's home as planned, but Joseph Smith's friend and counselor Frederick G. Williams performed the marriage. Woodruff wrote, "There is not a greater man than Joseph standing in this generation. The gentiles look upon him & he is to them like bed of Gold conceled from human view. They know not his principle, his spirit, his wisdom, virtue, phylanthropy, nor his calling. His mind like Enochs swells wide as eternity. Nothing short of a God can comprehend his Soul."[24]

We will close this section with one more excerpt from Wilford Woodruff's life—an experience so difficult for him that he could not even write down the details. This occurred on May 28 in the house of the Lord.

> Sunday I repaired to the House of the Lord to worship the GOD of Israel with the Congregation of the Saints....
>
> The same spirits of murmering, complaining, & of mutiny, that I spake of in Feb. 19th in this journal, hath not slept from that day to the present.... Untill many & some in high places had risen up against Joseph the servent whom God had raised up to lead Israel. And they were striving to overthrow his influence & cast him down untill Joseph was grieved in spirit to stand in such perils among fals brethren.
>
> But notwithstanding this thick cloud of darkness standing over Kirtland Joseph being unmoved in the cause entered the Congregation of the Saints arose in the stand & spake to the people in the name of the Lord in his own defence. The Lord was with him by his power & spirit to the Convinceing of the honest that he would stand & his enemies fall.

Sidney followed him ... but; Alas, one arose, once a friend, (not now) in the blackness of his face & corruption of his heart stretched out his puny arm and proclaimed against Joseph. Joseph acted wisely while all saw the spirit of his foe.[25]

The one who raised his arm against Joseph was Joseph's scribe Warren Parrish, one of Woodruff's friends. Woodruff was so beside himself with pain that he could not even write details of the experience. He said simply, "Let memory speak upon this subject. . . . The Presidents withdrew. The council closed without transacting business."[26]

Gratefully, Mary Fielding attended that same meeting. Although Woodruff could not bring himself to write about it, Mary did. Parrish openly denounced Joseph Smith, and not content with this, he also pronounced a curse upon him. He then declared by the God of heaven that this curse would be sealed upon Joseph because of Joseph's wickedness. Not surprisingly, the whole meeting ended in confusion. We can only imagine the feelings of the Saints when two weeks later Joseph fell deathly ill and his life was despaired of. This proved to be a trial of faith for many. Though Mary Fielding made it through what was to come, I am not sure all of us would have.

June 1837: Mission to England and More Trouble at Home

At this very time, Joseph Smith was inspired to do something different for the salvation of the Church. At a meeting in the temple on June 4, he approached Heber C. Kimball and said, in essence: "Brother Kimball, you've got to go to England and fulfill the mission that the Quorum of the Twelve is preparing for. But the quorum is now divided and, despite the difficulties, you must go alone." Elder Kimball was planning on going, but as one of the Twelve, not the leader of the mission. The prospect frightened him; he was uneducated and felt unprepared, believing that he could not do this alone. "Let me at least take Brother Brigham," he asked. "No, I need Brigham here," said Joseph Smith, and indeed as things unfolded during the rest of 1837, he very much needed Brigham Young there. Reluctantly, Heber said that he would do his duty; he would do what the Prophet had asked of him. Just before he was set apart on June 11, Orson Hyde, who had been disaffected for a time, came back and begged for the privilege of going with them. So Heber Kimball, Orson Hyde, Joseph Fielding, and several of the Canadian Saints were sent on this great mission.

Heber Kimball was absolutely the right man for this mission. Within eight months, the missionaries had performed nearly two thousand baptisms and laid the foundation for what the Quorum of the Twelve would do two years later. That later mission would elevate the membership in Great Britain from two thousand to over six thousand. And those British converts, with their skills, resources, and faith, were the ones who indeed saved the Church. It is hard to imagine the city of Nauvoo or the Nauvoo Temple without their skills, dedication, and numbers. In the midst of the darkness of 1837, Joseph was inspired to send these missionaries, and they had faith enough to do their duty.

Joseph Smith set the missionaries apart on June 11. When they went to see the Prophet on the thirteenth to bid him farewell, he was so sick that he could not raise his head from his pillow to visit with them. By the following day, he was worse and suffering intensely. This story we know largely from the letters of Mary Fielding written to her sister Mercy. Mary reports that "on June 18th, our beloved Brother Joseph appeared to be so far gone that Brother Rigdon told us that he should not wonder, naturally speaking, if he did not live until night."[27]

According to Mary, Parley Pratt spoke that day in a great meeting in the assembly room of the temple. In his talk, Parley attempted to show how all the Church had departed from the good way. Parley was disaffected from the Church at that time, as was Orson. Unwilling to hear more from dissenters, President Sidney Rigdon dismissed the meeting, but some stayed. The afternoon meeting presented another unforgettable "scene of confusion," to use Mary Fielding's language. Both of the Pratt brothers, Warren Parrish, and others of the disaffected were present. President Rigdon, carrying this burden almost alone and "bowed down with the sad condition of the Church and the situation of dear Brother Joseph," stood before the Church "and in language that is impossible . . . to describe"[28] rehearsed the dissenters' actions and declared that he would bear no more the public insulting of Joseph. When Rigdon left the building, many of the Saints left with him. Mary herself stayed to hear Oliver Cowdery attempt to justify his position, but when Orson Pratt attempted to do the same, she felt he was so far off track that she left too. As she passed Joseph Smith's home on her way back to her own dwelling, she wondered if he would live until morning.

That night, according to Mary Fielding, a number of the brethren fasted and prayed for Joseph in the temple. From that time, wrote Mary, to the great relief and joy of his friends, Joseph began to recover, and she predicted "he shall yet stand in his place and accomplish the work God has given him to do however much many seek his removal."[29] By Sunday, June 25, Joseph Smith was still too unwell to attend meetings. Warren Parrish arrived at the temple early enough to seat himself in the place usually occupied by the Prophet. Hyrum conducted the meeting. He spoke until tears forced him to his seat. When he took the stand again, "he seemed to be filled with the spirit and power of God" and prophesied "with great energy that from that hour the Church should begin to rise."³⁰

July and August 1837: Relief, Riot, and Reprisal

The next week brought favorable changes. On Sunday, July 2, Joseph Smith attended meetings for the first time in several weeks. With Joseph back among his people, Mary Fielding called the meeting "a quiet comfortable waiting upon God in his House."³¹ President Rigdon prophesied that the kingdom "should never be destroyed, nor be left to other people."³² Many who lived in Kirtland said that they had never before seen "such a time of love and refreshing" as they had that day. Mary Fielding, who had not lived in Kirtland long, wrote, "I do assure you Brother Hyrum Smith's prediction that from that hour the Lord would begin to bless his people has been verily fulfilled. ... What I felt that day seemed to outweigh all the affliction and distress of mind I have suffered since I came here."³³

In the meantime, interesting things were going on among some of the dissenters. Though at the moment he lacked confidence in Joseph Smith, Parley Pratt still wanted to go to England and claimed to have faith in the gospel and in his own calling. He refused to listen to Brigham Young, who urged him to stay in Kirtland and work things through. Instead he took off for Missouri, a nearly nine-hundred-mile trip. On his way there, he met his quorum leaders Thomas B. Marsh and David W. Patten, who were traveling from Missouri to Kirtland. Marsh succeeded where Brigham Young had failed; he convinced Parley to turn around, and they all went back to Kirtland.

Meanwhile, David Patten had his own brief crisis of faith. Although he had heard all the criticisms of Joseph, he had confidence in Joseph, loved Joseph, and believed in Joseph. Still, Patten wanted to hear both sides of the issue. He determined to hear the worst there was to hear and then see the Prophet. Thomas B. Marsh tried to convince Patten that his proposed approach was backward: he should go see the Prophet first, then talk to the dissenters. Once they arrived at Kirtland, however, Patten visited the dissenters first and got an earful. What he heard got him so worked up that when he went to see the Prophet, according to Brigham Young, "he insulted Joseph," who kicked him out of the yard, and this experience "done David good" and quickly brought him to his senses.[34] It was later said in Nauvoo that of all the original Quorum of the Twelve, only Brigham Young and Heber Kimball never lifted their heel against Joseph Smith.

By now, things were finally looking more orderly, and Joseph Smith was ready to go on another business trip. He went to visit the Saints in Canada and also sent Brigham Young to conduct business in the East. While they were gone, there was a great row in the temple. Apostle was pitted against Apostle, pistols and knives were brandished, people jumped out of windows, and stovepipes were knocked over—it was a horrible melee with the dissenters, who remained unrepentant. When Joseph Smith Sr., who was conducting the meeting, could not impose order, he called in the police, who expanded the melee. At the end of the day, nobody had been killed, but many blows had been struck, and a horrible scene had transpired in the House of the Lord. Reminiscences preserve memories of the awful scene, but without the resulting lawsuit, it may have been impossible to date the event. Dissenters who had been arrested by the police filed a lawsuit for false arrest, resulting in Joseph Smith Sr., William Smith, and others being hauled into court to defend the arrests. They were acquitted, but, as one can imagine, the ruling did not help heal feelings among the apostates.

When Joseph returned in late August, he was of course appalled at what had happened. At this point he apparently came to the conclusion that the faithful Saints could no longer tolerate the dissenters' actions, nor could he. But why did the Prophet tolerate it this long? How could Warren Parrish still get into the temple, after all he had done, and sit in Joseph's own seat? Why were wayward leaders still part of the congregation? Joseph never said why, but it appears that he felt that patience was a virtue and that until this point it was not time to move against his critics. The time had now come to cut the apostates off from the Church and have a fresh start with those that were willing to support him. Had he done it earlier, he might have lost Parley P. Pratt, Orson Pratt, or Orson Hyde. Gratefully, Joseph was willing to tolerate this spring and summer of rebellion, mutiny, and pain before finally acting definitively. A number of repentant leaders who came back stayed with him and helped lead the Church throughout the nineteenth century.

September through December 1837: Restoring Order and Leaving Kirtland

In September Joseph decided to convene a major conference in order to confront those still in rebellion and cut them off. Dissent had been widespread enough that some must have wondered how such a meeting would turn out. Brigham Young, for one, was not going to take any chances. He had defended Joseph Smith throughout the summer against the apostates, he had defended the Prophet's life against anti-Mormon threats, and now he was going to pack the house with the faithful so they could voice their support for the Prophet and his decisions. Brigham Young later described how, early in the morning, he gathered supporters so that when the meeting opened at 9:00 a.m. on September 3, the faithful were front and center as the apostates and wavering members were called to account. Several were repentant, while others tried to give excuses or justification. John F. Boynton of the Quorum of the Twelve is perhaps the best example of this. He was not sustained, but he was allowed time to try and give satisfaction. He came back a few days later with a more humble and complete apology and was allowed to remain in his position a while longer, until he again went off the rails. Overall, the conference resulted in a much-needed housecleaning, and finally the leadership could once again be united and prepare for the things that were ahead.

But the task was not yet finished. The Saints in Missouri also needed to sustain the changes in Church leadership, and the dissenters living there also needed to be called to account. So later in September, Joseph Smith, Hyrum Smith, and a few other leaders traveled to Missouri to hold another conference. In this Missouri conference, Hyrum was sustained as a member of the First Presidency in place of Frederick G. Williams. Hyrum Smith served in the Presidency from that point forward, although Frederick G. Williams later returned to the Church and died a faithful Latter-day Saint.

While he and Joseph were in Missouri, Hyrum's wife, Jerusha Barden Smith, became ill and died during childbirth. Hyrum's brothers Don Carlos and Samuel wrote him a heart-wrenching letter declaring that despite "all our diligence of care and our prayers [she] did not prevail" and "Jerusha has gone from a world of trouble and affliction and toil . . . to rest until the morning of the resurrection." Of course they would care for his children until his return.[35] When the letter reached him, Hyrum left immediately for home. Now that Hyrum was in the First Presidency, Joseph needed him more than ever, and bereaved Hyrum did not know how to take care of his family, let alone how to help Joseph lead the Church. According to family tradition, Joseph said to Hyrum, "Take Mary Fielding as your wife," and once she agreed, he did.³⁶

Mary's story is interesting. She had had opportunities to be married but had elected not to. A surviving letter indicates that she declined one suitor because she did not want to be a stepmother, something her own mother had warned her against. In Hyrum's case, despite her general preference, Mary felt it was the will of the Lord and accepted the proposal. Mary came to love Hyrum and the children, but, as she had understood, being a stepmother meant certain inescapable and difficult realities. In a fall 1842 letter to Hyrum, who was traveling on Church business, Mary conveyed to him the continuing challenge inherent in being a stepmother to his children (who occasionally stung her feelings by insisting she was only a stepmother) by signing the letter as "your faithful Companion and Friend but unhappy StepMother M. Smith."³⁷ Thanks to the new arrangement, at the end of 1837 the Hyrum Smith family again had a wife and mother, and the family was ready to go forward the best it could.

After a period of relative calm, by late fall dissent erupted again in Kirtland, this time violently. Apostates had set up another organization and were ridiculing the faithful Saints who still followed Joseph, whom they called the Lick-Skillets. Finally Church leaders cut off nearly thirty people, but even that did not end the Church's problems. The apostates were angry, the anti-Mormons were coming after Joseph, the bank had failed, and the economy was in crisis. Emotions ran high, and many lives were threatened—none more so than Brigham Young's. During an entire year of boldly defending Joseph, Brigham had angered many people and feared for his life. Though his ailing wife Mary Ann was about to give birth to twins, he fled to

Missouri on December 22, leaving his wife and family to follow later. When they did, the Youngs settled not in Far West with the largest body of the Saints but on a quiet farm some miles away. This was because Joseph counseled Brigham to settle his family there so he could nurse his wife back to health; this counsel was ratified by revelation on April 17, 1838.[38] So it was that when the crisis came in late 1838, Brigham Young was not among those arrested, and he was able to step forward and lead when Joseph and other leaders were imprisoned in Liberty.

Back in Kirtland, meanwhile, Joseph and Sidney Rigdon had received a revelation which confirmed that their labors were "finished in this place for a season" and instructed them to leave with their families for Missouri "as soon as it is practicable."[39] They had already been planning to leave for Missouri when circumstances permitted, but there had not yet come a time when they could all depart. An earlier revelation had indicated that Kirtland would be a place of safety and refuge, "a strong hold," but for only five years (see Doctrine and Covenants 64:21–22). Those five years had passed, and on January 12, 1838, Joseph Smith and Sidney Rigdon departed for Missouri. Their families soon caught up with them, and together they made a winter migration—nearly nine hundred miles overland—to get their families and themselves safely to Missouri, where they arrived on March 13.

Conclusion

That, then, is the story of Joseph Smith's 1837. It was a year he would never want to repeat, but a year that had held great lessons and great beginnings, especially in Britain, that would bless the Church for years to come. In Missouri the Prophet hoped to continue the progress of the Church and advance projects that could not be completed in 1837. In 1836 Joseph

Smith's diary had ended, as I mentioned before, with section 110 of the Doctrine and Covenants. Elijah had brought the sealing keys and now, at the beginning of 1838, Joseph was separated from the only temple where he could use them. With little prospect of returning to Kirtland, Joseph moved on, ready to build another temple in another place. Not surprisingly, a temple site was designated at Far West just a month after his arrival, but he could not fulfill the promises of 1836 and 1837 until Nauvoo, when he would have both the keys and a temple and could pass on the blessings of the temple to the Saints.

I have learned a great deal studying Joseph Smith's life in 1836–38. The story ranges from the highs of the temple to the lows of apostasy and open rebellion, the military confrontation of the Mormon war, and the imprisonment of Joseph Smith for six months, mostly in Liberty Jail. At the end of that period, Joseph Smith emerged as a man who was prepared to face new challenges and succeed, who had learned, who had become stronger in the right ways for the calling and responsibility of finishing his work in Nauvoo. Nauvoo would have been very different had Joseph not gone through what he did during those difficult years of 1837 and 1838. Those were difficult in the most dramatic way, but they made him who he was.

Just one example that helps illustrate this change: On December 16, 1838, Joseph wrote an angry letter from prison about his enemies, about what the Saints had gone through, about their pain and suffering, and about all their difficulties. Indeed, the Saints had suffered, and the circumstances they were in merited an angry letter. Three months later, his epistle to the Church from Liberty Jail, parts of which became Doctrine and Covenants 121, 122, and 123, breathed a different spirit. And when Joseph emerged from Liberty Jail, he published in Commerce, before it became Nauvoo, what he called "an extract from the private journal of Joseph Smith." He composed this document to record his sufferings in Missouri, but compared to his December 16 letter, its tone was tempered rather than angry. He had mellowed; he had come to understand that his trials were part of the lot of mortality, and he had renewed confidence that he and the Saints could make it through their difficulties and come out the better for it.

I am grateful that Joseph Smith had the calling, the vision, the fortitude, and the Spirit of God within him to accomplish the things he did even in those dark times of late Kirtland in 1837 and the Missouri difficulties of 1838, and that he emerged from these difficulties with the steel and vision to finish his mission in Nauvoo.

Notes

1. For a more detailed account of many of these events and for access to the original sources supporting this retelling, see Ronald K. Esplin, *The Emergence of Brigham Young and the Twelve to Mormon Leadership, 1830–1841*, Dissertations in Latter-day Saint History series (Provo, UT: BYU Studies, 2006); chapters 5–8. Citations to many of the sources used in this article are to the most widely accessible version.

2. Orson F. Whitney, *Life of Heber C. Kimball* (Salt Lake City: Kimball Family, 1888), 111.

3. Warren A. Cowdery, *Messenger and Advocate*, May 1837, 509.

4. Warren A. Cowdery, *Messenger and Advocate*, July 1837, 538.

5. Cowdery, *Messenger and Advocate*, July 1837, 538.

6. Cowdery, *Messenger and Advocate*, July 1837, 538.

7. Oliver Cowdery to Edward Partridge, Far West, Missouri, April 12, 1838, in Joseph Smith, *History of the Church of Jesus Christ of Latter-day Saints*, ed. B. H. Roberts, 2nd ed. rev. (Salt Lake City: Deseret Book, 1957), 3:18.

8. Mary Fielding to Mercy Fielding, June 15, 1837, Church History Library, The Church of Jesus Christ of Latter-day Saints, Salt Lake City.

9. *Wilford Woodruff's Journal: 1833–1878, Typescript*, ed. Scott G. Kenney (Midvale, UT: Signature Books, 1983), 1:106–7.

10. *Wilford Woodruff's Journal*, 1:107.

11. *Wilford Woodruff's Journal*, 1:107–8.

12. *Wilford Woodruff's Journal*, 1:108.

13. *Wilford Woodruff's Journal*, 1:109.

14. *Wilford Woodruff's Journal*, 1:111.

15. *Wilford Woodruff's Journal*, 1:115.

16. *Wilford Woodruff's Journal*, 1:121.

17. *Wilford Woodruff's Journal*, 1:121.

18. *Wilford Woodruff's Journal*, 1:122.

19. *Wilford Woodruff's Journal*, 1:122.

20. *Wilford Woodruff's Journal*, 1:124.

21. *Wilford Woodruff's Journal*, 1:125.

22. *Wilford Woodruff's Journal*, 1:133–34.

23. *Wilford Woodruff's Journal*, 1:138.

24. *Wilford Woodruff's Journal*, 1:139.

25. *Wilford Woodruff's Journal*, 1:147–48.

26. *Wilford Woodruff's Journal*, 1:148.

27. Mary Fielding to Mercy Fielding, ca. June 15, 1837, Church History Library.

28. Mary Fielding to Mercy Fielding, ca. June 15, 1837.

29. Mary Fielding to Mercy Fielding, ca. June 15, 1837.

30. Mary Fielding to Mercy Fielding, ca. June 15, 1837.

31. Mary Fielding to Mercy Fielding, July 8, 1837, Church History Library.

32. Mary Fielding to Mercy Fielding, July 8, 1837.

33. Mary Fielding, 1837 Letters, Church History Library, 60–61.

34. *Wilford Woodruff's Journal*, 5:63.

35. Samuel H. Smith to Hyrum Smith with Don Carlos Smith postscript, October 13, 1837, Church History Library.

36. Joseph Fielding Smith, comp., *Life of Joseph F. Smith: Sixth President of the Church of Jesus Christ of Latter-day Saints* (Salt Lake City: Deseret Book, 1938), 120.

37. Mary Fielding Smith to Hyrum Smith, September 14, 1842, Church History Library.

38. Dean C. Jessee, Mark Ashurst-McGee, and Richard L. Jensen, eds., *Journals, Volume 1: 1832–1839*, vol. 1 of the Journals series of *The Joseph Smith Papers*, ed. Dean C. Jessee, Ronald K. Esplin, and Richard Lyman Bushman (Salt Lake City: Church Historian's Press, 2008), 257–58; see also *History of the Church*, 3:23.

39. Jessee, Ashurst-McGee, and Jensen, *Journals, Volume 1*, 283–84.

The Mormon War. *During a period of nearly four months, August through the end of November, 1838, seven major confrontations took place, and the Saints were required to defend themselves. Above is a depiction of the Haun's Mill Massacre, where a mob killed seventeen men, women, and children. (C. C. A. Christensen [1831–1912],* Haun's Mill, *1865 ca., tempera on muslin, 78 x 114 inches. Brigham Young University Museum of Art, gift of the Christensen grandchildren.)*

ALEXANDER L. BAUGH

1838
Joseph Smith in Northern Missouri

During late 1837, the Church in Kirtland was in turmoil. Dissatisfied with Joseph Smith's leadership, several hundred Saints questioned his divine calling and withdrew from the Church or were excommunicated. At the core of the dissension was the failure of the Kirtland Safety Society, organized and established by Joseph Smith and other Church leaders in late 1836. However, from its beginnings the institution experienced major problems. Unable to secure a legal charter from the Ohio legislature, the officers restructured the enterprise as a joint stock company known as the Kirtland Safety Society Anti-Banking Company in January 1837. Because it lacked state backing, however, other financial institutions questioned the legitimacy of its notes as legal tender. Furthermore,

Alexander L. Baugh is an associate professor of Church history and doctrine at Brigham Young University and an editor of The Joseph Smith Papers.

lacking capital (most of the society's assets were tied up in land and property) and hard specie, the company was forced to seek loans from other banks, leading to additional institutional debt. On a larger scale, during this time the entire U.S. experienced its own nationwide economic crises. Known as the "panic of 1837," the economic downturn and subsequent depression forced the closure of hundreds of lending institutions and businesses nationwide. In July 1837, the Kirtland Safety Society was forced to close its doors, leaving the pockets of its investors empty. Creditors were angry, and charges of mismanagement and lawsuits followed.

Joseph Flees Kirtland

Most of the two hundred individuals who invested in the Safety Society were Church members, many of whom blamed Joseph Smith for their losses, thereafter questioning his authority and ability to receive divine direction. Lacking confidence in Joseph and the First Presidency's leadership, a number of men sought to take control of the Church with the intent to force the First Presidency from office and then oust them from Kirtland entirely. The opposition group was led by Warren Parrish, one-time scribe and secretary to Joseph Smith. Other dissenters included Apostles John F. Boynton and Luke and Lyman E. Johnson; Seventies Hazen Aldrich, Leonard Rich, Sylvester Smith, John Gould, and John Grayson; and even Martin Harris, one of the witnesses to the Book of Mormon. The dissenters not only openly opposed the Mormon leadership but also pursued civil action and criminal lawsuits and in some instances threatened their lives. Joseph Smith's published history states, "The bitterness of the spirit of apostate mobocracy . . . continued to rage and grow hotter and hotter until Elder Rigdon and myself were obliged to flee from its deadly influence, as did the Apostles and Prophets of old, and as Jesus said, 'when they persecute you in one city, flee to another.'"¹ The decision to abandon Kirtland and relocate with the body of Saints then living in Far West, Caldwell County, Missouri, was directed by the following revelation dated January 12, 1838:

> Thus saith the Lord Let the presidency of my Church take their families as soon as it is praticable and a door is open for them and move on to the west as fast as the way is made plain before their faces and let their hearts be comforted for I will be with them
>
> Verily I say unto you the time [has] . . . come that your laibours are finished in this place, for a season, Therefore arise and get yourselves on to a land which I shall show unto you even a land flowing with milk and honey you are clean from the blood of this people and wo unto those who have become your enimies who <have> professed my name saith the Lord, for their judgement lingereth not and their damnation slumbereth not, let all your faithfull friends arise with their families also and get out of this place and gather themselves together unto Zion and be at peace among yourselves O ye inhabitants of Zion or there shall be no safty for you.²

Joseph and Sidney made their departure on the evening of January 12, the very date the revelation instructing them to leave was received. Their hasty departure was necessitated by the fact that the local sheriff planned to arrest Joseph Smith, which likely would have resulted in a lawsuit or imprisonment.³ Lucy Mack Smith reported that her son left in the "dead hour of the night."⁴ Zerah Pulsipher reported that in making the getaway, the Prophet was "carried away in a box nailed on an ox sled." After making their way a safe distance from Kirtland, the pair mounted horses and rode all night before arriving at Norton,

Ohio (southwest of present-day Akron), where they waited for their families to join them.[5]

Joseph Smith's Arrival at Far West, Missouri

The Smith and Rigdon families left Norton, Ohio, for Missouri on January 16, 1838. Although their journey began in the middle of an extremely cold winter, the weather was not their main problem. "We were obliged to secrete ourselves in our wagons . . . to elude the grasp of our pursuers, who continued their pursuit of us more than two hundred miles from Kirtland, armed, with pistols and guns, seeking our lives."[6] After Joseph and Sidney made their way out of Ohio, their antagonists eventually gave up. At Dayton the company picked up the national road, continuing on to Dublin, Indiana, where they had an extended stay with Lorenzo Dow Young, brother of Brigham Young.[7] Leaving Dublin, Joseph and his family parted ways with the Rigdons and headed due west through Indianapolis and Terre Haute, then further west to Quincy, Illinois. A short while after crossing the Mississippi River, the Prophet's party was met by a company from Far West who provided additional teams and money to complete the journey. On March 14, Joseph and his family arrived at Far West. In a letter to the Kirtland presidency, written two weeks after his arrival, the Prophet described the elation he felt to be united with his fellow Saints:

> Through the grace & mercy of our God, after a long & tedious Journey of two months & one day, I and my family arrived in the City of Far West Having been met at Huntsville 120 Miles from this by brotheren with teams & money to forward us on our Journey When within eight miles of the City of Far West We were met by an escort of bretheren from

the City . . . who received us with open armes and warm hearts and welcomed us to the bosom of their Sosciety On our arrival in the City we were greeted on Every hand by the Saints who bid us welcome; Welcome; to the land of their inheritance.[8]

At Far West, Joseph, Emma, and their family took up temporary residence with George Washington Harris, a member of the Missouri high council, and his wife, Lucinda Morgan.[9] A short while later, the Church provided the Smith family with a modest two-room frame home about a quarter of a mile southwest of the public square. Joseph lived here until his arrest in late October 1838. Emma lived in the home until February 1839, when she and the children made their way out of the state.[10]

Revelation Explaining Isaiah 11 and 52

Within just a few days of his arrival, probably during an informal meeting with perhaps several men, Joseph Smith was asked to clarify passages from Isaiah. His explanations regarding verses found in the eleventh and fifty-second chapters were noted in his "Scriptory Book" by his secretary George W. Robinson. Significantly, in his 1839 history, Joseph Smith indicated that on the occasion of the visit of the angel Moroni on September 21–22, 1823, the heavenly messenger "quoted the Eleventh Chapter of Isaiah saying that it was about to be fulfilled" (see Joseph Smith—History 1:40). Regarding Isaiah 11:1–5, 10–11, the general interpretation among Christian scholars is that the passage is a prophetic allusion to the life and ministry of Jesus. While the Latter-day Saints accept this interpretation, they believe the passage has dual meaning because Joseph Smith indicated that the fulfillment of Isaiah 11 was yet future. Given this, Latter-day Saints believe the "stem" and the "root" of Jesse spoken of by Isaiah is none other than the Prophet Joseph Smith himself.[11]

Excommunications

The Prophet probably expected that Missouri would bring a respite from the internal opposition he experienced in the Kirtland community. However, at the time of his arrival at Far West on March 14, the Missouri Church was in the middle of a crisis of its own. In 1836, using Church funds, W. W. Phelps and John Whitmer, two members of the Missouri presidency (David Whitmer was president), made land purchases in the newly created Caldwell County. Later, the two men were charged with buying and selling Church property in their own names and retaining some of the profits from the sales. However, perhaps more incriminating was the charge against the presidency for selling Church property in Jackson County, an act interpreted by their brethren as totally disregarding the commandments given in revelation (see D&C 57:1–4; 101:67–75; 105:26–29). In early February 1838 (before Joseph Smith's arrival at Far West), the high council met to discuss the actions of the Missouri presidency, and a vote was taken wherein they were rejected as a presidency but retained their Church membership. Thomas B. Marsh and David W. Patten, the two senior members of the Twelve, were then sustained as presidents pro tem. A month later, on March 10, the three former presidents still had not made adequate reconciliation concerning the situation, so the council voted unanimously to excommunicate the two counselors, W. W. Phelps and John Whitmer. Marcellus Cowdery, nephew of Oliver, objected to the action taken by the council and was disfellowshipped as a result of his protest. The Prophet arrived at Far West four days later and in a meeting on March 15 gave his approval to the action taken by the high council.[12]

The council waited for the Prophet's arrival at Far West before taking any action in the cases of the assistant president, Oliver Cowdery, and the Missouri president, David Whitmer. Cowdery moved to Missouri during the late summer or fall of 1837 after being accused of adultery (a charge which was not true) as well as mismanagement in connection with the Kirtland Society and its collapse. Joseph, aware that Oliver was teetering, issued a formal announcement concerning his status in the Church. "Oliver Cowdery has been in transgression," he reported, "I trust [however] that he will yet humble himself and magnify his calling, but if he should not, the Church will be under the necessity of raising their hands against him."[13] After he arrived in Missouri, Oliver's dissatisfaction deepened, and he began stirring up trouble and making his own accusations, particularly against Joseph. Being accused of infidelity himself, and knowing the Prophet had entered into a polygamous relationship in Ohio, Cowdery violated the personal trust he shared with Joseph and spread information concerning the Prophet's plural marriage to Fanny Alger, accusing him of adultery.[14] The second elder also became partner with the Missouri presidency in selling property in Jackson County contrary to the revelations, and he informed others that he did not believe the Church had any authority to dictate in temporal matters. One month after the Prophet's arrival in Far West, the Missouri high council met to discuss Oliver's attitude and conduct. Cowdery received notice of the hearing and the nine allegations made against him but chose not to appear before the body. Instead, he wrote a formal letter wherein he preferred discussing only two of the accusations. After lengthy discussion, six of the charges were sustained by the council, and the body severed his membership on April 12, 1838.[15]

The day after Oliver Cowdery's hearing, April 13, the council met to consider David Whitmer. Upon learning that his brother-in-law Oliver had been excommunicated, Whitmer addressed a letter to John Murdock, stating that he had decided to "withdraw from your fellowship and communion." The council met to consider the matter anyway, and Alanson Ripley preferred five charges against Whitmer, all of which were sustained, whereupon the council voted in favor of excommunication. During the same meeting, the high council also ruled against Lyman E. Johnson, one of the Twelve.[16] There was one additional Whitmer casualty, Jacob. Although there are no Church records extant indicating his formal separation from the Church, following the departure of his brothers from the faith, he likewise alienated himself from the main body of believers.[17]

Two other leaders became disaffected with the Church. First was Apostle William E. McLellin. According to his own statements, McLellin's disenchantment with Mormonism and its leaders began in 1836, when he left the main body of the Church for a brief time. He returned, however, and was sustained as a member of the Twelve as late as November 1837. During that same month, he apparently settled in Far West, because records indicate he accepted a commission in the Missouri state militia. However, by April 1838, his loyalty to the Church was again brought into question. On May 11 a trial was held for McLellin wherein he stated he had no confidence in the leaders of the Church. It is not known whether this trial constituted his excommunication, but his complete break with Mormonism occurred about this time. Unlike the other dissidents, who chose to remain in the Mormon community, he relocated in Clay County soon after losing his membership.[18]

Second was Frederick G. Williams, counselor to Joseph Smith in the First Presidency. As early as May 1837, Williams was wavering. According to one source, his problems started when he began to believe in the revelations of an unnamed sister in the Church. The matter was investigated, but apparently no action was taken. Incidents surrounding the collapse of the Kirtland Safety Society during the summer generated more discord between the Prophet and his counselor, leading Joseph to drop him from the presidency. In spite of the rift with the Prophet, Williams moved to Missouri, where he remained a member of the Church but took up a close association with the Missouri presidency and other dissidents. At a conference of the Church held in Far West on November 7, Williams's vacancy in the First Presidency was filled by Hyrum Smith, who was officially sustained as the new Second Counselor. Even though Williams was not as active in his opposition, his association with the dissidents put him in their camp.[19] The departure of these leading men from the Church, especially the disaffections of Oliver Cowdery and David and John Whitmer—three of Joseph's closest friends—must have been devastating to him. Perhaps he believed they would make a quick return to the Church; however, this was not the case.

April Revelations

During the month of April 1838, Joseph Smith received three revelations—two which have been canonized, and one that has not. On April 17, 1838, just over a month after the Prophet's arrival at Far West, David W. Patten and Brigham Young were both named in revelation. At the time, Patten was second in seniority in the Twelve, and Young third.

Both revelations are brief, containing personal direction and instruction. In his revelation, Patten was instructed to settle his personal affairs so that he could embark on a collective mission with the other members of the Twelve the following spring, 1839. Although the revelation does not mention where the Twelve would be sent, reports had been received regarding the success of Apostles Heber C. Kimball, Orson Hyde, and five other missionaries then serving in north-central Great Britain. The revelation implied that the entire Twelve would perform a follow-up mission to the British Isles the next year.[20] Tragically, Patten was never able to fulfill the revelation because he died on October 25, 1838, after being wounded in the Battle of Crooked River in northern Ray County. Patten's revelation is now included as section 114 in the Doctrine and Covenants.[21]

Brigham Young's revelation is more personal than Patten's, which possibly explains why this revelation was not chosen to be included in the Doctrine and Covenants. Young left Kirtland on December 22, 1837, arriving in Far West, Missouri, on March 14, 1838, in company with Joseph Smith. Shortly thereafter he purchased land on Mill Creek (probably in Kingston Township), about four miles east of Far West, where he built a home and began to provide for his family. The revelation states, "Verrily thus Saith the Lord, Let my Servant Brigham Young go unto the place which he has bought on Mill Creek and there provide for his family until an effectual door is op[e]ned for the suport of his family untill I shall command to go hence, and not to leave his family untill they are amply provided for Amen."[22] At the time Brigham's family consisted of his wife Mary Ann (Angell) and five children—Elizabeth and Vilate (daughters from Brigham's first wife, Miriam Works, who died in 1832), Joseph A., and twins Brigham Jr. and Mary, the last two born on December 18, 1837, just four days before Brigham's departure from Kirtland. Due to the delivery, Mary Ann and the children came to Missouri separate from her husband, and the travel and care of the newborns and other children seriously affected her health. The wording of the revelation suggests that Mary Ann and the children had arrived, hence the instruction to Brigham that he provide for his children due to his wife's precarious health.

The most important of the April revelations was the one received by Joseph Smith on April 26, 1838, and it contains three major elements. First, the revelation specifies that a change be made in the name of the Church. When the Church was organized on April 6, 1830, it bore the name the Church of Christ (see D&C 20:1). Then, beginning on May 3, 1834, the Church officially adopted the title the Church of the Latter Day Saints.[23] However, the revelation specifies that from that time forward the Church be called the Church of Jesus Christ of Latter Day Saints, albeit with minor changes to the punctuation and capitalization.

Second, the revelation instructed the Saints to move forward with the construction of a temple at Far West. Following the creation of Caldwell County in December 1836, Church leaders discussed plans regarding the building of a temple at Far West. As early as April 1837, nearly a year before the Prophet's arrival, the Missouri presidency, high council, and bishopric were "appointed to superintend the building of the house of the Lord in . . . Far West."[24] A site was subsequently chosen in the northeast corner of the Far West public square, and work began on July 3, 1837. W. W. Phelps noted that on that day some fifteen hundred Saints assembled and broke ground, digging an excavation 110 feet long by 80 feet wide.[25] Although the digging of the foundation marked an important beginning, further construction was suspended until Joseph Smith could give instruction and direction. When the Prophet visited Far West during the first week of November 1837, a council was held in which it was decided that "the building of the House of the Lord be postponed until the Lord shall reveal it to be His will to have it commenced."[26] That understanding came on April 26, 1838, less than six weeks after Joseph Smith's arrival in northern Missouri. A portion of the revelation reads as follows:

> Let the City Far West, be a holy and consecrated land unto me, and <it shall> be called <most> holy for the ground upon which thou Standest is holy Therefore I command you to build an house unto me for the gathering togethering of my Saints that they may worship me, and let there be a begining of this work; and a foundation and a preparatory work, this following Summer; and let the begining be made on the 4th day of July next; and from that time forth let my people labour diligently to build an house, unto my name, and in one year from this day, let them recommence laying the foundation of my house; thus let them from that time forth laibour diligently untill it Shall be finished, from the Corner Stone thereof unto the top thereof, untill there Shall not any thing remain that is not finished.[27]

Thus the Saints were to dedicate the Far West temple site or foundation on July 4, 1838. Thereafter they were to make preparations (i.e., secure rock, lumber, and other building materials) and begin construction "in one year from this day," namely on April 26, 1839.

A final element of the revelation specified that Far West was to be the main place of Mormon gathering, with additional localities being designated as settlement areas as needed. The revelation reads, "Verrily I Say unto you it is my will, that the

City Far West Should be built up spedily, by the gathering of my Saints, and also that other places Should be appointed for Stakes in the regions round about as they shall be manifested unto my Servant Joseph from time to time."[28] To encourage the Saints living in the East to immigrate to northern Missouri, on May 4, just a week after the revelation, the Prophet prepared an editorial, later published in the *Elders' Journal*, describing the favorable conditions of the region: "No part of the world can produce a superior to Caldwell County," he exclaimed, "the country is healthy, and the farming . . . is equal to that in any part of the world, . . . the means of living are very easily obtained, not even luxuries excepted."[29] Throughout the spring, summer, and early fall, Church members by the hundreds heeded the revelation and Joseph Smith's call to relocate to northern Missouri. Significantly, by the end of 1838 the Saints had established a dozen settlement communities in Caldwell and Daviess Counties, and Far West could claim the distinction of being the largest frontier settlement in northern Missouri. In summary, the revelation specified the name of the Church, instructions regarding the dedication and construction of a temple, and the call to gather. The revelation comprises what is today section 115 in the Doctrine and Covenants.

Expeditions into Daviess County

With the expectation that a large number of Latter-day Saints would be relocating to Missouri that summer, and in accordance with the April 26 revelation which indicated that besides Far West "other places should be appointed for stakes in the regions round about," Joseph Smith conducted at least three exploratory expeditions to Daviess County, north of Caldwell County, between May 18 and June 5, to search for possible settlement locations.[30] On May 18, the Prophet and a number of others left Far West on the first of three exploratory expeditions to Daviess County "for the purpose of . . . making Locations & laying claims for the gathering of the Saints for the benefit of the poor."[31] The following day, May 19, the company arrived at the home of Lyman Wight. In February 1838, Wight secured a property claim about twenty-three miles north of Far West on the Grand River in the Grand River Township in Daviess County, where he farmed and operated a ferry during the high-water season. On this occasion, the first time Joseph Smith visited the region, the Prophet's secretary George W. Robinson recorded the following significant entry in the Prophet's Scriptory Book: "Spring Hill a name appropriated by the bretheren present, But afterwards named by the mouth of [the] Lord and was called Adam Ondi Awmen [Adam-ondi-Ahman], because said he it is the place where Adam shall come to visit his people, or the Ancient of days shall sit as spoken of by Daniel the Prophet."[32] The entry is significant for two reasons. First, it reveals that the region of Spring Hill where Lyman Wight was living was the ancient homeland of Adam following his and Eve's expulsion from the Garden of Eden. And second, Latter-day Saints familiar with Daniel's biblical prophecy in Daniel 7:9–10 and 13–14 will understand that before the Second Coming of Christ to all the world the resurrected Jesus and the resurrected Adam, the "ancient of days," will visit and preside at an assemblage of Adam's posterity at Adam-ondi-Ahman. Immediately following Joseph's mid-May visit to the region and his pronouncement, people began to identify the region as Adam-ondi-Ahman, or Diahman for short. The Scriptory Book passage, with two minor variations, now comprises Doctrine and Covenants section 116 and is the shortest revelation in the book.[33]

The Altar on Tower Hill

While at the base of a large hill near Lyman Wight's cabin, George W. Robinson recorded that they discovered "the remains of an old Nephitish Alter." To commemorate the discovery, Joseph Smith called the place Tower Hill. The wording of Robinson's statement as recorded in the Prophet's Scriptory book has led to a number of erroneous conclusions by historians and others regarding what the party actually came across or discovered. In fact, in editing the Prophet's manuscript history, which B. H. Roberts later edited and published as the *History of the Church*, the editors changed Robinson's narrative to read in first person as if Joseph Smith were writing it and then changed the statement to read that the Prophet discovered "the remains of an old *Nephite* [italics mine] altar or tower."[34] Such a change has led to the erroneous conclusion that the structure was in fact an actual Nephite altar from the Book of Mormon period and culture. However, this is simply not true. So what did Robinson mean when he said they discovered the remains of a "Nephitish" structure? It is important to note that the early Latter-day Saints clearly believed that the native North American tribes were descendants of the earlier Nephite-Lamanite civilization. With this belief, Robinson probably used the word "Nephitish" to indicate that the structure or altar was built by, or originated with, the North American Indians. He may have also used "Nephitish" to mean that the altar was of ancient origin. Therefore, what Robinson was attempting to describe were the remains of what appeared to be a sacred altar structure erected by early Native Americans.

The matter is further complicated by the fact that a number of Joseph Smith's contemporaries made statements about visiting Tower Hill and seeing the ancient ruins and then reported them as being Adamic or that the structure was in fact part of the original altar used by Adam to offer sacrifices. Archaeologically speaking, it is extremely rare for almost any type of physical structure, large or small, to survive some five or six thousand years under any circumstances. Furthermore, it is important to note that nowhere in Joseph's personal record book (the Scriptory Book) he was keeping in 1838 is there any statement by him identifying the ruins on Tower Hill as being Adamic. So how did the idea come about that the peculiar ruins on Tower Hill originated with Adam?

Although a full treatment cannot be given here, the following will have to suffice. During the summer and fall of 1838, Joseph Smith visited Adam-ondi-Ahman, and on a number of occasions he, along with others, went to Tower Hill. In the reminiscences of those of the Prophet's contemporaries who visited the site, either with Joseph or not, there is consistent agreement that the Prophet specifically identified Tower Hill as the location where Adam offered ancient sacrifices. Given this, one can see how after visiting the site and seeing the ruins and being told by Joseph that this was where Adam sacrificed, they would naturally associate the ancient remains with Adam when they were in fact of much later origin.

In summary, the following conclusions can be made. First, on May 19, 1838, Joseph Smith revealed that the location known as Spring Hill, in Daviess County, Missouri, was anciently known as Adam-ondi-Ahman, or the homeland of Adam and his posterity, and that at a future day, before the Second Coming of the Savior Jesus Christ, a great and marvelous council meeting will take place at that location. Second, the archaeological remains which the Prophet's party discovered on May 19, 1838, could not have originated with Adam; rather, they were of Native American origin. Third, since Joseph Smith taught that Tower Hill was the location where Adam offered sacrifice, many of his contemporaries mistakenly identified the remains of the ancient structure still present there in 1838 as being of Adamic rather than of Native American origin.

Birth of Alexander Hale Smith

In late May, while Joseph Smith was on one of the expeditions to Daviess County, word came from Far West that Emma was in labor and about to deliver. George W. Robinson recorded on June 1 that Joseph returned to Far West to attend to Emma.[35] The baby was born June 2 and was given the name Alexander Hale Smith. Family tradition says he was named after Alexander W. Doniphan. Doniphan had acted as chief legal counsel to the Saints since 1833 and was highly respected by the entire Latter-day Saint community. Joseph's acquaintance with Doniphan was much shorter, only a few months, but both men had a mutual admiration for each other. The birth of Alexander brought the number of Smith children to four—Julia (the adopted Murdock daughter, age seven), Joseph III (age five), Frederick Granger (almost two), and Alexander.

Creation of the Adam-ondi-Ahman Stake

Unfortunately, Robinson failed to make any entries in Joseph Smith's personal history from June 5 to July 4, so historians are left in the dark regarding the Prophet's day-to-day activities during this time. However, an important entry in the *Elders' Journal* indicates that in late June Joseph was once again in Daviess County. On June 28, during a conference held in a small grove near Lyman Wight's cabin, Joseph Smith organized the Adam-ondi-Ahman stake, the third stake organized in the Church, with John Smith (the Prophet's uncle) as president and Reynolds Cahoon and Lyman Wight as counselors. The stake, however, would be short-lived. Following the expulsion of the Saints from Daviess County in November 1838, it was dissolved.[36]

Far West Temple Site Dedication

As instructed by Joseph Smith's April 26, 1838, revelation, on July 4 perhaps as many as two to three thousand persons assembled on the public square for the temple site dedication and cornerstone-laying ceremonies for the Far West temple.[37] The day's activities were conducted in grand style. The festivities commenced at 10 a.m. with a grand parade consisting of military infantry, Church leaders according to their offices, "ladies and gentlemen," and cavalry. The entire procession marched to the public square to the music of a brass band led by Dimick B. Huntington. After assembling at the temple site, the entire company formed a circle around the excavation, with the ladies in front. Joseph Smith offered the opening prayer.[38]

Early temple site dedications were characterized by the placement of a large cornerstone, cut and roughly shaped beforehand, at each of the corners of the excavated foundation, after which a prayer of dedication was offered. The Far West cornerstones were cut by Elisha Averett (chief mason), Dimick B. Huntington, and Cornelius Lott.[39] Each stone was approximately seven feet long, four feet wide, and two feet thick.[40] The cornerstones were dedicated in the following order by the following leaders, each of whom was assisted by twelve men: (1) southeast (Missouri stake presidency), (2) southwest (presidents of the elders), (3) northwest (the bishop), and (4) northeast (president of the teachers). After each stone was laid, the band struck up a number.[41]

The day before the July 4 dedication and festivities, Joseph Smith asked Levi Hancock to compose a song for the ceremonies.

"He worked on it much in the night, and had it ready for the occasion," wrote Levi's son, Mosiah Hancock. The song, titled "Song of Freedom," consisted of twelve stanzas.[42]

At the conclusion of the cornerstone ceremonies, Church leaders and dignitaries next took their places on a stand constructed for the occasion. Sidney Rigdon, first counselor in the First Presidency, gave the oration. Rigdon used the occasion to eloquently recount the principles of freedom by which the founders established the government and the rights that religious societies are entitled to under its provisions. Speaking in general terms, he also spoke of the false reports circulated about Mormonism as well as the persecution and suffering experienced by the Church from its earliest beginnings. But in his closing statements the speech took on a different tone. Buoyed by the relative peace that had existed in northern Missouri since 1836, and secure in the notion that continued immigration would result in a steady increase in their population, Rigdon announced that the Latter-day Saints would no longer suffer abuse at the hands of their enemies. His final words were words of warning: "That mob that comes on us to disturb us; it shall be between us and them a war of extermination, for we will follow them, till the last drop of their blood is spilled, or else they will have to exterminate us; for we will carry the seat of war to their own houses, and their own families, and one party or the other shall be destroyed." In the end, Rigdon's expressions proved to be partly prophetic.[43]

Following Rigdon's speech, those assembled participated in the "Hosanna Shout," a sacred vocal expression in which the Saints exclaim in unison, "Hosanna, Hosanna, Hosanna, to God and the Lamb. Amen, Amen, and Amen," repeated three times.[44] With the ceremonies completed, Church leaders left the stand and took a position on the south side of the temple excavation. Here the military officers and troops paraded and passed in review before the Church leaders, after which the entire procession was dismissed.[45] A grand celebration indeed!

July 8, a Day of Revelation

July 8 could very well be called a day of revelation. On this day, the Prophet received five separate revelations—the most known to have been recorded on one single day. The first of these revelations included instructions addressed in a letter from the First Presidency to Newel K. Whitney, William Marks, and Oliver Granger. Following Joseph's departure from Kirtland, Marks was appointed to preside over the Saints who remained there. Newel K. Whitney, the bishop in Kirtland, also remained to oversee the temporal operations of the Church. However, it was fully expected that both men would, in short order, settle their affairs and relocate along with the rest of the Saints in Missouri. However, by July, the two men were still living in Kirtland, while the majority of members had made their way or were en route to the West. The revelation made clear in no uncertain terms that Marks and Whitney were to relocate to Missouri before winter. The revelation implied that, once in Missouri, they would preside over the Saints in their respective callings—Marks as president of the Missouri stake, and Whitney as a bishop at Adam-ondi-Ahman. To expedite the process, Oliver Granger was dispatched to Kirtland to act as an agent for the First Presidency in settling some of their business affairs.[46] The revelation constitutes what is today section 117.

Pursuant to the instructions given in the revelation, Newel K. Whitney and his family left Kirtland in the fall of 1838. However, after arriving in St. Louis, the Whitneys learned of the expulsion of the Saints from Missouri, so they relocated temporarily in Greene County, Illinois, later moving to Commerce in 1839. The Marks family settled for a short time in Quincy before their move to Commerce. Marks subsequently became the Nauvoo stake president. Whitney became one of the first four bishops in Nauvoo.

A second revelation received on July 8 was directed specifically to the Twelve. As noted, the April 17 revelation to David W. Patten stated that the Twelve would be appointed to fill a quorum mission beginning in the spring of 1839 (see D&C 114). The July 8 revelation was a follow-up revelation, instructing them that the 1839 mission would be overseas, namely to Great Britain. Furthermore, specific instruction was given regarding their date and place of departure. The revelation stated, "Let them take leave . . . of Far West, on the twenty-sixth day of April next [April 26, 1839], on the building-spot of my house." Furthermore, because of the excommunications of four of the original members of the quorum of the Twelve during the previous months—John F. Boynton, brothers Luke S. and Lyman E. Johnson, and William E. McLellin—the quorum was incomplete, necessitating that new members be called. Those appointed in the revelation to fill the vacancies were John Taylor, John E. Page, Wilford Woodruff, and Willard Richards.[47] The revelation is now section 118.

Probably the best known and most often cited of the five revelations received by Joseph Smith on July 8 was the revelation on tithing, which presently constitutes section 119. In 1837, Church leaders in both Kirtland and Missouri had discussed the idea of implementing some sort of tithing system in the Church, but no action had been taken. However, by the summer of 1838, Far West was bustling with economic enterprise, a temple was planned, hundreds of Latter-day Saints from Ohio and other eastern branches had gathered to Missouri, and more were expected throughout the summer, all of which necessitated immediate capital and property. Because of the Church's pressing economic needs, coupled with the need to standardize the financial contributions made by Church members, Joseph Smith sought revelatory direction. The Prophet's history states that the revelation came as a direct result of personal inquiry. It reads, "O! Lord. show unto thy servents how much thou requirest of the properties of thy people for a Tithing?" The answer received was essentially twofold. The first part reads, "Verrily thus saith the Lord, I require all their surpluss property to be put into the hands of the Bishop of my Church of Zion, for the building of mine house, and for the Laying the foundation of Zion, and for the priesthood, and for the debts of the presidency of my Church, and this shall be the begining of the tithing of my people." In other words, in order to jump-start the program, the Saints were directed to give all their surplus assets, resources, or property to the Church. This would enable to Church to have the immediate resources it needed. The second part of the revelation then reads, "and after that," meaning after they have consecrated any surplus, "those who have thus been tithed, shall pay one tenth of all their interest [or increase] annually."[48]

After the instructions on tithing were received, a companion revelation was given identifying the officers appointed to oversee the expenditure of the tithing funds received: "Verily thus saith the Lord, the time has now come that it shall be disposed of by a council composed of the first Presidency of my Church and of the Bishop and his council and by <my> high Council, and <by> mine own voice unto them saith the Lord, even so Amen."[49] In short, the revelation called for the tithing funds to be disbursed by a council comprising the First Presidency, the Missouri bishopric, and the Missouri high council. Today, however, there is a slightly different arrangement. The council, referred to as the Council on the Disposition of the Tithes, comprises the First Presidency, the Presiding Bishopric, and the Quorum of the Twelve.

The fifth and final July 8 revelation is one directed to Frederick G. Williams and William W. Phelps. As noted, for over a year Williams's standing in the Church was up and down. In November 1837 he was dropped from the First Presidency, although he remained in the Church. Phelps had also wavered, resulting in his excommunication by the Missouri high council in March 1838. However, by July both Williams and Phelps had apparently made satisfactory restitution and were reinstated into the Church as evidenced by the following uncanonized revelation: "Verrily thus Saith the Lord in consequence of their transgressions, their former standing has been taken away from them and now if they will be saved, Let them be ordained as Elders, in my Church, to preach my gospel and travel abroad from land to land and from place to place, to gather mine Elect unto me Saith the Lord, and let this be their labors from hence forth Even So Amen."[50] Once again, because of the personal nature of the revelation, one can understand why it was never included in the canon of scripture.

An Interesting July 1838 Editorial

In late 1837, Joseph Smith made a relatively short trip to Missouri (September 27–December 10).[51] Upon his return, the Prophet included an account of his travels in the *Elders' Journal* (then being published in Kirtland), noting that while on the journey, people of all classes "daily and hourly" posed questions to him. At the conclusion of his narrative, he listed twenty questions he had been asked from time to time. Sensing that the answers to some of the questions would be beneficial to honest inquirers as well as to the Saints, he indicated that he would answer them in the next issue of the *Elders' Journal*.[52] However, due to the relocation of the Church to Far West in 1838, the next issue of the *Elders' Journal* did not appear until July of that year. Nonetheless, that issue included the Prophet's responses. A few of the more interesting and even comical questions, and Joseph's responses, are noted below:

> Question 3rd. Will every body be damned but Mormons?
>
> Answer. Yes, and a great portion of them, unless they repent and work righteousness. . . .
>
> Question 10. Was not Jo Smith a money digger[?]
>
> Answer. Yes, but it was never a very profitable job to him, as he only got fourteen dollars a month for it. . . .
>
> Question 11th. Did not Jo Smith steal his wife[?]
>
> Answer. Ask her; she was of age, she can answer for herself. . . .
>
> Question 15th. Do the Mormons baptize in the name of Jo Smith[?]
>
> Answer. No, but if they did, it would be as valid as the baptism administered by the sectarian priests. . . .
>
> Question 20th. What are the fundamental principles of your religion[?]
>
> Answer. The fundamental principles of our religion is the testimony of the apostles and prophets concerning Jesus Christ, "that he died, was buried, and rose again the third day, and ascended up into heaven;" and all other things are only appendages to these, which pertain to our religion.[53]

The Mormon War

On August 6, 1838, hostilities between the Latter-day Saints and the Missourians erupted when a group of Mormons came to Gallatin in Daviess County to exercise their right to vote in the state elections, and historians mark the beginning of the Missouri Mormon War with the election-day skirmish. During a period of nearly four months, from August through the end of November, seven major confrontations or military campaigns took place which included the following: (1) the confrontation between Mormons and Missouri vigilantes in Daviess County, including the intercession made by regional militia (August through mid-September); (2) the Latter-day Saint defense of the Mormon population residing in Carroll County against county regulators, and the response of the regional militia to the disturbances (August through October 10); (3) the burning of Millport and Gallatin and the expulsion of the non-Mormon residents of Daviess County by Mormon militia (mid-October); (4) the encounter between Mormon and Missouri militia at Crooked River in Ray County (October 25); (5) the attack of the Mormon settlement of Haun's Mill by Missouri vigilantes (October 30); (6) the Mormon defense of Far West against vigilante and state militia forces (October 28–31); and (7) the Mormon surrender and the military occupation conducted by authorized militia (November 1–29).

During the entire Mormon War, Joseph Smith played an active role, but he did so as a private citizen. He held no rank in the county or state militia and in fact claimed exemption from militia duty based on his ministerial responsibilities. Throughout the conflict, the Prophet was content to have the legally authorized and commissioned Mormon officers conduct the military activities. Frequently, these officers sought his advice and counsel, but they did so because he was the President of the

Church, one who they thought could provide proper counsel. However, in the capacity of a private citizen and Mormon defender, Joseph Smith participated or was on the scene in three of the seven confrontations. He went with some two hundred other Mormon defenders to Daviess County in mid-October, but he did not participate in any of the company's activities. When Carroll and Daviess citizens conducted the siege of the Mormon community of De Witt in early October, Joseph visited the settlement to assess the situation, but he did not engage in any fighting. Finally, he was present at Far West during the last days of the war when the Mormons made their final stand to defend the community, but no hostilities between the Mormon troops and the state militia took place. That said, at the time of the Mormon surrender, Missouri authorities had every intention of arresting Joseph Smith with the hope of prosecuting him for his involvement in the Missouri Mormon War.

Arrests at Far West

On October 27, 1838, after nearly three months of hostilities between Mormon and Missouri settlers in Daviess, Carroll, Ray, and Caldwell counties, Governor Lilburn W. Boggs signed an executive order authorizing the state militia to subdue the Mormon populace, force their surrender, and compel them to evacuate the state.[54] The order was carried out by Samuel D. Lucas, a major general in the state militia and the commander of the troops from Jackson and Lafayette counties. The day before issuing the extermination order, Boggs relieved Major General David R. Atchison of his command of the state militia in the Northern District.[55] Atchison was likely released because he had served as legal counsel to Joseph Smith and was sympathetic to the Mormons. Boggs replaced Atchison with John B. Clark of Howard County. However, because Clark was not on the scene to take charge, Lucas assumed command. On October 31, Lucas and his officers negotiated a peaceful albeit unfair settlement with a five-man Mormon delegation led by George M. Hinckle, commander of the Caldwell County militia. The final conditions of surrender called for the Mormons to surrender property to cover any damages caused during the Missouri conflict, give up their arms, and agree to leave the state. A final stipulation required their leaders to be turned over to Missouri authorities.[56]

Lucas wasted no time in apprehending those who he thought were the chief instigators behind the Mormon insurgence, namely, Joseph Smith, Sidney Rigdon, Parley P. Pratt, Lyman Wight, and George W. Robinson. On November 1, Hyrum Smith and Amasa M. Lyman were arrested. The reasons why these seven men were apprehended appear evident. Joseph Smith, Rigdon, and Hyrum Smith comprised the Church's First Presidency. Robinson was the Prophet's secretary. Lyman Wight was the highest-ranking Mormon militia officer in Daviess County and had played a leading role in the Mormon retaliatory strikes in Daviess County in October. Amasa Lyman was a leader of a spy company that reconnoitered throughout southern Caldwell and northern Ray counties during the days just preceding the surrender. Finally, Parley P. Pratt, a member of the Church's Quorum of the Twelve, had been a participant in the battle between Mormon and Missouri militia at Crooked River on October 25.

On the evening of November 1, Lucas made a rash and hasty decision to hold a military court for the seven prisoners. He believed he had to act quickly—before Clark arrived, while he still had command of the operation, since the Howard County general, who was less familiar with the Mormon problem, might be disposed to render more lenient justice in behalf of the Church's leaders. With these considerations in mind, the Jackson County general decided to move ahead immediately with the court-martial. Details concerning the hearing are sketchy, but the evidence is clear that at the time of the hearing, Joseph Smith and his cohorts were in custody at Alexander W. Doniphan's camp and were not even allowed to be present to defend themselves.[57]

The deliberation did not last long. Upon hearing the evidence, Lucas called for a vote from officers of the court, who voted three to one in favor of conviction on the charge of treason, a capital offense.[58] Doniphan vehemently opposed the decision, telling his fellow officers that not one of them was familiar with military law and then leaving the hearing in protest.[59] Nonetheless, with the verdict rendered, Lucas drafted the execution order and dispatched it to Doniphan, expecting his compliance. The order read, "Brigadier-General Doniphan.—Sir: You will take Joseph Smith and the other prisoners into the public square of Far West, and shoot them at 9 o'clock to-morrow morning. [Signed] Samuel D. Lucas Major-General Commanding."[60] However, Doniphan was not about to be an accessory to such an order, and he issued a brusque response. Not only did he inform Lucas that he considered the order illegal and that he would not obey it, but he threatened legal action if the execution was carried out. The illegality of the entire order centered on the fact that at least three of the prisoners, namely, Joseph and Hyrum Smith and Sidney Rigdon of the First Presidency, claimed exemption from state militia service and therefore did not come under military authority.[61] Doniphan had previously acted as Joseph Smith's legal counsel and knew firsthand concerning his military exemption. One of Doniphan's own brigade members reported, "These men had never belonged to any lawful military organization, and could not, therefore, have violated military law. The law of the soldier could not apply to them, as they had not been soldiers in any legal sense."[62] However, the same was not true for the other four prisoners—Lyman Wight, Parley P. Pratt, George W. Robinson, and Amasa Lyman—who were commissioned or elected state militia officers. Despite the fact that four of the seven could have come under military authority, Doniphan's dauntless refusal to carry out Lucas's order, in addition to his warning that he would pursue legal action if the executions were carried out, led Lucas to reconsider his decision and to ultimately decide to keep all seven men in custody until they could be turned over to the appropriate civil authorities.[63]

During the forenoon of November 2, a heavily guarded wagon containing the seven prisoners pulled into Far West. Lucas put Brigadier General Moses Wilson in charge of three hundred men and assigned him to take the Church leaders to Independence while he finalized the surrender.[64] Lucas remained overnight, leaving Far West the next day in order to catch up with Wilson. Around three p.m. on Sunday, November 4, Lucas and Wilson arrived in Independence with the prisoners, who were immediately incarcerated in a vacant log house just north of and across the street from Independence's public square.[65] While incarcerated, Joseph Smith penned a short letter to Emma Smith wherein he provided some details regarding the events since they left Far West. In the letter, Joseph mentions that Lucas, Wilson, and their guards were treating them with considerable kindness. He then shares his concerns for her and the children:

> My dear and beloved companion, of my bosam, in tribulation, and affliction, I woud inform you that I am well, and I am that we are all of us in good spirits as regards our own fate, we have been protected by the Jackson County

boys, in the most genteel manner, and arrived here in <the> midst of a splended perade, ~~this~~ a little after noon, instead <of> going to ~~J~~ goal [jail] we have a good house provided for us and the kindst treatment, I have great anxiety about you, and my lovely children, my heart morns <and> bleeds for the brotheren, and sisters, and for the slain <of the> people of God. . . . I want you to stay where you are untill you here from me again, I may send for you to ~~bl~~ bring you to me, I cannot learn much for certainty in the situation that I am in, and can only pray for deliverance, untill it is meeted out, and take every thing as it comes, with patience and fortitude, I hope you will be faithful and true to every trust, I cant write much in my situa[t]ion, conduct all matters as your circumstances and necesities require, may God give you wisdom and prudance and sobriety which <I> have every reason to believe you will, those little <childrens> are subjects of my meditation continually, tell them that Father is yet alive, God grant that he may see them again Oh Emma for God sake do not forsake me nor the truth but remember, if I do <not> meet you again in this life may God grant that we may <may we> meet in heaven, I cannot express my feelings, my heart is full, Farewell Oh my kind and affectionate Emma I am yours forever your Hu[s]band and true friend
[Joseph Smith, Jr.][66]

On the second day of their confinement in Independence (November 5), in consideration of their hospitable treatment, the seven prisoners drafted and signed a card expressing appreciation to the militia officers (Lucas and Wilson are mentioned by name) and their subordinates for the kindness and civility shown to them. Lucas and Wilson were so pleased by the prisoners' expression of appreciation that they mailed the card to the newspaper editor of the *Boonslick Democrat*, published in

Fayette, Howard County, Missouri, requesting that it be printed. The document was published on November 10, 1838.

> It is with feelings of no ordinary kind that the undersigned take this method of tendering their most unfeigned gratitude to you for the kind treatment and great attention they have received at your hands since they were committed to your charge as prisoners; having received every degree of kindness that could be expected at the hands of a magnanimous and honorable people. This, gentlemen, is not designed as flattery, but a debt that they feel they owe to you. We hope that Generals Lucas and Wilson, and all the officers and privates under their command, will receive this expression of our feelings, as due to them from us, in return for the kind treatment received at their hands. Gentlemen, we found you as friends at a time when we most needed them; and since the time we arrived at this village, we have not received the first insult from any individual.
>
> Gentlemen, we are prisoners in your hands, and such has been your magnanimity, that while we remain prisoners, we shall desire to continue in your care.
>
> For your prosperity in this life, and rest eternal in that which is to come, you have the sincere desire and devout prayer of your prisoners in tribulation.[67]

A day or two after their arrival in Independence, the seven prisoners were moved from the log house a short distance east to the Noland House, a hotel situated on the northwest corner of Main and Maple. Here they waited for word regarding where their hearing would be held. They were treated hospitably and were even permitted to come and go as they pleased.[68]

Transfer to Richmond

On November 4, the same day that Lucas and Wilson arrived in Independence with Joseph Smith and the other six prisoners, Major General John B. Clark arrived at Far West, where he supervised the final activities of the Mormon surrender and conducted additional arrests. The following day, November 5, Clark interrogated Latter-day Saint colonel George M. Hinckle and a number of other Church leaders, who supplied him with information regarding which Saints had played the most active role in the conflict. Later that afternoon, Clark ordered the arrest of forty-six Latter-day Saint men.[69] Clark also dispatched Colonel Sterling G. Price and two companies of state militia to travel to Richmond to meet up with General Lucas and secure Joseph Smith and the other six prisoners. However, at the time, Clark and Price were not aware that Lucas had not gone to Richmond but had proceeded to Independence. When Clark learned that Lucas had taken the seven prisoners to Jackson County, he sent a small detachment to Independence with orders for Lucas to turn over the prisoners so they could be taken to Richmond for examination.[70] On November 7, Clark's men arrived in Independence and took charge of the prisoners. Accordingly, the next day, accompanied by a small military escort, the prisoners proceeded fifteen miles, crossed the Missouri River, and lodged that evening in an old frame house. The following day, November 9, while en route to Richmond, they were met by a strong guard commanded by Colonel Price, who conducted them the rest of the way. Upon their arrival that evening at the Ray County seat, Joseph and Hyrum Smith, Sidney Rigdon, George W. Robinson, Parley P. Pratt, Lyman Wight, and Amasa Lyman were put into an old log house about one block north of Richmond's public square and courthouse, where they were placed under guard and chained together in heavy irons.⁷¹ For three weeks (November 9–29) the log house served as the ad hoc jail for the seven Church leaders. Athalia R. Robinson, Rigdon's seventeen-year-old daughter and wife of George Robinson, also lodged with the prisoners for a time. Because of Rigdon's tenuous health, Athalia was permitted to take care of her ailing father and to be with her husband.⁷²

On the afternoon of Tuesday, November 6, General Clark left Far West and marched to Richmond with the forty-six Mormon men he had taken prisoner. He arrived at the Ray County seat on November 9, where he discharged the remainder of his division, with the exception of a small force he retained to guard the Latter-day Saint prisoners brought to Richmond for the court examination.⁷³ Meanwhile, Captain Samuel Bogart of the Ray County militia made additional arrests of Latter-day Saints suspected of having taken part in the Mormon War who still had not been apprehended. Ultimately, Bogart rounded up an additional eleven Mormon prisoners, bringing the total number of Mormon defendants to sixty-four.⁷⁴ Excluding Joseph Smith and the six other leaders who were incarcerated in the log house, the remaining fifty-seven Mormon prisoners were confined in the Ray County courthouse, the only building large enough to accommodate that many men.

The Richmond Court of Inquiry

Beginning on November 12, court was convened by Fifth Circuit Court judge Austin A. King to examine the charges raised against the Mormons. It is important to understand that the Richmond Court of Inquiry was not a trial per se, but only an investigation or preliminary hearing to determine if there was sufficient evidence or probable cause against the Mormon defendants to bind over the defendants for trial. The court of inquiry began on November 12 and continued through

November 29 (with the likely exception of November 18 and 25, which were Sundays). Thomas Burch and William Wood prosecuted in behalf of the state. The prisoners were represented by Alexander Doniphan and Amos Rees.[75]

Sometime during the opening day of the Richmond hearing (November 12), Joseph Smith penned a letter to Emma from the log house where he and his six other prison companions were shackled. He begins the letter by declaring his innocence: "[W]e are pr prisoners in chains, and under strong guards, for Christ sake and for no other cause, although there has been things that were unbeknown to us, and altogether beyond our controal, that might seem, to the mob to be a pretext, for them to persacute us, but on examination, I think that the authorities, will discover our inocence, and set us free, but if this blessing cannot be done obtained, I have this consolation that I am an innocent man, let what will befall me." He next expresses his love and concern for his family: "Oh God grant that I may have the privaliege of seeing once more my lovely Family, in the injoyment, of the sweets of liberty, and sotiaial life, to press them to my bosam and kissng their lovely cheeks would fill my heart with unspeakable great grattitude, tell the chilldren that I am alive and trust I shall come and see them before long, comfort their hearts all you can, and try to be comforted yourself, all you can." Continuing, he mentions each of his children: "[T]ell little Joseph, he must be a good boy, Father loves him <with> a perfect Hove, he is the Eldest must not hurt those that <are> smaller then him, but cumfor<t> them tell little Frederick, Father, loves him, with all his heart, he is a lovely boy. Julia is a lovely little girl, I love hir also She is a promising child, tell her Father wants her to remember him and be a good girl, tell all the rest that I think of them and pray for them all; . . . little baby Elexander is on my mind continuly." He then concludes the letter with a personal expression of love for Emma: "Oh my affectionate Emma, I want you to remember that I am <a> true and faithful friend, to you and the chilldren, forever, my heart is intwined around you[r]s forever and ever, oh may God bless you all amen ~~you~~ I am your husband and am in bands and tribulations &c."[76]

Each day court was held, Joseph and Hyrum Smith, Sidney Rigdon, George Robinson, Parley P. Pratt, Lyman Wight, and Amasa Lyman were escorted by a small contingent of militia guards under the command of Sterling Price from the log house to the Ray County courthouse, where they joined the other Latter-day Saint prisoners to hear the evidence presented against them. When the hearing recessed at the end of each day, the Smith brothers, Rigdon, Robinson, Pratt, Wight, and Lyman were conducted back to the log house for the night, while the remaining Latter-day Saint prisoners spent the evening confined in the unfinished courthouse. Pratt later reported that one evening during their confinement in the log house Joseph Smith issued a scathing rebuke of the militia guards, an event memorialized in Church history.[77]

Following nearly three weeks of testimony, the court released twenty-nine of the sixty-four defendants. However, Judge King determined that sufficient evidence existed to bind thirty-five over for trial. Twenty-four Mormons were bound over for trial for crimes committed in Daviess County. These defendants were charged with arson, burglary, larceny, and robbery, and were ordered to appear at the circuit court in Daviess County on March 28. After posting bail, these men were released.[78] King ruled that there was sufficient evidence to charge five men—Parley P. Pratt, Norman Shearer, Darwin Chase, Luman Gibbs, and Morris Phelps—in the death of Moses Rowland, which occurred during the attack at Crooked

River. Since the charge of murder was nonbailable, these five men were ordered to remain confined in the Richmond Jail until March 11, 1839, when the circuit trial would convene there. Finally, probable cause was also found against Joseph Smith, Sidney Rigdon, Hyrum Smith, Lyman Wight, Alexander McRae, and Caleb Baldwin on the charge of treason, also a nonbailable offense. Their trial was set to begin on March 7, 1839, in Daviess County. However, because there was no jail in Daviess, King ordered that they be taken to Liberty Jail in Clay County to await their court appearance.[79] The six Church leaders were immediately transferred to Liberty to begin their confinement.

Liberty Jail

In the late afternoon of December 1, 1838, accompanied by an armed guard, Joseph Smith and his five prison companions arrived at the Liberty Jail and were placed under the charge of jailor Samuel Tillery. Lyman Littlefield, a Latter-day Saint, was present at the time the prisoners first entered the jail and years later described the scene:

> This large, clumsy built wagon—the box of which was highest at each end—finally halted close to the platform in front of the jail, which platform had to be reached by means of about half a dozen steps, constructed on the south and north sides of the same. The jail fronted the street at the east.
>
> The prisoners left the wagon and immediately ascended the south steps to the platform, around which no banisters were constructed. The door was open, and, one by one, the tall and well proportioned forms of the prisoners entered. The Prophet Joseph was the last of the number who lingered

behind. He turned partly around, with a slow and dignified movement, and looked upon the multitude. Then turning away, and lifting his hat, he said in a distinct voice, "Good afternoon, gentlemen." The next moment he had passed out of sight. The heavy door swung upon its strong hinges and the Prophet was hid from the gaze of the curious populace who had so eagerly watched.[80]

Originally built in 1833, the jail measured twenty-two by twenty-two and one-half feet and was made of mortared limestone blocks two feet thick. Separating the outer limestone wall from the foot-thick square interior wood timbers was a twelve-inch space of loose rock, making the total wall structure four feet thick. The interior of the jail consisted of a main level upper room and a lower dungeon cell, the latter accessed by means of a trapdoor. Small, grated windows provided ventilation. A small stove provided heat for the upper story, the dungeon being unheated.[81] It was under these conditions that Joseph and Hyrum Smith, Wight, Baldwin, and McRae would spend the next 127 days (December 1, 1838, to April 6, 1839). Rigdon's confinement would be considerably less. On January 25, 1839, he successfully argued his case before Judge Joel Turnham and was released, although he did not leave the jail until February 5.[82] Because the scope of this chapter is the year 1838, I will focus only briefly on Joseph Smith's activities in Liberty Jail during the month of December.

On the evening of his first day of confinement in Liberty, the Prophet wrote the following letter to Emma at Far West to inform her of their removal to the jail and their present situation. "My Dear companion I take this oppertunity to inform you that I we arrived in Liberty and [were] commited to Jaol this Evening but we are all in good spirits Captain bogard [Samuel Bogart] will hand you this line my respects to all remain where you are at preasant Ʝ yours &c. Joseph Smith Jr."⁸³ The short note is one of eight extant letters written or dictated by Joseph Smith from Liberty Jail.

Missouri authorities were considerate enough to allow visitors to the jail, some of whom were also permitted to remain for a few days. One can only imagine how visits from family and friends raised the prisoners' spirits. More often than not, they would bring food, clothing, letters, blankets, and other necessities. Emma visited the jail on three occasions—December 8–9, December 20–22, and finally January 21, 1839.⁸⁴ On two of her visits, six-year-old Joseph III is known to have accompanied her. Years later, Joseph III recalled his father giving him a blessing during one of these two visits.⁸⁵ After the middle of February 1839, the number of visitors dropped off dramatically, primarily because most Saints were making their way out of the state.

More often than not, the prisoners' lives were monotonous. Most of their time was spent conversing with each other. Reading provided some diversion. And there was always plenty of thinking time. Most of all, they were downright uncomfortable. Since they were confined during the winter, the cold took its toll. When confined to the dungeon area in the lower story, it was almost like being exposed to the outside because there was no stove or fireplace to provide any type of indoor heat. Occasionally, they lit a fire, but the room would fill with smoke. About the best they could do to keep warm was to block the grated open windows and bundle up in blankets. Exposure to the cold, combined with filthy and coarse food, led to sickness—nausea, fever, headaches, and body aches, not to mention frazzled nerves. Honey buckets were their latrines, which caused additional stench in the room. They remained in the same clothes for days, and their personal appearance soon became very haggard. Only on rare occasions were they taken outside to get a little exercise and an occasional good meal at a local tavern or to visit with their attorneys—all the while being kept under a strong guard.

By mid-December, Joseph had already had enough of his dreary cell. Full of indignation against those who he perceived were the cause for his imprisonment, his doleful circumstances, and frustrated by the thought of spending the winter in jail, on December 16 he vented his innermost feelings in a lengthy letter addressed to the Church. In the letter, Joseph emphatically declared his innocence. He saw himself, like the ancient prophets and apostles of old, as a victim of religious persecution in the cause of truth. Moreover, he openly named and condemned his accusers, particularly his former friends and associates, most notably George M. Hinckle, Reed Peck, John Corrill, William W. Phelps, Sampson Avard, and John Clemenson, who, during the Mormon surrender and military occupation, cooperated with the Missouri militia officers and later testified as witnesses in behalf of the state during the Richmond hearing. In addition to these men, the Prophet mentioned Martin Harris, David Whitmer, John Whitmer, Oliver Cowdery, William E. McLellin, Thomas B. Marsh, and Orson Hyde, each of whom had apostatized from the Church during the past year and whom Smith also characterized as traitors to the cause. Finally, he emphatically condemned the actions of the state militia and those who carried out acts of aggression against the Saints, labeling them as murderers and robbers. In spite of the letter's condemnatory tone, the Prophet expressed confidence and optimism in the future and a personal conviction that God was still with him and the Latter-day Saint people.[86]

Conclusion

On December 23, 1838, Joseph commemorated his thirty-third birthday. Given his circumstances, it was an extremely difficult time for him. I am certain that as the year came to a close, he reflected considerably on the events of the past twelve months. The year 1838 was not good to him. In fact, if it were possible to ask Joseph Smith, "Looking back over your life, when did you experience the most discouragement? When did you experience the most disappointment? When was life the toughest? When did you hit rock bottom?" my guess is that he would answer, "1838." The events of that year challenged him like no other. The year 1838 stands out to me as the most trial-filled year of his life, 1844 not excepted. Threatened with vexatious lawsuits from apostates and non-Mormon antagonists, he was compelled to leave Kirtland in the middle of winter, only to take up a new residence in the harsh frontier environment of northern Missouri. The Kirtland apostasy of 1837 was serious, but consider whom the Church lost in 1838. First and foremost, there was Oliver Cowdery, Joseph's closest and dearest friend, who abandoned him. Other prominent figures and close associates of the Prophet included David Whitmer, one of the witnesses to the Book of Mormon and the president of the Church in Missouri; John Whitmer, one of the eight witnesses, Church historian, and a member of the Missouri presidency; Frederick G. Williams, former counselor in the First Presidency; W. W. Phelps, a member of the Missouri presidency and Church printer; William E. McLellin, Thomas B. Marsh, and Orson Hyde, members of the Twelve; Hiram Page and Jacob Whitmer, two of the eight witnesses to the Book of Mormon; George M. Hinckle, military commander; Reed Peck; John Corrill; and Sampson Avard. All of these men turned their backs on Mormonism and Joseph Smith. Fortunately, a few eventually found their way back, but for those who did not, while their names appear in the pages of our early history, one wonders what contributions they could have made had they remained faithful.

And then there was the 1838 Missouri Mormon War. Where in the annals of American history is there an equal to the persecutions experienced by a religious minority? Nowhere! When Joseph took up permanent residency at Far West in March 1838, the geographic and political circumstances seemed to indicate that the Mormons would be able to experience relative peace and long-term cooperation with their Missouri neighbors. Yet within just a few months the Latter-day Saints became embroiled in armed conflict, not only with Missouri vigilantes but with authorized state militia. The hostility, mistreatment, and illegal action taken against the Saints by Missouri's citizens and state officials caused unbelievable physical and emotional hardships. But I submit that perhaps Joseph Smith suffered as much as anyone. As President of the Church, he knew that the Saints experienced persecution because they believed in his message and his testimony. Nearly two dozen Saints died as a direct result of the Mormon War—seventeen at Haun's Mill alone. And why were they killed? Because they believed Joseph Smith was God's prophet. No one but Joseph himself will ever comprehend the emotional, psychological, and spiritual pain he felt in behalf of those who suffered because they believed in him.

And finally, there was Liberty Jail—hardly the right name for a prison. Wrongfully and falsely accused, Joseph faced the threat of legal prosecution while in state custody for what would be a period of five and one-half months. Could things get any worse? No wonder in March of 1839 he would exclaim in writing, "O God, where art thou?" (Doctrine and

Covenants 121:1). Fortunately, he could take some reassurance from personal revelation that things would work out. On the morning of November 3, only four days after being taken into custody by Major General Samuel D. Lucas, Parley P. Pratt wrote, "Joseph Smith spoke to me and the other prisoners, in a low, but cheerful and confidential tone; said he: 'Be of good cheer, brethren; the word of the Lord came to me last night that our lives should be given us, and that whatever we may suffer during this captivity, not one of our lives should be taken.'"[87] Little did he realize at the time that it would be five and one-half months before he would be free and clear of Missouri's captivity. Nearing the end of his incarceration, he was reassured once again, "Thy friends do stand by thee, and they shall hail thee again with warm hearts and friendly hands" (Doctrine and Covenants 121:9).

Fortunately, better days were ahead, but freedom would not come until April 22, 1839, when he would leave Missouri for the last time, never to set foot on her soil again, cross the Mississippi, and find permanent refuge in Illinois.

Notes

1. Joseph Smith Jr., *History of the Church of Jesus Christ of Latter-day Saints*, ed. B. H. Roberts, 2nd ed. rev. (Salt Lake City: Deseret Book, 1971), 3:1.

2. Joseph Smith, Revelation, January 12, 1838, Joseph Smith Papers, Church History Library, The Church of Jesus Christ of Latter-day Saints, Salt Lake City. A slightly different version of the revelation was recorded in Joseph Smith's Scriptory Book (see Joseph Smith, Scriptory Book, Joseph Smith Papers, Church History Library; published in *The Papers of Joseph Smith*, vol. 2, *Journal, 1832–1842*, ed. Dean C. Jessee [Salt Lake City: Deseret Book, 1992], 255).

3. See Luke S. Johnson, "History of Luke S. Johnson," *Millennial Star*, January 1, 1865, 5–6. Although Luke Johnson was one of the dissenters who had been excommunicated from the Church, he helped Joseph Smith at the time of his escape from Kirtland.

4. Lucy Mack Smith, *Biographical Sketches of Joseph Smith, the Prophet, and His Progenitors for Many Generations* (London: Published for Orson Pratt by S. W. Richards, 1853), 216.

5. See Smith, *History of the Church*, 3:2. It is significant to note that the revelation instructed the entire presidency of the Church to leave Kirtland. At the time, the First Presidency consisted of Joseph Smith, Sidney Rigdon, and Hyrum Smith, who had replaced Frederick G. Williams as second counselor in the First Presidency in November 1837. In addition to the three First Presidency members, Joseph Sr. (the Prophet's father) and John Smith (the Prophet's uncle) had both been sustained in September 1837 as Assistant Presidents in the First Presidency. Finally, Oliver Cowdery held the office of Assistant President of the Church. Taken together, these six men made up the presidency of the Church. With the exception of Cowdery, who was already in Missouri, Hyrum, Joseph Sr., and John Smith were also compelled to leave Kirtland. Hyrum left in March. John Smith arrived in Missouri sometime in June. Joseph Sr. and Lucy took up temporary residence in New Portage, Ohio, before traveling to Missouri, where they arrived in late July or August.

6. Smith, *History of the Church*, 3:2–3.

7. Leonard J. Arrington, *Brigham Young: American Moses* (New York: Alfred A. Knopf, 1985), 62. Arrington mistakenly identifies Dublin, Indiana, as Dublin, Illinois.

8. Joseph Smith to the Presidency of the Church of Jesus Christ of Latter Day Saints at Kirtland, March 29, 1838, Scriptory Book, 22–23; see also Smith, *History of the Church*, 3:10.

9. Linda King Newell and Valeen Tippetts Avery, *Mormon Enigma: Emma Hale Smith: Prophet's Wife, "Elect Lady," Polygamy's Foe* (Garden City, NY: Doubleday, 1984), 70.

10. In July 1862 or 1863, a newspaper reporter visited Far West and noted seeing the Joseph Smith home, which was still standing at the time. His report, which was not published until 1875, is as follows: "The third feature of interest, perhaps the most attractive on the spot, is the former residence of Joseph Smith, the Mormon prophet, and founder of the Church of Jesus Christ of Latter Day Saints. . . . This is a rude, old fashioned, one story frame building, with two rooms situated about a quarter of mile southwest of the temple site on the n[orth] e[ast] q[uarte]r of sec. 15 T[ownship]. 56, R[ange] 29. . . . The house is at present occupied as a residence by N. Howard. The farm on which it stands was once the property of J. Hughes, but now belongs to Col. Calvin F. Burnes, of St. Joseph" (*Daily Morning Herald* [St. Joseph, Missouri], January 1, 1875). An 1876 plat drawing of Mirable township shows the locality and ownership of the home as described by the reporter, indicating the home was still standing at that time. (*An Illustrated Historical Atlas of Caldwell County, Missouri* [Philadelphia: Edwards Brothers of Missouri, 1876], 37). In 1907, photographer George Edward Anderson visited Far West, where he was shown the location of the home, but by this time the home was no longer standing. However, in Anderson's image one can clearly see a ground depression indicating the location of the home (Richard Neitzel Holzapfel, T. Jeffery Cottle, and Ted D. Stoddard, *Church History in Black and White: George Edward Anderson's Photographic Mission to Latter-day Saint Historical Sites* [Provo, UT: Religious Studies Center, Brigham Young University, 1995], 83).

11. Donald W. Parry, Jay A. Parry and Tina M. Peterson, *Understanding Isaiah* (Salt Lake City: Deseret Book, 1998), 116–17; Victor L. Ludlow, *Isaiah: Prophet, Seer, and Poet* (Salt Lake City: Deseret Book, 1982), 170–74; Monte S. Nyman, *"Great Are the Words*

of Isaiah" (Salt Lake City: Bookcraft, 1980), 71–74; and Sidney B. Sperry, *The Voice of Israel's Prophets* (Salt Lake City: Deseret Book, 1952), 34–35.

12. Donald Q. Cannon and Lyndon W. Cook, eds., *The Far West Record: Minutes of The Church of Jesus Christ of Latter-day Saints, 1830–1844* (Salt Lake City: Deseret Book, 1983), 70–71, 135–41, 145–51; see also Smith, *History of the Church*, 3:3–8.

13. Smith, *History of the Church*, 2:511.

14. Oliver Cowdery to Warren Cowdery, January 21, 1838, Huntington Library, San Marino, California. For information concerning Cowdery's possible infidelity, as well as his charges of adultery against Joseph Smith, see Robert G. Mouritsen, "The Office of Associate President of the Church of Jesus Christ of Latter-day Saints" (master's thesis, Brigham Young University, 1972), 107–11.

15. Cannon and Cook, *Far West Record*, 162–71; and Smith, *History of the Church*, 3:16–18. Historian Kenneth H. Winn contends that Cowdery hoped his resistance would help to maintain the original purity of the Church. Believing he could no longer compromise his "individual rights and liberties [which were] affirmed by republican culture," and feeling the Church was becoming more and more theocratic, Cowdery decided to separate from Mormonism (Kenneth H. Winn, "Republican Dissent in the Kingdom of God," in *Exiles in a Land of Liberty* [Chapel Hill: University of North Carolina Press, 1989], 106–28).

16. Cannon and Cook, *Far West Record*, 171–78; and Smith, *History of the Church*, 3:18–20.

17. Richard Lloyd Anderson, *Investigating the Book of Mormon Witnesses* (Salt Lake City: Deseret Book, 1989), 127.

18. Larry C. Porter, "The Odyssey of William Earl McLellin: Man of Diversity, 1806–83," in Jan Shipps and John W. Welch, eds., *The Journals of William E. McLellin* (Provo, UT: BYU Studies and Brigham

Young University; Urbana and Chicago: University of Illinois Press, 1994), 321–23; see also 368, n. 178.

19. Frederick Granger Williams, "Frederick Granger Williams of the First Presidency of the Church," *BYU Studies* 12 (Spring 1972): 252–59.

20. Joseph Smith, Revelation to David W. Patten, April 17, 1838, Scriptory Book, 32.

21. For an interpretive account of the Patten's death and the Battle of Crooked River, see Alexander L. Baugh, "The Battle Between Mormon and Missouri Militia at Crooked River," in *Regional Studies in Latter-day Saint Church History: Missouri*, ed. Arnold K. Garr and Clark V. Johnson (Provo, UT: Department of Church History and Doctrine, Brigham Young University, 1994), 85–103.

22. Joseph Smith, Revelation to Brigham Young, April 17, 1838, Scriptory Book, 32.

23. *The Evening and the Morning Star*, May 1834, 160. David Whitmer recalled that Rigdon was primarily responsible for changing the name from "The Church of Christ" to "The Church of the Latter Day Saints" (*An Address to all Believers in Christ* [Richmond, MO: By the Author: 1887], 73). Whitmer also said he objected to the name because it did not contain the name of Christ (*An Address to All Believers in Christ*, 62, 74).

24. Cannon and Cook, *Far West Record*, 103–4; also in *History of the Church*, 2:481.

25. See W. W. Phelps letter, July 7, 1837, in *Latter Day Saints' Messenger and Advocate*, July 1837, 529; also in Smith, *History of the Church*, 2:496–97.

26. Smith, *History of the Church*, 2:521.

27. Joseph Smith, Revelation, April 26, 1838, Scriptory Book, 33, now canonized as Doctrine and Covenants 115:7–12.

28. Joseph Smith, Revelation, April 26, 1838, Scriptory Book, 34, now canonized as Doctrine and Covenants 115:18–19.

29. Joseph Smith, editorial, May 4, 1838, in *Elders' Journal*, July 1838, 33–34. Although the editorial does not bear the signature of Joseph Smith, he was the editor of the periodical.

30. See Smith, Scriptory Book, 42–46. Joseph Smith was probably in Daviess County after June 5, but Robinson failed to record the Prophet's activities in the Scriptory Book from June 5 until July 4. Daviess County appealed to the Latter-day Saints because of the preemption laws that existed at the time regarding land acquisition. In Missouri in the 1830s, as new regions were surveyed, the federal government made large tracts of land available to the public. Individuals wanting to settle in these new regions were permitted to file a preemption claim for a specified tract of land (up to 160 acres) and then settle on the property without having to actually buy it. When the land came up for sale by the government, by right of their preemption claim, a person would then be entitled to purchase the property outright. Mormon leaders were very much aware of this program and saw it as benefitting the Saints since, at least initially, Church members relocating in Missouri could acquire property in Daviess County without having to purchase it. For a detailed explanation and analysis of the Mormons and their preemption claims in Daviess County, see Jeffrey N. Walker, "Mormon Land Rights in Caldwell and Daviess Counties and the Mormon Conflict of 1838," *BYU Studies* 47, no.1 (2008): 4–55.

31. Smith, Scriptory Book, 42.

32. Smith, Scriptory Book, 43–44.

33. The variation made by Orson Pratt from that contained in the Scriptory Book is not significant. He introduces the verse with the phrase "Spring Hill is named by the Lord," then includes a more accepted spelling of "Adam-ondi-Ahman."

34. Smith, Scriptory Book, 42.

35. Smith, Scriptory Book, 45.

36. See "Conference Minutes," *Elders' Journal*, August 1838, 60–61.

37. Owen H. McGee, a non-Mormon, escorted two young Mormon women to the all-day affair and estimated that some five thousand Latter-day Saints were in attendance (Joseph H. McGee, "History of Daviess County: Incidents and Reminiscences in its Early Settlement, Etc., &c," *North Missourian* [Gallatin, MO], March 4, 1888). Owen's estimate is probably too high, but it indicates that perhaps even a few thousand were present and that even non-Latter-day Saints were in attendance.

38. "Celebration of the 4th of July," *Elders' Journal*, August 1838, 60; see also Smith, *History of the Church*, 3:41–42.

39. Elijah Averett wrote, "Elisha Averett, my brother, Demick [*sic*] Huntington and Cornelius Lot[t] quarried the rock for the temple, Elisha being the chief mason laying the foundation that day" (A History of Elijah Averett, typescript, 1, L. Tom Perry Special Collections, Harold B. Lee Library, Brigham Young University, Provo, Utah; hereafter cited as Perry Special Collections).

40. Joseph Holbrook, Autobiography of Joseph Holbrook, 39, Perry Special Collections. Holbrook helped haul the cornerstones from the quarry to the temple excavation.

41. "Celebration of the 4th of July," 60. Some of the leaders involved in the cornerstone dedications can be identified. As indicated, the southeast cornerstone was dedicated by the "Presidents of the stake," or what would have been the Missouri presidency. At the time of the July 4 activities, the Missouri stake presidency consisted of Thomas B. Marsh, David W. Patten, and Brigham Young, the three senior members of the Twelve. On April 6, 1838, Marsh, Patten, and Young replaced David Whitmer, W. W. Phelps, and John Whitmer as the presidency of the Missouri stake (Cannon and Cook, *Far West Record*, 158). The northwest cornerstone would have been dedicated by Edward Partridge, the bishop in Missouri. The "presidents of the

elders [quorums]" and the "president of the teachers [quorum]," who dedicated the southwest and northeast cornerstones, respectively, could not be precisely identified.

42. See Mosiah L. Hancock, Autobiography, typescript, 5–8, Perry Special Collections. In his autobiography, Mosiah recalls that his father, Levi Hancock, sang the song, and that his uncle, Solomon Hancock, "helped father sing the song" (Hancock, Autobiography, 5, 8). However, the *Elders' Journal* newspaper report of the dedication published in August, just a month after the event, clearly states that Solomon sang a solo ("Celebration of the 4th of July," 60). Mosiah was only fourteen at the time and probably confused the facts.

43. Sidney Rigdon, *Oration Delivered by Mr. S. Rigdon, on the 4th of July, 1838, at Far West, Caldwell County, Missouri* (Far West, MO: Printed at the Journal Office, 1838), 12. The entire document has subsequently been published in Peter Crawley, "Two Rare Missouri Documents," *BYU Studies* 14, no. 4 (Summer 1974): 517–27.

44. It is not known if this was the exact phrase used on the occasion, but it would have been something similar. In more recent times when the shout was performed, the congregation exclaimed, "Hosanna, Hosanna, Hosanna, to God and the Lamb," repeated three times, followed by "Amen, Amen, and Amen," while waving a white handkerchief in the air. It does not appear at the time of the temple site cornerstone dedication at Far West that the Mormons waved handkerchiefs. For an explanation of the history of the Hosanna Shout in Church history, see Jacob W. Olmstead, "From Pentecost to Administration: A Reappraisal of the History of the Hosanna Shout," *Mormon Historical Studies* 2, no. 2 (Fall 2001): 7–37. Parley P. Pratt briefly mentions the Hosanna Shout being performed at the dedication of the Far West temple cornerstone dedication (*Autobiography of Parley P. Pratt*, ed. Parley P. Pratt Jr. [Salt Lake City: Deseret Book, 1985], 149–50).

45. "Celebration of the 4th of July," 60; also Smith, *History of the Church*, 3:42. One other activity was done in conjunction with the Far West temple site dedication, namely the erection of a liberty pole, or flag pole, adjacent to the excavation (Luman A. Shurtliff, Biographical Sketch of the Life of Luman Andros Shurtliff, typescript, 33, Perry Special Collections).

46. Joseph Smith, Sidney Rigdon, and Hyrum Smith to William Marks and Newel K. Whitney, July 8, 1838, Joseph Smith Papers, Church History Library.

47. Smith, Scriptory Book, 53–54. The manuscript of this document was removed from the Scriptory Book and is currently part of the Revelations Collection.

48. Smith, Scriptory Book, 56.

49. Smith, Scriptory Book, 57.

50. Smith, Scriptory Book, 57.

51. Smith, *History of the Church*, 2:518, 528.

52. *Elders' Journal*, November 1837, 28–29. The November issue of the *Elders' Journal* was not published until after Joseph Smith's return in December.

53. *Elders' Journal*, July 1838, 42–43.

54. Lilburn W. Boggs to John B. Clark, October 27, 1838, in *Document Containing the Correspondence, Orders, &c. in Relation to the Disturbances with the Mormons; And the Evidence Given Before the Hon. Austin A. King, Judge of the Fifth Judicial Circuit of the State of Missouri, at the Court-House in Richmond, in a Criminal Court of Inquiry, Begun November 12, 1838, on the Trial of Joseph Smith, Jr., and Others, for High Treason and Other Crimes Against the State* (Fayette, MO: Boonslick Democrat, 1841), 61 (hereafter cited as *Document*).

55. Lilburn W. Boggs to John B. Clark, October 26, 1838, in *Document*, 62–63. Although the order was signed by B. M. Lisle, an adjutant general in the state militia, Lisle wrote by order of Boggs.

56. Samuel D. Lucas to Lilburn W. Boggs, November 5, 1838, in *Document*, 70.

57. *Autobiography of Parley P. Pratt*, 160; and Sidney Rigdon, *An Appeal to the American People: Being an Account of the Persecutions of the Church of Latter Day Saints; and of the Barbarities Inflicted on Them by the Inhabitants of the State of Missouri* (Cincinnati: Glesen and Shepard, Stereotypers and Printers, 1840), 51.

58. See *History of Clay and Platte Counties, Missouri, Written and Compiled From the Most Authentic Official and Private Sources, Including a History of Their Townships, Towns and Villages, Together With a Condensed History of Missouri; a Reliable and Detailed History of Clay and Platte Counties—Their Pioneer Record, Resources, Biographical Sketches of Prominent Citizens; General and Local Statistics of Great Value; Incidents and Reminiscences* (St. Louis: National Historical Company, 1885), 134, n. 1.

59. Rigdon, *An Appeal to the American People*, 51; Rigdon petition in Clark S. Johnson, *Mormon Redress Petitions: Documents of the 1833–1838 Missouri Conflict* (Provo, UT: Religious Studies Center, Brigham Young University, 1992), 675–76; also in Smith, *History of the Church*, 3:460; and Parley P. Pratt, *History of the Late Persecution Inflicted by the State of Missouri Upon the Mormons, in which Ten Thousand American Citizens Were Robbed, Plundered, and Driven From the State, and Many Others Imprisoned, Martyred, &C. for Their Religion, and All This by Military Force, by Order of the Executive* (Detroit: Dawson and Bates, Printers, 1839), 40 (hereafter *History of the Late Persecution*).

60. *History of Caldwell and Livingston Counties, Missouri, Written and Compiled From the Most Authentic Official and Private Sources, Including a History of Their Townships and Villages, Together With a Condensed History of Missouri; a Reliable and Detailed History of Caldwell and Livingston Counties—Their Pioneer Record, Resources, Biographical Sketches of Prominent Citizens; General and Local*

Statistics of Great Value; Incidents and Reminiscences (St. Louis: National Historical Company, 1886), 137.

61. For statements concerning Joseph Smith's exemption from state militia duty, see Alanson Ripley, Heber C. Kimball, William Huntington, Joseph B. Noble, and Joseph Smith Jr. petition, in John P. Greene, *Facts Relative to the Expulsion of the Mormons or Latter Day Saints from the State of Missouri, under the "Exterminating Order"* (Cincinnati: R. P. Brooks, 1839), 32; and Lyman Wight petition in Johnson, *Missouri Redress Petitions*, 656; also in Smith, *History of the Church*, 3:441. Hyrum Smith claimed the entire First Presidency was exempt because of their ministerial status, while Sidney Rigdon stated he was excluded because he was over age (Smith and Rigdon petitions in Johnson, *Mormon Redress Petitions*, 632, 634; also in Smith, *History of the Church*, 3:417, 459).

62. Peter H. Burnett, *An Old California Pioneer by Peter H. Burnett, First Governor of the State* (Oakland, CA: Biobooks, 1946), 37–38.

63. The significance of Doniphan's intervention in behalf of the Mormon leaders cannot be overstated. Had he not blocked Lucas, Joseph Smith and the other prisoners would most assuredly have lost their lives. Missourian Peter H. Burnett wrote, "Had it not been for the efforts of Doniphan and others from Clay, I think it most probable that the prisoners would have been summarily tried, condemned, and executed" (*An Old California Pioneer*, 38).

64. Samuel D. Lucas to Lilburn W. Boggs, November 2, 1838, in *Document*, 75; also Samuel D. Lucas to Lilburn W. Boggs, November 5, 1838 in *Document*, 71; see also Lyman Wight, Journal, in Joseph Smith III and Heman C. Smith, *History of the Reorganized Church of Jesus Christ of Latter Day Saints* (Independence, MO: Herald House, 1967), 2:295; and Wight petition in Johnson, *Mormon Redress Petitions*, 662; also in Smith, *History of the Church*, 3:447.

65. Wight, Journal, 295–96; *Autobiography of Parley P. Pratt*, 164; and Smith, *History of the Church*, 3:201. In his journal, Wight

incorrectly indicated that the prisoners arrived in Independence on November 3, whereas Smith and Pratt place the date as November 4. November 4 was a Sunday (as noted by Pratt) and is the correct date. It was on this same day that both Joseph Smith and Parley P. Pratt penned letters to their wives, Emma and Mary Ann, respectively (Parley P. Pratt to Mary Ann Frost Pratt, November 4, 1838, Church History Library; and Joseph Smith Jr. to Emma Smith, November 4, 1838, Community of Christ Library-Archives, Independence, Missouri; also published in *Personal Writings of Joseph Smith*, ed. Dean C. Jessee [Salt Lake City: Deseret Book, 2002], 399).

66. Joseph Smith Jr. to Emma Smith, November 4, 1838, Community of Christ Library-Archives; also published in *Personal Writings of Joseph Smith*, 399.

67. As explained, the message issued by Joseph Smith and the other six Mormon prisoners thanking Lucas, Wilson, and other members of the militia originally appeared in the *Boonslick Democrat* on November 10, 1838, five days after it was written. The article was subsequently picked up and printed on November 28, 1838, in the *Ohio Statesman*, published in Columbus. No extant copy of the *Boonslick Democrat* for the date of November 5, 1838, could be found, so the *Statesman* version is provided here. The card was signed by each of the seven prisoners.

68. Lyman Wight indicated their move from the log house to the Noland Hotel occurred on November 6 (Lyman Wight, Journal, in Joseph Smith III and Heman C. Smith, *History of the Reorganized Church of Jesus Christ of Latter Day Saints* [Independence, MO: Herald House, 1967], 2:296). Parley P. Pratt recorded: "[After our arrival in Independence] the troops were then disbanded. In the meantime we were kept under a small guard, and were treated with some degree of humanity, while hundreds flocked to see us day after day. We spent most of our time in preaching and conversation, explanatory of our doctrines and practice. Much prejudice was removed, and the

feelings of the populace began to be in our favor.... In a day or two we were at liberty to walk the streets without a guard. We were finally removed from our house of confinement to a hotel, where we boarded at the public table, and lodged on the floor, with a block of wood for a pillow. We no longer had any guard; we went out and came in when we pleased—a certain keeper being appointed merely to watch over us, and look to our wants" (*Autobiography of Parley P. Pratt*, 166).

69. Clark stated in two separate documents that the number of Mormon prisoners taken was forty-six (John B. Clark to Lilburn W. Boggs, November 10 and November 29, 1838, in *Document*, 66, 90). The number of men arrested by General Clark is given differently in Mormon sources, ranging from fifty to seventy-five. For example, see Smith, *History of the Church*, 3:202; and Albert Perry Rockwood, Journal, in Dean C. Jessee and David J. Whittaker, eds., "The Last Months of Mormonism in Missouri: The Albert Perry Rockwood Journal," *BYU Studies* 28, no. 1 (Winter 1988): 27.

70. John B. Clark to Lilburn W. Boggs, November 10 and November 29, 1838, in *Document*, 66, 90.

71. Smith, *History of the Church*, 3:205–6; *Autobiography of Parley P. Pratt*, 168; Wight, Journal, 296–98. Pratt indicated that immediately upon their arrival in Richmond they were confined in chains. Wight said that they were not put into chains until the following day, November 10. For a general location of the old log house, see LaMar C. Berrett and others, eds., *Sacred Places*, vol. 4: *Missouri* (Salt Lake City: Deseret Book, 2004), 238.

72. *Autobiography of Parley P. Pratt*, 179.

73. John B. Clark to Lilburn W. Boggs, November 10, 1838, in *Document*, 66–67.

74. The eleven men who were added to the original fifty-three defendants were Lemuel Bent, Jonathan Dunham, King Follett, Clark Hallett, Joseph Hunter, Joel S. Miles, George W. Morris, Morris

Phelps, Thomas Rich, James Henry Rollins, and William Whitman. The names were obtained by comparing the list of the original fifty-three defendants who were in custody at the beginning of the hearing with that of the defendants cited in Judge King's final ruling (*Document*, 93, 149–51).

75. *Document*, 97; and Smith, *History of the Church*, 3:209, 212. For an examination of the Richmond hearing, see Stephen C. LeSueur, "'High Treason and Murder': The Examination of Mormon Prisoners at Richmond, Missouri, in November 1838," *BYU Studies* 26, no. 2 (Spring 1986): 3–30; and H. Michael Marquardt, "Judge Austin A. King's Preliminary Hearing: Joseph Smith and the Mormons on Trial," *John Whitmer Historical Association Journal* 24 (2004): 41–55. The hearing is also discussed in general terms in Susan Easton Black, "The Evils of Rumor: Richmond, Missouri, 1836–1838," in *Regional Studies in Latter-day Saint Church History: Missouri*, 125–30.

76. Joseph Smith Jr. to Emma Hale Smith, Community of Christ Library-Archives, also published in *Personal Writings of Joseph Smith*, 399.

77. *Autobiography of Parley P. Pratt*, 179–80. In a March 1839 letter to the Church in Quincy, Illinois, Joseph Smith may have alluded to the event of his rebuking the guards when he wrote, "And although<ugh> their influance shall cast the[e] into trouble and into barrs and walls thou shalt be had in honor and but for a small moment and thy voice shall be more terible in the midst of thine enemies than the fierce Lion because of thy ritiousness [righteousness] and thy God shall stand by the[e] forever" (Joseph Smith Jr. to the Church at Quincy, March 20, 1839, Church History Library; also in *Personal Writings of Joseph Smith*, 441). The passage has been canonized as Doctrine and Covenants 122:4.

78. *Document*, 150. By the time the Daviess trial was to begin most of the Mormon defendants had left the state, thus they did not appear and the case was eventually dismissed.

79. *Document*, 150; Smith, *History of the Church*, 3:212. Joseph and Hyrum Smith, McRae, Baldwin, and Wight were all charged with the crime of treason in Daviess County, while Rigdon was charged with treason in Caldwell.

80. Lyman Omer Littlefield, *Reminiscences of Latter-day Saints* (Logan, UT: Utah Journal, 1888), 80–81.

81. See Dean C. Jessee, "'Walls, Grates and Screeking Iron Doors': The Prison Experience of Mormon Leaders in Missouri, 1838–1839," in *New Views in Mormon History: A Collection of Essays in Honor of Leonard J. Arrington*, ed. Davis Bitton and Maureen Ursenbach Beecher (Salt Lake City: University of Utah Press, 1987), 25.

82. See Richard S. Van Wagoner, *Sidney Rigdon: A Portrait of Religious Excess* (Salt Lake City: Signature Books, 1994), 254–55.

83. Joseph Smith to Emma Smith, December 1, 1838, Joseph Smith Papers, Church History Library.

84. See Joseph Smith III and Heman C. Smith, *History of the Reorganized Church of Jesus Christ of Latter Day Saints* (Independence, MO: Herald House, 1967), 2:309, 315.

85. See Joseph Smith, "The Memoirs of President Joseph Smith (1832–1914)," *Saints' Herald* (November 6, 1934, 1414–15. Lyman Wight recalled seeing Joseph "lay [his] hands on the head of a youth [Joseph III] and heard him cry aloud 'You are my successor when I depart'" (Lyman Wight to Editor, *Northern Islander*, July 1855: Lyman Wight Letterbook, Community of Christ Library-Archives; as cited in Roger D. Launius, *Joseph Smith III: Pragmatic Patriarch* [Urbana and Chicago: University of Illinois Press, 1988], 10).

86. Joseph Smith to the Church of the Latter Day Saints in Caldwell County, December 16, 1838, Scriptory Book, 101–8.

87. *Autobiography of Parley P. Pratt*, 164.

WILLIAM G. HARTLEY

1839
The Saints' Forced Exodus from Missouri

Tucked between popular Church history chapters about Liberty Jail and Nauvoo is a little-known but vitally important chapter dealing with the Latter-day Saints' seven-month struggle to survive the winter of 1838–39 in Missouri and to leave there by spring 1839. Triggered by Missouri governor Lilburn Boggs's October 1838 extermination order against them, some ten thousand Saints engaged in a mass exodus, many going to Quincy, Illinois. It was difficult, dramatic, sometimes harrowing, and only partly organized. Their tough experiences produced definite impacts—both short- and long-term—on Missouri and Illinois, on the course of the Church, and on individual members.[1]

William G. Hartley is a professor emeritus of history at Brigham Young University.

The Saints' exodus from Missouri took place mostly during winter and involved four main arenas: Far West, Missouri; Quincy, Illinois; a road network between the two cities; and the west shore mudflats across the Mississippi River from Quincy. Because Joseph Smith was in prison during the exodus, attention focuses here on Joseph Smith's parents, his wife Emma, Elders Brigham Young and Heber C. Kimball, and four selected families: the John and Caroline Butler family, the Newel and Lydia Knight family, the Daniel and Martha Thomas family, and the Levi and Clarissa Hancock family.

Ordered to Leave

On October 27, 1838, three days after Missouri and Mormon militias engaged in the Battle of Crooked River, Governor Boggs issued his infamous extermination order. To his military leaders, it decreed, "The Mormons must be treated as enemies and must be exterminated or driven from the state, if necessary for the public good."[2] Four days later, that order reached Church leaders and members in northwest Missouri. At the time, perhaps ten thousand Mormons were concentrated in two particular counties. Their chief settlement was Far West in Caldwell County. Far West had a population by then of about five thousand Saints, and another five thousand lived in at least nineteen other Latter-day Saint communities in Caldwell County. In Daviess County on Caldwell County's north side, Saints had begun building about 150 log houses at Adam-ondi-Ahman, and as many as 1,500 Saints in total lived in Daviess County.[3]

By October 1838, Newel and Lydia Knight and their three children were among the Saints living in and near Far West, the Church's headquarters city. They belonged to a large extended family headed by Joseph Knight Sr., who converted to Mormonism in New York state in 1830, the year the Church was organized. They numbered twelve families with more than sixty souls, having surnames of Knight, DeMille, Peck, Slade, Culver, and Stringham. Joseph Knight's son Newel was Joseph Smith's close friend—the Prophet had performed his and Lydia's wedding in Kirtland and had no followers more loyal than Newel and Lydia.[4]

November 1 brought heartbreak for all Saints in Far West. Newel and all men in the city had to surrender their arms. The next day, Missouri troops brought Joseph and Hyrum Smith and five other prisoners into town in wagons to pick up personal effects and say good-bye. Then three hundred militiamen escorted them away to face trial and prison. That same day Latter-day Saint men assembled at the town square at bayonet point and, one by one, signed deeds that gave their land to the state of Missouri to pay the costs of the "Mormon War." On November 6, soldiers took more prisoners and then ordered all Saints out of Missouri by spring.[5] Meanwhile, a militia force headed to Adam-ondi-Ahman, made the Mormons there surrender, and on November 10 gave them ten days to relocate to Far West or elsewhere in Caldwell County.[6]

Mormon Militiamen Escape First

In the exodus, Mormon militiamen were the first to leave—or rather escape. John Lowe Butler, age thirty, and wife Caroline, twenty-six, who had converted in Kentucky three years earlier, lived in Mirabile just south of Far West with their four children. John, tall and strong, had fought off Missourians trying to block Mormons from voting. He rode with the Mormon militia who fought in the Battle of Crooked River. Because the Missouri militia wanted to arrest him, he fled from home on November 2, leaving Caroline and the children to fend as best they could.

Slipping through "the guard," he had to cross a creek by taking off his clothes and wading across the "bitter cold" water. Then he had to be very careful for days to avoid capture. At times he hid in members' homes as he headed east. John was one of dozens of Mormon militiamen who fled from Missouri in November. They formed the first wave of the exodus.[7]

The shortest way out of state was to go north sixty to eighty miles into unsettled regions of present-day Iowa. Church leaders told fugitive Charles C. Rich to "flee north into the wilderness and take all that I Could find of the Brethren that was in the Crooked river Battle." So he and others left Far West at midnight on November 1. At Adam-ondi-Ahman they obtained provisions from fellow Saints. They organized into a company with Rich as captain. Learning that Missouri militia were looking for them, they "set out for Iowa thrugh the wilderness," enduring snow and cold with "little to eat." Among the twenty-eight men in this group were Samuel Smith and Phineas and Lorenzo Young. Samuel said they traveled "the most secluded route" they could find. They ran out of provisions and became so weak they couldn't continue, so they held a council and prayed to know where to hunt. Taking a direction shown him by the Spirit, Samuel and two others found a wigwam where an Indian woman baked cakes for all the company.[8] After eleven days' travel, they reached "white Settlements on the Desmoine River" in Iowa. Lorenzo said that his pants were so shredded by bushes that he refused to face the Iowans until someone brought him better pants.[9] The men split into two groups to avoid attention.[10] They crossed the icy Mississippi River, some at Quincy, where Charles C. Rich said, "We found friends and was kindly received."[11]

Another half dozen Mormon militiamen led by Dimick Huntington left separately. At least one man escaped west to

Fort Leavenworth. Some sneaked southward to the Missouri River and took boat passage to St. Louis.[12] John Butler's escape route apparently was across northern Missouri. On horseback, he, fellow Kentuckian David Lewis, and Elias Higbee endured December snows, cold, and meager food to reach Quincy, Illinois. By primitive Missouri roads, the distance from Far West to Quincy was about 180 miles. At Quincy, where some Church members lived, John taught school for a short period. An old man who was sympathetic to the needy Saints hired John to teach his children and grandchildren and neighbors' children. John marked time until his family and his mother and brothers could join him in Quincy.[13]

Hard Winter of Waiting

During November 1838, Latter-day Saint settlements in Caldwell and Daviess counties endured a military occupation. "We were not permitted to leave Far West," Anson Call said, "only to get our firewood. We had not the privilege of hunting our cattle and horses."[14] Newel Knight noted that because the Saints were unarmed, they became prey for small parties of armed men "insulting our women, driving off our stock, and plundering." To him "it seemed as though all hell was aroused to do us injury."[15] Newel's cousin Reed Peck said that "some horses, wagons and much other property were stolen from the Mormons by some of the militia who were villains enough to plunder."[16] By late November, most crops around Far West were unharvested, and potatoes still in the ground were "frose solid." Soldiers "rifled" through homes, Albert Rockwood said, and "our sheep & hogs, & horses [are] drove off before our eyes by the Missourians who come in small companies well armed."[17]

In neighboring Daviess County, Missouri militia ordered all the Saints out and gave William Huntington and eleven other Mormons four weeks to round up the Latter-day Saints' livestock, wagons, and personal property. Huntington estimated that in Daviess County the Saints lost nearly thirty thousand bushels of corn because of the militia takeover.[18]

Far West was ill equipped to become a refugee center for Saints displaced by Missouri militia. Food was scarce and housing inadequate. Those coming from outside Far West suffered because as John Greene wrote, "we have been robbed of our corn, wheat, horses, cattle, cows, hogs, wearing apparel, houses and homes, and indeed, of all that renders life tolerable."[19] On November 9 the *Missouri Republican Daily* reported that the Saints' situation was "a case of great difficulty" because "they are generally poor" and facing starvation. "And where shall they be sent?" the newspaper asked. "Their numbers exceed 5,000 people—without any means and literally beggars—to be thrust upon the charities of Illinois, Iowa, or Wisconsin." Joseph Holbrook, thirty-two, said his wife Nancy "had verry poor health" that fall and winter because of being exposed to "inclement weather by having to remove from place to place as our house had been burned and we were yet left to seek a home whenever our friends could accommodate us and for my safety." Saints "in flourishing condition but a few months before," he said, "were now destitute. I could have commanded some two thousand dollars but now I had only 1 yoke of old oxen and 2 cows left."[20]

Two families moved in with Newel Knight's family. "Many could not get into houses," Newel said, "and had to take shelter in wagons, tents, and under bedclothes and while in this situation we had a severe snow storm, which rendered their suffering intense." An acre of land in front of Lucy Mack

Smith's home became "completely covered with beds, lying in the open sun, where families were compelled to sleep, exposed to all kinds of weather." Houses in Far West were so full, Mother Smith said, that people could not find shelter. "It was enough to make the heart ache to see the children, sick with colds, and crying around their mothers for food, whilst their parents were destitute of the means of making them comfortable."[21]

Northwest Missouri winters can be harsh. During November and December, Joseph C. Kingsbury and Caroline, his wife of two years, lived in a little cabin with meager provisions. Caroline suffered from dropsy, or painful swellings, and the cold intensified her pain.[22] Aroet Lucius Hale, age ten, recalled that while his father was helping others, "My dear mother was lying sick in a wagon box in a tent."[23] James Carroll said that his family had to "remain in an open frame in the Cold weather when the Snow fell in torrents and would Blow upon us in the Night and we with our Little ones would have to Crawl out of our Beds while the[y] were Coverd frequently with Snow that would blow in to the frame from the north and we had to endure it."[24] William F. Cahoon said, "Both me and my family Suffred much on account of Could & hunger because we was not permitted to go out Side of the guard to obtain wood and provision."[25]

After her husband John left, Caroline Butler faced three difficult tasks. She worried if John had escaped Missouri or been caught. She had to provide for the family after being deprived of the corn they had grown on their farm, which vigilantes had prevented them from harvesting. John later filed claim for the loss of 240 acres of land, three yoke of oxen, a corn crop, and hogs. Caroline's third task was to find some way to move the family and belongings from Missouri before spring. Caroline said that at one point that winter, Joseph Smith got word to

Emma to send him quilts or bed clothes. "Sister Emma cried and said that they [thieves] had taken all of her bed clothes, except one quilt and blanket, and what could she do?" So Caroline and other sisters told Emma to send hers to Joseph, which she did, and they gave her replacement bedding for her family.[26]

Negotiations to Halt the Exodus Fail

Some opinions downstate held that Mormons would not have to leave at all. *The Missouri Argus*'s editor argued incorrectly on December 20, 1838, that "they cannot be driven beyond the limits of the state—that is certain. To do so, would be to act with extreme cruelty. . . . If they choose to remain, we must be content. The day has gone by when masses of men can be outlawed, and driven from society to the wilderness, unprotected. . . . The refinement, the charity of our age, will not brook it. . . . Mercy should be the watchword—not blood, not extermination, not misery."

In December 1838 and early January 1839, the Missouri state legislature, by a close vote, refused to overturn Governor Boggs's extermination order.[27] That left the Saints no choice but to leave Missouri as soon as possible.

Committee for Removal

Hundreds still lacked the means to leave. "Many were stripped of clothing and bedding," John P. Greene reported, and "many without cattle, horses, or waggons, had no means of conveyance."[28] To provide them help required leadership. On January 16, the imprisoned First Presidency sent instructions to Heber C. Kimball and Brigham Young that said, "Inasmuch as we are in prison, . . . the management of the affairs of the Church devolves on you, that is the Twelve . . . appoint the

THE SAINTS' FORCED EXODUS FROM MISSOURI

oldest of those of the Twelve, who were first appointed, to be the president of your quorum."

Brigham Young was the senior Apostle, hence the presiding Church officer on the ground. Far West Saints met in a public meeting on January 26 to consider measures to expedite the move out of state, given the "seeming impossibility" of moving "in consequence of the extreme poverty of many."[29] A seven-man committee was appointed to find out how many needed help and how much help members could give to those in need.[30] A second meeting on January 29 heard a partial report from the committee, after which Brigham Young proposed that Saints covenant "to stand by and assist each other to the utmost of our abilities in removing from the state, and that we will never desert the poor who are worthy" until they are safely out of state. Nearly three hundred made that covenant and signed pledges.[31]

William Huntington headed up a Committee of Removal. Its seven members, soon expanded to eleven, agreed to move first the families of the Presidency and of the other prisoners.[32] The committee surveyed the needs and weighed requests for help. They collected donations of furniture, farm implements, and money from farm sales.[33] They sent agents eastward to deposit corn for Saints to use along the way, to contract for ferries, and to ensure security for the travelers.[34] Saints used existing roads as much as possible, although some took detours to avoid problems with local residents or to avoid being recognized. An upper route ran directly east from Far West; a lower route ran southeast from Far West and then east through the towns of Keytesville and Huntsville. Both routes merged southwest of the town of Palymra, twenty miles south of Quincy. From there, refugees had to cross the South and North Fabius rivers and mudflats to reach the Mississippi opposite Quincy.[35]

On February 11 the committee accepted applications for assistance, and the next day they appointed Theodore Turley to "superintend the management of the teams provided for removing the poor." The plan was for some wagons to go east, unload passengers and belongings at the Mississippi, and then return empty to help others move out. On February 19 the committee sent Charles Bird to visit Caldwell County and William Huntington Far West to determine how many families still needed assistance to move and to solicit means to help them.[36] With Joseph Smith's approval, leaders in Far West decided to sell Church properties in Jackson County to help raise money for the exodus. Also, three men were sent to locate possible settlement sites up the Mississippi River in Illinois.[37]

Elders Young and Kimball kept in constant contact with the imprisoned First Presidency by correspondence, messenger, and visits. On February 7 and 8, both men visited Liberty Jail, then returned to Far West. Elder Young, when his life seemed in danger, left Far West for Illinois on February 14, but Elder Kimball stayed behind to help with the removals.[38]

Getting Out of Missouri

Saints had until late March to vacate Missouri, but they started leaving in earnest during January. Five reasons best explain why Saints moved during winter conditions: (1) by January, armed patrols were showing up and threatening the Saints, so in the January 26 public meeting the people agreed to begin moving immediately; (2) the Saints had been told that Joseph Smith would not be released from prison until they all had left Missouri, and the sooner that happened, the better;[39] (3) individuals were running out of food and supplies; (4) in February, Far West experienced some stretches of weather that seemed favorable for traveling; and (5) wagons going to Illinois and then returning to take others needed four to six weeks to make the two trips before the late March deadline.

The exodus had no large, organized wagon trains. Refugees moved as individuals, by families, or in small clusters of wagons whenever they were ready. As one said, those who moved during the winter traveled "in colde weather thinly clad and porly furnished with provisions."[40] Women without their husbands had harder times of it than those with husbands.

January Removals

Albert Rockwood and his family left Far West with another family on January 10. Their difficult trip to the Mississippi River took twelve days: "We had snow and rain every day but 2. We had heavy loads, were obliged to walk from 2 to 8 miles a day thro mud and water, camped out on the wet ground 3 nights before we arrived at the River.... The river froze over & we were obliged to camp close to the river 3 days and nights before we could cross in the boat, 6 waggons were with us at the time."[41]

By mid-January, Saints were leaving Far West daily.[42] Joseph Holbrook and two other men, to escape "those that would like to do us harm," moved out the night of January 20. Holbrook left behind his wife Nancy, who a week later gave birth to their fourth child, and three small children ages seven, five, and two. He and his friends traveled on foot. They reached Quincy on January 29 "and found ourselves in a land of Freedom once more by the help of God and his blessings." Holbrook observed that "brethren were continually coming to Quincy from the Missouri as I had done."[43] In late January, Ebenezer Robinson and three other men walked from Far West to Quincy "through the snow."[44]

In January some Missourians gave Levi Hancock, one of the seven presidents of the Seventy, three days to leave. So Levi "rigged up a foot lathe and soon had two hubs turned out" and built a cart. The family filled the cart with corn. Levi's nearly five-year-old son Mosiah recalled, "The snow was deep enough to take me to the middle of the thigh, and I was bare footed and in my shirt tail." They hitched their horse "old Tom" to the cart, Mosiah said, "and father drove the horse and carried the rifle on his shoulder. Mother followed the cart carrying my little brother, Francis Marion in her arms." Barefooted Mosiah "tried to follow in her tracks." A little girl, Amy, rode in the cart and felt bad that the others had to "tramp through the snow."[45] At the Mississippi River they camped, and "Oh! What a cold night that was!" Mosiah recalled:

> The next morning the river was frozen over with ice—great blocks of frozen ice all over the river, and it was slick and clear. That morning we crossed over to Quincy, Illinois. I being barefooted and the ice so rough, I staggered all over. We finally got across, and we were so glad, for before we reached the other side, the river had started to swell and break up. Father said, "Run, Mosiah," and I did run! We all just made it on the opposite bank when the ice started to snap and pile up in great heaps, and the water broke thru![46]

February Accounts

The Murdock family. During February the migration became more intense. The John Murdock family left on February 4 without "any team or animal or carriage of any kind." They put Mrs. Murdock and the household furniture in a Brother Humphrey's wagon. John and his son Orrice walked. Three days later they reached De Witt, where they sold a property deed and bought a yoke of steers for $25 and a wagon for $30. They restarted on February 14 and reached the Mississippi two weeks later, on March 1, where they camped and waited for more than a week.[47]

The Smith family. Joseph Smith's parents tried to leave early in February, but Lucy said, "Just as we got our goods into the waggon, a man came to us and said, that Sidney Rigdon's family were ready to start, and must have the waggon immediately. Accordingly, our goods were taken out." They waited until another team came for them. "We put our goods into the wagon a second time, but the wagon was wanted for Emma and her family, so our goods were again taken out."[48] Stephen Markham, a member of the Committee of Removal, helped Emma Smith leave on February 7. They reached the bank of the Mississippi in eight days and found the river frozen over. Emma crossed the ice carefully, walking apart from the wagon. She carried two children while two others hung on to her skirt. Tied to her waist were heavy bags containing Joseph's papers.[49] Brother Markham then drove the wagon back to Far West to bring others out.

Anson Call. In mid-February, Anson Call headed east. "The weather was cold and severe, with snow to the depth of 1 foot. The first night, our wagon tipped over into the creek. The second day we had to cross a long prairie, and were not able to reach the settlement. Twas a very cold and blustering night." They put clothes over the wagon tongue to make a tent and put their beds underneath. As they moved on they found "camp fires and tent poles already struck nearly all the way after this," apparently provided by the Committee of Removal.[50]

The Young and Kimball families. Brigham Young, in danger from anti-Mormons, joined the exodus on February 14. He helped shepherd Saints across Missouri by "advancing with one part of the camp as rapidly and as far as possible" and then returning with the teams to move others out.[51] Elder Heber C.

Kimball sent his family with the Youngs. "I fitted up a small wagon, procured a span of ponies, and sent my Wife and three children, in company with Bro. Brigham Young and his family, with several others," Kimball said. "Every thing my family took with them out of Missouri, could have been packed on the backs of two horses; the mob took all the rest."[52]

The Knight family. Newel Knight had a wagon but no team. So, he said, "Sold my cook stove and the only cow the mob had not killed." With that money he hired a man with a team to drive him, Lydia, and their three children east. They pulled out of Far West on February 18, leaving behind a house and farm. At times, deep snows rubbed their wagon hubs during the journey. In intense cold, Lydia recalled, they sometimes scraped away snow beside the wagon so they could put down their beds at night. At Huntsville, the driver said his horses could not go on, so the Knights unhitched the wagon and camped. Newel prayed for help, for "I knew not how to extricate myself but as I had never been forsaken by my Heavenly Father I commited myself and family into his care." For a week they were stranded, but finally a man asked his son to drive the Knights the rest of the way. Brigham Young's family was also stranded at Huntsville, having too many goods for their wagon to haul. Newel said, "Bro. Young put on board some of his goods" into the wagon carrying the Knights, and both families resumed their journeys. A few days later, the horses ran away. The oxen they had left could not pull all the load, so Newel unloaded part of his and Brigham Young's goods and left them in the care of a friendly resident. Constant delays meant that the Knights did not reach the Mississippi River until early May.

Joseph Smith's parents. On February 19 or 20, Joseph Smith's parents, Joseph Sr. and Lucy, finally joined the exodus. "After a long time," Mother Smith said, "We succeeded . . . in getting one single wagon to convey beds, clothing, and provisions for our family," and luggage. Her son Don Carlos, "with his family and the remainder of his baggage, was crowded into a buggy, and went in the same company with us." They encountered continuous rains and had to travel through mud. "When we came to within six miles of the Mississippi river, the weather grew colder, and, in the place of rain we had snow and hail." They walked six miles across low and swampy ground, sinking to their ankles in mud. Reaching the river, they joined other Saints waiting to cross who had no shelter. Snow was six inches deep. "The next morning our beds were covered with snow," Lucy said, and they were unable to light a fire. Her fugitive son Samuel came from Quincy and arranged for a ferryman to take the Smith party across. "About sunset we landed in Quincy," Lucy said. "Here Samuel had hired a house and we moved into it, with four other families."[53]

The Thomas family. A later First Presidency report about the exodus noted that "women and children marked their footsteps on the frozen ground with blood, it being the dead of winter."[54] Was this an exaggeration? Not for Daniel Stillwell and Martha Payne Jones Thomas and their family. They left Far West on February 14. "We loaded up our little efects into a wagon and with one small pair of stears we started out with five children [ages twelve, nine, seven, four, and two] in our family and only one pair of shoes amongst them," Daniel wrote. Their first twenty miles was through snow six inches deep. Martha, about eight months pregnant, said, "To hear them [children] crying at night with their feet cracked and bleeding" was hardly bearable. When the family arrived opposite Quincy, they became "ice bound for two weeks." While they waited, a Brother Brunson came from Quincy and asked campers to donate their outfits to go back and assist in removing the poor.

The Thomases complied. "Out went everything by the log," Martha said, "the looking glass by a stump." That night Martha, soon to give birth, became ill, so Daniel rigged up a bed frame made of forked sticks and rope strands, and then drove in the frozen ground four six-foot poles topped by cross poles, hung quilts all around, and left openings at the bottom "so the heat of the log fire would shine in" to keep them warm. After one severe storm, Daniel said, "Our corn bread was frosen so hard I had to take the ax and break it and give it to the children to gnaw at, the bread looking like chunks of ice." As many as one hundred families were camped along the banks, he said.

When the river opened, the Thomases used two boats to move their effects across, while Daniel and son Morgan, twelve, stayed behind to ferry the cow across later.[55] Martha and the children reached the Quincy side and waited, sitting at night on their bed, wrapped in bed clothes and shivering in the cold wind until Daniel arrived. They moved into a Brother Wiswanger's crowded home. A few days later, Martha gave birth to a son she named after the Prophet.[56]

The Hammer family. Another story about bleeding feet involves Nancy Hammer, whose husband Austin was murdered in the Haun's Mill Massacre a few months earlier. With other refugees, she and six children ages two through nine accompanied their small wagon, pulled by a blind horse. They took what "scanty provisions we could muster." They walked and slept under the sky. There was "scarcely a day while we were on the road that it did not either snow or rain," son John said. At night they would build fires if they could find firewood. Only his mother and sisters had shoes, but these wore out and became almost useless before they reached Illinois. All but the youngest two "had to walk every step of the entire distance." They "were almost barefooted and some had to wrap their feet in clothes in order to keep them from freezing and protect them from the sharp points of the frozen ground." Son John, nine, later said that "often the blood from our feet marked the frozen earth."[57]

The Butler and Smoot families. Caroline Butler, whose husband had fled Missouri in November, couldn't care for her four young children, ages seven years to two months, and drive her wagon at the same time. So she made a deal with Abraham O. Smoot and Martha, his bride of three months. The Smoots lacked a team, so their wagon was useless. Abraham agreed to drive the Butlers' wagon and two-horse team for Caroline, and Caroline let the Smoots put their baggage in the Butler wagon. The group then included one man, two women, and children ages seven, four, three, and one. They started in February, "but it was bitter cold," and they suffered fearfully, Caroline said. Soon after starting, her eyes became infected, so Martha Smoot walked beside her and led her along for five or six days. Baggage filled the wagon, so Martha and Caroline sometimes took turns riding next to Abraham, the driver, while the other walked with and carried children. They averaged ten miles per day.

One day while Martha was sitting in the front of the wagon with three-year-old Keziah Butler on her lap, one of the horses began to kick. It struck Martha on the knees and little Keziah above the eyes. Both screamed loudly, and Caroline ran back to aid them. She found them both bleeding badly. A woman living in a nearby house ran to find out what was wrong. Seeing the injuries, she rushed back to her house and brought back camphor, brown paper, and a pan of warm water. She said she was sorry to see the Mormons suffer so much and be driven from their homes. Caroline went ahead and brought back some elders from a camp ahead to give Martha and Keziah blessings. "They got some better," Caroline said.[58]

The Butlers and Smoots reached the Mississippi on March 10 or 11. Fugitive John Butler, in Quincy, learned of their arrival, and he rowed across the river in a canoe, dodging ice. He had been separated from the family for three months or more. He could find no way to bring the Butlers' wagon across the river, so he spent the night with his family. When morning came, he and Abraham Smoot crossed to Quincy, leaving their families with the wagon. A day or two later, a ferry finally dodged through the ice and brought the women and children across.[59]

At Far West on February 22, Eliza R. Snow reported that a man who had just arrived from Illinois had counted 220 wagons between Far West and the Mississippi."[60] If that figure is accurate, and if wagons helped transport an average of four people each, then the man had passed about a thousand Saints on the road.

March Accounts

On March 5, Bishop Edward Partridge reported in Quincy that ice had been running for three days so that no one could cross the Mississippi. Quincy, he said, was full of members—even though Saints were scattering out from there almost constantly.[61] That same day, Eliza R. Snow and relatives, who had wintered seven miles from Far West, started for Illinois.[62] "After a night of rain, which changed to snow and covered the ground in the morning," she said, "we thawed our tent which was stiffly frozen, by holding and turning it alternately before a blazing fire, until it could be folded for packing, and, while we all shivered and shook with cold, we started." Sun melted the snow, increasing the depth of the mud and rendering travel almost impossible. She said, "The teams were puffing and the wagons dragging so heavily that we were all on foot, tugging along as best we could."[63]

During Zera Pulsipher's exodus that March, he and his son-in-law lost horses. Along the way, he said he "had to stop among strangers with my daughter who had given birth to a child on the prairie."[64] Elisha Whiting said his family was "driven in the month of March through cold storms of snow and rain, having to make our beds on the cold wet ground which when we arose in the morning we often found drenched with water and then obliged to load our wet bedding into the waggon and move slowly forward."[65]

About March 18, Wilford Woodruff, in Quincy and newly back from a mission, went to the river and looked across "and saw a great many of the Saints, old and young, lying in the mud and water, in a rainstorm, without tent or covering. . . . The sight filled my eyes with tears, while my heart was made glad at the cheerfulness of the Saints in the midst of their affliction."[66] He visited Saints on his side of the river who were camped "in a sufering Condition with Cold, rain & mud & some want of food."[67]

Fugitive Joseph Holbrook, two months after leaving his expectant wife and three children on January 20, learned of their arrival at the Mississippi River late in March. He crossed the river "and found some hundred of the brethren waiting for the new ferry boat to be completed, which was done the next day. I found my family in good health though in the mud and snow half a leg deep in the camp. I now saw my little daughter, Nancy Jane, for the first time about two months old. . . . My family . . . had not heard anything from me during this time, neither dare I write to [them]."[68]

At a March 17 meeting, Saints in Quincy heard a letter read from the Committee of Removal in Far West asking for "teams

& money for the removing of fifty families of poor Saints from far west to Quincy."⁶⁹ On March 29 the committee in Quincy wrote to their counterparts in Far West sympathizing with their "extreme labor and travail" to move out the last poor Saints. "We are sensible, brethren, that you have done all that you could do in removing the poor Saints," they said, adding that "nor have we, brethren, been backward in exerting our energies" for that purpose. After "deliberating on the best means" to finish the job, "we have thought that considering the bad state of the roads, the expense of ferrage in consequence of high water, that the teams are all nearly worn out, and the brethren here very poor and very much scattered" that the best solution was to "forward the remainder of the poor brethren by water." By contracting with a steam boat, "the poor brethren might all be removed at once" and the Far West committee would be free to get out of the state.⁷⁰

Kind Hearts in Quincy

Saints chose to go to Quincy for several reasons. To reach safety in Illinois, the closest state, they had to cross the broad Mississippi River, and Quincy had ferryboat facilities. Quincy was the closest Illinois city to Far West. Scores of Church members were living there, including Mary Jane York, William Hickman, John P. Greene, and Wandle Mace. Greene, a Quincy innkeeper and cousin by marriage to Brigham Young and Heber C. Kimball, encouraged the Apostles and other Saints to come there. Another attraction was that unsettled lands were available in the vicinity.⁷¹

Quincy is on the east bank of the Mississippi on a limestone bluff 125 feet above the river.⁷² It is about 130 miles upriver from St. Louis and 45 miles directly south of where Nauvoo now is. It is the county seat for Adams County. Adams County, organized in 1825, was named after John Quincy Adams, who that year became America's sixth president, and the town of Quincy received his middle name. By 1838 Quincy had a strong population base of sixteen hundred residents, mostly Germans and New Englanders, and several industries and businesses, including "its share of coopers and cabinet-makers, saddlers and leather-makers, and a pork packing and meat processing center." Quincy was on its way to prosperity.[73]

Assistance by Mormons Living in Quincy

Church members living in Quincy and nearby tried to help the refugees when they crossed the river. John P. Greene reported that during the months of February and March, "the Mormons who were already in Quincy, formed a committee among themselves, to aid to the best of their power the committee of Far West in giving assistance to their suffering brethren. They received them as they came, sent forward all who had means and strength into the interior, provided the poor and sick with lodgings, fuel, food and clothing."[74] Wandle Mace opened his house to the refugees. "Many of the Saints were glad to find shelter in my house from the storms," he said. "Many nights the floors, upstairs and down, were covered with beds so closely it was impossible to set a foot anywhere without stepping on someone else's bed."[75]

Emma Smith and the children arrived on February 15.[76] They moved in with Judge John Cleveland and his Latter-day Saint wife, Sarah, four miles east of Quincy. Sarah later became Emma's first counselor in the Nauvoo Relief Society.[77]

Quincy's Compassion

On February 23, the *Quincy Whig* reported that Saints were "coming in from all quarters" and that "for several days they have been crossing at this place, bringing with them the wreck of what they could save from their ruthless oppressors. . . . They appear, so far as we have seen, to be a mild, inoffensive people, who could not have given cause for the persecution they have met with." City leaders and residents suddenly had to deal with a humanitarian crisis thrust upon them. Their hospitality stemmed more from pity than anything else. While locals let the suffering Saints crowd into farms, sheds, huts, and tents, they judged the refugees to be "generally of the poorer and more illiterate classes."[78] On February 25, Quincy leaders met and adopted measures to provide relief. They asked a committee of Latter-day Saints to provide them facts about the needy. The response, signed by Elias Higbee and John P. Greene, stated that "if we should say what our present wants are, it would be beyond all calculation; as we have been robbed of our corn, wheat, horses, cattle, cows, hogs, wearing apparel, houses and homes." Twenty widows were entirely destitute. Innumerable able-bodied men needed jobs. "Give us employment," the Saints pleaded, "rent us farms, and allow us the protection and privileges of other citizens."

The Quincy citizens' committee passed a resolution which said that the Saints "are entitled to our sympathy and kindest regard." Any Saints who because of sickness or destitution found themselves homeless, the committee decided, should appeal directly for assistance. Further, the committee agreed to find employment for those willing and able to labor.[79] In its March 2 issue, the *Quincy Whig* termed the Saints crossing the Mississippi River "objects of charity." Because they had been "thrown upon our shores destitute, through the oppressive people of Missouri, common humanity must oblige us to aid and relieve them all in our power."[80]

On March 5, Bishop Partridge reported from Quincy to Joseph Smith, "The people here receive us kindly" and "are willing that we should enjoy the privileges guaranteed to all civil people without molestation."[81]

Joseph Smith Sr. and wife Lucy rented a house or part of it on the northeast corner of Sixth and Hampshire streets.[82] Lucy said ladies in Quincy sent them "every delicacy which the city afforded."[83] Residents proffered employment. Aroet Hale said a Mr. Stilson employed his father.[84] William Cahoon noted that a family named Travis offered him employment;[85] Mr. Travis also hired refugee Truman Angell to frame a barn.[86]

As soon as John Butler's family arrived, they "had no place to go and it was bitter cold," John said. The old man for whom John taught school treated them generously. He operated a large butcher shop by the river and a wholesale store by the boat landing. He also owned and rented out ten or twelve small houses he had built. When the man saw the Saints' plight, he told his tenants to go elsewhere, "for the Mormons were coming and they had no place to go and he was going to let his apartments to them." He invited John to bring his family up to one of his houses where they could live for a while. He never charged them rent. He told the Butlers to go to his butcher shop and take meat when they wanted some. Three or four Latter-day Saint families lived in his houses adjoining the Butlers', and the man treated them all with kindness, which "seemed a new thing to us," John confessed. John said that Quincy residents "generally were kind" to the Saints "all over the place." The Butlers stayed in Quincy for three or four weeks. Then, because it was planting season, they moved about ten miles out and rented a farm.[87]

It is not known how many Saints temporarily took refuge in Quincy. Many found refuge not only in Quincy but throughout Adams County and all over western Illinois. Quincy's compassion, noted historian Richard E. Bennett, "saved the saints as a people and may even have saved the Church as an institution."[88]

Completing the Exodus

Assigned by the Committee of Removal, David Rogers visited Jackson County on March 15, sold Church properties, raised some $2,700, and brought the funds to Far West by mid-April.[89] "In consequence of the sale of Lands in Jackson County," William Huntington, head of the Committee of Removal, said, "We ware able to remove All the poor who had a desire To leave the state" by April 13, the day he left Far West. Isaac Laney said the committee had moved all but thirty or forty families when armed men from Daviess County ordered him and others to be "out of the County by the next Friday night which was giving us Six dayes for to do that that Requird a month." So the committee urgently hired teams and sent families to Tenney's Grove, twenty miles away, with a minimum of personal belongings. A number of teams arrived from Illinois to help move the last families.[90]

By mid-April, the mobs lost patience with the Saints still in Caldwell County. Elder Kimball said he stayed behind to assist members of the Committee of Removal and to "wait upon those in prison." In Far West he had to hide out in the woods during daytime.[91] On April 18, when a group of anti-Mormons found him at the public square, they threatened to blow his brains out and tried to ride over him with their horses. He went to the room where the Committee of Removal was meeting and told them to wind up affairs and "be off" to save their lives.

Shortly, twelve mobbers with rifles entered the tithing office and broke windows, tables, chairs, and "seventeen clocks into matchwood." One threw iron pots at Theodore Turley, hitting him in the shoulder. Mobbers shot cows while girls were milking them. They threatened to send the committee "to hell jumping" and "put daylight through them." The men gathered up what they could and hastily fled from Far West within the hour. After they left, the mob plundered thousands of dollars' worth of property donated to help the poor move. One mobber shot a cow and, while it was still alive, skinned off a strip of hide from its nose to its tail, and tied his horse to a stump with it. During the vandalism spree, "a great portion of the records of the committee, accounts, history, etc. were destroyed or lost."[92]

A year earlier, Joseph Smith had received a commandment for the Twelve to leave for missions "over the great waters" from the Far West temple site on April 26, 1839 (Doctrine and Covenants 118). Anti-Mormons had vowed to keep that ceremony from happening. Some members of the Twelve left Quincy on April 18, 1839, to travel secretly to Far West to fulfill their instruction. That party came to include Brigham Young, Orson Pratt, and John Taylor. Also there were Wilford Woodruff and George A. Smith, who were soon to be ordained as Apostles. They passed Saints heading east, including Elder John E. Page, who turned around and joined them. On March 21 Wilford Woodruff said the apostolic company passed through Huntsville and found "the roads were full of Saints that were fleeing Missouri."[93] On April 24 they met three members of the Committee of Removal who had just been driven from Far West, who also joined them. The Apostles' group arrived at Far West soon after midnight on April 26. They held a short conference in one of the homes and excommunicated thirty-one "unworthies." In addition to the Apostles, six members of the committee and about a dozen other members were present. A stone weighing about a ton was rolled to the southeast corner of the site. Alpheus Cutler placed it in position. The five Apostles who were present—Brigham Young, Heber C. Kimball, Orson Pratt, John E. Page, and John Taylor—ordained Wilford Woodruff and George A. Smith as Apostles and two men who had just been liberated from the Richmond prison, Darwin Chase and Norman Shearer, as Seventies. The Twelve then offered kneeling prayer at the southeast cornerstone, sang "Adam-ondi-Ahman," and dismissed so they could leave there for their missions to England. They had fulfilled the commandment.[94]

In the dark the group reached Tenney's Grove and there added to their group the "last company of the poor" needing help to reach Quincy.[95] At that point, Brigham Young felt that the covenant to move the poor Saints had been fulfilled: "We had entered into a covenant to see the poor Saints all moved out of Missouri to Illinois, that they might be delivered out of the hands of such vile persecutors, and we spared no pains to accomplish this object until the Lord gave us the desires of our heart. We had the last company of the poor with us that could be removed."[96]

But the exodus was not quite complete because five prisoners were still in Liberty Jail and six in Richmond's jail, including King Follett, who had just been arrested that month while trying to leave Missouri.[97] During a change of venue from Daviess to Boone County, Joseph Smith and the four others who had been in Liberty Jail were allowed to escape on April 16, and they found their way to Illinois safely.[98] That summer the prisoners who had been at Richmond escaped confinement, except King Follett. By October 1839, King Follett had his trial, and because the charges of robbery were unsubstantiated, he was set free.⁹⁹ At that point the Saints' exodus from Missouri was finished, and Governor Boggs's extermination order had succeeded in removing Saints from northwest Missouri. However, a significant number had taken refuge in St. Louis, a Missouri city that became "an oasis of tolerance" for Mormons.¹⁰⁰

Joseph Smith's Return

In the morning of April 22, Dimick Huntington, at Emma Smith's request, went down to the river's edge to inquire about news from the West and spotted the Prophet. "My God is it you Bro. Joseph. He raised his hand and stopped me saying Hush, Hush." Huntington said that Joseph had come by ferryboat about 8:00 a.m. and "was drest in an old pair of boots full of holes, pants torn, tucked inside of boots, blue cloak with collar turned up, wide brim black hat, rim sloped down, not been shaved for some time, looked pale & haggard." Dimick asked if he wished to see his father and mother, but Joseph wanted to see Emma and the children first. When he reached the Clevelands', Emma recognized him as he dismounted from his horse and met him half way to the gate."¹⁰¹

A Quincy newspaper reporter publicized the arrival of Joseph Smith and his prison companions, concluding with a favorable description of the Church President and Prophet: "We had supposed from the stories and statements we had read of 'Jo Smith' (as he is termed in the papers) to find him a very illiterate, uncouth sort of man; but from a long conversation, we acknowledge an agreeable disappointment. In conversation, he appears intelligent and candid, and divested of all malicious thought and feeling towards his relentless persecutors."¹⁰²

Joseph Smith quickly finalized plans for a new gathering place for the homeless Saints upriver at Commerce, soon to be renamed Nauvoo. When the Twelve returned from Far West in early May, they rejoiced to see him a free man in Illinois. Saints gathered for a general conference on May 4–6 held in a Presbyterian campground two miles north of Quincy. Joseph Smith presided. "Much business of consequence was accomplished during the day," Elder Woodruff noted, adding, "It truly gave us great Joy to once more sit in conference with Br. Joseph."[103] Perrigrine Sessions said that Joseph being there "gave us much joy to see his face among the Saints and here the voice of inspiration that flowed from his lips this caused our drooping spirits to revive as we were like sheap with out a shepherd that had been scatered in a cloudy and dark day."[104] After Joseph heard the congregation enthusiastically sing the hymn "Zion, City of Our God," Wandle Mace observed that Joseph rose to speak but had difficulty controlling his emotions: "To look upon the Saints who had been driven from their homes, and scattered as they were, among strangers, without homes, robbed of everything, and to see them under all these trying circumstances assemble to this General Conference from all the region around, and sing of Zion, the city of our God, with so much spirit, showing their love and confidence in the gospel, and the pleasure he felt in meeting with them. He could scarcely refrain from weeping."[105]

Petitions for Redress

Once safely in Illinois, the Saints still had some unfinished business related to their expulsion from Missouri. While in Liberty Jail, Joseph Smith had instructed them to compile statements and affidavits about their losses and sufferings "with the design of securing redress from the federal government for the losses they suffered in Missouri" (Doctrine and Covenants 123:1–13). In response, when Saints reached safety they began filling out petitions for redress and having them notarized by justices of the peace and court clerks in two counties in Iowa and ten in Illinois.[106] Fortunately, 678 petitions survive. In total, these petitioners' losses totaled $2,275,789—an average of $3,761 per petitioner.[107] In 2007 dollars, that equals $52,325,000 total, or $87,000 per petitioner.[108] The extended Knight family's losses were at least $14,562, or about $335,000 in today's currency. Joseph Knight Jr., for one, claimed $200 for a mill burned down, $50 for a house burned, $50 for 3 acres of land and 50 peach trees, $25 for hay and corn, $475 for losses of land and town properties, and $150 for expenses for moving twice. Leaders compiled these petitions and affidavits and presented them three times, possibly four, to U.S. president Martin Van Buren and to Congress, but the federal government refused to act on them.[109]

Nauvoo Becomes the New Gathering Center

After inspections, the Church agreed to buy twenty thousand acres of land at Commerce, Illinois, and across the river in Lee County, Iowa. On May 10, Joseph Smith and his family moved into a small, two-story log house at Commerce, fifty miles north of Quincy, "hoping that I and my friends may here find a resting place for a little season at least."[110] Church headquarters moved there, as did large numbers of the exiled Saints. These souls, by and large, were poor, bedraggled, and sickly. Many of them started from scratch and built up religious communities in Illinois and Iowa.

Short- and Long-Term Consequences

This forced expulsion of Saints from Missouri produced short- and long-term consequences, as enumerated here for various of the parties involved.

Mormon regard for Quincy. In April 1839, Eliza R. Snow wrote a poem titled "To the Citizens of Quincy" to thank "Ye noble, gen'rous hearted Citizens."[111] It was published on page 1 of the *Quincy Whig* on May 11, 1839. The poem praised those "who have put forth your liberal hand to meet / The urgent wants of the oppress'd and poor!" In 1841 Joseph and Hyrum Smith and Sidney Rigdon, the First Presidency, issued a proclamation of appreciation, saying, "It would be impossible to enumerate all those who in our time of deep distress, nobly came forward to our relief and like the good Samaritan poured oil into our wounds and contributed liberally to our necessities as the citizens of Quincy en masse and the people of Illinois generally seemed to emulate each other in the labor of love."[112]

In Quincy's Washington Park stands a simple historical marker erected in 1976 to memorialize the Saints' exodus. It notes, "Many of them crossed into Illinois at Quincy and were made welcome by the people here." In recent years, several related commemoration events have taken place in Quincy.[113]

A test passed by the faithful. Being forced from Missouri posed a test of faith that most Saints passed, but some failed, as the extended Knight family illustrates. When those families reached Illinois early in 1839, they were poor, worn out, and ragged looking. No one could have recognized them as the prosperous Yankees they had once been in New York before embracing Mormonism. First in Ohio and then three times in Missouri, they had practiced starting over. To begin again in Illinois was heartbreaking. But only three of the two dozen adults in Knight family network faltered. About sixty individuals in that network restructured their everyday lives in or near Nauvoo and continued to follow Joseph Smith.[114] John Lowe Butler became a trusted workhorse for Joseph Smith and Brigham Young, serving as one of Joseph's official, ordained bodyguards and later as a bishop in Spanish Fork, Utah. The Thomas family stayed strong in the faith and emigrated to Utah in 1849. Levi Ward Hancock continued as a President of the Seventy, marched to California in the Mormon Battalion, was a pioneer in Manti and southern Utah, and served as a patriarch. Abraham O. Smoot became mayor of Salt Lake City and later Provo, president of the Utah Stake, and a promoter of Brigham Young Academy.

A decision to continue to gather. President Sidney Rigdon, Bishop Edward Partridge, and a few others felt the Saints could avoid problems like the ones they had in Missouri by spreading out rather than gathering together into Latter-day Saint communities. However, President Young advised the Saints to gather in order to help each other better. Joseph Smith, when asked, advised leaders to obtain properties where the Saints could collect rather than scatter, and he developed Nauvoo to be the next gathering place.[115]

Health problems and deaths. Winter exposure and food shortages in Caldwell County and during exodus caused health problems for many and a host of deaths during 1839. During the exodus, Truman Angell's wife Elizabeth, already ill, took a "cold upon cold" and was expected to die. Her health "partially returned, but she has never been able to work much since," her husband wrote in 1845.[116] A plague of sickness that befell Nauvoo residents in the summer of 1839 was due in large measure to physical debility caused by sufferings during the previous year.[117] Benjamin F. Johnson observed that during the rest of 1839 in the Nauvoo area, "the people had flocked in from the terible exposures of the past and Nearly every one was Sick with intemitant or other fevers of which many died—In this time of great Sickness poverty & death."[118] Henry Jackson claimed the March's "Stormy blasts of Snow & rain" so affected his sight that he was "not able to work."[119] The exodus caused "considrable sickness" for the Levi Hancock family."[120] Mosiah Hancock, the boy who had crossed the Mississippi ice barefoot, was an emaciated lad for many months. "My mother called my legs pipe stems, and my arms straws!" he said.[121] James Golligher claimed he was "exposed to the weather in which sickness followed & the loss of one of my Children."[122] Innumerable such examples can be cited.

Mental and emotional scars. The Saints' persecution in several states and then expulsion by order of a state governor helps explain why they obtained a charter for a self-defensive city-state in Nauvoo with the Nauvoo Legion; why some Saints justified retaliation against persecutors; why many gladly exited the United States and headed toward Mexican territory in 1846; and why many Saints, if not the Church, expressed distaste for judges, courts, deputies, the federal army during the Utah War, and antipolygamy laws. Some participants in the Missouri exodus vented powerful feelings of anger, horror, outrage, and persecution. John Lowe Butler, for one, wanted his written record to stand as a witness against Missourians who were cruel to his suffering family during the exodus and earlier.[123]

Ghost towns and farms. When the Saints pulled out of Far West, their houses, barns, fences, stores, schools, farms, farm equipment, household goods, livestock, and stored grain fell into non-Mormons' hands. In time, most of the houses were torn down for firewood or hauled away. The streets and city square became corn fields. The temple site has since been salvaged and given modern landscaping, but no houses remain. The city cemetery's tombstones marking where some two hundred Saints are buried are long gone, and the site has become farmland. At Adam-ondi-Ahman, Saints in October

1838 were building about 150 log houses, but most of them were not finished by the time the Saints left. In 1888 Lyman Wight's cabin was the only building standing in "Ahman," and by 1970 it was totally gone.[124]

Economic impact on Illinois and Iowa. The large body of displaced Saints became an economic force and political presence in Illinois and Iowa Territory. They developed communities, farms, roads, livestock herds, commerce, and trade in parts of Adam and Hancock counties, Illinois, and in Lee County, Iowa.

A storehouse of historical documents and records. The exodus from Missouri generated a rich store of documents and records. These include the petitions for redress, prison letters, other correspondence, diaries, autobiographies and memoirs, pamphlets, newspaper articles, and a mass of official Missouri government records.

Extermination order not rescinded for 137 years. Governor Bogg's infamous extermination order remained a stain on Missouri's character for 137 years until June 25, 1976, when Missouri governor Christopher S. Bond signed an executive order rescinding it.[125] Animosity toward Missourians by Mormons and by Missourians toward Mormons lasted for generations.

Training experience for 1846 exodus. Finally, in some respects, the exodus from Missouri was a training exercise for the Saints' exodus from Nauvoo seven years later. That larger move was led by Brigham Young and other Apostles whose first tutorial about moving a mass of people came during the Missouri exodus. Brigham Young, remembering the covenant he had asked the Saints in Far West to make to help move those in need, had members similarly covenant when preparing to leave Nauvoo for the West. That covenant became the foundation for the Church's emigration programs from then until 1869, producing the Perpetual Emigrating Fund in 1849, the handcart program from 1856 to 1860, and the 1860s team trains going "down and back" from Utah to provide transportation to Utah for emigrants in need.[126]

Notes

1. William G. Hartley, "'Almost Too Intolerable a Burthen': The Winter Exodus from Missouri, 1838–1839," *Journal of Mormon History* 18 (Fall 1992): 6–40.

2. Leland H. Gentry, "A History of the Latter-day Saints in Northern Missouri, from 1836 to 1839" (PhD diss., Brigham Young University, 1965), 273–85; Stephen C. LeSueur, *The 1838 Mormon War in Missouri* (Columbia: University of Missouri Press, 1987), 150–53.

3. LaMar C. Berrett and others, eds., *Sacred Places*, vol. 4: *Missouri* (Salt Lake City: Deseret Book, 2004), 288–89, 361, 402.

4. William G. Hartley, *"Stand by My Servant Joseph": The Story of the Joseph Knight Family and the Restoration* (Salt Lake City: Joseph Fielding Smith Institute for Latter-day Saint History at Brigham Young University and Deseret Book, 2003); and William G. Hartley, "Newel and Lydia Bailey Knight's Kirtland Love Story and Historic Wedding," *BYU Studies* 39, no. 4 (2000): 6–22.

5. Gentry, "Latter-day Saints in Northern Missouri," 325–27; Alexander L. Baugh, "A Call to Arms: The 1838 Mormon Defense of Northern Missouri" (PhD diss., Brigham Young University, 1996), 340–47.

6. Baugh, "A Call to Arms," 326–29.

7. William G. Hartley, *My Best for the Kingdom: The History and Autobiography of John Lowe Butler, a Mormon Frontiersman* (Salt Lake City: Aspen Books, 1993), 81–84; Baugh, "Call to Arms," 392–96.

8. Lavina Fielding Anderson, ed., *Lucy's Book: A Critical Edition of Lucy Mack Smith's Family Memoir* (Salt Lake City: Signature Books, 2001), 691–92.

9. Leonard J. Arrington, *Charles C. Rich* (Provo, UT: BYU Press, 1974), 60; Juanita Brooks, ed., *On the Mormon Frontier: The Diary of Hosea Stout, 1844–1861* (Salt Lake City, Utah: University of Utah Press and the Utah State Historical Society, 1964), xvi; Lorenzo Dow Young, "Recollections," *Four Faith Promoting Classics* (Salt Lake City: Bookcraft, 1968), 52–54.

10. Arrington, *Charles C. Rich*, 60–61.

11. Charles C. Rich, "A Sketch that I was an eye witness to in the state of Missouri," holograph, Charles C. Rich Papers, Church History Library, The Church of Jesus Christ of Latter-day Saints, Salt Lake City.

12. Baugh, "Call to Arms," 328–29.

13. Hartley, *My Best for the Kingdom*, 82–84.

14. "Autobiography of Anson Call," typescript, 13, L. Tom Perry Special Collections, Harold B. Lee Library, Brigham Young University.

15. Hartley, *Stand by My Servant Joseph*, 291; Reed Peck, *Reed Peck Manuscript* (Salt Lake City: Modern Microfilms reprint, n.d.), 29.

16. Baugh, "Call to Arms," 395; *Reed Peck Manuscript*, 29.

17. Dean C. Jessee and David J. Whittaker, "The Last Months of Mormonism in Missouri: The Albert Perry Rockwood Journal," *BYU Studies* 28 (Winter 1988): 27–29.

18. "Diaries of William Huntington," typescript, in Miscellaneous Mormon Diaries, vol. 16, Lee Library, 6–7; Joseph Smith, *History of the Church of Jesus Christ of Latter-day Saints*, ed. B. H. Roberts, 2nd ed. rev. (Salt Lake City: Deseret Book, 1976 reprint), 3:210.

19. John P. Greene, *Facts Relative to the Expulsion of the Mormons or Latter-day Saints from the State of Missouri, Under the "Exterminating Order"* (Cincinnati: R. P. Brooks, 1839), 8.

20. "The Life of Joseph Holbrook, 1806–1871," typescript, 46, Perry Special Collections.

21. Anderson, *Lucy's Book*, 676.

22. William Huntington Diary, 7; Lyndon W. Cook, *Joseph C. Kingsbury: A Biography* (Provo, UT: Grandin Book, 1985), 61.

23. Heber Quincy Hale, *Bishop Jonathan H. Hale of Nauvoo: His Life and Ministry* (Salt Lake City: The Author, 1938), 64.

24. James Carroll Petition in Clark V. Johnson, *Mormon Redress Petitions: Documents of the 1833–1838 Missouri Conflict* (Provo, UT: Religious Studies Center, Brigham Young University, 1992), 155; see biographical sketch in Donald Q. Cannon and Lyndon W. Cook, eds., *Far West Record* (Salt Lake City: Deseret Book, 1983), 252.

25. William F. Cahoon Petition in Johnson, *Mormon Redress Petitions*, 152–53.

26. Hartley, *My Best for the Kingdom*, 85–86.

27. Gentry, "Latter-day Saints in Northern Missouri," 414–19.

28. Greene, *Expulsion of the Saints from Missouri*, 8.

29. Smith, *History of the Church*, 3:249.

30. The committee was composed of John Taylor, Alanson Ripley, Brigham Young, Theodore Turley, Heber C. Kimball, John Smith (the Prophet's uncle), and Don Carlos Smith (the Prophet's brother).

31. Smith, *History of the Church*, 3:250–54.

32. Committee of Removal members were William Huntington, Charles Bird, Alanson Ripley, Theodore Turley, Daniel Shearer, Shadrach Roundy, and Jonathan H. Hale. The additions were Elias Smith, Erastus Bingham, Stephen Markham, and James Newberry (Smith, *History of the Church*, 3:249–54, includes 214 names of those who pledged).

33. William Huntington Diary, 8.

34. Smith, *History of the Church*, 3:255.

35. A Missouri map published in 1840 by L. Augustus Mitchell, on file in the National Archives Branch in College Park, Maryland,

shows roads that provided two possible routes, an upper and a lower one.

36. Brigham H. Roberts, *A Comprehensive History of the Church of Jesus Christ of Latter-day Saints, Century I* (reprint, Provo, UT: Brigham Young University Press, 1965), 1:510–511, and Smith, *History of the Church*, 3:261–63.

37. David Rogers Report, 1839, in Leo Ritchie Rogers, *Willis Rogers and Elizabeth (Bessie) Ritchie with Their Ancestors and Descendants* (Salt Lake City: Leo R. Rogers, 1981), 230.

38. Larry C. Porter, "Brigham Young and the Twelve in Quincy: A Return to the Eye of the Missouri Storm, 26 April 1839," in *A City of Refuge: Quincy, Illinois*, ed. Susan Easton Black and Richard E. Bennett (Salt Lake City: Millennial Press, 2000), 134.

39. Joseph Holbrook said that Saints understood that "if the Church would make haste and move as fast as possible it would [do] much to the relieve our brethren who were now in jail as our enemies were determined to hold them as hostages until the church left the state so that every exertion was made in the dead of the winter to remove as fast as possible" ("Life of Joseph Holbrook," 46).

40. "[Auto]Biographical Sketch of George Washington Gill Averett," typescript, 8, in Miscellaneous Mormon Diaries, vol. 11. A painting by C. C. A. Christensen, *Exodus of the Saints from Missouri*, is the only depiction the author has seen of the winter exodus experience.

41. Jessee and Whittaker, Albert Perry Rockwood Journal, 34.

42. Jessee and Whittaker, Albert Perry Rockwood Journal, 34.

43. "Life of Joseph Holbrook," 47.

44. Ebenezer Robinson, "Items of Personal History of the Editor, Including Some items of Church History Not Generally Known. Taken from 'The Return,'" typescript, 243, Perry Special Collections.

45. *The Mosiah Hancock Journal* (Salt Lake City: reprint by Pioneer Press, n.d.), 11.

46. *Mosiah Hancock Journal*, 12.

47. Dated entries in "An Abridged Record of the Life of John Murdock, Taken from His Journal by Himself," typescript, n.p., n.d., Perry Special Collections.

48. Anderson, *Lucy's Book*, 680.

49. Linda King Newell and Valeen Tippetts Avery, *Mormon Enigma: Emma Hale Smith* (Garden City, NY: Doubleday, 1984), 79.

50. "Autobiography of Anson Call," 17.

51. Ronald K. Esplin, "The Emergence of Brigham Young and the Twelve in Mormon Leadership, 1830–1841" (PhD diss., Brigham Young University, 1981), 370; *Times and Seasons*, September 1840, 165.

52. Heber C. Kimball Journals, 1838–1839, in Porter, "Brigham Young and the Twelve," 134.

53. Anderson, *Lucy's Book*, 680–87.

54. "The Saint's Petition to Congress," November 1839, in Smith, *History of the Church*, 4:24–38; the mention of bloody footsteps is on p. 36.

55. The shoes belonged to the oldest boy, Morgan. Thomas's version is in E. Kay Kirkham, *Daniel Stillwell Thomas, Utah Pioneer of 1849*, bound typescript, 26; wife Martha Pane Jones Thomas's version in Kate Woodhouse Kirkham, ed., *Daniel Stillwell Thomas Family History*, bound typescript, n.d., n.p., 25; copies in author's possession.

56. *Daniel Stillwell Thomas Family History*, 27–29.

57. Quoted in Lyman O. Littlefield, *Reminiscences of Latter-day Saints* (Logan, UT: Journal Company Printers, 1888), 72–73.

58. Hartley, *My Best for the Kingdom*, 87–90.

59. Hartley, *My Best for the Kingdom*, 90.

60. Eliza R. Snow to Esqr. [Isaac] Streator, Feb. 22, 1839, in "Eliza R. Snow Letter from Missouri," *BYU Studies* 13 (Summer 1973): 549.

61. Journal History, March 5, 1839.

62. Eliza Roxey (Snow) Smith, *Biography and Family Record of Lorenzo Snow* (Salt Lake City: Deseret News, 1884), 45.

63. *Eliza R. Snow, an Immortal: Selected Works by Eliza R. Snow*, ed. Nicholas G. Morgan Sr. (Salt Lake City: Nicholas G. Morgan Sr., 1957), 10–11.

64. History of Zera Pulsipher As Written by Himself, typescript, 15–16, Perry Special Collections.

65. Elisha Whiting Petition, in Johnson, *Mormon Redress Petitions*, 374.

66. Journal History, March 16, 1839.

67. *Wilford Woodruff's Journal, 1833–1898, Typescript*, ed. Scott G. Kenney (Midvale, UT: Signature Books, 1983–85), 1:322.

68. "Life of Joseph Holbrook," 48.

69. *Wilford Woodruff's Journal*, 1:322.

70. John Taylor, Brigham Young, Isaac Higbee, Israel Barlow, John P. Greene to Dear Brethren, March 29, 1839, at Quincy, reprinted in Kate B. Carter, comp., *Our Pioneer Heritage* (Salt Lake City: Daughters of Utah Pioneers, 1960), 3:122.

71. In 1837 the population was 1,653 according to Pat. H. Redmond, *History of Quincy and Its Men of Mark* (Quincy, IL: Heirs and Russell, 1863), 15; Richard E. Bennett, "'Quincy—the Home of Our Adoption': A Study of the Mormons in Quincy, Illinois, 1838–1839," 87–88, and Susan Easton Black, "Quincy—A City of Refuge," 69, in *A City of Refuge*.

72. Roberts, *Comprehensive History*, 2:3.

73. Bennett, "'Quincy—the Home of Our Adoption,'" 86.

74. Greene, *Expulsion of the Saints from Missouri*, 40.

75. Wandle Mace Autobiography, typescript, 31–32, Perry Special Collections.

76. Smith, *History of the Church*, 3:262.

77. *Wilford Woodruff's Journal*, 1:329–30.

78. *Quincy Whig*, February 23, 1839.

79. Smith, *History of the Church*, 3:270.
80. "The Mormons," *Quincy Whig*, March 2, 1839.
81. Journal History, March 5, 1839.
82. Bennett, "'Quincy—the Home of Our Adoption,'" 92.
83. Anderson, *Lucy's Book*, 695.
84. Aroet Hale, Autobiography, typescript, 6, Perry Special Collections.
85. William Cahoon, Autobiography, in Susan Easton Black, "Quincy—A City of Refuge," 73, n. 34.
86. Truman O. Angell Journal, reprinted in Kate B. Carter, comp., *Our Pioneer Heritage* (Salt Lake City: Daughters of Utah Pioneers, 1967), 10:199.
87. Hartley, *My Best for the Kingdom*, 91–92.
88. Bennett, "'Quincy—the Home of Our Adoption,'" 101.
89. Rogers, *Willis Rogers and Elizabeth (Bessie) Ritchie*, 230–31.
90. Diaries of William Huntington, 8; Isaac Leany Petition in Johnson, *Mormon Redress Petitions*, 485.
91. Porter, "Brigham Young and the Twelve," 137.
92. Smith, *History of the Church*, 3:322–23.
93. *Wilford Woodruff's Journal*, 1:325.
94. Porter, "Brigham Young and the Twelve," 141–49.
95. *Wilford Woodruff's Journal*, 1:329.
96. Manuscript History of Brigham Young, Church History Library, 28.
97. The Liberty Jail prisoners were Joseph Smith, Hyrum Smith, Lyman Wight, Alexander McRae, and Caleb Baldwin. Sidney Rigdon had been released in January. In jail in Richmond were Parley P. Pratt, Norman Shearer, Darwin Chase, Luman Gibbs, Morris Phelps, and King Follett.
98. Alex Baugh, "'We Took a Change of Venue for the State of Illinois': The Gallatin Hearing and the Escape of Joseph Smith and the

Mormon Prisoners from Missouri, April 1839," in *A City of Refuge*, 31–66.

99. Smith, *History of the Church*, 4:17.

100. Stanley B. Kimball, "The Saints and St. Louis, 1831–1857: An Oasis of Tolerance and Security," *BYU Studies* 13 (Summer 1973): 489–519.

101. Cited in Baugh, "'We Took Our Change of Venue,'" 52.

102. See *Missouri Republican* (St. Louis), May 3, 1839.

103. *Wilford Woodruff's Journal*, 1:330, entry for May 4, 1839.

104. Donna Toland Smart, *Exemplary Elder: The Life and Missionary Diaries of Perrigrine Sessions, 1814–1893* (Provo, UT: BYU Studies and Joseph Fielding Smith Institute for Latter-day Saint History, 2002), 43.

105. Mace Autobiography, 31–32.

106. Johnson, *Mormon Redress Petitions*, xix.

107. Johnson, *Mormon Redress Petitions*, xix–xxvii.

108. According to calculations found in Samuel H. Williamson, "Six Ways to Compute the Relative Value of a U.S. Dollar Amount, 1774 to Present," a dollar in the year 2007 was 22.99 times what a dollar in 1839 was worth based on consumer price indexes (Measuring Worth, 2009, http://www.measuringworth.com/calculators/uscompare).

109. Johnson, *Mormon Redress Petitions*, xix–xxvii. This book contains copies of the individual and group petitions and provides excellent explanations about each of the petition drives and how the petitions were used by the Church to seek redress for its members.

110. Smith, *History of the Church*, 3:349.

111. Starting with this poem, Eliza R. Snow published a total of eighteen poems in the *Quincy Whig* during the 1839–41 period.

112. "A Proclamation to the Saints Scattered Abroad—Greeting," *Times and Seasons*, January 15, 1841, 6.

113. On February 10, 1989, Mayor Vern Hagstrom gave the key to the city of Quincy to Elder Loren C. Dunn of the First Quorum of

Seventy and declared February 15 the city's Latter-day Saints Day to honor Emma Smith's crossing for the frozen Mississippi River and entering Quincy. In May that year the Mormon History Association held their annual meetings there. A Quincy Heritage Celebration was held July 24, 1999. More than 1,400 descendants of 1839 exiled Mormons came to Quincy and, attired like pioneers, represented their ancestors and walked across the Memorial Bridge to reach Quincy from Missouri. Then on November 5 and 6, 1999, a Quincy History Symposium honored the city's humanitarian efforts for Saints who fled Missouri.

114. "Close Friends as Witnesses: Joseph Smith and the Joseph Knight Families," in *Joseph Smith: The Prophet, the Man*, ed. Susan Easton Black and Charles D. Tate Jr. (Provo, UT: Religious Studies Center, Brigham Young University, 1993), 271–84.

115. Joseph Smith and Others to Edward Partridge and the Church, March 25, 1839, in *Times and Seasons*, May 1840, 102, and July 1840, 131–32. Bishop Partridge felt the poor could be better served if scattered in various communities and not gathered in one place. Uncertain which policy to push, the conference voted against accepting the land offer (Journal History, February 1, 1839).

116. Truman O. Angell Journal, 199–200.

117. "Weakened by the rigorous trek in midwinter after the severe ordeal of persecution in Missouri, the exiles who were camped along the Mississippi River began to feel the effects of the hardships" such that "almost every family succumbed to the ague and bilious fever" (Ivan J. Barrett, *Joseph Smith and the Restoration* [Provo, UT: BYU Press, 1973], 439).

118. Dean R. Zimmerman, *I Knew the Prophets: An Analysis of the Letters of Benjamin F. Johnson to George F. Gibbs Reporting Doctrinal Views of Joseph Smith and Brigham Young* (Bountiful, UT: Horizon, 1976), 10–11.

119. Henry Jackson petition in Johnson, *Mormon Redress Petitions*, 247.

120. Levi W. Hancock petition in Johnson, *Mormon Redress Petitions*, 225.

121. *The Mosiah Hancock Journal*, 12.

122. James Galligher Petition in Johnson, *Mormon Redress Petitions*, 218.

123. Butler denounced the hard-heartedness that Missourians had shown his wife and children and Church authorities. Such souls "will have to suffer for the ill treatment of the Saints," he wrote, adding that "they need not think that they will escape, for the Lord is just and He will punish those that have ill treated His children" (Hartley, *My Best for the Kingdom*, 89).

124. Berrett and others, *Sacred Places: Missouri*, 329, 402, 411.

125. Photocopy of order, filed June 25, 1976, copy in author's file; also see transcript in *LDS Church News*, July 3, 1976, 4.

126. Hartley, "How Shall I Gather?" *Ensign*, October 1997, 5–17.

The Prophet Joseph Smith went to Washington to meet with Congress and the president of the United States regarding the Saints' plea for redress and restoration of their rights. After Joseph addressed President Martin Van Buren (pictured here), the president said, "What can I do? I can do nothing for you,—if I do anything, I shall come in contact with the whole State of Missouri." (Library of Congress.)

RONALD O. BARNEY

1839–40
Joseph Smith Goes to Washington

This chapter focuses on events during one winter of Joseph Smith's life. I preface it with a disclaimer: this information is provisional, even tentative, and is part of my work editing and annotating the fifth volume in the Documents Series of *The Joseph Smith Papers*. My purpose as documentary editor is, first, to create accurate transcriptions of the records and, second, to prepare annotation providing the context by which the records associated with the Prophet's life can best be understood. This will be accomplished by the team of Joseph Smith Papers scholars through published volumes, thirty of which are planned, and an Internet

---

Ronald O. Barney is a historian in the Church History Department, a series and volume editor of The Joseph Smith Papers, *and executive producer of the television series* The Joseph Smith Papers.

site, josephsmithpapers.org, where material too unwieldy to include in the already substantial books will be made available. While there has been a great deal of publicity regarding the work of the Joseph Smith Papers project, I will briefly introduce the project to provide some background for Joseph Smith's trip to Washington DC.

As currently planned, there will be six series in the publication of the Prophet Joseph Smith's papers, with several volumes produced within each series. For example, the first volume released the fall of 2008 is from the Journal Series, which will include three volumes. Multiple volumes will compose the Revelation and Translation, History, Legal, and Administrative series. The volume on which I am working as editor is the fifth in the projected thirteen-book Document Series, the largest of the series within the *Papers*. This latter series will include a variety of contemporary records evidencing Joseph Smith's life and ministry and his role as President of the Church. The Documents Series will contain his outgoing and incoming correspondence, scribal reports of his sermons (because the scribal reports are all that exist of his speeches), his written epistles, his revelations in context, minutes of meetings—including conferences—at which he spoke, and essays and articles that he wrote, dictated, or commissioned to be written under his name, along with various and sundry ephemeral documentation.

Each of the volumes within *The Joseph Smith Papers* will have multiple coeditors contributing to each book. The volume on which I am working covers two years of the Prophet's life, 1839 and 1840, and includes all of the extant records for that period that I have mentioned above. I base my essay on several of these documents.

Joseph Smith Goes to Washington

Expulsion from Missouri and Regrouping in Illinois

The story begins in 1838. It was a complicated time for the national government. The unanticipated baggage Van Buren had inherited from his predecessor, Andrew Jackson, had led to the economic reversal known as the Panic of 1837, which still held its grip on Americans. Earlier in the year the Underground Railroad had clandestinely begun operation, spiriting black slaves to liberation in the free states of the North. Sectional issues intensified as the first abolitionist was elected to the House of Representatives. And at the same time as the Saints' expulsion from Missouri, the winter of 1838–39, a somewhat comparable number of Cherokee Indians were banished by the federal government from Georgia to designated lands in what is now Oklahoma. The weighty matters occupying America's citizenry in 1838 subordinated the catastrophe consuming the Latter-day Saints in America's westernmost state, Missouri.

With the Prophet's followers in a panic after the state of Missouri pressed them into submission and flight, Joseph Smith was subjected to sequential incarcerations beginning the first week of November 1838—first in Independence, then in Richmond, then in Liberty, Clay County, Missouri, where he arrived on December 1, 1838. Four and a half months later, after surviving a bitter winter in the jail's stone dungeon, Joseph "escaped" with four fellow inmates in collaboration with their sympathetic guards. A week later he was reunited with his wife and children in the Mississippi River city of Quincy, Illinois, on April 22, 1839.

The Prophet and several thousand of his fellow impoverished Latter-day Saint refugees soon made plans to relocate forty-some miles upriver to the villages of Commerce, Illinois, and Montrose, Iowa. On May 10, 1839, Joseph and Emma Smith moved with their four children into a log home near the bank of the huge river, in what would later be called Nauvoo. The emerging city had antecedents that stretched back to the beginning of the century; as early as 1805, government explorer Zebulon Pike marched across the site. The first permanent white settler moved to this bend in the Mississippi River in 1823. Others followed. Six years later, the same year Hancock County was organized, the few who inhabited the future Mormon site established a post office with the exotic name of Venus. Five years later the small frontier village became Commerce, and a sister settlement, Commerce City, was organized three years later. The beauty of the peninsula, located within the westernmost county in Illinois, drew the Saints enthusiastically into the region. Here Joseph Smith's vision for a flourishing metropolis quickly materialized.

The city's initial success masked the difficulties that confronted the new settlers in the late spring and summer of 1839. Indeed, there was nothing easy about preparing the site for occupation by a poverty-stricken people. Joseph Smith's work as director of operations, city developer, and institutional strategist complemented the Saints' significant efforts to build the new city. During the village's first summer, Joseph shared the malarial sickbed with his fellow Saints. It was during this discouraging and difficult—though optimistic—period that the Lord inspired the Prophet to call the nascent Quorum of the Twelve Apostles to missionary service in the British Isles. Within weeks most of the Twelve embarked on their missions. While he did not join them in their apostolic mission, neither did Joseph Smith remain behind merely to enjoy the fruits of their season's work in the new city. A significant enterprise that portended great advance for the Church was in the making.

Mission to Washington

Though their frozen limbs had barely thawed from their winter ordeal, the Saints convened a Church conference in May 1839 in Quincy, Illinois, where many were rehabilitating. In the aftermath of their horrific expulsion from their lands and rights in Missouri, they had something on their minds. After all, Missouri officials had purged the state of American citizens whose forbears bore scars evidencing their patriotic sacrifice for free institutions. Because the Church had no representation in the nation's capital, Sidney Rigdon, forty-six-year-old counselor in the Church's First Presidency, was appointed by the conference to be the first Church agent to present the Saints' Missouri plight to the federal government. However, by the time of the October conference that fall a revised strategy emerged. President Rigdon was to be accompanied by Elias Higbee, a very capable former Caldwell County, Missouri, judge, then forty-four; they would also be joined by the thirty-three-year-old Prophet Joseph Smith.

In an interesting window into Church government at the time, the Washington mission was authorized two weeks after the conference, not by the First Presidency or the Quorum of the Twelve, most of whom had left Nauvoo for Great Britain earlier in the year, but by the Nauvoo Stake high council. The next week the council affixed their final approval to a document ratifying the Prophet's proposal for the trip. The following day, October 29, 1839, Joseph Smith and his small team, which included twenty-five-year-old Orrin Porter Rockwell, departed Commerce for Washington. Although Sidney Rigdon, suffering from malaria, was in no shape for travel, he went with the group.

After traveling only a hundred miles to the newly designated Illinois state capital of Springfield, Sidney's worsening condition forced a decision. He needed help or he would have to be left behind. There in Springfield, on November 8 they found a young physician, a twenty-eight-year-old who had apparently just joined the Church by the name of Robert D. Foster, whom they induced to join them and tend to Sidney Rigdon.

With President Rigdon's debilitation, he turned over all of the letters of introduction written for him and endorsed them to Joseph Smith, along with his own affirmation of Joseph, the latter a document dated November 9, 1839. With the expanded entourage, the group continued eastward, likely traveling by way of the National Road once they were in Indiana. On November 18, the group paused to allow Sidney some relief near Columbus, Ohio. But Joseph could not bear the delay and decided to continue accompanied only by Elias Higbee, allowing Sidney time for recovery.

The information discussed to this point comes from disparate contemporary records that provide data describing the Washington mission, as I will refer to it. Hereafter we rely on documents incident to the mission itself. But there is a consideration that we must include here that actually bears on other events surrounding Joseph Smith's ministry; in particular it informs our understanding of this time in the Prophet's life. Oftentimes, details of events reconstructed from memory years afterward—especially in the absence of contemporary records— have acquired an enduring shelf life, keeping them in the public discussion of the past. In some cases, though certainly not in all, the memory does not mirror the reality of the incidents. One example concerns the story at hand.

We will begin with the trip itself, where after nearly a month on the road, a notable event occurred that endures as an indicator of Joseph Smith's character. Dr. Foster, the young physician who joined the Prophet's small entourage en route to Washington, later wrote in 1874:

> After we got to Dayton, Ohio, we left our horses in care of a brother in the church, and proceeded by stage, part of us; and the same coach that conveyed us over the Allegheny Mountains also had on board, as passengers, Senator Aaron of Missouri, and a Mr. Ingersol, a member of congress, from New Jersey or Pennsylvania, I forget which, and at the top of the mountain called Cumberland Ridge, the driver left the stage and his four horses drinking at the trough in the road, while he went into the tavern to take what is very common to stage drivers, a glass of spirits. While he was gone the horses took fright and ran away with the coach and passengers. There was also in the coach a lady with a small child, who was terribly frightened. Some of the passengers leaped from the coach, but in doing so none escaped more or less injury, as the horses were running at a fearful speed, and it was down the side of a very steep mountain. The woman was about to throw out the child, and said she intended to jump out herself, as she felt sure all would be dashed to pieces that remained, as there was quite a curve in the road, and on one side the mountain loomed up hundreds of feet above the horses, and the other side was a deep chasm or ravine, and the road only a very narrow cut on the side of the mountain, about midway between the highest and lowest parts. At the time the lady was going to throw out the child, Joseph Smith . . . caught the woman and very imperiously told her to sit down, and that not a hair of her head or any one on the coach should be hurt. He did this in such confident manner that all on board seemed spell-bound; and after admonishing and encouraging the passengers he pushed open one of the

doors, caught by the railing around the driver's seat with one hand, and with a spring and a bound he was in the seat of the driver. The lines were all coiled around the rail above, to hold them from falling while the driver was away; he loosened them, took them in his hands, and although those horses were running at their utmost speed, he, with more than herculean strength, brought them down to a moderate canter, a trot, a walk, and at the foot of Cumberland Ridge to a halt, without the least accident or injury to passenger, horse or coach, and the horses appeared as quiet and easy afterward as though they had never run away.[1]

Of course, this is quite a story. And there are parts of it that are demonstrably true based on other documentation. But as one can ascertain from the narrative, the writer presented himself as an eyewitness to the event. The difficulty with this inference is that the narrator, Dr. Foster, who had stayed behind in Ohio with Sidney Rigdon to help him recuperate, was likely not on board the stage. He constructed the story, including names of government officials, from a source or sources other than his own experience for reasons that we do not know. However, there is an eyewitness report by Joseph's companion, Elias Higbee, written on December 5, 1839, within two weeks of the event, that allows the modern reader to be much closer to the incident. It reads as follows:

> we came with one of the Missouri members [of Congress] from Wheeling to this place, who was drunk but once and that however was most of the time; there was but one day but what he could navigate and that day he was keel^d over so he could eat no dinner—The horses ran away with the stage, they ran about 3 miles; several passengers jumped out and were hurt. bro.^{r} Jo^s clum [climbed] out of the stage—got the

lines and stoped the horses, and also saved the life of a lady & child. He was highly commended by the whole company for his great exertions and presence of mind through the whole affair.—E[lias] Higbee [who reported this event, said of himself that he] jumped out of the stage at a favourable moment, just before they stoped with a view to assist in stopping them and was but slightly injured—We were not known to the stage company until after our arrival.[2]

Elias Higbee, now mostly unknown in historical circles because of his premature death in 1843 and the absence of surviving personal papers, had risen to play a significant role in the Prophet's life at this time. The Twelve, of course, were not available to augment the delegation to Washington. Sidney Rigdon would have undoubtedly played a much more visible and influential part of this venture had his health not precluded him from doing so, and his absence elevated Elias Higbee to the important status of the Church's first emissary, unofficial as it was, to Washington DC. After Joseph Smith's encounter with Martin Van Buren, which will be discussed later, the Prophet stayed in or around Washington for three more weeks, trying to muster support for the Saints by lobbying primarily the Illinois delegation to Washington. But after determining that he could do no more in Washington, with confidence he left Elias Higbee alone in the nation's capital to carry the Saints' message to all who would listen. Joseph then conducted a ministry tour to groups of Latter-day Saints in Pennsylvania and New Jersey. We know that the Prophet then returned to Washington DC to continue his endeavor with the Congress, along with other enterprises.

Elias Higbee wrote two letters to the Saints in Nauvoo while he was with Joseph Smith in December 1839, and he penned six subsequent letters to Joseph in February and March 1840, after the Prophet's departure from Washington. These, along with the communications Higbee received from congressional members, serve as the best primary sources of information about Joseph's and the Church's efforts with the U.S. president and Congress regarding the Saints' plea for redress and restoration of their rights in 1839–40.

Arrival in Washington

What we know about the petitioners' arrival in Washington DC is best represented in Elias Higbee's letter of December 5, 1839, written to Hyrum Smith in Nauvoo. Higbee reported, "we arrived in this City on the morning of the 28th of November, and spent the most of that day in looking up a boarding house which we succeeded in finding, We found as cheap boarding as can be had in this city."[3] In 1839, Washington DC was not the pride of American city making. In fact, it was considered a disappointment by many, if not most, Americans, and almost all Europeans, who were accustomed to the glitter and elegance of the flourishing capitals of Europe. One Viennese-born gentleman, Francis Grund, visited Washington somewhat contemporarily to Joseph Smith and wrote upon arriving in the nation's capital:

> The approach to the metropolis is anything but striking. . . .
>
> Washington is, indeed, a city sui generis, of which no European who has not actually seen it can form an adequate idea. [This was not a compliment.] Mr. Serullier, formerly minister of France, used to call it "a city of magnificent distances;" but, though this be true, I should rather call it "a city without streets." The Capitol, a magnificent palace, situated on an eminence called Capitol-hill, and the White-house, the dwelling of the President, are the only two

specimens of architecture in the whole town; the rest being mere hovels, and even the public buildings, such as the Treasury, War and Navy Departments, and the General Post-office, little superior to the most ordinary dwelling-houses in Europe. The whole town is, in fact, but an appendix to those two public buildings, a sort of ante-chamber either to the Capitol or to the house of the chief magistrate. If such a town were situated in Europe, one would imagine those buildings to be the residences of princes, and the rest of the humble dwellings of their dependents.

The only thing that approaches a street in Washington is Pennsylvania Avenue, a sometimes single, sometimes double row of houses, leading from the Capitol to the White-house. In this street are the two principal hotels of the city, and a considerable number of boarding-houses. The former are two large barracks, capable of holding each from one hundred and fifty to two hundred people; the latter are, for the most part, mean insignificant-looking dens, in which a man finds the worst accommodations at the most exorbitant prices, and must often be glad to be accommodated at all.[4]

While we cannot claim that Joseph Smith and Elias Higbee's experience was identical to Grund's, the generalities described here conform to other similar opinions of the city and its residents. Grund continues:

The first thing that struck me in Washington was the unusual number of persons perambulating the streets without any apparent occupation, of which every other American city, with the exception of Philadelphia, seems to be entirely drained. If there be poor and idle persons walking the streets of New York, Boston, or Baltimore, it is, I am sorry to say, generally owing to some late arrival from Europe,—some of the steerage passengers being yet left without employment. Washington, however, is a city of *American* idlers,—a set of gentlemen of such peculiar merit as well to deserve a public comment. They live in what is called "elegant style," rise in the morning at eight or nine, have breakfast in their own rooms, then smoke five or six cigars until twelve, at which time they dress for the Senate. . . .

The Senate of the United States is, indeed, the finest drawing-room in Washington; for it is there the young women of fashion resort for the purpose of exhibiting their attractions. The Capitol is, in point of fashion, the opera-house of the city; the House of Representatives being the crush-room. In the absence of a decent theatre, the Capitol furnishes a tolerable place of rendezvous, and is on that account frequented during the whole season—from December until April or May—by every lounger in the place, and by every belle that wishes to become the fashion.

After speaking and talking is over in the Senate, the idlers commence the regular performance of eating, which is no sort of amusement to any one in America who is obliged to dine at an ordinary [table]. For this reason they club together in numbers from four to six, to dine at their rooms; single dinners being too expensive, and the people who have the means of entertaining in Washington being not sufficiently numerous to secure every dandy a place at a private gentleman's table.[5]

It is probably safe to say that, like Grund, Joseph Smith was equally underwhelmed by Washington and its adornments.

President Smith and his associate found lodging for a modest sum just west of the U.S. capitol building on the corner of Missouri and 3rd streets, a site that would today be located on Washington's National Mall. Elias Higbee's report to his brethren in Nauvoo continued, "On friday morning [November] 29th, we proceeded to the house of the President— We found a very large and splendid palace, surrounded with a splendid enclosure decorated with all the finiries and elegancies of this world. we went to the door and requested to see the President."[6]

Audience with the President

We now arrive at the center of the traditional story of Joseph Smith's audience with the president of the United States, Martin Van Buren. This story has often been repeated by Latter-day Saints and others, although Joseph Smith and Elias Higbee's efforts with the Illinois delegation to Congress in December 1839 and Higbee's subsequent efforts on behalf of the Saints with the Senate Judiciary Committee were likely more important and held more promise than their brief encounter with the country's president.

A contemporary newspaper account dated December 21, 1839, reported on the Mormon delegation (by then including Sidney Rigdon) after they had been in Washington for three weeks:

> Several of the Mormon leaders are at present in the city. Their object is to obtain recompense for losses sustained by them in consequence of the outrages committed on them in Missouri. The statement which they have addressed to the President and Congress, presents details of robbery & butchery, at which the heart sickens. Houses burned, men slaughtered in cold blood, women driven into the woods to give birth to their off-spring in the den of the wolf, are pictures too horrible for contemplation. They appear to be

peaceful and harmless, and if fanaticism has led them into error, reason, not violence, should be used to reclaim them.

Joe Smith, the leader and prophet of the sect, who professes to have received the golden plates on which the Mormon creed was transcribed, and who has figured so conspicuously in fight, is a tall muscular man, with a countenance not absolutely unintellectual. On the contrary, [he] exhibits much shrewdness of character. His height is full six feet, and his general appearance is that of a plain yeoman, intended rather for the cultivation of the soil, than the expounding of prophecy. Without the advantage of education, he has applied himself, with much industry, to the acquisition of knowledge; and although his diction is inaccurate, and his selection of words not always in good taste, he converses very fluently on the subject nearest to his heart, and whatever may be thought of the correctness of his opinions, no one who talks with him, can doubt that his convictions of their truth are sincere and settled. His eye betokens a resolute spirit, and he would doubtless go to the stake to attest his firmness and devotion, with as little hesitation as did any of the leaders of the olden time. It is not probable that any relief will be obtained by these persons from the Federal Government. Their remedy lies against the State of Missouri. But it is to be apprehended, from the deep sense of their wrongs, which rankles in their hearts, and the determination they evince to right themselves, if they cannot be protected by the law, that they will return to Missouri, and commence a retributive course of action, which, from their number may be productive of greater evils than those which have already occurred. I understand that the followers of this new creed, throughout the United States, already exceeds

200,000, and they are still on the increase. Persecution swells their ranks.[7]

Despite this newspaperman's view of Latter-day Saint objectives at the time, only Mormons and Mormon observers, for the most part, were interested in Joseph Smith's visit with Martin Van Buren. Van Buren's biographers do not mention Joseph Smith or his visit with the president; Van Buren's own nearly eight-hundred-page autobiography does not mention Joseph Smith or the Mormons (although it doesn't mention his wife or marriage either). In Van Buren's own papers, now part of the Library of Congress, Manuscript Division, the visit is not described. The several newspaper reports that later noted Joseph Smith and his small entourage's presence in Washington did not mention him visiting with Van Buren. And other than two letters of introduction (one from Sidney Rigdon and the other from James Adams, a friend of Joseph Smith's from Springfield, Illinois) presented by Joseph Smith to the president (now part of the president's papers), no other documentation that I know of survives, except the following.[8]

Sixteen years after the fact, John Reynolds, the former governor of Illinois who became a U.S. congressman from Illinois in 1834, penned a memoir published in 1855. In it he described his role in the historic encounter:

> In December, 1839, the prophet, Joseph Smith, appeared at Washington City and presented his claims to Congress for relief for the losses he and the Mormons sustained in Missouri at the City of the Far West.
>
> When the prophet reached the city of Washington, he desired to be presented to President Van Buren.
>
> I had received letters, as well as the other Democratic members of congress, that Smith was a very important

character in Illinois, and to give him the civilities and attention that was due him. He stood at the time fair and honorable, as far as we knew at the city of Washington, except his fanaticism on religion. The sympathies of the people were in his favor.

It fell to my lot to introduce him to the President, and one morning the prophet Smith and I called at the white house to see the chief magistrate. When we were about to enter the apartment of Mr. Van Buren, the prophet asked me to introduce him as a "Latter-Day Saint." It was so unexpected and so strange to me . . . that I could scarcely believe he would urge such nonsense on this occasion to the President. But he repeated the request, when I asked him if I understood him. I introduced him as a "Latter-Day Saint," which made the President smile.[9]

Regrettably, Congressman Reynolds failed to include a report of the meeting's contents, leaving Higbee's report as the primary source of information about the Prophet's audience with the president.

It should be remembered that Van Buren was of Joseph's father's generation, having been born in 1782. When Joseph met him, the president was fifty-seven; Joseph, as mentioned, was thirty-three. Upon their arrival at the president's mansion, the White House, Elias Higbee wrote, "we were immediately introduced into an upper apartment where we met the President and were introduced into his parlor, where we presented him with our Letters of introduction;—as soon as he had read one of them, he looked upon us with a kind of half frown and said, what can I do? I can do nothing for you,—if I do anything, I shall come in contact with the whole State of Missouri."[10]

For generations this statement has been the iconic symbol of the Saints' poor treatment by the federal government. At one time I tried to track the expression in Church literature and from tabernacle pulpits. Before long it became evident that the account had been so pervasively recounted that calculating its breadth and distribution was of little value. It is etched into the corpus of our identity.

Before we move on to investigate the meaning of this encounter more broadly, let us consider the other things that Elias Higbee mentioned in his letter to his Nauvoo brethren. Even though the president had dismissed their plea, Higbee wrote: "we were not to be intimidated, and demanded a hearing and constitutional rights – Before we left him he promised to reconsider what he had said, and observed that he felt to sympathize with us on account of our sufferings,—Now we shall endeavor to express our feelings and views concerning the President, as we have been eye witnesses of his Majisty."[11] While Higbee mocked the president's regal air in biblical language—having been "eye witnesses of his Majisty" (2 Peter 1:16)—he also suggested that Van Buren may have been willing to give further consideration of the plea.

There is some dispute as to whether Van Buren's willingness to reconsider the Saints' plight resulted in a second visit by the Mormon delegation to the White House. Traditionally, only one meeting of Joseph Smith and Martin Van Buren is recounted. However, one could conclude from a reading of the *History of the Church* for the last part of January and the first part of February 1840 that, indeed, there was a subsequent encounter. (Joseph Smith had returned by this time to Washington after having visited Pennsylvania and New Jersey.) Having already included in the *History of the Church* Elias Higbee's December 5, 1839, letter chronicling the delegation's first visit on November 29,

1839, an entry from the *History* for the period covering the late January to early February 1840 period, which of course, is not a contemporary document but was assembled some years after the event, reads: "During My stay I had interview with Martin Van Buren, the President, who treated me very insolently, & it was with great reluctance he listened to our message, which, when he heard, he said, *'Gentlemen your cause is just but I can do nothing for you.'*—and 'If I take up for you I shall lose the vote of Mo.'"[12] While the wording of meeting or meetings' descriptions are somewhat similar, the aftermath of the meetings, if indeed there were two, is demonstrably different. The accounts of speeches given by Joseph Smith upon his return to Illinois after his Washington venture, as noted below, suggest that the hostility felt by Joseph Smith toward Martin Van Buren was the result of a second visit, the first visit having produced primarily disappointment rather than disgust and contempt. To be sure, as will be reported below, there are contradictory particulars in the extant documentation regarding the Smith/Van Buren encounter that may preclude certainty regarding the issue of whether there were one or two events.

Report of John Reynolds

Before continuing, I want to return to some other things that John Reynolds said about Joseph Smith and the Mormons. Given his forthright declarations in his memoir, one particular acknowledgment is consequential, in light of what may appear to be dismissive criticism. Reynolds wrote in 1855:

> In all the great events and revolutions in the various nations of the earth nothing surpasses the extraordinary history of the Mormons. The facts in relation to this singular people are so strange, so opposite to common-sense, and so great

and important, that they would not obtain our belief if we did not see the events transpire before our eyes. No argument, or mode of reasoning, could induce any one to believe that in the nineteenth century, in the United States, and in the blaze of science, literature, and civilization, a sect of religionists could arise on *delusion* and *imposition*. But such are the facts, and we are forced to believe them. This sect, amid persecutions and perils of all sorts, has reached almost half a million souls, scattered over various countries, within twenty-five or thirty years.[13]

As Joseph and Elias entreated the Illinois congressional delegation to the Mormons' Missouri plight, John Reynolds drew some conclusions about the Mormon leader: "Smith, the prophet, remained in Washington a great part of the winter, and preached often in the city. I became well acquainted with him. He was a person rather larger than ordinary stature, well proportioned, and would weigh, I presume, about one hundred and eighty pounds. He was rather fleshy, but was in his appearance amiable and benevolent. He did not appear to possess any harshness or barbarity in his composition, nor did he appear to possess that great talent and boundless mind that would enable him to accomplish the wonders he performed."[14]

While Reynolds remained stumped by the contrast of Joseph's humble circumstance and demeanor in juxtaposition to his notable accomplishments, he made this remarkable deduction: "No one can fore tell the destiny of this sect, and it would be blasphemy, at this day, to compare its founder to the Saviour, but, nevertheless it may become veritable history, in a thousand years, that the standing and character of Joseph Smith, as a prophet, may rank equal to any of the prophets who have preceded him."[15]

There is also something else to note about John Reynolds before we leave him, and though it sounds like trivia, it is a coincidence much more than that. John's brother was Thomas Reynolds, then the governor of Missouri. At the time of John's acquaintance with Joseph Smith, Thomas Reynolds began efforts to extradite Joseph Smith to Missouri for alleged crimes that Thomas, as a Missouri judge, had dismissed before his ascension to the governorship.

Views about Van Buren

As mentioned previously, there is regrettably no record extant from President Van Buren that describes Joseph Smith, their visit together, or his opinion of the Mormons. However, we do have one viewpoint of the event and its outcome; the importance of Elias Higbee's record, again, is noted. In his December 5th, 1839, portrait of the eighth president, he said:

> He is a small man, sandy complexion, and ordinary features; with frowning brow and considerable body but not well proportioned, as [are] his arms and legs—and to use his own words is quite fat—On the whole we think he is without boddy or parts, as no one part seems to be proportioned to another—therefore instead of saying boddy and parts we say boddy and part, or partyism if you please to call it, and in fine to come directly to the point, he [is] so much a fop or a fool, (for he judged our cause before he knew it,) we could find no place to put truth into him—We do not say the Saints shall not vote for him, but we do say boldly, (though, it need not be published in the streets of Nauvoo, neither among the daughters of the Gentiles,) That we do not intend [that] he shall have our votes.[16]

While this statement and subsequent ones by Joseph Smith indict Martin Van Buren in person and principal, the story is much larger than this encounter. While some of Van Buren's contemporaries disliked the president immensely, a condition applicable to many who have political rivals, there is a fairly uniform consensus among modern scholars that Van Buren was an honorable man and somewhat of a remarkable politician. Indeed, he is acknowledged by many to be the founding father of modern political parties. How can we explain the incongruity of Van Buren being an honorable man and yet completely indifferent to the Saints' plight? There were three primary factors, in my judgment, that help explain this dilemma. I will identify these only generally and briefly. The first factor was Van Buren's preoccupation with getting reelected. In late 1839, Van Buren's return to the White House as a Democratic president, like that of his two-term predecessor Andrew Jackson, was by no means guaranteed. The second factor was the condition of the country. The entirety of Van Buren's administration had been a struggle; many considered the country to be in a mess. Not only were most national issues filtered through the contentions of sectionalism, not the least of which was slavery (something that Van Buren adamantly defended), but the residual effects of the Panic of 1837 also pulled down the country's economic-bearing walls within two months of his assuming office, crippling any economic advance that he had hoped to make. Plus, there were international troubles with Great Britain that some thought might explode into war. The third and probably most important factor was that Mormons did not matter in the political landscape, especially in light of what they asked of the president.

Interceding on the Saints' behalf against the state of Missouri would have required Van Buren to violate the very foundation of his political persona, the premise upon which he believed he had made his career and achieved his ascension to the presidency—the protection of states' rights. Many have discussed Van Buren's apparent inability to initiate federal intervention to protect American citizens and execute their demands for redress from an offending state. It is true that post–Civil War constitutional amendments that arguably provided for such intervention were not enacted at this time. But even if there had been statutes on the books that provided for federal action, it is my judgment that Van Buren was so concerned about keeping sectional animosity at bay that he would not have acted on the Saints' behalf, even if he had had the law and the means to do so. Mormons did not matter. They were on nobody's "radar," to use today's parlance. They especially were of no concern when it came to pitting the president's entire career against what would have accelerated the unthinkable at the time—the unraveling of the republic.

This political worldview of the primacy of states' rights was so fundamental to Van Buren, and his posture was so widely known among Americans, that is implausible to me that Joseph Smith went to Washington ignorant of what he would likely encounter. It is difficult to believe that the Mormons were that naïve about the instincts and disposition of their nation's president regarding the matter of states' rights. If there was one word to describe what everyone knew about Van Buren, and it has been used repeatedly to describe him even by modern scholars, it was the word *cautious*. A cautious states' rights advocate likely never would have considered what the Saints proposed.

And, frankly, the president had other matters on his mind. The president's annual message to Congress, delivered on December 2, 1839, just three days after his visit with Joseph

Smith, was filled with his national agenda, including the mismanagement of Native American Indian difficulties, which he called an "embarrassment." But his message centered on his continuing emphasis regarding the primary ambition of his presidency, the establishment of an independent national treasury. This goal was of such importance to the president, and he pushed so hard for its enactment, that until 1840 it dominated the discussions of the 26th Congress.[17]

Importuning at the Feet of the President

So how do we account for Joseph Smith's venture to Washington? It may be rooted in a December 1833 revelation received by Joseph Smith regarding the eventual redemption of Zion—which, of course, was what underlay the redress petitions. My views about the effect of this revelation in the Prophet's subsequent thinking and behaviors are informed by the work of my colleague Mark Ashurst-McGee. In his recently completed doctoral dissertation, he argues that the divine counsel in section 101 of the Doctrine and Covenants regarding the Saints' petition for government intervention in the aftermath of their expulsion from Jackson County provided directives that motivated much of their future strategy. What I am advancing now, however, is my own interpretation of what compelled Joseph Smith to go to Washington. The divine logistics in applying for redress for wrongs committed against the Saints included this provision: "Let them importune at the feet of the judge; and if he heed them not, let them importune at the feet of the governor; and if the governor heed them not, let them importune at the feet of the president; and if the president heed them not, then will the Lord arise and come forth out of his hiding place, and in his fury vex the nation" (Doctrine and Covenants 101:86–89).

It appears that there was nothing received by Joseph Smith later to mute this strategy. This revelatory directive was not necessarily a formula that anticipated the president's refusal to act on behalf of the Saints. Joseph Smith apparently went to Washington informed of the president and his policies but with the expectation that Van Buren would somehow intuit through divine inspiration the necessity of aiding the Saints. The Saints, after all, were primarily Democrats. They had reason to believe not only that they would be heard, but that they would be justified. Joseph Smith's disappointment came when it was apparent that Van Buren's politics not only preempted the divinely granted freedoms of the Constitution but also spurred a heart hardened to the revelation and inspiration of God. The parallel to Moses' encounter with Egypt's pharaoh is vivid. It appears to me that Joseph Smith went to Washington thinking that Martin Van Buren would acquiesce and accept the pleas of a "much injured people." John Reynolds explained the reversal in Joseph's views in light of both the president and Congress: "His claim for damages done to the Mormons in Missouri, was submitted to the Senate, and both the senators of Missouri, Messrs. Benton and Lynn [Linn], attacked his petition with such force and violence that it could obtain scarcely a decent burial. Smith returned to the State of Illinois a red-hot Whig."[18]

Frustration after the Visit

Joseph Smith arrived back in Nauvoo in early March of 1840. Coincidentally, his arrival at home intersected with the Whig Party's assault of Martin Van Buren, determined to unseat him in the fall election. Three newspaper reports in the spring of 1840 captured Joseph Smith's immediate views upon his return to Nauvoo after his education in Washington. They illustrate, with whatever journalistic license we allow newspapermen or newspaper stringers, the Prophet's thinking. On Sunday, March 22, a writer for the *New York Journal of Commerce* reported a discourse by Joseph Smith given to the Illinois Saints explaining his Washington experience:

> After engaging in prayer to the Most High and reading a chapter of sacred writ, he [Joseph Smith] commenced his discourse. He told his people he was their servant; that they had a right to know all the incidents of his journey; he would therefore endeavor to give them a minute account. He did [not] like to preach politics on the Sabbath, but he must free his mind, must tell the whole story.
>
> The object of his visit at Washington, you well know, was to make application to congress for relief, touching their troubles in Missouri. But to the discourse. He said, on his arrival at Washington, he, with two of his elders, (Rigdon and Higbee,) called on Mr. Van Buren at the "White House" with a letter of introduction, and after making known to him the subject of their visit, and soliciting him to help them, Mr. Van Buren replied "Help you! How can I help you? All Missouri would turn against me." But they demanded of Mr. Van Buren a hearing, and he, after listening a few moments to their tale of injured innocence, abruptly left the room. After waiting some time for his return, they were under the necessity of departing, disappointed, and chagrined.[19]

Apparently one of the reasons that Joseph Smith was so outraged over Van Buren's response was that he had been subjected to personal insult, even though the president's general reputation was one of respectful deportment. Not having Van Buren's side of the story, we do not know whether the president was busy or irritated about something else that would have influenced his treatment of the small delegation. The newspaper report continued: "He thought Mr. Van Buren treated them with great disrespect and neglect, and in conversation, among other things, [Joseph] told the president that he (the president) was getting fat. The president replied that he was aware of the fact; that he had to go every few days to the tailor's to get his clothes let out, or purchase a new coat. The 'prophet' here added, at the top of his voice,—*'he hoped he would continue to grow fat, and swell, and, before the next election burst!'*"[20]

While the strong words could have been rhetorical hyperbole to arouse in the audience antipathy for the manner in which the nation's president had rejected the Saints' plight, the language conforms to other expression by Joseph Smith regarding the personal affront he felt at the hands of the president, an affront that the Prophet apparently took every occasion to recount upon his return from Washington. At the general conference of April 7, Joseph's rehearsal of what happened in Washington was reported by a Peoria, Illinois, newspaper:

> On the first day [of the conference] Mr. S[mith], took occasion to give to the assembled multitude, consisting of about 3000 persons, a detailed account of his mission, which was related with great clearness, and heard with deep interest. He said that soon after reaching Washington, he called on Mr. Van Buren, and asked permission to leave with him the memorial with which he had been entrusted, at the same time briefly stating its contents. Mr. Van Buren's manner was very repulsive, and it was only after his (Smith's) urgent request that he consented to receive the paper and to give an answer on the morrow. The next day Smith again called [here is one of those contradictory sources that we have to sort out], when Mr. Van Buren cut short the interview by saying, "I can do nothing for you, gentlemen. If I were you, I should go against the whole state of Missouri, and that state would go against me in the next election." Mr. Smith

said he was thunderstruck at this avowel. He had always believed Mr. Van Buren to be a high-minded statesman, and had uniformly supported him as such; but he now saw that he was only a huckstering politician, who would sacrifice any and every thing to promote his re-election. He left him abruptly, and rejoiced when without the walls of the palace, that he could once more breathe the air of a freeman.[21]

In April 1840, another journalist-traveler, this one from the *Alexandria* [Virginia] *Gazette*, gave this report of Joseph Smith's description of his visit to Washington by way of personal conversation:

> It was a beautiful morning towards the close of April last [1840], when the writer of the foregoing sketch, accompanied by a friend, crossed the Mississippi River, from Montrose [Iowa], to pay a visit to the prophet.... We descended from his chamber, and the conversation turned upon his recent visit to Washington, and his talk with the President of the United States. He gave us distinctly to understand that his political views had undergone an entire change; and his description of the reception given him at the executive mansion was anything but flattering to the distinguished individual who presides over its hospitalities.
>
> Before he had heard the story of our wrongs, said the indignant Prophet, Mr. Van Buren gave us to understand that he could do nothing for the redress of our grievances lest it should interfere with his political prospects in Missouri. *He is not as fit* said he, *as my dog, for the chair of state;* for my dog will make an effort to protect his abused and insulted master, while the present chief magistrate will not so much as lift his finger to relieve an oppressed and persecuted community of

freemen, whose glory it has been that they were citizens of the United States.²²

The net effect of the Mormon delegation to Washington in 1839–40 was frustrated disappointment, their entreaties dismissed by both the president and Congress. I previously implied that Joseph Smith changed his thinking about American policies and political personalities in the aftermath of his experience in Washington, as illustrated by the newspaper reports quoted above. But he had not given up on the foundational premise of American institutions being beholden to the people. In what was perhaps the first sermon he delivered upon his arrival home after the Washington venture, he reminded the Saints, as reported by his uncle John Smith, that "the affairs now before Congress [concerning the Saints] was the only thing that ought to interest the Saints at present. . . . He requested every exertion to be made to forward affidavits to Washington, and also letters to members of Congress."²³

In a subject for another time, what Joseph Smith did subsequent to his encounter with the president and Congress inaugurated what has been described as his role as statesman-prophet. Certainly Joseph Smith's view of his prophetic ministry had expanded through his defense of his fellow Saints before the chief magistrates of the time, and he would petition another day.

Notes

1. Robert D. Foster, "A Testimony of the Past: Loda, Illinois, February 14, 1874," *The True Latter Day Saints' Herald* (April 15, 1875): 225–26.

2. Joseph Smith and Elias Higbee to Hyrum Smith, December 5, 1839, Washington City, "Corner Missouri and 3d Street," Joseph

Smith Collection, Letterbook 2:85–88, Church History Library, Salt Lake City.

3. Joseph Smith and Elias Higbee to Hyrum Smith, "Corner Missouri and 3d Street," Letterbook 2:85–88.

4. Francis J. Grund, *Aristocracy in America: From the Sketch-Book of a German Nobleman* (New York: Harper & Brothers, 1959), 229–30.

5. Grund, *Aristocracy in America*, 231.

6. Joseph Smith and Elias Higbee to Hyrum Smith, "Corner Missouri and 3d Street," Letterbook 2:85–88.

7. *Adams Sentinel* (Gettysburg, Pennsylvania), December 30, 1839.

8. November 9, 1839: Rigdon, Sidney. Springfield, Ill. To Martin Van Buren and the Heads of Departments, Washington. Introducing Joseph Smith, Jr., and Elias Higbee, Mormons. A.L.S. 1 p.; and November 9, 1839: Adams, J. Springfield, Illinois, To M[artin] Van Buren, Washington. Introducing two Mormons, Joseph Smith, Jr., and [Elias] Higbee. A.L.S. 1p. *Library of Congress: Calendar of the Papers of Martin Van Buren* (Washington: Government Printing Office, 1910), 382.

9. John Reynolds, *My Own Times: Embracing Also the History of My Life* ([Belleville,] Illinois: [B. H. Perryman and H. L. Davidson, printers], 1855), 367.

10. Joseph Smith and Elias Higbee to Hyrum Smith, "Corner Missouri and 3d Street," Letterbook 2:85–88.

11. Joseph Smith and Elias Higbee to Hyrum Smith, "Corner Missouri and 3d Street," Letterbook 2:85–88.

12. Draft of Historian's Office, History of the Church [ca. 1840s–1880], Church History Library. Besides the newspaper reports described above of Joseph Smith's accounts of his Washington visit, other evidence also suggests a second audience with the U.S. president. See, for example, claims that Sidney Rigdon was with the delegation when they visited the president. This could only have happened during a second visit (Richard S. Van Wagoner, *Sidney Rigdon: A Portrait of*

Religious Excess [Salt Lake City: Signature Books, 1994], 270; see also Wandle Mace, Autobiography [ca. 1890], typescript page 54, Church History Library).

13. Reynolds, *My Own Times*, 359.
14. Reynolds, *My Own Times*, 367.
15. Reynolds, *My Own Times*, 359.
16. Joseph Smith and Elias Higbee to Hyrum Smith, "Corner Missouri and 3d Street," Letterbook 2:85–88.
17. *The Congressional Globe: Containing Sketches of the Debates and Proceedings of the Twenty-Sixth Congress, First Session, Volume VIII* (Washington: Globe, 1840).
18. Reynolds, *My Own Times*, 368.
19. Reprinted in "The Mormons for Harrison," *Peoria Register and North-Western Gazetteer*, April 17, 1840.
20. "The Mormons for Harrison."
21. "The Mormons for Harrison."
22. *The* [New York] *Sun*, July 28, 1840. This article, which received wide circulation, initially appeared in the *Alexandria* [Virginia] *Gazette*. It also appeared in the [Hartford] Connecticut *Courant*, August 29, 1840; and the *Quincy* [Illinois] *Whig*, October 17, 1840.
23. Iowa Stake, Records, 1839–41, March 6, 1840, Church History Library.

RICHARD NEITZEL HOLZAPFEL

1841
The Nauvoo Temple

At the beginning of 1841, Joseph Smith was thirty-five years old and living in Nauvoo, Illinois.[1] This chapter will briefly review some of the important events in the Prophet's life that year and then focus on the revelation he received on January 19, known today as Doctrine and Covenants section 124.[2]

The year 1841 was a busy one for Joseph Smith.[3] In a meeting held on Tuesday, January 5, he organized the Nauvoo Lyceum (an adult study and discussion group that met weekly for a brief period).[4] Two weeks later, on Tuesday, January 19, the Prophet recorded a rather long revelation known today as section 124.

On Sunday, January 24, as commanded in Doctrine and Covenants 124:95, the Prophet ordained Hyrum

---

Richard Neitzel Holzapfel is a professor of Church history and doctrine at Brigham Young University.

Smith as the Assistant President and Patriarch of the Church, replacing Oliver Cowdery as Assistant President of the Church and Joseph Smith Sr. as Patriarch.[5]

On Saturday, January 30, the Saints sustained the Prophet as the Church's sole trustee in trust.[6] A few days later, Joseph was elected to the newly formed Nauvoo City Council on Wednesday, February 3. The following day, the Illinois governor appointed Joseph Smith as lieutenant general in the Nauvoo Legion.[7]

On Monday, March 1, in a Nauvoo City Council meeting, Joseph Smith presented a bill to allow "free toleration and equal privileges" to each religious sect and denomination, including Christianity, Islam, and others.[8] In late March, the Prophet received a revelation commanding the Saints in Iowa to organize a new stake of Zion (Doctrine and Covenants 125).

The Prophet presided at the laying of the four Nauvoo Temple cornerstones during general conference on Tuesday, April 6, the eleventh anniversary of the organization of the Church.[9]

On Saturday, July 3, Joseph spoke to the Nauvoo Legion. The legion's minutes for that day note that "Joseph Smith . . . made an eloquent and patriotic speech to the troops, and strongly testified of his regard for our national welfare, and his willingness to lay down his life in defense of his country, and closed with these remarkable words, 'I would ask no greater boon, than to lay down my life for my country.'"[10]

The Prophet received a revelation on Friday, July 9, for Brigham Young, who had recently returned from a mission to the British Isles: "Verily thus saith the Lord unto you: My servant Brigham, it is no more required at your hand to leave your family as in times past, for your offering is acceptable to me" (Doctrine and Covenants 126:1).

Three days later on Monday, July 12, Joseph Smith appointed John Patton to be one of the three recorders of the baptisms for the dead performed in the Mississippi River on the Iowa side of the river.[11]

On Sunday, July 25, the Prophet spoke on the resurrection of the dead in a meeting in the grove near the temple.[12] Don Carlos Smith, Joseph Smith's twenty-five-year-old brother, died in Nauvoo on Saturday, August 7.[13]

On Thursday, August 12, the Prophet spoke to one hundred Native Americans in Nauvoo.[14] Three days later, on Sunday, August 15, Joseph and Emma's infant son, Don Carlos, died.[15] Robert B. Thompson, the Prophet's clerk, died on Friday, August 27.[16]

The Saints gathered for conference after the cornerstone ceremony of the Nauvoo House (see Doctrine and Covenants 124:22–24) on Saturday, October 2.[17] The Prophet decided to place the original manuscript of the Book of Mormon in the southeast cornerstone during the celebration. Warren Foote later recalled, "I was standing very near the corner stone when Joseph Smith came up with the manuscript of the Book of Mormon and said that he wanted to put that in there, as he had had trouble enough with it."[18]

On Sunday, November 7, Joseph warned the Saints of the dangers of pointing out sins and accusing others. The Prophet said, "If you do not accuse each other, God will not accuse you. If you have no accuser you will enter heaven, and if you will follow the revelations and instructions which God gives you through me, I will take you into heaven as my back load. If you will not accuse me, I will not accuse you. If you will throw a cloak of charity over my sins, I will over yours—for charity covereth a multitude of sins."[19]

On Monday, November 8, Joseph attended the dedication of the baptismal font in the basement of the uncompleted Nauvoo Temple (see Doctrine and Covenants 124:29).[20] This first font was made of wood, but a stone font replaced it in 1845.[21]

On Sunday, November 28, the Prophet told the Twelve that "the Book of Mormon was the most correct of any book on earth, and the keystone of our religion, and a man would get nearer to God by abiding by its precepts than by any other book."[22]

On Sunday, December 5, Joseph began to proofread a new printing of the Book of Mormon.[23]

Joseph appointed Willard Richards to be his personal scribe and a recorder for the Nauvoo Temple on Monday, December 13.[24]

The Prophet turned thirty-six years old on Thursday, December 23. Four days later, on Monday, December 27, Joseph showed the seer stone, sometimes called the Urim and Thummin, to the Twelve. Wilford Woodruff recorded the event in his journal: "The Twelve or a part of them spent the day with Joseph the Seer & he unfolded unto them many glorious things of the kingdom of God the privileges & blessings of the priesthood, [etc.]. I had the privilege of seeing for the first time in my day the URIM & THUMMIM."[25]

Joseph performed several baptisms for the dead in the wooden baptismal font in the basement of the uncompleted Nauvoo Temple on Tuesday, December 28. Those acting as proxies included Sidney Rigdon and Reynolds Cahoon.[26]

Doctrine and Covenants 124

Joseph Smith's reception of section 124, the longest revelation in the current Doctrine and Covenants, was a significant event. Steven C. Harper argues, "The revelation oriented [Joseph Smith's] life and that of the Church."[27]

On January 19, 1841, the Lord spoke to Joseph Smith: "Verily, thus saith the Lord unto you, my servant Joseph Smith, I am well pleased with your offering and acknowledgments, which you have made; for unto this end have I raised you up, that I might show forth my wisdom through the weak things of the earth" (Doctrine and Covenants 124:1–2).

It is interesting to note that the Lord often identified his disciples, including the Prophet, as "the weak things of the earth." Joseph characterized himself as being "like a huge, rough stone rolling down from a high mountain; and the only polishing I get is when some corner gets rubbed off by coming in contact with something else."[28]

Although Doctrine and Covenants 124 contains many specific commandments on a variety of issues, there seems to be four general commands. First, Church leaders were commanded to prepare a solemn proclamation (see v. 2).[29] Second, the Saints were commanded to build a hotel in Nauvoo called the Nauvoo House, to provide lodging for visitors (v. 23).[30] Third, the revelation commanded the Saints to build a temple in Nauvoo (see vv. 25–28). Fourth, the revelation called for the reorganization of the priesthood quorums that had been depleted by death and by apostasy in Ohio and Missouri (see vv. 123–43).

The revelation commanded the Prophet to prepare a solemn proclamation: "I say unto you, that you are now called immediately to make a solemn proclamation of my gospel" (v. 2). The revelation indicated that it was to be written by the Holy Ghost in meekness (see v. 4) and sent to the U.S. president-elect (William Henry Harrison), to state governors (for example, Thomas Carlin of Illinois), and to the leaders of the earth (such as King Louis Philippe of France, Queen Victoria of Great Britain, and Isabella II of Spain), announcing the new gospel dispensation and the establishment of a stake of Zion in the kingdom of God (see v. 3).[31]

The revelation also reemphasized the call to gather at Nauvoo: "And again, verily, I say unto you, let all my saints come from afar" (v. 25). It also mentions several individuals who were commanded to help support the Prophet. William Law, for example, was commanded to help specifically Joseph's efforts to publish the New Translation of the Bible, known today as the Joseph Smith Translation (vv. 82, 89). Law was a Canadian and the first non-U.S. citizen to become a member of the First Presidency.[32]

The Lord also mentioned three individuals who had died: David W. Patten, the first apostolic martyr; Edward Partridge, the first bishop; and Joseph Smith Sr., the first patriarch (see v. 19).

The Nauvoo Temple

The Latter-day Saints attempted to build several temples during the Church's first decade: Independence, Missouri (see Doctrine and Covenants 57:3); Kirtland, Ohio (see Doctrine and Covenants 88:119); Far West, Missouri (Doctrine and Covenants 115:8); and apparently, Adam-ondi-Ahman, Missouri.[33]

Poverty and persecution prevented the Saints from completing these temples, with the exception of the Kirtland Temple (dedicated in 1836). In the Kirtland Temple, the Lord restored important priesthood authority, keys, and ordinances (washings and anointings) that prepared the Saints to receive additional blessings in the Nauvoo Temple (see Doctrine and Covenants 110).

In Nauvoo, the Lord commanded the Saints to "build a house to my name, for the Most High to dwell therein" (Doctrine and Covenants 124:27). He said, "Verily I say unto you, that your anointings and your washings, and your baptisms for the dead, and your solemn assemblies, and your memorials for your sacrifices by the sons of Levi, and for your oracles in your most holy places wherein you received conversations, and your statutes and judgments, for the beginning of the revelations and foundation of Zion, and for the glory, honor, and endowment of all her municipals, are ordained by the ordinance of my holy house, which my people are always commanded to build unto my holy name" (v. 39). Additionally, the Lord informed the Church that he would reveal a great blessing in the Nauvoo Temple, "even the fulness of the priesthood," if they did as he commanded (v. 28).

The Fulness of the Priesthood

Even though the Aaronic and Melchizedek priesthoods had been restored, including the offices of deacon, teacher, priest, bishop, seventy, high priest, patriarch, and apostle, by January 1841, the Lord wanted to give the Saints another blessing and gift, "even the fulness of the priesthood" (v. 23).

Later, the Prophet taught, "Those holding the fulness of the Melchizedek Priesthood are kings and priests unto the Most High God, holding the keys of power and blessings."[34] An allusion to the fulness of the priesthood had been made in February 1832 when the Lord described those sanctified beings in the celestial kingdom: "They are they who are *priests and kings*, who have received of his fulness, and of his glory" (Doctrine and Covenants 76:56; emphasis added).

Shortly after the January 19 revelation was given, the Lord restored the temple ordinances that were necessary to prepare the Saints to receive the fulness of the priesthood. Based on a divinely appointed time frame, the Lord asked Joseph to begin this work with a small group of men and women before the temple was completed. The group of faithful Saints was known as the "Quorum of the Anointed" or the "Holy Order." Later, these Saints assisted the general body of the Church to receive the same blessings bestowed upon them in the Nauvoo Temple in December 1845 through February 1846. The Prophet explained that there are "certain signs & words ... which cannot be revealed to the Elders till the Temple is completed.—The rich can only get them in the Temple. The poor may get them on the mountain top as did Moses."[35] Therefore, before his death, Joseph Smith dedicated a few upper rooms in Nauvoo (the Homestead, the Mansion House, and the red brick store) to perform these sacred ordinances to a select group of men and women. Later, the Saints completed the temple so that the rest of the Saints could receive the ordinances.

Preparations

The Lord prepared the Saints in Nauvoo to receive these ordinances. For example, during a Relief Society meeting, the Prophet "gave a lecture on the Priesthood, showing how the sisters would come in possession of the privileges, blessings and gifts of the Priesthood."[36] He then "exhorted the sisters always to concentrate their faith and prayers for, and place confidence in their husbands, whom God has appointed for them to honor, and in those faithful men whom God has placed at the head of the Church to lead His people; that we should arm and sustain them with our prayers; for the keys of the kingdom are about to be given to them [Church leaders], that they may be able to detect everything false."[37]

Joseph indicated that the "keys of the Priesthood" (presumably referring in this case to the fulness of the priesthood) would be given to members of the Church, both men and women. Elder George A. Smith amplified the Relief Society minutes in Joseph Smith's history, as represented by the italicized additions in the following paragraph: "He spoke of delivering the *keys of the Priesthood* to the Church, and said that the *faithful members* of the Relief Society *should receive them in connection with their husbands*, that *the Saints who integrity has been tried and proved faithful, might know how to ask the Lord and receive an answer*."[38]

Six days following this Relief Society meeting in 1842, nine Church members met in the upper room of Joseph's store in a special meeting and received their temple blessings from Joseph. They became the first in this dispensation to receive their "washings, anointing, endowments and the communication of keys pertaining to the Aaronic Priesthood, and so on to the highest order of the Melchisedek Priesthood, setting forth the order pertaining to the Ancient of Days, and all those plans and principles by which any one is enabled to secure the fullness of those blessings which have been prepared for the Church of the First Born, and come up and abide in the presence of the Eloheim in the eternal worlds."[39]

Shortly following this introduction of these sacred priesthood ordinances, Bishop Newel K. Whitney, one of the men endowed on May 4, 1842, spoke to the sisters: "Rejoice while contemplating the blessings which will be poured out on the heads of the Saints. God has many precious things to bestow, ever to our astonishment, if we are faithful." The society's secretary noted that Bishop Whitney then "rejoiced at the formation of the society, that we might improve our talents and ... prepare for those blessings which God is soon to bestow upon us."[40] The stage was now set for the Lord to fulfill his promise in restoring the fulness of the priesthood. The first members to receive this blessing were Joseph and Emma Smith on September 28, 1843.[41] Others received the same blessing soon thereafter.

Priesthood and Keys

As mentioned, the Lord commanded that the priesthood quorums be reconstituted. The First Presidency was one of the quorums to be reconstituted, as well as the Quorum of the Twelve Apostles, which was reorganized with Brigham Young as President (see v. 127). The Nauvoo high council and high priests quorum were also to be organized (see vv. 131–36). The elders quorum presidencies, the seven Presidents of the Seventy, and the Aaronic Priesthood presidency were also addressed (see vv. 137–42).

In the revelation of January 19, 1841, Hyrum Smith was called to fill both positions simultaneously, as Patriarch and Assistant President of the Church: "That my servant Hyrum may take the office of Priesthood and Patriarch, which was appointed unto him by his father, by blessing and also by right; that from henceforth he shall hold the keys of the patriarchal blessings upon the heads of all my people, that whoever he blesses shall be blessed, and whoever he curses shall be cursed; that whatsoever he shall bind on earth shall be bound in heaven; and whatsoever he shall loose on earth shall be loosed in heaven" (vv. 91–93).

Prayer

The revelation continued, "And from this time forth I appoint unto him that he may be a prophet, and a seer, and a revelator unto my church, as well as my servant Joseph; that he may act in concert also with my servant Joseph; and that he shall receive counsel from my servant Joseph, who shall show unto him the *keys whereby he may ask and receive*" (vv. 94–95; emphasis added). The keys spoken of here are the priesthood keys associated with temple worship. The keys of presidency had already been restored, but in Nauvoo the Lord introduced priesthood keys that allowed the Saints to ask and receive, and now the Lord commanded Joseph to show them unto Hyrum. This the Prophet did on May 4, 1842, when Joseph Smith revealed the endowment for the first time.[42]

One of the blessings reported as a result of the endowment was the enhancement of the power of prayer. Bathsheba W. Smith recalled that Joseph "said that we did not know how to pray to have our prayers answered. But when I and my husband had our endowments in [December 1843], Joseph Smith presiding, he taught us the order of prayer."[43] On another occasion she said, "[He also] showed us . . . how to detect them when true or false angels come to us."[44]

By late December 1843, some fifty individuals met every Saturday and Sunday evening for prayer. Besides praying for the sick and those in need, time in the meetings was taken up by Joseph's lectures on various gospel themes and explanations of the sacred ordinances. In some cases, the sacrament was administered and brief testimonies were offered. Meetings were held regularly during the winter, bringing much joy and comfort. On January 27, 1844, for example, Joseph met with the group. One participant noted: "The [Quorum of the Anointed] met for a meeting in the evening at Joseph's store. [We] had a number of prayers and exhortations upon the subject of holiness of heart. Brother [Willard] and Sister [Jennetta] Richards were present. They had both been unwell for a number of days before, but were able to attend meetings this evening and seemed to enjoy themselves well. They had received blessings by the prayer of faith."[45]

Four Commandments

Among the four major commands given in Doctrine and Covenants 124, only one was fully completed before Joseph Smith's death in June 1844. Nevertheless, the Twelve Apostles eventually issued the solemn proclamation and dedicated the Nauvoo Temple before the exodus from Nauvoo in 1846. However, the Nauvoo House was never completed. The Prophet's diligent efforts to fulfill the Lord's commandment meant that he had to prioritize his actions, focusing on the most important first. Reorganizing the priesthood quorums and preparing the Twelve to succeed him were the most important steps as the Prophet's ministry was about to end.

Some have wondered about the meaning and implications of verse 32: "But behold, at the end of this appointment your baptisms for your dead shall not be acceptable unto me; and if you do not these things at the end of the appointment ye shall be rejected as a church, with your dead, saith the Lord your God." Steven C. Harper argues that those examining these verses place too much emphasis on completing the temple itself. He believes that the revelation instead points to the fact that the Prophet was to give the ordinances into the hands of those who would succeed him before the end of the appointment was complete. The historical record details how Joseph Smith accomplished this before his death in 1844.[46]

The Prophet's Mission

Section 124 provides some important insights into Joseph Smith's mission in Nauvoo. First, the Lord approved the site for the temple: "And ye shall build it on the place where you have contemplated building it, for that is the spot which I have chosen for you to build it. If ye labor with all your might, I will consecrate that spot that it shall be made holy" (vv. 43–44). Second, the Saints were promised that if they would hearken unto the Lord's voice and unto the voice of his servants, "they shall not be moved out of their place" (v. 45). Third, the Saints learned that the Lord would "deign to reveal unto my church things which have been kept hid from before the foundation of the world, things that pertain to the dispensation of the fulness of times" (v. 41). Finally, the Lord told the Saints that it was Joseph Smith's mission to be the instrument to receive these things for the Church: "And I will show unto my servant Joseph all things pertaining to this house [the temple], and the priesthood thereof" (v. 42). Thus, the year 1841 laid the foundation for the Saints to receive the fulness of the priesthood and other significant truths hidden from before the foundation of the world.

Notes

1. For a biographical treatment of this period, see Richard Lyman Bushman, *Joseph Smith: Rough Stone Rolling* (New York: Alfred A. Knopf, 2005), 403–35.

2. My colleague, Steven C. Harper, has influenced some of the major themes discussed in this essay about Doctrine and Covenants 124; see Steven C. Harper, *Making Sense of the Doctrine and Covenants: A Guided Tour through Modern Revelations* (Salt Lake City: Deseret Book, 2008), 455–61.

3. For a complete chronology of Joseph Smith, see *BYU Studies* 46, no. 4 (2007).

4. *The Words of Joseph Smith: The Contemporary Accounts of the Nauvoo Discourses of the Prophet Joseph*, ed. Andrew F. Ehat and

Lyndon W. Cook (Provo, UT: Religious Studies Center, Brigham Young University, 1980), 82 n. 1.

5. Joseph Smith, *History of the Church of Jesus Christ of Latter-day Saints*, ed. B. H. Roberts, 2nd ed. rev. (Salt Lake City: Deseret Book, 1976), 4:286.

6. Smith, *History of the Church*, 4:286.

7. Smith, *History of the Church*, 4:295–96.

8. John C. Bennett, "An Ordinance in Relation to Religious Societies," *Times and Seasons*, March 1 1841, 336–37.

9. Smith, *History of the Church*, 4:326–30.

10. Smith, *History of the Church*, 4:382.

11. Smith, *History of the Church*, 4:382–83.

12. *Words of Joseph Smith*, 75.

13. Smith, *History of the Church*, 4:393–99.

14. Smith, *History of the Church*, 4:401–2.

15. Smith, *History of the Church*, 4:402.

16. Smith, *History of the Church*, 4:411.

17. Smith, *History of the Church*, 4:423.

18. Warren Foote Autobiography, typescript, L. Tom Perry Special Collections, Harold B. Lee Library, Brigham Young University.

19. Smith, *History of the Church*, 4:445.

20. Smith, *History of the Church*, 4:446–47.

21. See Matthew S. McBride, *A House for the Most High: The Story of the Original Nauvoo Temple* (Salt Lake City: Greg Kofford, 2007), 233–37; and Don F. Colvin, *Nauvoo Temple: A Story of Faith* (Provo, UT: Religious Studies Center, Brigham Young University, 2002), 184–87.

22. Smith, *History of the Church*, 4:461.

23. Smith, *History of the Church*, 4:468.

24. Smith, *History of the Church*, 4:470.

25. *Wilford Woodruff's Journal*, ed. Scott G. Kenney (Midvale, UT: Signature Books, 1983), 2:144; see also Terryl L. Givens, *By the Hand*

of Mormon: The American Scripture that Launched a New World Religion (New York: Oxford University Press, 2003), 266 n. 91.

26. Smith, *History of the Church*, 4:486.

27. Harper, *Making Sense of the Doctrine and Covenants*, 460.

28. Smith, *History of the Church*, 5:401.

29. Jack L. Rushton, "Proclamations," in *Encyclopedia of Latter-day Saint History*, ed. Arnold H. Garr, Donald Q. Cannon, and Richard O. Cowan (Salt Lake City: Deseret Book, 2000), 954–55.

30. Susan Easton Black, "Nauvoo House," in *Encyclopedia of Latter-day Saint History*, 825–26.

31. Robert B. Thompson began work on drafting the proclamation under the supervision of Joseph Smith in 1841, but his efforts were cut short by his death. The topic was apparently not revisited again until 1843, when Smith instructed Willard Richards, Orson Hyde, John Taylor, and W. W. Phelps to draft a new document. Their efforts were interrupted by other matters. Finally, after Joseph Smith's death in 1844, the proclamation was written principally by Elder Parley P. Pratt and published in 1845 as *Proclamation of the Twelve Apostles of the Church of Jesus Christ, of Latter-day Saints, "To all the Kings of the World; To the President of the United States of America; To the Governors of the several States; And to the Rulers and People of all Nations"* (New York, April 6, 1845). See Peter Crawley, *A Descriptive Bibliography of the Mormon Church, Volume One, 1830–1847* (Provo, UT: Religious Studies Center, Brigham Young University, 1997), 294–96.

32. For more on William Law, see Lyndon W. Cook, "William Law, Nauvoo Dissenter," *BYU Studies* 22, no. 1 (Winter 1982): 47–72.

33. See Robert J. Matthews, "Adam-ondi-Ahman," *BYU Studies* 13, no. 1 (Autumn 1972): 33–34.

34. *Teachings of the Prophet Joseph Smith*, comp. Joseph Fielding Smith (Salt Lake City: Deseret Book, 1938), 322.

35. Joseph Smith Journal, May 1, 1842; in *The Papers of Joseph Smith* vol. 2: *Journal, 1832–1842*, ed. Dean C. Jessee (Salt Lake City: Deseret Book, 1992), 379.

36. Smith, *History of the Church*, 4:602.

37. Smith, *History of the Church*, 4:602–5.

38. Smith, *History of the Church*, 4:604.

39. Smith, *History of the Church*, 5:2.

40. Relief Society Minutes, May 27, 1842.

41. Scott H. Faulring, ed., *An American Prophet's Record: The Diaries and Journals of Joseph Smith* (Salt Lake City: Signature Books, 1989), 416.

42. Smith, *History of the Church*, 5:1–2.

43. "Recollections of the Prophet Joseph Smith," *Juvenile Instructor*, June 1, 1892, 345.

44. "A Notable Event—The Weber Stake Reunion," *Deseret Evening News*, June 23, 1903.

45. "A Notable Event," January 27, 1844.

46. Harper, *Making Sense of the Doctrine and Covenants*, 457–58.

ANDREW H. HEDGES AND ALEX D. SMITH

1842
Joseph Smith, John C. Bennett, and the Extradition Attempt

As a careful study of Joseph Smith's journal shows, the months between December 1841 and March 1843 were busy ones for the Prophet. While much of his time was spent on ecclesiastical affairs, numerous other issues demanded his attention as well. This paper provides a brief overview of the Prophet's activities during this fifteen-month period, followed by more detailed discussions of two issues that dominated Joseph's life during this time. These were, first, John C. Bennett's estrangement from the Church; and second, Joseph's and his friends' efforts to keep him out of the hands of the Missourians after he was charged with being accessory to the May 1842 assassination attempt on

---

Andrew H. Hedges and Alex D. Smith are editors of The Joseph Smith Papers.

former Missouri governor Lilburn W. Boggs. This paper draws heavily on research conducted under the auspices of the Joseph Smith Papers Project, and we want to thank our colleagues—particularly Dean Jessee, Richard Anderson, David Grue, and Kay Darowski and her team of researchers—for all their help in bringing together much of the information presented here.

Joseph in Nauvoo, 1842

Numerous references throughout Joseph's journal to buying and selling land reflect the frontier nature of Nauvoo as well as the growth of the Church. Consistent with the doctrine of "gathering," Church members from the eastern states, Canada, and England had settled in and around Nauvoo by 1842; in January 1843, Joseph estimated that some twelve thousand lived in the area. Many of these lived on land purchased from Isaac Galland and brothers William and Hugh White following the expulsion of the Saints from Missouri in 1839. Joseph also contracted with Connecticut land speculators Horace R. Hotchkiss, John Gillet, and Smith Tuttle for an additional five hundred acres on the "Flats" near the Mississippi River. Under the terms of the contract, the Latter-day Saints were to have immediate use of the land, but no deeds were to be issued until the land was paid for. Among other methods, Joseph hoped to make the required payments for the land by selling lots to those moving into the city. Speculators also courted Joseph and other Church members to purchase land in nearby areas like Warren, Warsaw, Ramus, and Shokokin, leading to similar land contracts in some of these places. Other land speculators, however, who owned land on the "Hill" or the "Bluff" east of the Flats were able to sell that land at a lower price than Joseph, threatening his ability to meet the terms of his real estate contracts.

Joseph was also heavily involved with building the Nauvoo Temple and the Nauvoo House—the latter intended to be a hotel where "strangers may come from afar to lodge, . . . [where] the weary traveler may find health and safety while he shall contemplate the word of the Lord" (Doctrine and Covenants 124:23). Donations from Church members funded the construction of the temple, which was built on a bluff overlooking the Flats, while money for the Nauvoo House was to come through selling stock in the project according to guidelines received by revelation. Having been commanded by God to build the two structures, Joseph viewed both as of paramount importance; also, as the duly appointed trustee-in-trust for the Church, he was legally accountable for the building funds, which added urgency to the situation. In spite of a hearty response from many Church members, both undertakings suffered from a lack of capital and occasional mismanagement on the part of the committees overseeing them. Both projects also suffered from the competition of private developers' projects. The same economic jealousies between the Flats and the Hill that plagued Joseph's efforts to pay off land debts hindered the temple and the Nauvoo House. Addressing workers' concerns, improving the methods for collecting funds, and keeping the Saints on task with these construction projects occupied no small amount of Joseph's time and energy. On more than one occasion he publicly denounced developers like Robert Foster, Amos Davis, and Hiram Kimball, whose private land sales and business enterprises were seen as an impediment to accomplishing larger Church goals.

Other concerns vied for Joseph's attention as well. By the end of 1842, Joseph and Emma had four living children to support and raise, ranging from eleven-year-old Julia to four-year-old Alexander. One means of providing for his family was his red brick store. While he seems to have spent relatively little time directly managing or operating the store, journal entries indicate his continued involvement with stocking the store with hard-to-find goods. Similarly, while he turned his farm over to Cornelius Lott for management, any given day in the summer might find him riding the three miles out of Nauvoo to visit Lott and hoe potatoes. Both enterprises—the store and the farm—as well as Joseph's other business concerns and the building projects he oversaw as trustee for the Church, were significant factors in the overall economy of Nauvoo. "Let me assure you," wrote Emma to Illinois governor Thomas Carlin in August 1842, "that there are many whole families that are entirely dependent upon the prosecution and success of Mr Smiths temporal business for their support."[1]

A large part of Joseph's time was taken up with managing the details of a number of enterprises. For example, most of 1842 he served as editor of the Church's newspaper, the *Times and Seasons*. As lieutenant general of the Nauvoo Legion, Joseph was ultimately responsible for training, staffing, and supplying some three thousand troops of the Illinois militia. As a city councilman and then, after May 1842, the mayor of Nauvoo, he spent several hours most weeks drafting ordinances, discussing proposals, and attending city council meetings. As a councilman he was required to serve as a justice on the appellate municipal court, and as mayor he served occasionally as judge of that court and as chief justice of the mayor's court. Cases involving charges of slander, assault, petty thievery, and disorderly conduct were the usual bill of fare for these courts, although more specialized and technical cases occasionally appeared, including the *Dana v. Brink* medical malpractice suit. The forty-one manuscript pages of Joseph's journal dedicated to recording the graphic testimony of the witnesses in this trial—which involved a case of childbirth—probably reflect his scribe's professional interest in the details more than Joseph's. The scribe was Willard Richards of the Twelve, who had practiced medicine. With the journal's numerous references to legal precedence, haggling over expert witnesses, and technical language, it also illustrates how well versed Joseph and his associates needed to be, and were, in the law.

Through all this, Joseph continued to direct and oversee important developments in the Church. These included publishing the book of Abraham and the first pages of his history as well as writing two lengthy letters detailing how baptisms for the dead were to be recorded—all of which have since been accepted into the standard works of the Church. Building on Sarah M. Kimball's efforts to create a women's charitable organization, Joseph at this time also organized the "Female Relief Society of Nauvoo." Charging the society with "searching after objects of charity, and ... correcting the morals and strengthening the virtues of the female community,"[2] Joseph appointed his wife Emma to preside over the organization. Joseph also revealed new temple ordinances to a few trusted associates during this time.

By December 1841, Joseph had revealed the doctrine of plural marriage to his closest associates and was practicing it himself. Contemporary sources, reminiscent accounts, and later affidavits indicate that he took a number of plural wives over the course of the next two years. It was probably inevitable that some of the people to whom Joseph revealed the doctrine of plural marriage would misunderstand or reject it—several pieces of information, for example, suggest the practice was at least partly behind Sidney Rigdon's and George Robinson's estrangement from Joseph during this time. It was also probably inevitable that some of Joseph's confidants would abuse Joseph's understanding of plural marriage. This abuse often took the form of men seducing women by telling them that Joseph had sanctioned extramarital affairs—a charge Joseph strenuously denied. Among those who "made use of his name to carry on their iniquitous designs"[3] was John C. Bennett, general in the Nauvoo Legion, a prominent Mason, first mayor of Nauvoo, and one-time member of the First Presidency. While Joseph's journal and other documents indicate that the Prophet initially sought to resolve the problem privately, mounting evidence of Bennett's rascality eventually brought the city council, the Nauvoo Legion, and the Masonic lodge into the picture. Faced with censure from all quarters, Bennett fled Nauvoo and launched a smear campaign against Joseph through the pages of the *Sangamo Journal* and other newspapers. Most prominent among those who took Bennett's accusations seriously was Elder Orson Pratt, whose wife, Sarah, accused Joseph of making improper advances toward her during her husband's absence.

Along with misrepresenting Joseph's intentions regarding plural marriage, Bennett joined others in charging the Prophet with masterminding the May 6, 1842, assassination attempt of Lilburn W. Boggs, who had ordered the removal of the Mormons from Missouri in 1838. Initially appearing as editorials and letters in newspapers, these accusations eventually led to formal legal charges being leveled against Joseph and formal requests to the governor of Illinois and Iowa Territory that Joseph, if captured, be extradited to Missouri for trial. Having barely survived his most recent encounter with Missouri justice and not daring to trust himself in the hands of the Missourians a second time, Joseph accordingly spent a good part of the last five months of 1842 hiding in and around Nauvoo.

The Fall of John C. Bennett

Bennett's fall from grace began shortly after he moved to Nauvoo in August 1840, when Joseph received a letter "from a person of respectable character" in Ohio who lived "in the vicinity where Bennett had lived."[4] The letter warned Church officials that their new convert, ostensibly a bachelor, was "a very mean man" who had a wife and children in McConnelsville, Morgan County, Ohio. Joseph, "knowing that it is no uncommon thing for good men to be evil spoken against," tried to keep the matter quiet but was apparently forced into confronting Bennett with it after the latter began courting a young lady in Nauvoo. Only after Joseph threatened to publicly expose him, however, did Bennett end the relationship.[5]

Seeing that Joseph, at least, was suspicious of his marital status, Bennett took his amorous designs underground. Failing in his efforts to convince unsuspecting women that promiscuity "was a doctrine believed in by the Latter-Day Saints," Bennett tried to convince them that "the authorities of the church"—including Joseph—"not only sanctioned, but practiced" it themselves. The argument proved to be an effective one, Joseph wrote, with Bennett eventually seducing several women "by the same plausible tale."[6]

Meanwhile, in July 1841, Joseph received a letter from his brother Hyrum and William Law, who presented further evidence of Bennett's wife and children and the "ill-treatment" they had received at his hands. Bennett "candidly acknowledged" the truth of the letter's contents, then attempted suicide by taking poison. An antidote saved his life but did little to bring about the "thorough reformation in his character" that Joseph was hoping for. Adding to the "aggravating nature of this case," Joseph wrote, Bennett's statement that Joseph sanctioned illicit relationships had convinced other men "to persue the same adulterous practice" and to make use "of the same language insinuated by Bennett" to convince unsuspecting women of the propriety of what they were doing. Faced with a growing body of evidence from victims and perpetrators alike, mortified that Joseph's name was being invoked to justify the deeds, and "seeing no prospects of any satisfaction from his future life," the First Presidency, nine members of the Quorum of the Twelve, and the Presiding Bishopric quietly withdrew the hand of fellowship from Bennett on May 11, 1842.[7]

"Some four or five days" later, William Law informed Bennett concerning the Church leaders' action. "He plead with me to intercede for him," Law wrote, "assuring me that he would turn from his iniquity, and never would be guilty of such crimes again.—He said that if he were exposed it would break his mother's heart—that she was old, and if such things reached her ears it would bring her down with sorrow to the grave." Moved by Bennett's pleas, Law asked Joseph to "spare Bennett from public exposure, on account of his mother."[8]

A similar scene played itself out shortly afterward on May 17, 1842, when Hyrum Smith learned of Bennett's continuing perfidy, including evidence that he had promised to give his victims "medicine to produce abortions, providing they should become pregnant." "On becoming acquainted with these facts," Hyrum wrote, "I was determined to prosecute him, and bring him to justice." Learning of Hyrum's intentions, Bennett tearfully pleaded with Hyrum not to expose him, then asked Joseph for the same favor.[9] "On account of his earnestly requesting that we would not publish him to the world," Joseph wrote later, "we concluded not to do so at that time, but would let the matter rest until we saw the effect of what we had already done."[10] Concerned with how Bennett had been using his name to convince men and women alike of the correctness of his actions, however, Joseph required Bennett at this time to make a sworn deposition to the effect that he, Bennett, had never known Joseph to teach or practice anything contrary to the highest standards of virtue. Bennett immediately repaired to city alderman Daniel H. Wells, where, in the presence of William Clayton, Hyrum Smith, and Wells, he "stood at the desk" and wrote "that he was never taught any thing in the least cantrary to the strictest principles of the Gospel, or of virtue, or of the laws of God, or man, under any occasion either directly or indirectly, in word or deed, by Joseph Smith; and that he never knew the said Smith to countenance any improper conduct whatever, either in public or private;" and that Joseph had never taught him or anyone else that illicit relationships were, "under any circumstances, justifiable." Joseph accepted the statement and agreed to keep silent.[11]

Bennett resigned as mayor the same day and also confessed his sins in the Masonic lodge later in the afternoon. "He seemed to be very penitent and wept much," Hyrum recorded. "His penitence excited sympathy in the minds of the brethren, and they withdrew the charge for the time being."[12] A similar confession followed two days later in the city council—the same day Joseph was elected as mayor—when Bennett again defended Joseph's character, expressed his desire to continue his association with the Saints, and looked forward to the time, he said, "when I may be restored to full confidence, and fellowship, and my former standing in the church."[13]

Even as Bennett was proclaiming his loyalty to Joseph and the Church, however, evidence was accruing that he had been expelled from a Masonic lodge in Ohio before moving to Nauvoo. The evidence was reviewed in a special lodge meeting on June 16, 1842, at which time it was determined that the lodge in question was the Pickaway lodge. At the meeting, however,

Bennett presented laudatory character references from men in Ohio dated about the time of his alleged expulsion and claimed that he had never been informed of his expulsion from Pickaway lodge. Choosing to err on the side of caution, the Nauvoo lodge postponed his case until more testimony could be gathered. By July 7 the Nauvoo lodge became "fully satisfied" that he had been expelled from Pickaway and summarily expelled him as a Mason for falsely claiming Ohio membership and for being unworthy of fellowship. When additional charges against Bennett's character and activities were substantiated over the course of the following month, the action was confirmed and elaborated upon, with Bennett being expelled from the Nauvoo lodge "and from all the priviledges of Masonry" for seduction, adultery, using Joseph Smith's name to justify immoral acts, perjury, embezzlement, and seducing a master mason's wife.[14]

Long before the lodge took action against him, however, Bennett had skipped town and begun attacking Joseph and the Church through the press. In his letters, Bennett claimed that Joseph, not he, had been the immoral one and that he had left the Church because of the wickedness of the Saints. Bennett also claimed that the statements he had made defending Joseph's character had been made under duress and in the face of threats.[15] Joseph responded to Bennett's defection quietly at first by simply publishing a short "Notice" on the last page of the June 15, 1842, issue of the *Times and Seasons* announcing that Church leaders had withdrawn the hand of fellowship from Bennett on May 11.[16] The following issue—that of July 1 —called forth a lengthy account of Bennett's rascality and Joseph's efforts to reform him, Bennett's May 17 affidavit and May 19 statement before the city council, and excerpts from letters that "gentlemen in this city" had received from various correspondents regarding Bennett's less-than-savory character.¹⁷ Bennett's claims about being under duress when he defended Joseph's character and that he had left the Church before being excommunicated brought forth additional affidavits and testimonials in the August 1 issue of the *Times and Seasons* explicitly denying the charges.¹⁸

The 1842 Extradition Attempt

At the same time Bennett's true colors were making themselves publicly known, events of a far more sinister aspect were coming to a head. On the evening of May 6, 1842, an unknown assailant shot Lilburn W. Boggs, former governor of Missouri, as he sat in his home in Independence, Missouri.¹⁹ Eight days later, on May 14, news of the event reached Nauvoo, apparently with the erroneous report that Boggs had been killed in the attack.²⁰ Joseph Smith's enemies in the area were quick to connect him with the attack. The same day Joseph heard about it, for example, David Kilbourn—a presbyterian merchant, land speculator, and lawyer with ties to John C. Bennett—wrote to Missouri governor Thomas Reynolds accusing Joseph of complicity in the assassination attempt and calling for his arrest.²¹ One week later, on May 21, Sylvester M. Bartlett, editor of the *Quincy Whig*, addressed the issue in the pages of his paper: "There are several rumors in circulation in regard to the horrid affair," wrote Bartlett. "One of which throws the crime upon the Mormons—from the fact, we suppose, that Mr. Boggs was governor at the time, and no small degree instrumental in driving them from the state.—Smith too, the Mormon Prophet, as we understand, prophesied a year or so ago, his death by violent means. Hence, there is plenty of foundation for rumor."²² Joseph was quick to deny the charge, complaining by letter to the Whig's editor the following day of the "manifest injustice" he had done him. "He died not through my instrumentality," wrote Joseph, pointing out that Boggs might simply have been the victim of political intrigue. "I am tired of the misrepresentation, calumny and detraction heaped upon me by wicked men," Joseph added, "and desire and claim only those privileges guaranteed to all men by the Constitution and Laws of the United States and Illinois."[23]

The issue might have died there had not John C. Bennett kept it alive in letters published in the *Sangamo Journal* on July 15. "In 1841," reported Bennett, "Joe Smith predicted or prophesied in a public congregation in Nauvoo, that Lilburn W Boggs, ex-Governor of Missouri, should die by violent hands within one year. From one or two months prior to the attempted assassination of Gov. Boggs, Mr. O. P. Rockwell left Nauvoo for parts unknown to the citizens at large. I was then on terms of close intimacy with Joe Smith, and asked him where Rockwell had gone? 'Gone,' said he, 'GONE TO FULFILL PROPHECY!'" Bennett provided affidavits from other individuals to the same effect, openly acknowledging his "determination ... [to] arouse the public indignation" against Joseph, "if there is yet virtue and courage left in man."[24]

Authorities could do nothing on the basis of the circumstantial evidence and rumor provided by Kilbourne, Bartlett, Bennett, and others. But when Boggs himself—who fully recovered from the attack—signed an affidavit on July 20 accusing Joseph of being "accessary before the fact of the intended murder" and requesting Governor Reynolds to extradite Joseph to Missouri for trial, officials from Illinois and Missouri sprang into action.[25] Acting on Boggs's affidavit, Reynolds signed a requisition on July 22 requiring Illinois governor Thomas Carlin to deliver Joseph to Missouri for trial.[26] Concerned for Joseph's well-being, "about eight hundred, or upwards" of the citizens of Nauvoo signed a petition that same day urging Carlin not to issue a writ for Joseph "to be given up to the authorities of Missouri" but to try him in Illinois if he really thought the Prophet may have committed the crime.[27] Carlin received the Saints' petition on July 26 but chose to honor Reynolds's requisition instead, issuing a writ for Joseph's arrest on August 2.[28]

Reynolds's requisition, based on Boggs's affidavit, was ill-conceived. Extradition, as defined in the Constitution, requires that one be charged with committing a crime in one state and then fleeing to another.[29] Boggs's affidavit, upon which the extradition proceedings were based, accused Joseph of being "accessary before the fact" and identified him as "a citizen or resident of the State of Illinois" but failed to accuse him of actually committing a crime in Missouri and then fleeing to Illinois. Without such an accusation, Reynolds had no constitutional grounds for calling on Carlin to deliver Joseph to Missouri for trial—meaning, in effect, that Carlin's arrest warrant for Joseph was not issued on legal grounds.

Six days after Carlin issued his warrant, Thomas King of Adams County and two other officers showed up in Nauvoo with the warrant in hand and arrested Joseph Smith and Orrin Porter Rockwell, "the latter being charged with shooting ex-Governor Boggs of Missouri with intent to kill . . . and Joseph with being accessory."[30] The municipal court immediately convened and issued a writ of habeas corpus.[31] Unsure of the authority of the municipal court's writ in this particular case, King and his men left Joseph and Rockwell in the custody of Henry G. Sherwood, Nauvoo city marshal, and returned to Quincy with the arrest warrant to seek instructions from Carlin.

Without the arrest warrant in his possession, Sherwood had no legal authority to retain Joseph and Rockwell in custody. Neither man was anywhere to be found when King returned two days later. Convinced, apparently, that "Governor Carlin's course which he had pursued was unjustifiable and illegal" and that "the whole business [was] but another evidence of the effects of prejudice,"[32] both men had gone into hiding—Rockwell back east to Pennsylvania and New Jersey, and Joseph in various locations in and around Nauvoo.[33] King, no doubt furious with this new development, reportedly "endeavored to alarm sister Emma & the Brethren by his threats, but could not do it they understanding the nature of the Law in that case."[34] The sheriff and his men remained in the area for several days, "utter[ing] heavy threats . . . that if they could not find Joseph they would lay the city in ashes," William Clayton reported. "They say they will tarry in the city a month but they will find him."[35]

Joseph first stayed at the home of his uncle John Smith in Zarahemla, across the river from Nauvoo, in Iowa Territory. Pursuant to instructions from Joseph, on the night of August 11, Emma, Hyrum, William Law, Newel K. Whitney, George Miller, William Clayton, and Dimick B. Huntington rowed out to the island between Nauvoo and Montrose to meet with the Prophet and Erastus H. Derby. There it was decided that Joseph should "abide for a season" at the home of Edward Sayers, some distance upriver from Nauvoo on the Illinois side.[36]

Joseph stayed at Sayers's home six days. After accidentally meeting Martin Henderson Harris, nephew of Martin Harris, while getting some exercise in the woods and then hearing of rumors in Nauvoo that his hiding place had been discovered, Joseph retired to Carlos Granger's home in the northeast part of Nauvoo on the night of August 17.[37] Here he remained another six days, when he received a "few lines from sister Emma informing him that she would expect him home this evening believing that she could take care of him better at home than elsewhere." Joseph accordingly left Granger's home "soon after dark" on August 23 and arrived home "without being noticed by any person."[38]

Joseph kept a low profile for several more days, meeting with members of the Twelve and a few others at his home or in the red brick store.[39] After another six days, however, he felt sufficiently secure to make an unannounced appearance at a special conference on August 29. "The brethren were rejoiced to see him," recorded William Clayton. "He had not been seen for three weeks and his appearance amongst the brethren under present circumstances caused much animation and joy, it being unexpected. Some had supposed that he was gone to Europe and some to Washington.... Every one rejoiced to see him." As he addressed the conference, Joseph called for volunteers to go out and disabuse the public mind concerning his character—a call some three hundred and eighty answered immediately.[40]

Five days later, however, Joseph was back on the run. The day began with the Prophet entertaining former Apostle John Boynton in his home, when a note was brought in from David Hollister, who was acting as an informant of sorts for Joseph, "to the effect that the Missourians were again on the move." Shortly after noon, three officers showed up at Joseph's house, having apparently reached it undetected by "com[ing] up the river side and hitch[ing] their horses below the Nauvoo House and then proceed[ing] on foot." While Boynton stalled for time, Joseph, who had been eating lunch with his family, "passed out at the back door and through the corn in his garden" to the red brick store, where Newel K. Whitney's family was living at the time. By this time Emma was talking with the officers, who insisted on searching the house even though they had no search warrant with them. Joseph remained at the red brick store until nine that evening—thereby avoiding another search conducted at his home "soon after Sun down"—after which he retreated to the home of Edward Hunter, "where he was welcomed and made comfortable by the family."[41]

The following day, Sunday, Joseph sent William Clayton a letter he had written September 1, shortly after his unexpected conference appearance. Pursuant to Joseph's request, the letter—which outlined procedures for how baptisms for the dead were to be recorded—was read to the Saints assembled in the grove near the temple.[42]

The week Joseph remained in hiding was not an idle one. Several trusted friends, such as Brigham Young, Heber C. Kimball, William Clayton, and Newel K. Whitney dropped by for instruction. George Adams and David Rogers delivered several letters from Saints in the east, including one from Willard Richards. Joseph dictated a lengthy letter to Mormon sympathizer James Arlington Bennet in New York and dictated a "long Epistle to the Saints" on September 7, which provided further instruction about recording baptisms for the dead and which he "ordered to be read next sabbath."[43] Emma, Wilson Law, Amasa Lyman, and George A. Smith paid him a visit after dark on the evening of September 9.[44] The following day was one of the designated "training days" for the Nauvoo Legion, during which Nauvoo swarmed with people. After spending the day "very close and still; lest on account of the quantity of people passing two and fro he should accidently be discovered," Joseph received word from Emma "that she wished him to come home, as she thought he would be as safe at home as any where for the present." Heeding his wife's request a second time, Joseph arrived home after dark "safe and undiscovered."[45]

Joseph slowly came out of hiding over the course of the next four weeks, although a lingering sickness of Emma kept him at home a good part of the time. Gathering rumors that "many of the Missourians were coming to unite with the Militia of this State" to search for him, however, sent him off to the home of James Taylor—John Taylor's father—after dark the evening of October 7.[46] There he remained—except for one brief visit to his family[47]—until October 28, when, "from the appearance of thinks [things] abroad" he was "encouraged to believe that his enemies wont trouble him much more at present" and moved back home.[48]

Joseph's first big break on the extradition issue came several weeks later, when Stephen A. Douglas recommended to several of Joseph's associates that Joseph petition Thomas Ford, the newly elected governor of Illinois, to revoke former governor Carlin's arrest warrant for Joseph. Taking Douglas's advice, Joseph's associates asked U.S. district attorney Justin Butterfield to prepare the petition, which he did, at the same time remarking, William Clayton recorded, that "[Joseph's] arrest was based upon far weaker premises than he had previously supposed, inasmuch as the affidavit of Ex Gov. Boggs said nothing about Joseph having fled from justice, . . . and the constitution only authorizes the delivery up of a 'fugitive from Justice to the Executive authority of the State from which he fled.'"[49] Unsure of his authority to revoke an act of the previous governor, Ford consulted with six justices of the Illinois Supreme Court concerning Joseph's petition. The justices, Ford wrote to Joseph, "were unanimous in the opinion that the requisition from Missouri was illegal and insufficient to cause your arrest, but were equally divided as to the propriety and Justice of my interference with the acts of Governor Carlin." Ford, playing it safe, declined to revoke Carlin's writ and recommended that Joseph "submit to the laws and have a Judicial investigation" into his rights.[50] In a letter to Joseph, Butterfield confirmed Ford's report of the justices' advice and recommended that Joseph immediately come to Springfield, where the charges against him were sure to be discharged by habeas corpus either through the Illinois Supreme Court or the U.S. Circuit Court currently in session.[51]

Joseph and several trusted friends complied with Butterfield's request. The party arrived in Springfield on December 30 with Joseph in custody of Wilson Law, who had arrested him four days earlier on the authority of Carlin's Proclamation—an executive order of sorts that Carlin had issued September 20, 1842, giving any citizen the right to arrest Joseph.[52] Unsure of where Carlin's original writ for Joseph's arrest was and not wanting to leave any room for Joseph's enemies to make a competing arrest on the authority of that writ, Joseph petitioned Ford the following day for a new writ for his arrest, which was promptly granted. Joseph was then arrested on the authority of this new writ by William F. Elkin, sheriff of Sangamon County.[53] This placed him, for the time being, in custody of both Elkin and Law, and secure from arrest by someone in possession of Carlin's original warrant.

In the meantime, Butterfield had decided that since this habeas corpus hearing dealt with extradition and since extradition was a constitutional concern, the federal U.S. Circuit Court was the most appropriate venue for it. Disregarding Ford's earlier suggestion that Joseph's hearing be held before the Illinois State Supreme Court, Butterfield petitioned Nathaniel Pope, judge of the U.S. Circuit Court then in session in Springfield, that Joseph be allowed a hearing there and that he also be released on bail. Pope agreed to both, appointing Monday, January 2, for the hearing and setting Joseph's bail at $4,000.[54]

Joseph's presence in Springfield did not go unnoticed by her citizens, nor by members of the state legislature then in session. As Joseph and his party came "to the head of the stairs" after leaving Judge Pope, for example, "some man observd there goes Smith the prophet and a good looking man he is. & (said another) as damnd a rascal as ever lived. . . . & any one that takes his part is as damed a rascal as he is." Wilson Law retorted, "I am th[e] man. & I take his part." The confrontation quickly turned into a name-calling match and was moving outside into the street when the marshal interfered and restored order.[55] Later in the day, the Illinois House of Representatives effected an impromptu adjournment when a team of horses spooked and went clattering down the road past the State House, and someone yelled, "Joe Smith is running away."[56]

Joseph spent the remainder of Saturday, December 31, conversing with friends and new acquaintances on topics ranging from the Nauvoo Legion to the Nauvoo Charter. A good part of Sunday was spent in worship services held in the hall used by the House of Representatives. The following day, Monday, which had been set aside for Joseph's habeas corpus hearing, opened with Josiah Lamborn, the state attorney, requesting the hearing be pushed back a day. Pope scheduled it for Wednesday, January 4, giving Joseph and his associates another two days of downtime.[57] These were spent in conversation, as well as in watching the state Senate in action. While Joseph's thoughts on the Senate's activities are unknown, it is clear that this latter activity afforded Willard Richards no small entertainment. This was especially so when it came to watching the antics of Edward D. Baker, a senator from Sangamon county. The "Senator. appears much like an african Monken [Monkey]," Richards recorded, "at <one> moment standing by one stove. the next by another on the opposite side of the chamber. setting down in every senators chair in his way & he never gooes out of his way for his way is every where & and his nose in every mans face. eating apples staring at & pointing & staring at every one, ... a monkey without a monkey's wit."[58]

The hearing, when it was finally held, went relatively smoothly. The only real opposition was provided by state attorney Josiah Lamborn, who argued, first, that extradition was a state matter and that this federal circuit court therefore had no jurisdiction in this case; and second, that it was inappropriate in a habeas corpus hearing—which is simply a review of the arresting documents—to ask whether Joseph was in Missouri when Boggs was shot because that was delving into the evidence concerning guilt or innocence that could only be heard in a trial. Butterfield challenged Lamborn's objections by arguing that extradition was a federal matter, and therefore the federal court had jurisdiction, and that discussing Joseph's whereabouts was not an attempt to establish guilt or innocence but simply to point out that Joseph had not committed a crime in one state and then fled to another as extradition requires. Butterfield then pointed out the illegality of the documents— especially Boggs's affidavit—used to arrest Joseph, which said nothing about Joseph having fled from justice in Missouri. Lamborn's rebuttals were weak at best, Richards recorded, with the state attorney "apparently saying littl[e] more than the natu[r]e of his situation required—& no more than would be usefull in satisfying the public mind—that there had been a fair investigation—of the whole matter."[59]

In his decision given the following day, Pope agreed with Butterfield's arguments and discharged Joseph.[60] The five-month-long ordeal ended with Joseph and his party leaving Springfield for Nauvoo on January 7 in high spirits. On the journey home, Wilson Law composed a song, with the assistance of Willard Richards, for the occasion—sung to the tune of *Auld Lang Syne* and later known as the Mormon Jubilee—in which he praised those who had had a hand in bringing the whole affair to a successful close. "And are you sure the news is true?" ran the opening verse,

> And are you sure he's free?
> Then let us Join with one accord,
> And have a Jubilee.
>
> *Chorus*
> We'll have a Jubilee. my frie[n]ds
> We'll have a Jubilee
> With heart & voice we'll all rejoice
> In that our Prophet's free.[61]

Along with demonstrating the resiliency of Joseph and his associates, the 1842 extradition attempt also provides an important glimpse into the character and talents of Emma. Often a silent figure in Church history, Emma emerges from the background following a letter she received early on from Joseph instructing her on what to do should the need arise for them to flee to Wisconsin, as some of Joseph's associates were urging him to do. Evidently following up on an earlier conversation, Joseph also advised Emma in this letter against personally visiting Thomas Carlin in Quincy: "You may write to him," he wrote his wife, "whatever you see proper, but to go and see him, I do not give my consent at present."[62] Emma responded she was ready to go to Wisconsin if necessary, but that she was still confident that Joseph could "be protected without leaving this country."[63]

Emma then wrote a lengthy letter to the governor maintaining Joseph's innocence and asking, even begging, him to recall the writs he had issued for Joseph's and Rockwell's arrest. "You must be aware that Mr Smith was not in Missouri, and of course he could not have left there," she wrote, evidently in an effort to draw Carlin's attention to the inappropriateness of extradition in this case.[64] Carlin wrote back that he was simply fulfilling his duty as governor to deliver fugitives from justice to the executives of other states, so long as those other executives have "complied with the requisitions of the act of congress in that case made and provided."[65] Emma responded, in a follow-up letter, that that was precisely the point—the "requisitions of the act of congress" regarding extradition had not been complied with in this case, as there was ample evidence that Joseph "was not in Missouri" when the crime was committed, and that therefore "he is not a fugitive from justice." "It only requires a knowledge of the constitution of the United States, and statute of the State of Missouri," Emma informed the governor, "and a knowledge of the outrages committed by some of the inhabitants of that State [Missouri] upon the people called Mormons, . . . to know that there is not the least confidence to be placed" in Boggs and other Missouri officials.[66]

Choosing to take issue with another point Emma brought up—that of the legality of the municipal court's writ of habeas corpus in this case—Carlin sidestepped Emma's point about extradition in his response the following month. Nor would he acknowledge the very real threats that had been leveled against the Prophet in the past, writing that he had "not the most distant thought that any person in Illinois, or Missouri, contemplated personal injury to Mr Smith by violence in any manner whatever."[67] No record has been found of Emma responding to this second letter of Carlin.

In the end, Emma failed in her effort to persuade Carlin to recall the arrest warrant he had issued against her husband. In the correspondence surrounding that effort, however, one gets a rare glimpse into the personality and thoughts of

Joseph's wife. As her expressive and thoughtful letters show, she was a woman of extraordinary ability and temperament who understood the finer points of the complex issue and articulated an intelligent argument. Carlin himself, we are told, "expressed astonishment at the judgement and talent manifest in the manner of her address" after reading her first letter;[68] and while he was unwilling to concede any ground to Emma, one gets the distinct impression that when he closed his last letter to her "with sentiments of high regard and esteem," he really did mean it.[69]

One also sees, in the brief correspondence between Joseph and his wife during this time, the degree to which the Prophet himself relied on her judgment and support—a degree of dependence perhaps too few over the years have appreciated. In Joseph's letter to Emma about writing to Carlin, for example, he addresses the recommendation of some of his associates that he flee alone to Wisconsin, where his family would later join him. "My mind will eternally revolt at every suggestion of that kind," Joseph wrote his wife. "My safety is with you. . . . Any thing more or less than this cometh of evil. . . . If I go to the Pine County, you shall go along with me, and the children; and if you and the children go not with me, I don[']t go."[70] Emma's judgment carried a lot of weight with Joseph during this stressful time. As we have already seen, for example, Joseph twice followed Emma's advice on when it was safe for him to return home from hiding. The Prophet's soliloquy on meeting Emma on the island is too well known to repeat here but is further evidence of how much he relied on his wife for comfort and support.

Conclusion

Joseph employed a number of different clerks during the Nauvoo years, one of whom, William Clayton, we have quoted above. We conclude with a lengthy description of Joseph that Clayton provided for his friends back in England shortly after arriving in Nauvoo in 1840. It stands as an important testimony of Joseph's prophetic calling during the last few years of his life and reflects our own sentiments about the prophet of the Restoration. "He is . . . a man of sound judgment, and possessed of abundance of intelligence," Clayton wrote, responding to the negative reports he and his readers had heard about Joseph,

> and whilst you listen to his conversation you receive intelligence which expands your mind and causes your heart to rejoice. He is very familiar, and delights to instruct the poor saints. I can converse with him just as easy as I can with you, and with regard to being willing to communicate instruction he says "I receive it freely and I will give it freely". He is willing to answer any question I have put to him and is pleased when we ask him questions. He seems exceeding well versed in the scriptures, and whilst conversing upon any subject such light and beauty is revealed I never saw before. If I had come from England purposely to converse with him a few days I should have considered myself well paid for my trouble. He is no friend to iniquity but cuts at it wherever he sees it, & it is in vain to attempt to cloke it before him. He has a great measure of the spirit of God, and by this means he is preserved from imposition. He says "I am a man of like passions with yourselves," but truly I wish I was such a man.[71]

Notes

1. Emma Smith to Thomas Carlin, August 16 [17], 1842, recorded in Joseph Smith, Journal, August 21, 1842, Church History Library, The Church of Jesus Christ of Latter-day Saints, Salt Lake City.

2. Minutes of March 17, 1842, Relief Society Minutebook, 1842–1844, 7, Church History Library.

3. Joseph Smith, Journal, April 10, 1842.

4. "To the Church of Jesus Christ of Latter Day Saints, and to All the Honorable Part of Community," *Times and Seasons*, July 1, 1842, 839.

5. "To the Church," *Times and Seasons*, July 1, 1842, 839.

6. "To the Church," *Times and Seasons*, July 1, 1842, 840.

7. "To the Church," *Times and Seasons*, July 1, 1842, 840–41; "Notice," *Times and Seasons*, June 15, 1842, 830.

8. "Affidavit of William Law," *Times and Seasons*, August 1, 1842, 873.

9. "Affidavit of Hyrum Smith," *Times and Seasons*, August 1, 1842, 870.

10. "To the Church," *Times and Seasons*, July 1, 1842, 841.

11. "Affidavit of Hyrum Smith," *Times and Seasons*, August 1, 1842, 871.

12. "Affidavit of Hyrum Smith," *Times and Seasons*, August 1, 1842, 871.

13. "To the Church," *Times and Seasons*, July 1, 1842, 841; see also Joseph Smith, Journal, May 19, 1842.

14. Nauvoo Masonic Lodge Minute Book, June 16, July 7, and August 8, 1842, Church History Library.

15. *Sangamo Journal*, July 15, 1842.

16. "Notice," *Times and Seasons*, June 15, 1842, 830.

17. "To the Church," *Times and Seasons*, July 1, 1842, 839–42.

18. "John C. Bennett," *Times and Seasons*, August 1, 1842, 868–78.

19. Boggs served as governor of Missouri from 1836 to 1840.

20. Joseph Smith, Journal, May 14, May 22, 1842.

21. David Kilbourn to Thomas Reynolds, May 14, 1842, in David Kilbourn and Edward Kilbourn, "Latter-Dayism, No. 1," *Hawk-Eye and Iowa Patriot*, September 30, 1841, [1].

22. "Assassination of Ex-Governor Boggs of Missouri," *Quincy Whig*, May 21, 1842, 3.

23. Smith to Bartlett, May 22, 1842, in *Quincy Whig*, June 4, 1842, 2.

24. John C. Bennett, letters, July 2 and 4, 1842, in *Sangamo Journal*, July 15, 1842.

25. Lilburn W. Boggs, Affidavit, Jackson Co., MO, July 20, 1842, Abraham Lincoln Presidential Library, Springfield, Illinois; also copied in Joseph Smith, Journal, December 9–20, 1842.

26. State of Missouri, Requisition of Thomas Reynolds, Jefferson City, Missouri, July 22, 1842, Abraham Lincoln Presidential Library, Springfield, Illinois; also copied in Joseph Smith, Journal, December 9–20, 1842.

27. Nauvoo City Council Minutes, July 22, 1842, 95–97, Church History Library.

28. Thomas Carlin to Joseph Smith, July 27, 1842, Joseph Smith Letterbook 2, Joseph Smith Collection, Church History Library; also copied in Joseph Smith, Journal, August 21, 1842. While the original warrant from Carlin has not be located, a copy of the warrant made by clerk James Sloan before the Nauvoo municipal court dates the original to August 2, 1842 (Thomas Carlin, Writ, Springfield, Illinois, August 2, 1842, copy by James Sloan, Nauvoo City, *Records, 1841–1845*, Church History Library).

29. U. S. Constitution, article 4, section 2.

30. Joseph Smith, Journal, August 8, 1842.

31. The Nauvoo city charter, which was ratified by the Illinois legislature in December 1840, granted authority to the municipal court to issue writs of habeas corpus "in all cases arising under the ordinances of the City Council" ("An Act to Incorporate the City of

Nauvoo," sec. 17, 55; "An Act to Incorporate the City of Nauvoo," *Times and Seasons*, January 15, 1841, 283). Anticipating attempts by "enemies" of the Church to subject the citizens of Nauvoo to "illegal process," the Nauvoo city council had passed an ordinance in July declaring that "no Citizen of this City shall be taken out of the City by any Writs without the privilege of investigation before the Municipal Court, and the benefit of a Writ of Habeas Corpus" (Nauvoo City Council Minute Book, July 5, 1842, 86–87, Church History Library). Along with issuing the writ of habeas corpus, the city council passed a statute on this date granting the Nauvoo municipal court the power to inquire into both proper procedure and merits of the case for any arrest warrant served in Nauvoo. The Nauvoo statutes were attempts to codify the broadest interpretation of the habeas corpus grant in the charter, with the goal to prevent the legal system from being used for "religious or other persecution" (Nauvoo City Council Minute Book, July 5, 1842, 98–99, Church History Library).

32. Joseph Smith, Journal, August 11, 1842.

33. Orrin Porter Rockwell per S. Armstrong, Philadelphia, PA, to JS, Nauvoo, IL, December 1, 1842, Joseph Smith Collection, Church History Library; Joseph Smith, Journal, March 13, 1843.

34. Joseph Smith, Journal, August 10, 1842.

35. Joseph Smith, Journal, August 13, 1842.

36. Joseph Smith, Journal, August 11, 1842.

37. Joseph Smith, Journal, August 17, 1842.

38. Joseph Smith, Journal, August 23, 1842.

39. Joseph Smith, Journal, August 24–28, 1842.

40. Joseph Smith, Journal, August 29, 1842.

41. Joseph Smith, Journal, September 3, 1842.

42. Joseph Smith, Journal, September 4, 1842. The letter was published in the *Times and Seasons*, September 15, 1842, 919–20, and is now Doctrine and Covenants 127.

43. Joseph Smith, Journal, September 6–8, 1842. The September 7 letter to the Saints, incorrectly dated September 6 in the original manuscript and published sources, is now Doctrine and Covenants 128.

44. Joseph Smith, Journal, September 9, 1842.

45. Joseph Smith, Journal, September 10, 1842.

46. Joseph Smith, Journal, October 7, 1842.

47. Joseph Smith, Journal, October 20, 1842.

48. Joseph Smith, Journal, October 28, 1842.

49. Joseph Smith, Journal, December 9, 1842.

50. Thomas Ford to Joseph Smith, December 17, 1842, in Joseph Smith, Journal, December 9, 1842.

51. Justin Butterfield to Joseph Smith, December 17, 1842, in Joseph Smith, Journal, December 9, 1842.

52. Joseph Smith, Journal, 26, December 30, 1842, Church History Library; "Proclamation," *Illinois State Register*, September 30, 1842, [3], and "Four Hundred Dollars Reward!" *Sangamo Journal*, September 30, 1842, [3]. For the authority Carlin's proclamation gave to private citizens, see Joseph Smith, Journal, October 5, 1842.

53. Joseph Smith, Journal, December 31, 1842.

54. Joseph Smith, Journal, December 31, 1842.

55. Joseph Smith, Journal, January 4, 1843.

56. Joseph Smith, Journal, December 31, 1842.

57. Joseph Smith, Journal, December 31, 1842–January 2, 1843.

58. Joseph Smith, Journal, January 2, 1843.

59. Joseph Smith, Journal, January 4, 1843.

60. Joseph Smith, Journal, January 5, 1843.

61. Joseph Smith History, Draft Notes, January 7, 1843, Church History Library.

62. Joseph Smith to Emma Smith, August 16, 1842, copied in Joseph Smith, Journal, August 21, 1842. As noted below, Emma and others had delivered a petition to the governor in person on July 29 requesting protection for Joseph Smith.

63. Emma Smith to Joseph Smith, [August 16, 1842], copied in Joseph Smith, Journal, August 21, 1842.

64. Emma Smith to Thomas Carlin, August 16, 1842, copied in Joseph Smith, Journal, August 21, 1842.

65. Thomas Carlin to Emma Smith, August 24, 1842, copied in Joseph Smith, Journal, September 3, 1842. Carlin was quoting from "An Act Concerning Fugitives From Justice," January 6, 1827, in *The Revised Code of Laws, of Illinois, Enacted by the Fifth General Assembly* (Vandalia, Illinois: Robert Blackwell, 1827), 232–34. The "act of congress" that the Illinois law referred to is "An Act Respecting Fugitives from Justice, and Persons Escaping from the Service of their Masters," February 12, 1793, in *The Public Statutes at Large of the United States of America, 1789–1799* (Boston: Charles C. Little and James Brown, 1845), 1:302–5.

66. Emma Smith to Thomas Carlin, August 27, 1842, copied in Joseph Smith, Journal, September 3, 1842.

67. Thomas Carlin to Emma Smith, September 7, 1842, copied in Joseph Smith, Journal, September 12, 1842.

68. Joseph Smith, Journal, August 21, 1842. Carlin read the letter in the presence of Judge James A. Ralston, a member of the Church living in Quincy.

69. Thomas Carlin to Emma Smith, September 7, 1842, copied in Joseph Smith, Journal, September 12, 1842.

70. Joseph Smith to Emma Smith, August 16, 1842, copied in Joseph Smith, Journal, August 21, 1842.

71. William Clayton to the Saints in England, December 10, 1840, in James B. Allen, "To the Saints in England: Impressions of a Mormon Immigrant," *BYU Studies* 18, no. 3 (Spring 1978): 478–79.

Because of Joseph Smith and the authority restored to him, we know that the family unit can be preserved throughout the eternities. He taught how to prize the endearing relationships of father and mother, husband and wife; of brother and sister, son and daughter. Thus love truly becomes eternal. ("A Father's Gift," by Liz Lemon Swindle, courtesy of Foundation Arts, © 1998.)

ROBERT L. MILLET

1843
Doctrines, Covenants, and Sweet Consolation

When Aaron and Miriam allowed themselves to be embroiled in a critical spirit in regard to their brother Moses, Jehovah declared, "If there be a prophet among you, I the Lord will make myself known unto him in a vision, and will speak unto him in a dream. My servant Moses is not so, who is faithful in all mine house. With him will I speak mouth to mouth, even apparently, and not in dark speeches; and the similitude of the Lord shall he behold: wherefore then were ye not afraid to speak against my servant Moses?" (Numbers 12:6–8). We learn from this exchange an important principle: there are prophets, and then there are prophets. The Apostle Paul explained that "the spirits of the prophets are subject to the prophets" (1 Corinthians 14:32). There is an order,

---

Robert L. Millet is a professor of ancient scripture at Brigham Young University.

a hierarchy, even among those called as chosen oracles and mouthpieces of the Almighty.

Jesus Christ is the presiding High Priest. The Prophet Joseph Smith explained that after Christ in the government of the kingdom of God comes Adam and then Noah.[1] Elder Bruce R. McConkie observed, "You start out with the Lord Jesus, and then you have Adam and Noah. Thereafter come the dispensation heads. Then you step down, appreciably, and come to prophets and apostles, to the elders of Israel, and to wise and good and sagacious men who have the spirit of light and understanding."[2] Joseph Smith, like Adam, Enoch, Noah, Abraham, Moses, and Jesus, stands as a dispensation head. The dispensation head becomes the means by which the knowledge and power of God are channeled to men and women on earth. He becomes the means by which the gospel of Jesus Christ—the plan of salvation and exaltation—is revealed anew, the means by which divine transforming powers, including saving covenants and ordinances, are extended to people during an age of time. The dispensation head stands as the preeminent prophetic witness and revealer of Christ; he knows firsthand because of what he has seen and heard.

Because of his central place in the plan and because it is by means of the power of his testimony that men and women come to know the Lord and bask in the light of the Spirit, men and women of a particular dispensation who stand to express the witness which burns in their bosoms find themselves bearing testimony of Christ and of the dispensation head—the revealer of Christ—in almost the same breath. This is just as it should be. Elder McConkie thus pointed out, "Every prophet is a witness of Christ; every dispensation head is a revealer of Christ for his day; and every other prophet or apostle who comes is a reflection and an echo and an exponent of the dispensation head. All such come to echo to the world and to expound and unfold what God has revealed through the man who was appointed for that era to give his eternal word to the world. Such is the dispensation concept."[3]

Thus the Savior affirmed to Joseph Smith, "This generation shall have my word through you" (Doctrine and Covenants 5:10). Thomas B. Marsh was instructed to "declare glad tidings of great joy unto this generation." And what did that entail? "You shall declare the things which have been revealed to my servant, Joseph Smith, Jun." (Doctrine and Covenants 31:3–4). If the knowledge and power of God are to be had in this final period of the earth's history, they will be had through the work set in motion and the truths which flowed and the authorities which were transmitted by Joseph Smith, or they will be had not at all. To bear witness that Joseph Smith is a prophet or seer is to testify that he was a revealer of truth, divine truth, and that he was a legal administrator, a conduit by which the keys of the kingdom of God have been restored.

President Joseph F. Smith, nephew of the Prophet, declared, "I believe in the divinity of Jesus Christ, because more than ever I have come nearer the possession of the actual knowledge that Jesus is the Christ, the Son of the Living God, through the testimony of Joseph Smith . . . that he saw Him, that he heard Him, that he received instructions from Him, that he obeyed those instructions, and that he today stands before the world as the last great, actual, living, witness of the divinity of Christ's mission and [Christ's] power to redeem man. . . . Thank God for Joseph Smith."[4]

Teachings in 1843

My task is to discuss the work of Joseph Smith in the year 1843. I will first mention a sampling of the things revealed to him or that he taught during that significant year, and then I will focus more closely on three matters of deep doctrinal import.

It is appropriate that on January 1, the *History of the Church* records, "If any person should ask me if I were a prophet, I should not deny it, as that would give me the lie; for, according to John, the testimony of Jesus is the spirit of prophecy; therefore, if I profess to be a witness or teacher, and have not the spirit of prophecy, which is the testimony of Jesus, I must be a false witness; . . . and any man who says he is a teacher or preacher of righteousness, and denies the spirit of prophecy, is a liar."[5] On February 8 he explained that "a prophet [is] a prophet only when he [is] acting as such."[6]

On Sunday, January 22, the Prophet Joseph spoke on what it takes to set up the kingdom of God, including priesthood and the call of legal administrators.[7] One week later he spoke on the greatness of John the Baptist as a legal administrator and how to discern the interpretation of parables, using the parable of the prodigal son as an illustration.

The February 1 issue of the *Times and Seasons* contains Joseph's poetic version of the Vision of the Glories (based on Doctrine and Covenants section 76), a colorful, thoughtful, and doctrinally significant rewrite of a monumental vision he had received some eleven years earlier.[8]

Parley P. Pratt had been away on missionary service and missed some of the instruction the Twelve had received during that time. Thus on February 9 Joseph spent time conversing with Elder Pratt on how to discern spirits and angels (resurrected beings), giving what we now have as section 129 of the Doctrine and Covenants.[9]

On February 28 Joseph read in the Chicago *Express* that a man had reported seeing the "sign of the Son of Man." The Prophet replied that whatever the man may have seen, it was not the sign spoken of in the Savior's Olivet discourse (see Matthew 24:30). Why? Because he, Joseph Smith, knew nothing concerning it, and, according to the prophetic word, "Surely the Lord God will do nothing, but he revealeth his secret unto his servants the prophets" (Amos 3:7).[10]

On March 4 he wrote what is one of my favorite maxims, one that teaches us something about his cheerful personality: "On returning to my office after dinner, I spoke the following proverb: For a man to be great, he must not dwell on small things, though he may enjoy them; this shows that a Prophet cannot well be his own scribe, but must have some one to write for him." Following that light comment, he added: "The battle of Gog and Magog will be after the millennium."[11]

On March 2 at 10:00 a.m. (*The Words of Joseph Smith* has this as April 2), the Prophet went to a meeting where Orson Hyde spoke on Christ appearing at the time of his Second Coming as a warrior riding on a horse, and on how each of us can have the Father and the Son dwell in our hearts. "We dined with my sister Sophronia McCleary, when I told Elder Hyde that I was going to offer some corrections to his sermon this morning. He replied, 'They shall be thankfully received.'" Joseph then spoke and delivered what we now have as the first seventeen verses of section 130 of the Doctrine and Covenants, explaining that when the Savior appears he will appear as a man, and that the idea of the Father and Son dwelling in our hearts is "an old sectarian notion, and is false" (v. 3). Later that day, instructions that constitute verses 18–23 of section 130 were given.[12]

Also on April 2, William Clayton's diary contains the following interesting insight: "The Holy Ghost is a personage, and a person cannot have the personage of the H. G. in his heart."[13]

The following is recorded under Friday, April 7:

> To a remark of Elder Orson Pratt's, that a man's body changes every seven years, President Joseph Smith replied: There is no fundamental principle belonging to a human system that ever goes into another in this world or in the world to come; I care not what the theories of men are. We have the testimony that God will raise us up, and he has the power to do it. If any man supposes that any part of our bodies, that is, the fundamental parts thereof, ever goes into another body, he is mistaken.[14]

In the morning session of a conference on April 8, Joseph offered a remarkable commentary on the book of Revelation, including some guiding principles on understanding this kind of apocalyptic literature.[15]

On Sunday, May 21, Joseph Smith provided his now-classic characterization of himself: "I am like a huge, rough stone rolling down from a high mountain; and the only polishing I get is when some corner gets rubbed off by coming in contact with something else, striking with accelerated force against religious bigotry, priestcraft, lawyer-craft, doctor-craft, lying editors, suborned judges and jurors, and the authority of perjured executives, backed by mobs, blasphemers, licentious and corrupt men and women—all hell knocking off a corner here and a corner there. Thus will I become a smooth and polished shaft in the quiver of the Almighty."[16]

James Burgess recorded the following on May 6:

> In the month of May 1843. Several miles east of Nauvoo. The Nauvoo Legion was on parade and review. At the close of which Joseph Smith made some remarks upon our condition as a people and upon our future prospects, contrasting our present condition with our past trials and persecutions by the hands of our enemies. Also upon the constitution and

government of the United States, stating that the time would come when the Constitution and Government would hand [hang] by a brittle thread and would be ready to fall into other hands, but this people, the Latter-day Saints, would step forth and save it.[17]

According to the journals of Willard Richards and Wilford Woodruff, the Prophet explained on Sunday, June 11, that the grand purpose, the ultimate objective behind the gathering of the Saints, was to build temples, "whereby He could reveal unto His people the ordinances of His house and the glories of His kingdom." In that same sermon Joseph spoke of the importance of baptism for the dead, the nature of the spirit world, the suffering in hell, and of the meaning of the Savior's words to the thief on the cross, "This day shalt thou be with me in paradise."[18] Willard Richards also recorded the following from Joseph: "At one time God obtained a house where Peter washed and anointed on the day of Pentecost."[19]

On July 9, Joseph responded to the question, "Why is it this babbler gains so many followers, and retains them?" He answered, "It is because I possess the principle of love. All I can offer the world is a good heart and a good hand."[20] Exactly two weeks later the Prophet added, "Friendship is one of the grand fundamental principles of 'Mormonism': [it is designed] to revolutionize and civilize the world, and cause wars and contentions to cease and men to become friends and brothers. . . . It is a time-honored adage that love begets love."[21]

Also on July 9, he explained that he was just as eager to fight for and uphold "the rights of a Presbyterian, a Baptist or a good man of any denomination" to worship as he pleases. Why? "The same principle which would trample upon the rights of the Latter-day Saints would trample upon the rights of the Roman Catholics, or of any other denomination who may be unpopular and too weak to defend themselves."[22]

In the same address Joseph provides insight that would make a real difference in how we relate to those of other faiths today: "The inquiry is frequently made of me, 'Wherein do you differ from others in your religious views?' In reality and essence we do not differ so far in our religious views, but that we could all drink into one principle of love. One of the grand fundamental principles of 'Mormonism' is to receive truth, let it come from whence it may." Continuing, he advised, "If I esteem mankind to be in error, shall I bear them down? No. I will lift them up, and in their own way too, if I cannot persuade them my way is better; and I will not seek to compel any man to believe as I do, only by the force of reasoning, for truth will cut its own way. Do you believe in Jesus Christ and the Gospel of salvation which He revealed? So do I. Christians should cease wrangling and contending with each other, and cultivate the principle of union and friendship in their midst."[23]

On July 16, Joseph taught the following, as recorded by James Burgess: "After God had created the heavens and the earth, he came down and on the sixth day said, Let us make man in our own image. In whose image? In the image of Gods created they them, male and female: innocent, harmless, and spotless, bearing the same character and the same image as the Gods. And when man fell he did not lose his image but his character, still retain[ing] the image of his Maker."[24]

On October 9, a conference was held, and during his sermon Joseph Smith paid tribute to Judge James Adams, who had passed away recently:

> All men know they must die. And it is important that we should understand the reasons and causes of our exposure to the vicissitudes of life and of death, and the designs

and purposes of God in our coming into the world, our sufferings here, and our departure hence. What is the object of our coming into existence, then dying and falling away, to be here no more? It is but reasonable to suppose that God would reveal something in reference to the matter, and it is a subject we ought to study more than any other. . . . If we have any claim on our Heavenly Father for anything, it is for knowledge on this important subject. . . . Reading the experience of others, or the revelation given to them, can never give us a comprehensive view of our condition and true relation to God. Knowledge of these things can only be obtained by experience through the ordinances of God set forth for that purpose. Could you gaze into heaven five minutes, you would know more than you would by reading all that ever was written on the subject.

Joseph went on to explain how spirits and angels are often allowed to witness our actions on earth and how they may minister to us.[25]

On October 15, Willard Richards recorded the following from the Prophet: "I believe the bible, as it ought to be, as it came from the pen of the original writers."[26] In that same sermon, Joseph offered brief but poignant commentary on the conversation between Jesus and Nicodemus in John 3: "It is one thing to see the kingdom of God, and another thing to be in it. We must have a change of heart to see the kingdom of God, and subscribe the articles of adoption [the first principles and ordinances, the means whereby we are adopted into the family of the Lord Jesus Christ] to enter therein."[27]

Now, because of my own interests in doctrine, I have chosen not to emphasize trials and arrests and writs of habeas corpus and minutes of meetings and everyday affairs, although those matters were going on at the same time that Joseph Smith was inviting the Saints to gaze with him upon the visions of eternity. The revelations of God, and the prophetic counsel that directed the Church in its destined course and that served as marvelous puzzle pieces to the grand plan of salvation, did not come to us in a vacuum, in the solitary places or in monasteries, but amid the comings and goings of noble men and women, busily engaged in earning a living as well as learning line upon line how to live and what to live for.

In moving through 1843 I have purposely skipped three doctrinal matters that were either introduced or expanded upon that year and will now deal with them in a bit more detail. These sacred matters are distinctively Latter-day Saint doctrines.

Eternal Marriage

Because of Joseph Smith and the authority restored to him, we know that the family unit will be preserved throughout the eternities. Thus love truly becomes eternal, and the privilege of fatherhood and motherhood continues through all generations of time.

We know from historical sources that Joseph Smith first learned of eternal marriage (as well as plural marriage) in 1831, during the time that he was engaged in his inspired translation of the Bible. But it was not until July 12, 1843, that the revelation we know as section 132 of the Doctrine and Covenants was recorded. The early brethren took seriously the commission of the Lord given in November 1831: "And of as many as the Father shall bear record, to you shall be given power to seal them up unto eternal life" (Doctrine and Covenants 68:12). Indeed, the records indicate that entire congregations were so sealed.[28] Elijah had come to the Kirtland Temple in April of 1836 and restored the keys associated with sealing powers and the fullness of the Melchizedek Priesthood, an invitation and direction to bind mothers and fathers, sons and daughters together forever (see D&C 110:13–15).²⁹

The doctrine and practice of eternal marriage within The Church of Jesus Christ of Latter-day Saints is so prevalent, almost so common, that we often do not take the time to reflect seriously upon what a treasure, what a pearl of great price, we have in our midst. Consider this unsatisfying statement by a very dedicated modern Evangelical pastor-teacher:

> The question I'm most often asked about heaven is, *"Will I be married to the same spouse in heaven?"* Most are saying, "I don't want to lose my relationship with my wife; I can't imagine going to heaven and not being married to her." (Others, however, may be secretly hoping for a different answer. I'm not certain why so many ask this one!) . . .
>
> Marriage and other business of this life can sometimes intrude on more important matters of eternal concern. Paul writes, "He that is unmarried careth for the things that belong to the Lord, how he may please the Lord: but he that is married careth for the things that are of the world, how he may please his wife" (1 Cor. 7:32–33). So if you can remain single, do. Concentrate on the things of the Lord, because marriage is only a temporary provision. . . .
>
> While married couples are heirs together of the grace of *this* life (cf. 1 Peter 3:7), the institution of marriage is passing away. There are higher eternal values. . . .
>
> But what are those of us who are happily married supposed to think of this? I love my wife. She's my best friend and my dearest companion in every area of life. If those are your thoughts about your spouse as well, don't despair! You will enjoy an eternal companionship in heaven that is more perfect than any earthly partnership. The difference is that you will have such a perfect relationship with every other

person in heaven as well. If having such a deep relationship with your spouse here is so wonderful, imagine how glorious it will be to enjoy a perfect relationship with every human in the whole expanse of heaven—forever![30]

Joseph Smith placed all things in proper perspective. He helped us see that some things matter more than others, that family life, family associations, and family love matter more than fame and fortune, more than intellectual acclaim, more than the acquisition of this world's goods. Elder Parley P. Pratt wrote:

> It was at this time [in Philadelphia in 1839] that I received from [Joseph Smith] the first idea of eternal family organization, and the eternal union of the sexes in those inexpressibly endearing relationships which none but the highly intellectual, the refined and pure in heart, know how to prize, and which are at the very foundation of everything worthy to be called happiness.
>
> Till then I had learned to esteem kindred affections and sympathies as appertaining solely to this transitory state, as something from which the heart must be entirely weaned, in order to be fitted for its heavenly state.
>
> It was Joseph Smith who taught me how to prize the endearing relationships of father and mother, husband and wife; of brother and sister, son and daughter.
>
> It was from him that I learned that the wife of my bosom might be secured to me for time and all eternity; and that the refined sympathies and affections which endeared us to each other emanated from the fountain of divine eternal love. It was from him that I learned that we might cultivate these affections, and grow and increase in the same to all eternity. . . .

I had loved before, but I knew not why. But now I loved—with a pureness an intensity of elevated, exalted feeling, which would lift my soul from the transitory things of this grovelling sphere and expand it as the ocean. I felt that God was my heavenly Father indeed; that Jesus was my brother, and that the wife of my bosom was an immortal, eternal companion; a kind ministering angel, given to me as a comfort, and a crown of glory for ever and ever. In short, I could now love with the spirit and with the understanding also.[31]

On Tuesday, May 16, the Prophet placed his hand upon the knee of his secretary and scribe, William Clayton, and said: "Your life is his with Christ in God, and so are many others. Nothing but the unpardonable sin can prevent you from inheriting eternal life for you are sealed up by the power of the Priesthood unto eternal life, having taken the step necessary for that purpose."[32] The Prophet went on to say: "Except a man and his wife enter into an everlasting covenant and be married for eternity, while in this probation, by the power and authority of the Holy Priesthood, they will cease to increase when they die; that is, they will not have any children after the resurrection."[33] Then follows what we know as Doctrine and Covenants 131:1–4, the explanation that the highest degree of the celestial kingdom, what we call exaltation, will come only to those who enter into and keep the terms and conditions of the new and everlasting covenant of marriage.

More Sure Word of Prophecy

Because of the teachings of Joseph Smith, we understand that we can receive the assurance of eternal life. We can know that our lives are on course, that we are in covenant, in Christ, and bound for celestial glory. Early in his ministry, Joseph Smith taught that as men and women live in such a way as to cultivate the gift and gifts of the Holy Ghost, they eventually receive the assurance of eternal life—they make their calling and election sure. "After a person has faith in Christ, repents of his sins, and is baptized for the remission of his sins and receives the Holy Ghost (by the laying on of hands), which is the first Comforter, then let him continue to humble himself before God, and the Lord will soon say unto him, Son, thou shalt be exalted. When the Lord has thoroughly proved him, and finds that the man is willing to serve Him at all hazards, then the man will find his calling and his election made sure."[34] That is, the Lord seals an exaltation upon him, seals him up unto eternal life. In receiving the promise of salvation, the individual has thereby passed the tests of mortality and qualified for exaltation and glory hereafter.

On May 14, 1843, Wilford Woodruff recorded a sermon by Brother Joseph in which he explained Peter's words in his second epistle that the Apostles who ascended the Mount of Transfiguration possess a "more sure word of prophecy": "Though they might hear the voice of God and know that Jesus was the Son of God, this would be no evidence that their election and calling was made sure, that they had part with Christ, and were joint heirs with Him. They then would want that more sure word of prophecy, that they were sealed in the heavens and had the promise of eternal life in the kingdom of God [see Doctrine and Covenants 131:5–6]. Then, having this promise sealed unto them, it was an anchor to the soul, sure and steadfast. . . . Then I would exhort you to go on and continue to call upon God until you make your calling and election sure for yourselves, by obtaining this more sure word of prophecy, and wait patiently for the promise until you obtain it."[35]

In the fall of 1843, Joseph Smith began to confer upon men and women the fullness of the blessings of the priesthood. "Those holding the fullness of the Melchizedek Priesthood are kings and priests of the Most High God," Joseph explained, "holding the keys of power and blessings. In fact, that priesthood is a perfect law of theocracy, and stands as God to give laws to the people, administering endless lives to the sons and daughters of Adam. Abraham says to Melchizedek, I believe all that thou hast taught me concerning the priesthood and the coming of the Son of Man; so Melchizedek ordained Abraham and sent him away. Abraham rejoiced, saying, Now I have a priesthood."[36] James Burgess's record of this sermon is as follows: "Abraham gave a tenth part of all his spoils and then received a blessing under the hands of Melchizedek, even the last law or a fulness of the law or priesthood, which constituted him [Abraham] a king and priest after the order of Melchizedek, or an endless life."[37]

Securing Families through the Covenant

Because of Joseph Smith and the powers exercised in holy temples, there is power in the new and everlasting covenant to secure families forever. That power transcends our finite capacity to fully understand an infinite God's willingness and eternal plan to save all of those who will be saved. We know so little. In a world that presses for fairness, we too often close our eyes to the tender mercies of a loving Savior. The Master demonstrates his infinite mercy, for example, by refusing to condemn those who were ignorant of the gospel message and its requirements (see 2 Nephi 9:25–26; Mosiah 3:11; Moroni 8:22; Doctrine and Covenants 137:7–9), including little children who died before the age of accountability (see Mosiah 3:16; 15:25; Moroni 8:8–12, 22; Doctrine and Covenants 29:46–47;

74:7; 137:10). He offers the sublime gift—eternal life—to those laborers who join the work of the vineyard in the eleventh hour, the same gift he offers to those who have labored the entire day (see Matthew 20:1–16).

Speaking at a funeral for Judge Elias Higbee on August 13, 1843, the Prophet stated, "Had I inspiration, revelation, and lungs to communicate what my soul has contemplated in times past, there is not a soul in this congregation but would go to their homes and shut their mouths in everlasting silence on religion till they had learned something. Why be so certain that you comprehend the things of God, when all things with you are so uncertain. You are welcome to all the knowledge and intelligence I can impart to you." After thus preparing us for what was to come, he continued, "That which hath been hid from before the foundation of the world is revealed to babes and sucklings in the last days. The world is reserved unto burning in the last days. He shall send Elijah the prophet, and he shall reveal the covenants of the fathers in relation to the children, and the covenants of the children in relation to the fathers." He then referred to the four angels mentioned in Revelation 7, described in modern revelation as "four angels sent forth from God, to whom is given power over the four parts of the earth, to save life and to destroy; these are they who have the everlasting gospel to commit to every nation, kindred, tongue, and people; having power to shut up the heavens, to seal up unto life, or to cast down to the regions of darkness" (Doctrine and Covenants 77:8; emphasis added). The Prophet then declared, "Four destroying angels holding power over the four quarters of the earth until the servants of God are sealed in their foreheads, which signifies sealing the blessing upon their heads, meaning the everlasting covenant, thereby making their calling and election sure. When a seal is put upon the father and mother, it secures their posterity, so that they cannot be lost, but will be saved by virtue of the covenant of their father and mother."[38]

Howard and Martha Coray recorded that same sermon as follows: "God shall send unto them Elijah the prophet and he shall reveal unto them the covenants of the fathers with relation to the children and the covenants of the children in relation to the Fathers, that they may have the privilege of entering into the same in order to effect their mutual salvation."[39] President Franklin D. Richards recorded the Prophet's words in the following manner: "Covenants either there or here must be made in view of eternity and the covenant sealed on the foreheads of the parents secured the children from falling, that they shall all sit upon thrones as one with the godhead, joint heirs of God with Jesus Christ."[40]

What does this mean? To what degree can righteous parents—fathers and mothers who have entered into and kept sacred covenants—affect or even effect the salvation of their posterity? President Brigham Young taught, "Let the father and mother, who are members of this Church and kingdom, take a righteous course, and strive with all their might never to do a wrong, but to do good all their lives; if they have one child or one hundred children, if they conduct themselves towards them as they should, binding them to the Lord by their faith and prayers, I care not where those children go, they are bound up to their parents by an everlasting tie, and no power on earth or hell can separate them from their parents in eternity; they will return again to the fountain from whence they sprang."[41] We think of the sufferings and pleadings of Alma the elder and his wife and remember the words of the angel to the wandering son: "Behold, the Lord hath heard the prayers of his people, and also the prayers of his servant, Alma, who is thy father;

for he has prayed with much faith concerning thee that thou mightest be brought to the knowledge of the truth; therefore, for this purpose have I come to convince thee of the power and authority of God, that the prayers of his servants might be answered according to their faith" (Mosiah 27:14).

We believe that those who are faithful in their first estate come to the earth with certain predispositions to receive and embrace the truth. The Prophet himself declared that those of the house of Israel who come into the Church do so with quiet receptivity to the Spirit of the Lord and an openness to pure intelligence.[42] Similarly, we have no difficulty speaking of the "spirit of Elijah" reaching out, touching, directing, and impelling individuals to search out their dead and perform the saving ordinances. Why should we have difficulty accepting the fact that the power of the covenant can reach out, touch, redirect, and impel the wandering sheep? Could it be that that power is indeed the same spirit of Elijah, the spirit that turns the hearts of the children to the covenant made with their fathers?

Elder Orson F. Whitney offered the following powerful commentary on Joseph Smith's words:

> The Prophet Joseph Smith declared—and he never taught more comforting doctrine—that the eternal sealings of faithful parents and the divine promises made to them for valiant service in the Cause of Truth, would save not only themselves but likewise their posterity. Though some of the sheep may wander, the eye of the Shepherd is upon them, and sooner or later they will feel the tentacles of Divine Providence reaching out after them and drawing them back to the fold. Either in this life or the life to come, they will return. They will have to pay their debt to justice; they will suffer for their sins; and may tread a thorny path; but if it leads them at last, like the penitent Prodigal, to a loving and

forgiving father's heart and home, the painful experience will not have been in vain. Pray for your careless and disobedient children; hold on to them with your faith. Hope on, trust on, till you see the salvation of God. . . .

You parents of the wilful and the wayward! Don't give them up. Don't cast them off. They are not utterly lost. The Shepherd will find his sheep. They were his before they were yours—long before he entrusted them to your care; and you cannot begin to love them as he loves them. They have but strayed in ignorance from the Path of Right, and God is merciful to ignorance. Only the fulness of knowledge brings the fulness of accountability. Our Heavenly Father is far more merciful, infinitely more charitable, than even the best of his servants, and the Everlasting Gospel is mightier in power to save than our narrow finite minds can comprehend.[43]

In our own day, President Boyd K. Packer has provided a comforting context and reaffirmation for the promise to faithful parents. In discussing the "moral pollution" of the last days, he said:

> It is a great challenge to raise a family in the darkening mists of our moral environment.
>
> We emphasize that the greatest work you will do will be within the walls of your home, and that "no other success can compensate for failure in the home." The measure of our success as parents, however, will not rest solely on how our children turn out. That judgment would be just only if we could raise our families in a perfectly moral environment, and that now is not possible.
>
> It is not uncommon for responsible parents to lose one of their children, for a time, to influences over which they have no control. They agonize over rebellious sons and daughters.

They are puzzled over why they are so helpless when they have tried so hard to do what they should.

It is my conviction that those wicked influences one day will be overruled....

We cannot overemphasize the value of temple marriage, the binding ties of the sealing ordinance, and the standards of worthiness required of them. When parents keep the covenants they have made at the altar of the temple, their children will be forever bound to them.[44]

But doesn't the Prophet Joseph Smith's statement regarding the sealing of righteous parents seem to indicate that the parents' calling and election must be made sure? Latter-day Saints who have received the ordinances of salvation—including the blessings of the temple endowment and eternal marriage—may thus press forward in the work of the Lord and with quiet dignity and patient maturity seek to be worthy of gaining the certain assurance of salvation before the end of their mortal lives. But should they not formally receive the more sure word of prophecy in this life, they have the scriptural promise that faithfully enduring to the end—keeping the covenants and commandments from baptism to the end of their lives (see Mosiah 18:8–9)—eventuates in the promise of eternal life, whether that promise be received here or hereafter (see Doctrine and Covenants 14:7; 53:7; see also 2 Nephi 31:20; Mosiah 5:15). "But blessed are they who are faithful and endure, whether in life or in death, for they shall inherit eternal life" (Doctrine and Covenants 50:5).

Elder Bruce R. McConkie expressed the following sentiments at the funeral of Elder S. Dilworth Young: "If we die in the faith, that is the same thing as saying that our calling and election has been made sure and that we will go on to eternal reward hereafter. As far as faithful members of the Church are concerned, they have charted a course leading to eternal life. This life is the time that is appointed as a probationary estate for men to prepare to meet God, and as far as faithful people are concerned, if they are in the line of their duty, if they are doing what they ought to do, although they may not have been perfect in this sphere, their probation is ended. Now there will be some probation for some other people hereafter. But for the faithful saints of God, now is the time and the day, and their probation is ended with their death."[45]

Amulek did teach that the same spirit or disposition we have in this life will be with us in the world to come (see Alma 34:31–35), and the principle is true enough. Continuing in an evil habituated course makes it awfully difficult to change. But is such impossible?

We must never deny another person the opportunity to change. People change here. Why can they not change hereafter? So many things can weigh upon the mind and heart of an individual, pressures and challenges and crosses that only God can see and comprehend. Why does a person reject the gospel? Why does a child wander? Can we see the whole picture? Are we in a position to pass appropriate judgment and close the doors to future recovery and reconciliation? I have a conviction that when a person passes through the veil of death, all of those impediments and challenges that were beyond his or her power to control—abuse, neglect, immoral environment, weighty traditions, and so on—will be torn away like a film. Then perhaps they will see and feel things that they could not see and feel before.

But isn't this teaching risky? Won't this kind of teaching motivate some young people to neglect their duty and sow their wild oats? I suppose there will always be those who choose to take license in gospel liberty or who do despite to the saving grace of our Lord by knowingly violating the laws of God. There is always a risk on that end of the spectrum. There is, however, what I perceive to be a greater risk—that well-meaning, hardworking, and diligent mothers and fathers with straying children may draw false conclusions about themselves and maybe even throw in the towel in despair. To such persons, the prophetic word concerning the consummate power of the covenant is like manna to the soul, like living water to parched lips. It may also be the case that such doctrine is often more effectively delivered and applied in more intimate settings.

But is all of this really fair to those parents who have been successful in rearing their families or to those children who have kept themselves from serious sin? Stated bluntly, all of us are guilty of sin. All of us are in need of pardoning mercy. All of us fall short of the divine standard. During a long day of debate with his opponents, Jesus delivered the following parable: "A certain man had two sons; and he came to the first, and said, Son, go work to day in my vineyard. He [the son] answered and said, I will not: but afterward he repented, and went. And he came to the second, and said likewise. And he [the second son] answered and said, I go sir: and went not. Whether of them twain did the will of his father?" (Matthew 21:28–31). One "may wonder why Jesus does not include a third son who said, 'I will' and kept his word. Perhaps it is because this story characterizes humanity, and we all fall short. Thus Jesus could describe only two kinds of religious people: those who pretend to be obedient but are actually rebels, and those who begin as rebels but repent."[46]

Inasmuch as each of us is a recipient of unending and unmerited grace, how can we, in the spirit of Christian charity—or in the attitude of sane discourse—speak of the Lord's pardoning mercy toward wayward children as *unfair*? Of course it's unfair! It's all unfair! That a pure and innocent man should suffer and agonize over others' transgressions is not fair. That he who had never taken a backward step should tread the winepress alone, "even the wine-press of the fierceness of the wrath of Almighty God" (Doctrine and Covenants 76:107) and thereby descend below all things (see Doctrine and Covenants 88:6), is not fair. That the lowly Nazarene should be subjected to the ignominy and unspeakable torture of crucifixion is definitely unfair. But the plan of the Father is not a plan of fairness, at least as we judge fairness from our limited perspective; it is a plan of mercy. The Father and the Son love us in ways that we cannot comprehend. They will do all that is within the bounds of propriety to save as many of the posterity of Adam and Eve as will be saved.

President Lorenzo Snow explained:

> God has fulfilled his promises to us, and our prospects are grand and glorious. Yes, in the next life we will have our wives, and our sons and daughters. If we do not get them all at once, we will have them some time, for every knee shall bow and every tongue shall confess that Jesus is the Christ. You that are mourning about your children straying away will have your sons and your daughters. If you succeed in passing through these trials and afflictions and receive a resurrection, you will, by the power of the Priesthood, work and labor, as the Son of God has, until you get all your sons and daughters in the path of exaltation and glory. This is just as sure as that the sun rose this morning over yonder mountains. Therefore, mourn not because all your sons and daughters do not follow in the path that you have marked out to them, or give heed to your counsels. Inasmuch as we succeed in securing eternal glory, and stand as saviors, and as kings and priests to our God, we will save our posterity. ... God will have His own way in His own time, and He will accomplish His purposes in the salvation of His sons and

daughters.... God bless you, brethren and sisters. Do not be discouraged is the word I wish to pass to you; but remember that righteousness and joy in the Holy Ghost is what you and I have the privilege of possessing at all times.[47]

Conclusion

A prophet is first and foremost a witness of Christ (see Revelation 19:10). His competence as a witness is predicated on knowledge, that is, the extent to which he unveils the heavens and reveals the mind and will of the Almighty. He is then a revelator and a teacher; he reveals and teaches the principles of salvation. The message is not his own but the Father's who sent him. Yet the prophet must be a pure vessel in order that the message not be soiled. Of that which he taught, Joseph Smith said:

> This is good doctrine. It tastes good. I can taste the principles of eternal life, and so can you. They are given to me by the revelations of Jesus Christ; and I know that when I tell you these words of eternal life as they are given to me, you taste them, and I know that you believe them. You say honey is sweet, and so do I. I can also taste the spirit of eternal life. I know it is good; and when I tell you of these things which were given me by inspiration of the Holy Spirit, you are bound to receive them as sweet, and rejoice more and more.[48]

It is in those teachings that we rejoice. As we study them, and teach them, and write about them, we find ourselves rejoicing "more and more." Their taste *is* sweet. They *are* light and truth. They lift the soul and expand the mind. They carry within them, as all truth does, the evidence of their own truthfulness. Separately and collectively they testify that Joseph Smith was a prophet. Of all that the Prophet taught we can but say: It tastes good; it lifts the soul and enlightens the mind. I share my great love for the Prophet Joseph Smith. I desire to honor his name and his ministry, to be loyal to him. Through him I have come to know my Lord and Savior and to experience the sweet fruits that come only from living the gospel. It was the Lord Jesus himself who told the Prophet, "The ends of the earth shall inquire after thy name, and fools shall have thee in derision, and hell shall rage against thee; while the pure in heart, and the wise, and the noble, and the virtuous, shall seek counsel, and authority, and blessings constantly from under thy hand" (Doctrine and Covenants 122:1–2). I desire to be numbered always among those who have sought counsel, authority, and blessings from under his hand. I do not worship Joseph Smith, for my worship is reserved for God. Such is the source of salvation. But I gladly sing praise to and express undying gratitude for the preeminent prophetic witness of the one who has done more, save Jesus only, for the salvation of men and women, than any man who ever lived (see Doctrine and Covenants 135:3).

Elder Wilford Woodruff said of his beloved prophet-leader: "There is not so great a man as Joseph standing in this generation. The gentiles look upon him, and he is like a bed of gold, concealed from human view. They know not his principles, his wisdom, his virtue, his calling. His mind, like Enoch's, expands as eternity, and only God can comprehend his soul."[49]

Notes

1. *Teachings of the Prophet Joseph Smith*, comp. Joseph Fielding Smith (Salt Lake City: Deseret Book, 1976), 157.

2. Bruce R. McConkie, "This Generation Shall Have My Word through You," in *Hearken, O Ye People: Discourses on the Doctrine and Covenants* (Sandy, UT: Randall Book, 1984), 4.

3. McConkie, "This Generation Shall Have My Word," 4–5.

4. Joseph F. Smith, *Gospel Doctrine* (Salt Lake City: Deseret Book, 1939), 495.

5. Joseph Smith, *History of the Church of Jesus Christ of Latter-day Saints*, ed. B. H. Roberts, 2nd ed. rev. (Salt Lake City: Deseret Book, 1957), 5:215.

6. Smith, *History of the Church*, 5:265.

7. Smith, *History of the Church*, 5:256–59.

8. *Times and Seasons*, February 1, 1843, 82–85.

9. Smith, *History of the Church*, 5:267.

10. Smith, *History of the Church*, 5:290–91; see also 337 on the sign of the Son of Man.

11. Smith, *History of the Church*, 5:298.

12. Smith, *History of the Church*, 5:323; see also 336.

13. *The Words of Joseph Smith*, ed. Andrew F. Ehat and Lyndon W. Cook (Provo, UT: Religious Studies Center, Brigham Young University, 1980), 170; in all quotations from this source, I have modernized spelling and punctuation.

14. Smith, *History of the Church*, 5:339.

15. Smith, *History of the Church*, 5:339–45.

16. Smith, *History of the Church*, 5:401.

17. *Words of Joseph Smith*, 279.

18. Smith, *History of the Church*, 5:423–25.

19. *Words of Joseph Smith*, 211.

20. Smith, *History of the Church*, 5:498.

21. Smith, *History of the Church*, 5:517.

22. Smith, *History of the Church*, 5:498.

23. Smith, *History of the Church*, 5:499.

24. *Words of Joseph Smith*, 231.

25. Smith, *History of the Church*, 6:50–52.

26. *Words of Joseph Smith*, 256.

27. *Words of Joseph Smith*, 256.

28. See examples in Hyrum L. Andrus, *Principles of Perfection* (Salt Lake City: Bookcraft, 1970), 346–52.

29. *History of the Church*, 6:251.

30. John F. MacArthur Jr., *The Glory of Heaven: The Truth about Heaven, Angels, and Eternal Life* (Westchester, IL: Crossway Books, 1998), 135–38.

31. *The Autobiography of Parley P. Pratt*, ed. Parley P. Pratt Jr. (Salt Lake City: Deseret Book, 1976), 297–98.

32. Smith, *History of the Church*, 5:391.

33. Smith, *Teachings*, 300–301.

34. Smith, *History of the Church*, 3:380–81.

35. Smith, *History of the Church*, 5:388–89.

36. Smith, *History of the Church*, 5:555.

37. *Words of Joseph Smith*, 246.

38. Smith, *History of the Church*, 5:530.

39. *Words of Joseph Smith*, 240.

40. *Words of Joseph Smith*, 241.

41. Brigham Young, in *Journal of Discourses* (London: Latter-day Saints' Book Depot, 1854–86), 11:215.

42. Smith, *Teachings*, 149–50.

43. Orson F. Whitney, in Conference Report, April 1929, 110.

44. Boyd K. Packer, "Our Moral Environment," *Ensign*, May 1992, 66.

45. Bruce R. McConkie, funeral service for S. Dilworth Young, July 13, 1981, typescript, 5.

46. John F. MacArthur Jr., *The Gospel According to Jesus*, rev. ed. (Grand Rapids, MI: Zondervan, 1994), 183–84.

47. Lorenzo Snow, address delivered on October 6, 1893, in *Collected Discourses*, 3:364–65.

48. Smith, *Teachings*, 355.

49. Wilford Woodruff, Journal History of the Church, entry for April 9, 1837, Church History Library, Salt Lake City.

Oil on canvas. William W. Major captures details in the faces of this group of Mormon leaders: Hyrum Smith, Willard Richards, Joseph Smith, Orson Pratt, Parley Parker Pratt, Orson Hyde, Heber Chase Kimball, and Brigham Young.

RICHARD NEITZEL HOLZAPFEL

1844
The Prophet's Final Charge to the Twelve

An election year in the United States, 1844 was filled with political concerns and issues for the Saints as well as doctrinal insights, administrative challenges of a growing community in Nauvoo and Church in North America and the British Isles, and continued opposition to Joseph Smith and his prophetic mission.[1] B. H. Roberts observed, "Accusations were repeatedly being made about this time that President Smith was a fallen prophet. But when the mighty doctrines [in his final general conference address delivered on April 6, 1844] are taken into account, and the spiritual power with which he is delivering them is reckoned with, no more complete refutation of his being a fallen prophet could be made. The Prophet lived his life in *crescendo*. From

---

Richard Neitzel Holzapfel is a professor of Church history and doctrine at Brigham Young University.

small beginnings, it rose in breadth and power as he neared its close."[2]

This chapter will focus on the Prophet's last six months of life—the hectic months of January through June. It will also address the important transition of authority from his ministry to that of the Apostles, including the last charge he gave them in the spring of 1844.

Overview of Key Dates

On Friday, January 19, the Prophet gave a lecture on the Constitution of the United States and on the candidacy of those who were running for president.[3] Two days later, on Sunday, January 21, the Prophet preached to several thousand people on sealing the hearts of the fathers to the children and the hearts of the children to the fathers, providing for the first time a precise interpretation of Malachi 4, which he alluded to in September 1842.[4] "How are [the Saints] to become Saviors on Mount Zion?" the Prophet asked rhetorically and then answered his own question: "By building their temples, erecting their baptismal fonts, and going forth and receiving all the ordinances, baptisms, confirmations, washings, anointings, ordinations, and sealing powers upon our heads in behalf of all our progenitors who are dead and redeem them; that they may come forth in the first resurrection and be exalted to thrones of glory with us. Herein is the chain that binds the hearts of the fathers to the children and the children to the fathers, which fulfills the mission of Elijah."[5] Since the very first appearance of the angel Moroni in Palmyra in 1823, the Lord had been preparing Joseph for one of the culminating events of his ministry: the institution of the ordinances that would seal families together for eternity (see Doctrine and Covenants 2). Many of the scriptures cited by Moroni in 1823 pertain to the "family kingdom" of the patriarchal priesthood (see Joseph Smith—History 1:36–39).

At first the Restoration focused on the salvation and eternal life of individuals. The Book of Mormon, published in March 1830, outlined the fulness of the gospel—that by believing in Christ, repenting of one's sins, accepting baptism by one who has authority, receiving the gift of the Holy Ghost, and enduring to the end, individuals could be saved in Christ's kingdom and obtain eternal life (see 2 Nephi 31; 3 Nephi 27:19–20). But as the Restoration unfolded, the passages cited by the angel Moroni came into focus. It became apparent that God intended rewards in addition to salvation and eternal life. For example, in the Sermon on the Mount, Jesus said, "Great is your reward *in heaven*" (Matthew 5:12; emphasis added). Heaven is not the ultimate reward, but a further reward is promised after one is in heaven[6]—something in addition to salvation or eternal life. The Lord indicated that the reward was exaltation and eternal lives. The first of four exaltation revelations (Doctrine and Covenants 76; 84; 88; 93) was received in February 1832.[7] It was clear that salvation had two meanings: first, to come forth in the Resurrection in any kingdom of glory; and second, in the fullest sense, to enter into the glory of the celestial kingdom, or obtain eternal life. Eternal life is available to individuals, but exaltation and eternal lives are available only to families (see Doctrine and Covenants 131:1–2). Sealing families together—bringing them together in the temple—was the ultimate purpose of the Restoration and the focus of the Prophet's last years. Only at the end of his ministry did the passages cited by the angel Moroni become meaningful.

That same month, the Prophet was nominated by local Nauvoo citizens as a candidate for president of the United States.[8] It is impossible to know whether Joseph Smith actually believed that he could win the election or whether he ran as a protest against the leading candidates, who were unwilling to intervene in state affairs even when minorities were persecuted, as had been the case in Missouri in 1838 for Latter-day Saints.[9] His candidacy also gave the missionaries additional opportunities to talk about the Church and to publicize the injustices Church members had experienced in Missouri. It is not unusual for people in city, county, state, or even national elections to vote out of principle for a candidate who could not conceivably win, feeling they could not in good conscience support the other candidates. Joseph Smith probably felt he could not support the major political candidates, James K. Polk and Henry Clay, after attempting to ascertain what they would do for minority faiths, including the Latter-day Saints. The Prophet certainly was concerned for the Latter-day Saints' welfare, but he also was concerned about other persecuted minorities in America.[10] About six months earlier, Joseph noted:

> Why is it this babbler gains so many followers and retains them? Because I possess the principle of love. All I can offer the world is a good heart and a good hand.
>
> Mormons can testify whether I am willing to lay down my life for a Mormon. If it has been demonstrated that I have been willing to die for a Mormon, I am bold to declare before heaven that I am just as ready to die for a Presbyterian, a Baptist, or any other denomination.
>
> It is a love of liberty which inspires my soul. Civil and religious liberty were diffused into my soul by my grandfathers while they dandled me on their knees. And shall I want [for] friends? No![11]

Another possible reason for the Prophet's presidential run was that he intended to become an important political power broker for the region to protect his people through political influence.

For whatever reason, Joseph Smith's announcement raised some questions about the separation of church and state. Ironically in the American tradition, pastors, ministers, and rabbis have run for city, county, state, and national offices. Nevertheless, many people in Hancock County were concerned about Joseph Smith's increasing influence.[12]

On Sunday, February 4, Joseph related to temple architect William Weeks the vision he had received concerning the appearance and design of the Nauvoo Temple.[13] He spent the following day with Weeks trying to make the temple plans fit that pattern. When God commanded Moses to build the tabernacle, the first permanent temple-type structure mentioned in the Old Testament, the book of Exodus says, "And the Lord spake unto Moses, saying, . . . let them make me a sanctuary; that I may dwell among them. According to all that I shew thee, *after* the pattern of the tabernacle, and the pattern of all the instruments thereof, even so shall ye make it" (Exodus 25:1, 5–9, 27; emphasis added). The Nauvoo Temple, like the earlier Kirtland Temple, was planned as a multiuse building. The ground floor was dedicated to be a general assembly room (analogous to a modern chapel or a stake center). The second floor was reserved for education and training (analogous to BYU campuses, seminary and institute buildings, or one of the MTC complexes). The attic story was organized for performing temple ordinances (like temples today), and an administrative office (like the Church Administration Office in Salt Lake City).

However, unlike the Kirtland Temple, the Nauvoo Temple had a full basement that accommodated a baptismal font on the backs of twelve oxen (see 1 Kings 7:25). The font was used for baptisms, including baptisms for the dead.[14] Locating the font in the basement may have been symbolic of the grave. The exterior displayed additional symbolic features: a weather vane with the figure of the angel Moroni dressed in priestly sacral clothing with a cap and flowing robe and a square and a compass, as well as star stones, moon stones, and sun stones.[15]

Josiah Quincy

On Monday, February 12, Joseph Smith signed a document titled "A Memorial to Congress," which outlined the Latter-day Saints' sufferings in Missouri, and dispatched Elder Orson Pratt to present it before government officials in Washington DC.[16]

Beginning in early March 1844, Joseph Smith organized the kingdom of God, with a leadership composed of over fifty men and described as the Council of the Kingdom or the Council of Fifty. This body represented the legislative body of the government of God on earth.[17]

On Sunday, April 7, the Prophet delivered his last general conference address in the east grove, often called the King Follett discourse.[18] The death of King Follett on March 9, 1844, nearly a month earlier, influenced its subject matter—the eternity of man. "I want you to know the first principle of this law," the Prophet stated, "how consoling to the mourner when they part with a friend to know that though they lay down this body, it will rise and dwell . . . to be an heir of God and joint heir with Jesus Christ, enjoying the same rise, exaltation, and glory, until you arrive at the station of a God."[19] This discourse may be correctly identified as an official eulogy.[20]

Charles Francis Adams

On Wednesday, May 15, Josiah Quincy (future mayor of Boston), Charles Francis Adams (son of U.S. president John Quincy Adams and grandson of U.S. president John Adams), and Dr. William G. Goforth (campaign organizer for U.S. presidential candidate Henry Clay) visited Joseph Smith, providing an interesting outsider view of the Latter-day Saints and their Prophet.[21] Years later, Quincy suggested that "it is by no means improbable that some future textbook, for the use of generations yet unborn, will contain a question something like this: What historical American of the nineteenth century has exerted the most powerful influence upon the destinies of his countrymen? And it is by no means impossible that the answer to the interrogatory may thus be written: *Joseph Smith the Mormon prophet.*"[22]

On Friday, May 17, the Reform Party, a third-party ticket, officially nominated Joseph Smith as their presidential candidate at a state convention in Illinois.[23]

Opposition within the Church grew—from both former associates of the Prophet, such as William Law, and some lay members who wanted to return to the theologically conservative New York period (which emphasized salvation and eternal life) and the limited ecclesiastical administrative Kirtland era, rejecting the doctrinal revelations implemented at Nauvoo. On Friday, June 7, some of these dissident members published the first and only issue of the *Nauvoo Expositor* in an attempt to embarrass Church leaders and kindle animosity among non-Mormons in the region.[24] On Monday, June 10, the city council declared the *Nauvoo Expositor* a public nuisance because they thought it might incite additional acts of violence against the Saints.[25] According to one scholar, the city council legally decided to destroy the press on which the newspaper was printed, recalling "a legal basis for this action in the Illinois law of 1844.... The guarantee of freedom of the press in the United States Constitution was not declared applicable to the actions of city and state governments until 1931, and then only by a five-to-four Court's reliance on a constitutional amendment adopted in 1868."[26] Nevertheless, this act sparked opposition to the point that the mayor of Nauvoo (Joseph Smith) and the city council were arrested. This began a series of legal maneuvers that placed Joseph Smith in custody in Carthage without protection.[27]

Before he surrendered himself, Joseph gave a sermon on June 16 in the grove east of the temple regarding the Godhead.[28] Each member of the Godhead is "a different or separate person," the Prophet taught. "Separate persons, but they all agree in one or the self same thing."[29] The sermon was an important doctrinal statement and summary of his teachings of the Nauvoo period.

On Saturday, June 22, John and Patrick Calhoun, sons of U.S. presidential candidate John C. Calhoun, visited Joseph Smith in Nauvoo. According to Calhoun, Joseph "gave us a full exposition of his faith, frequently calling himself the Prophet, in the course of conversation." That same day, Illinois governor Thomas Ford ordered Joseph and other Church leaders to appear in Carthage, the county seat, to "submit yourself to be arrested."³⁰

The conspiracy to place Joseph Smith in custody in Carthage culminated in the murder of the Prophet and the Patriarch on Thursday, June 27.³¹ On Friday, June 28, their bodies were returned to the mourning citizens of Nauvoo, and on the following day, Joseph and Hyrum were secretly buried in Nauvoo.³²

The Kingdom of God Established

As part of the restoration of the fulness of times, the Prophet established the kingdom of God on earth in preparation for Christ's millennial reign. As noted, this effort antagonized some of the Prophet's enemies. Richard Bushman and Dean Jessee observed:

> To add to his unpopularity, in the final six months of his life Joseph Smith set out on a course of political action that outraged his critics. In January 1844, he announced his candidacy for president of the United States and a few months later organized a shadow government called the Kingdom of God, which may have been envisioned as a prototype of Christ's millennial government of the earth. Whether or not he believed he could win the presidency, he spoke optimistically, as candidates do in the beginning of a campaign. Certainly his patience with government had run out. The Mormons had been abused many times with no compensation for confiscated property from any level of government, and in 1844 they felt the tide of hatred rising again. Smith could not understand why the Constitution did not compel the government to protect the rights of Mormons. His platform defended all downtrodden people of his time:

slaves, whom he felt should be purchased from their masters with revenues from public lands; prisoners held under cruel and unsanitary conditions; court-martialed soldiers; and sailors, whose suffering at the hands of tyrannical ship captains was attracting the sympathy of reformers. To all, he promised justice.[33]

The Prophet believed that the kingdom of God grew out of The Church of Jesus Christ of Latter-day Saints and was a distinct organization. The Church of Jesus Christ, the ecclesiastical organization, provided the message of salvation, while the kingdom of God, the political or family kingdom—what Bushman and Jessee termed "a shadow government"—will rule during the Millennium when "the kingdoms of this world are become the kingdoms of our Lord, and of his Christ; and he shall reign for ever and ever" (Revelation 11:15).[34] Although the terms are often used synonymously today, it is important to understand their use in the 1840s to appreciate the Prophet's teachings on the subject. For Joseph Smith, the Church and the kingdom were linked together through temple covenants and ordinances. The Lord, through the Prophet, established the Church and the kingdom as part of the restoration of all things.

Joseph Smith believed that the establishment of the kingdom of God was part of the fulfillment of Daniel's prophecy: "And in the days of these kings shall the God of heaven set up a kingdom, which shall never be destroyed: and the kingdom shall not be left to other people, but it shall break in pieces and consume all these kingdoms, and it shall stand for ever. Forasmuch as thou sawest that the stone was cut out of the mountain without hands, and that it brake in pieces the iron, the brass, the clay, the silver, and the gold; the great God hath made known to the king what shall come to pass hereafter: and the dream is certain, and the interpretation thereof sure" (Daniel 2:44–45).

It is important to note that Daniel saw that the stone was cut out of the mountain without hands. This Old Testament metaphor is symbolic of God's activity, meaning without "human hands." The Lord began his work in 1842 when he revealed the name of the kingdom: "Verily thus saith the Lord, this is the name by which you shall be called, the Kingdom of God and his Laws, with the Keys and power thereof, and judgment in the hands of his servants, Ahman Christ."[35] The Church had received its full and complete name in April 1838 (see Doctrine and Covenants 115:4), and in April 1842 the Lord also revealed the name of God's kingdom.

Soon after receiving this revelation, the Prophet wrote an editorial, "The Government of God," in the *Times and Seasons* in July 1842.[36] Joseph Smith declared that the governments of men "have failed in all their attempts to promote eternal power, peace and happiness. . . . [Even] our nation, which possesses greater resources than any other, is rent, from center to circumference, with party strife, political intrigues, and sectional interest."[37] Joseph Smith knew that the Lord had a hand in founding the government of the United States and that he raised up wise men to prepare the Constitution (see Doctrine and Covenants 101:80). But even this government had failed to provide the protection and prosperity that God intended for human happiness in the promised land, especially among the large American slave population, native peoples, and religious minorities.

Speaking of ancient Israel, Joseph Smith taught that "their government was a theocracy."[38] The Prophet added, "They had God to make their laws, and men chosen by Him to administer them. . . . [They were led] in both civil and ecclesiastical affairs.

... So will it be when the purposes of God shall be accomplished: when 'the Lord shall be King over the whole earth' and 'Jerusalem His throne.' 'The law shall go forth from Zion, and the word of the Lord from Jerusalem.'"[39] The Prophet understood that part of his mission was to prepare the earth for that kingdom—to prepare the Church for the coming of Christ.

A Kingdom of Priests

Even though the Lord had revealed the name and purpose of the kingdom of God in 1842, the Council of the Kingdom was not officially organized until 1844. During the interval between the 1842 revelation and the organization in 1844, Joseph Smith knew that the kingdom could only be established after God's people had become a "kingdom of priests," as outlined in the book of Exodus: "Thus shalt thou say to the house of Jacob, and tell the children of Israel; Ye have seen what I did unto the Egyptians, and how I bare you on eagles' wings, and brought you unto myself. Now therefore, if ye will obey my voice indeed, and keep my covenant, then ye shall be a peculiar treasure unto me above all people: for all the earth is mine: And ye shall be unto me a *kingdom of priests*, and an holy nation" (Exodus 19:3–6; emphasis added). The Lord intended to gather modern Israel, as he did anciently, to prepare them to be a special treasure, a kingdom of priests, and a holy nation.

The Fulness of the Priesthood

The Prophet learned in a revelation given to the Church in January 1841 that the Nauvoo Temple was to be built so the fulness of the priesthood could be restored, "For there is not a place found on earth that he may come to and restore again that which was lost unto you, or which he hath taken away, even the *fulness of the priesthood*" (Doctrine and Covenants 124:28; emphasis added). Later the Prophet observed, "Those holding the fulness of the Melchizedek Priesthood are kings and priests of the Most High God, holding the keys of power and blessings. In fact, that Priesthood is a perfect law of theocracy, and stands as God to give laws to the people, administering endless lives to the sons and daughters of Adam."[40]

The endowment, as revealed in Nauvoo, prepared the Saints to become "kings and priests" and "queens and priestesses." Later, on September 28, 1843, Joseph and Emma received the fulness of the priesthood. Joseph Smith's journal entry for the day noted that he was "anointed and ordained to the highest and holiest order of the priesthood (and companion)."[41] Soon thereafter others also received the fulness of the priesthood. Once the fulness of the priesthood was restored, Joseph Smith was inspired to establish the Council of the Kingdom.[42]

The Prophet lived in a democracy and, like the Protestants, had a vision of a church of equals; however, he restored an administrative hierarchy of priesthood leaders consisting of a First Presidency, Quorum of the Twelve Apostles, and so forth. But often overlooked is the fact that he expanded and democratized the priesthood base by making the fulness of the priesthood available to all. In Nauvoo, both men and women received the ordinances associated with temple worship, including the fulness of the priesthood. The Prophet told the sisters of the Relief Society that every member of the Church who was worthy would be given the same priesthood blessings when a place was prepared for that purpose. No revelation or blessing was given to Joseph that the Lord would not give to all Saints when they were ready to receive it.[43]

Reigning with Christ

The restoration of temple worship and the establishment of the kingdom of God was part of the fulfillment of other visions that pointed to the last dispensation. For example, in Revelation 1, John notes: "Grace be unto you, and peace, from him which is, and which was, and which is to come; and from the seven Spirits which are before his throne; and from Jesus Christ, who is the faithful witness, and the first begotten of the dead, and the prince of the kings of the earth. Unto him that loved us, and washed us from our sins in his own blood, and hath made us *kings and priests* unto God and his Father" (Revelation 1:4–6; emphasis added).

John specifically notes that Jesus "hath made us kings and priests unto God." That the Saints would be "kings and priests" enthroned in power under Christ is also emphasized in Revelation 3: "Behold, I stand at the door, and knock: if any man hear my voice, and open the door, I will come in to him, and will sup with him, and he with me. To him that overcometh will *I grant to sit with me in my throne*, even as I also overcame, and am set down with my Father in his throne" (vv. 20–21; emphasis added).

John, like Isaiah and Joseph Smith, saw into the heavens and into the temple made without hands—the throne room in the celestial temple in heaven:

> And I beheld, and, lo, in the midst of the throne and of the four beasts, and in the midst of the elders, stood a Lamb as it had been slain, having seven horns and seven eyes, which are the seven Spirits of God sent forth into all the earth.
>
> And he came and took the book out of the right hand of him that sat upon the throne.

> And when he had taken the book, the four beasts and four and twenty elders fell down before the Lamb, having every one of them harps, and golden vials full of odours, which are the prayers of saints.
>
> And they sung a new song, saying, Thou art worthy to take the book, and to open the seals thereof: for thou wast slain, and hast redeemed us to God by thy blood out of every kindred, and tongue, and people, and nation;
>
> *And hast made us unto our God kings and priests: and we shall reign on the earth.* (Revelation 5:6–10, emphasis added)

These passages from Revelation provide an important context for Joseph Smith's teachings in April and June of 1844.[44]

John saw twelve thousand exalted high priests from each tribe (see Revelation 7:4; Doctrine and Covenants 77:11), saying, "After this I beheld, and, lo, a great multitude, which no man could number, of all nations, and kindreds, and people, and tongues, stood before the throne, and before the Lamb, clothed with white robes, and palms in their hands" (Revelation 7:9).

Old and New Testament symbols of temple worship included the colors white, red, and royal blue or purple (see Exodus 25:4–5). Latter-day Saints, like other Christians, interpret the white of the ancient temple to represent the sinless life of the Messiah, the purity of his sacrifice; the red represents blood sacrifice, his Atonement; and the royal blue or purple represents Jesus' kingship. But in John's heavenly vision, the temple colors change from white, red, and blue to white and green.

When the Maccabees entered Jerusalem to liberate the city from the Greeks in 164 BC, the people waved green palm fronds as a symbol of the Jewish victory against their enemies.[45] This action became a symbol of the Davidic Messiah's return in power and glory. When Jesus entered Jerusalem in his triumphal entry, John tells us that palm branches were brought up and waved there also (see John 12:13). Ultimately, the palm fronds in Revelation symbolize Jesus' victory over the demonic forces in the cosmos.

The vision in the book of Revelation continues:

> And [they] cried with a loud voice, saying, Salvation to our God which sitteth upon the throne, and unto the Lamb.
>
> And all the angels stood round about the throne, and about the elders and the four beasts, and fell before the throne on their faces, and worshipped God,
>
> Saying, Amen: Blessing, and glory, and wisdom, and thanksgiving, and honour, and power, and might, be unto our God for ever and ever. Amen.
>
> And one of the elders answered, saying unto me, What are these which are arrayed in white robes? and whence came they?
>
> And I said unto him, Sir, thou knowest. And he said to me, These are they which came out of great tribulation, and have washed their robes, and made them white in the blood of the Lamb. (Revelation 7:10–14)

John then reveals the state of those who endure:

> Therefore are they before the throne of God, and serve him day and night in his temple: and he that sitteth on the throne shall dwell among them.
>
> They shall hunger no more, neither thirst any more; neither shall the sun light on them, nor any heat.
>
> For the Lamb which is in the midst of the throne shall feed them, and shall lead them unto living fountains of waters: and God shall wipe away all tears from their eyes. (Revelation 7:15–17)

The Council of the Kingdom

With the fulness of the priesthood restored, the stage was set for an important meeting on April 18, 1844, when Joseph Smith organized the Council of the Kingdom.[46] After attempts to prepare a constitution for this body failed, the Prophet asked and the Lord responded: "Ye are my Constitution and I am your God and ye are my spokesmen, therefore from henceforth keep my commandments."[47] In other words, the kingdom of God would not have a written constitution but would instead have a "living constitution," made up of those who had been called to preside. President John Taylor said: "These words are pregnant with meaning and full of intelligence and point out our position in regard of these matters—it is expected of us that [we] can act right—that our interests [are] bound up in the K[ingdom] of God. That we should consider we are not acting for ourselves, but we are the Spokesmen of God selected for that purpose in the interest of God and to bless and exalt all humanity. We acknowledge him as our God and all men who enter this body must acknowledge him here. There is peculiar significance to these things which needs some consideration."[48] Elder Orson Pratt added, "In the Church we take the Law of God and his Priesthood as the Constitution of his Church—here in this Council we have a living constitution not a written one—which we must conform to."[49] However, rules governing this body were eventually recorded.

One of the rules of the kingdom was that "to pass, a motion must be unanimous in the affirmative. Voting is done after the ancient order: each person voting in turn from the oldest to the youngest member of the Council, commencing with the standing chairman. If any member has any objections he is under covenant to fully and freely make them known to the Council. But if he cannot be convinced of the rightness of the course pursued by the Council he must either yield or withdraw membership in the Council."[50]

The reason Joseph Smith waited until April 1844 to establish this council was that the kingdom of God could not be organized until there were men and women who had received the fulness of priesthood. Just as the high priesthood had to be restored before the First Presidency could be organized, the apostleship had to be restored before the Quorum of the Twelve was organized. So likewise, the fulness of the temple ordinances had to be restored before the kingdom of God could be organized.

When Christ comes, as the book of Revelation outlines, the kingdom of God will already be on the earth, prepared for Christ's millennial reign. The Lord revealed through Joseph Smith the kingdom's name, constitution, and governing rules. More importantly, he restored the ordinances necessary to prepare a people to receive the fulness of the priesthood. When the millennial day comes, the banner of heaven, or the flag of the kingdom of God, will be raised. Such sentiments are expressed nicely in Joel H. Johnson's oft-sung hymn:

> High on the mountain top
> A banner is unfurled.
> Ye nations, now look up;
> It waves to all the world.[51]

Christ will then reign as King of Kings and Lord of Lords and establish peace, prosperity, and justice for a thousand years (see Revelation 19:11–16).

Succession in Church Leadership

Joseph Smith took one final decisive step in his prophetic mission as he prepared the Church for his departure. The Prophet did not want to die without establishing proper succession of authority. He had already faced some difficult situations when early Church leaders like David Whitmer, Oliver Cowdery, and Martin Harris fell away. There must have been a concern in Joseph's mind that the people he had relied on at the beginning of his ministry, who had experienced many marvelous visions and revelations with him, did not remain in full fellowship. Sources suggest that Joseph contemplated various succession models during his ministry. Early on, Oliver Cowdery, the second elder of the Church, could have succeeded Joseph Smith. Another possible successor, as articulated in Doctrine and Covenants section 124, was Hyrum Smith, but Hyrum died in Carthage just minutes before the Prophet.

Another succession model was established in the spring of 1844 and focused on the Quorum of the Twelve Apostles. Brigham Young, Willard Richards, John Taylor, Wilford Woodruff, and others had already received the keys of the kingdom, and Young had become the President of the Twelve.[52] These men had been tested by the Lord and had remained faithful to the Church and to the prophetic mission of Joseph Smith.

The principal test in Nauvoo had been plural marriage. It tried the hearts and souls of both men and women in the Church. By 1844, some leaders, including William Law of the First Presidency, had failed the test and had become enemies to the Prophet and his work. They believed that Joseph had been called of God but that he was now a fallen prophet. With good humor Joseph said, "I had rather be a fallen true prophet, than a false prophet."[53] However, Joseph testified that "he was not a fallen prophet, and never in any nearer relationship to God than at the present time."[54]

In those early months of 1844, the dissident movement of former Church members grew. The numbers are difficult to determine, but maybe as many as three to five hundred people may have attached themselves to a reformed church, led by William Law as president (but not as prophet).[55] Law set up an organization that resembled the 1830s Kirtland-period Church, simply setting aside the Nauvoo period ordinances, practices, revelations, and teachings.

However, most Saints in Nauvoo, including the Twelve, remained faithful and testified that Joseph was still a prophet. William Clayton, a convert from England, noted after hearing the Prophet preach in Nauvoo, "It seems like heaven began on earth."[56] To him, the doctrinal revelations of Nauvoo were not only prophetic but exhilarating.

The Final Charge to the Apostles

An important meeting occurred in the spring of 1844 when Joseph gathered the Apostles to receive their last charge from the Prophet.[57] Years later, President Wilford Woodruff recalled:

> I, Wilford Woodruff, being the last man living in the flesh who was present upon that occasion feel it a duty I owe to the Church of Jesus Christ of Latter-day Saints, to the House of Israel, and to the whole world to bear this my last testimony to all nations, that in the winter of 1843–4, Joseph Smith, the Prophet of God, called the Twelve Apostles together in the City of Nauvoo, and spent many days with us in giving us our endowments, and teaching us those glorious principles which God had revealed to him. And upon one occasion he stood upon his feet in our midst for nearly three hours declaring unto us the great and last dispensation which God

THE PROPHET'S FINAL CHARGE TO THE TWELVE

had set His hand to perform upon the earth in these last days. The room was filled as if with consuming fire; the Prophet was clothed upon with much of the power of God, and his face shone and was transparently clear, and he closed that speech, never-to-be-forgotten in time or in eternity, with the following language:

"Brethren, I have had great sorrow of heart for fear that I might be taken from the earth with the keys of the Kingdom of God upon me, without sealing them upon the heads of other men. God has sealed upon my head all the keys of the Kingdom of God necessary for organizing and building up of the Church, Zion, and Kingdom of God upon the earth, and to prepare the Saints for the coming of the Son of Man. Now, brethren, I thank God I have lived to see the day that I have been enabled to give you your endowments, and I have now sealed upon your heads all the powers of the Aaronic and Melchizedek Priesthoods and Apostleship, with all the keys and powers thereof, which God has sealed upon me; and I now roll off all the labor, burden and care of this Church and Kingdom of God upon your shoulders, and I now command you in the name of the Lord Jesus Christ to round up your shoulders, and bear off this Church and Kingdom of God before heaven and earth, and before God, angels and men; and if you don't do it you will be damned."

And the same spirit that filled the room at that time burns in my bosom while I record this testimony, and the Prophet of God appointed no one else but the Twelve Apostles to stand at the head of the Church and direct its affairs.[58]

The Testimony of the Twelve

There is another important source about this monumental gathering that may be the earliest written document describing the meeting. Although it is unknown exactly when it was composed, it could have been written as early as September 1844. Speaking of the meeting, the Twelve recalled, "Joseph Smith seemed somewhat depressed in Spirit, and took the liberty to open his heart to us concerning his presentiments of the future." The document then records what the Prophet said on that occasion. Joseph told the Twelve, "The Lord bids me hasten the work in which we are engaged." The Prophet did not want the "keys and powers" to "be lost from the earth" so he placed them on the heads of the Twelve: "Upon the shoulders of the Twelve must the responsibility of leading this church henceforth rest until you shall appoint others to succeed you. Your enemies cannot kill you all at once and should any of you be killed you can lay your hands upon others and fill up the quorum. Thus can this power and these keys be perpetuated in the earth."[59]

Witnesses of Christ

On a cold winter day in December of 1805, Joseph Smith breathed his first breath. In 1844 on a hot and humid Thursday afternoon in Carthage, Illinois, the Prophet's heart stopped beating. His enemies killed him, but they could not slay his testimony. They took his life, but they could not steal his witness. Joseph had been a dutiful son, a loving father, a kind neighbor, a visionary community leader, and a prophet of God.

Prophets from the beginning of time have had specific responsibilities. Noah built an ark, Moses led the children of Israel out of bondage, Joshua led the Israelites into the promised land, Lehi and Jeremiah warned the inhabitants of Jerusalem about the impending exile, and Peter and Paul took the gospel to the people of the Mediterranean Basin. No matter the specific assignment they have had, all prophets have stood as witnesses of the Lord. The Prophet Joseph Smith was no different. He received numerous assignments from the Lord, but his greatest and most important work as a prophet was to be a modern witness of Jesus Christ. In 1820 he saw Jesus, who said to him: "Joseph, my son, thy sins are forgiven thee. Go thy way, walk in my statutes and keep my commandments. Behold I am the Lord of glory. I was crucified for the world that all those who believe on my name may have eternal life."[60] The Prophet saw the Lord again in Hiram, Ohio, standing on the right hand of God in 1832, and he heard the voice bear witness that "by him, and through him, and of him, the worlds are and were created, and the inhabitants thereof are begotten sons and daughters unto God" (Doctrine and Covenants 76:24).

Joseph also saw Jesus Christ in the Kirtland Temple in April of 1836. He described the Lord as "standing upon the breastwork of the pulpit, . . . and his voice was as the sound of the rushing of great waters, even the voice of Jehovah, saying: I am the first and the last; I am he who liveth, I am he who was slain; I am your advocate with the Father" (Doctrine and Covenants 110:2–4).

The Prophet's witness of the Savior was twofold. First, he was called to testify of Jesus as Savior and Redeemer. He did this primarily through the establishment of the Church of Jesus Christ and the bringing forth of the Book of Mormon, which teach that individual salvation and eternal life come only through Christ the Savior. Joseph's witness of the Savior as Redeemer culminated in the restoration of the principles and ordinances of Christ's gospel, which allow us to enter into the celestial kingdom of God; this is the fulness of the gospel of Jesus Christ. Second, the Prophet was called to testify of Jesus as the author and finisher of our faith. He did this primarily through the revelations he received beginning in 1832 regarding exaltation and eternal lives. This witness saw its culmination in the Nauvoo Temple, where the Saints received the ordinances of the Church of the Firstborn, allowing them to come up into the presence of Elohim. All of the blessings and promises that the Prophet Joseph Smith announced to the inhabitants of the earth in this dispensation come by and through Jesus Christ, God's own Son and were aimed at establishing "a society filled with love and peace."[61] Certainly it is all good news. Without Jesus Christ, we have nothing. The Prophet Joseph Smith said just a few days before he was martyred, "The Savior has the words of Eternal life; nothing else can profit us."[62] As we listen to Joseph Smith's witness of Jesus Christ, we appreciate that "Jesus anointed that Prophet and Seer."[63]

Notes

1. For a biographical treatment of this period, see Richard Lyman Bushman, *Joseph Smith: Rough Stone Rolling* (New York: Alfred A. Knopf, 2005), 526–50.

2. B. H. Roberts, "The King Follett Discourse: The Being and Kind of Being God Is; the Immortality of the Intelligence of Man," *Liahona, the Elders' Journal*, December 5, 1911, 376–77.

3. Joseph Smith, *History of the Church of Jesus Christ of Latter-day Saints*, ed. B. H. Roberts, 2nd ed. rev. (Salt Lake City: Deseret Book, 1980), 6:180.

4. Smith, *History of the Church*, 6:183–85; see Doctrine and Covenants 128:18.

5. *The Words of Joseph Smith: The Contemporary Accounts of the Nauvoo Discourses of the Prophet Joseph*, ed. Andrew F. Ehat and

Lyndon W. Cook (Provo, UT: Religious Studies Center, Brigham Young University, 1980), 318; spelling, punctuation, and grammar standardized.

6. See Ben Witherington II, *Smyth and Helwys Bible Commentary* (Macon, GA: Smyth and Helwys, 2006).

7. See Bushman, *Rough Stone Rolling*, 195–214.

8. Smith, *History of the Church*, 6:187–88.

9. For an example of this opinion—that Joseph Smith was dissatisfied with other candidates but did not necessarily believe he could win the election—see B. H. Roberts, *Comprehensive History of the Church of Jesus Christ of Latter-day Saints* (Salt Lake City: Deseret News, 1930), 2:209. For a brief discussion of various interpretations, see Richard D. Poll, "Joseph Smith and the Presidency, 1844," *Dialogue: A Journal of Mormon Thought* 3, no. 3 (Autumn 1968): 17–21; and James B. Allen, "I Have a Question," *Ensign*, September 1973, 21–22. For book-length treatments on his presidential campaign, see Robert S. Wicks and Fred R. Foister, *Junius and Joseph: Presidential Politics and the Assassination of the First Mormon Prophet* (Logan: Utah State University Press); Arnold K. Garr, *Setting the Record Straight: Joseph Smith: Presidential Candidate* (Orem, UT: Millennial Press, 2007); and Newell G. Bringhurst and Craig L. Foster, *The Mormon Quest for the Presidency* (Independence, MO: John Whitmer Books, 2008), 7–49.

10. Smith, *History of the Church*, 6:478.

11. *Words of Joseph Smith*, 229; spelling, punctuation, grammar, and paragraphing modernized.

12. See Wicks and Foister, *Junius and Joseph*.

13. Smith, *History of the Church*, 6:196–97. For more information on the history of the Nauvoo temple, see Matthew S. McBride, *A House for the Most High: The Story of the Original Nauvoo Temple* (Salt Lake City: Greg Kofford Books, 2007); and Don F. Colvin, *Nauvoo Temple:*

A Story of Faith (Provo, UT: Religious Studies Center, Brigham Young University, 2002).

14. See D. Michael Quinn, "The Practice of Rebaptism at Nauvoo," *BYU Studies* 18, no. 2 (Winter 1978): 226–32.

15. See Glen M. Leonard, *Nauvoo: A Place of Peace, a People of Promise* (Salt Lake City: Deseret Book, 2002), 242–65.

16. Smith, *History of the Church*, 6:212.

17. On the Council of Fifty, see D. Michael Quinn, "The Council of Fifty and Its Members, 1844–1945," *Brigham Young University Studies* 20, no. 3 (Winter 1980): 163–97; and Andrew F. Ehat, "It Seems Like Heaven Began on Earth: Joseph Smith and the Constitution of the Kingdom of God," *BYU Studies* 20, no. 3 (Winter 1980): 253–79.

18. See Bushman, *Rough Stone Rolling*, 533–37; LaMar C. Berrett and others, eds., *Sacred Places*, vol. 2: *Ohio and Illinois* (Salt Lake City: Deseret Book, 2002), 174–76.

19. *Words of Joseph Smith*, 345; spelling, punctuation, and grammar modernized.

20. Longhand notes of the King Follett sermon were recorded contemporaneously by four scribes; their notes were then amalgamated and edited into a coherent text on at least three different occasions. For transcriptions of the original notes, see *Words of Joseph Smith*, 340–62. The first amalgamation, done by Thomas Bullock, was published in *Times and Seasons*, August 15, 1844, 612–17; a new amalgamation by Jonathan Grimshaw was published in *Deseret News*, July 8, 1857; this became the standard text that was eventually published in *History of the Church*, 6:302–17, and Joseph Fielding Smith, comp., *Teachings of the Prophet Joseph Smith* (Salt Lake City: Deseret Book, 1976), 342–62. For a more recent amalgamation, see Stan Larson, "The King Follett Discourse: A Newly Amalgamated Text," *BYU Studies* 18, no. 2 (Winter 1978): 193–208. For a parallel-column comparison of notes and two of the amalgamations, see Larry E. Dahl and Donald Q. Cannon, *The Prophet Joseph Smith's*

King Follett Discourse: A Six-Column Comparison of Original Notes and Amalgamations with Introduction and Commentary (Provo, UT: Religious Studies Center, Brigham Young University, 1983); see also Van Hale, "The King Follett Discourse: Textual History and Criticism," *Sunstone* 41 (September–October 1983): 5–12.

21. Josiah Quincy, *Figures of the Past from the Leaves of Old Journals* (Boston: Roberts Brothers, 1883), 376–400.

22. Quincy, *Figures of the Past*, 382.

23. For the minutes of the convention, see Smith, *History of the Church*, 6:386–97; Berrett and others, *Sacred Places: Ohio and Illinois*, 141–43.

24. Smith, *History of the Church*, 6:430; see also Berrett and others, *Sacred Places: Ohio and Illinois*, 185–86.

25. Smith, *History of the Church*, 6:432–48.

26. Dallin H. Oaks, "Joseph Smith in a Personal World," in *The Worlds of Joseph Smith: A Bicentennial Conference at the Library of Congress*, ed. John W. Welch (Provo, UT: Brigham Young University Press, 2006), 160–61; and Dallin H. Oaks, "The Suppression of the *Nauvoo Expositor*," *Utah Law Review* 9 (1965): 862–903.

27. For more on the legal details of the Prophet's martyrdom and the subsequent trials of his murderers, see Dallin H. Oaks and Marvin S. Hill, *Carthage Conspiracy: The Trial of the Accused Assassins of Joseph Smith* (Chicago: University of Illinois Press, 1975).

28. *Words of Joseph Smith*, 378–82; see also Berrett and others, *Sacred Places: Ohio and Illinois*, 174–76.

29. *Words of Joseph Smith*, 382.

30. Brian Q. Cannon, "John C. Calhoun, Jr., Meets the Prophet Joseph Smith Shortly before the Departure for Carthage," *BYU Studies* 33, no. 4 (1993): 773–80.

31. *Times and Seasons*, July 15, 1844, 586; and *Times and Seasons*, August 1, 1844, 599.

32. Smith, *History of the Church,* 6:627–29; see also Berrett and others, *Sacred Places: Ohio and Illinois,* 139–40.

33. See Richard Lyman Bushman and Dean C. Jessee, "Joseph Smith and His Papers," in Dean C. Jessee, Mark Ashurst-McGee, and Richard C. Jensen, eds., *Journals, Volume 1: 1832–1839,* vol. 1 of the Journals series of *The Joseph Smith Papers,* ed. Dean C. Jessee, Ronald K. Esplin, and Richard Lyman Bushman (Salt Lake City: Church Historian's Press, 2008), xxxi.

34. Bushman and Jessee, "Joseph Smith and His Papers," xxxi; see also Quinn, "The Council of Fifty and Its Members," and Ehat, "'It Seems Like Heaven Began on Earth.'"

35. William Clayton, cited in Ehat, "'It Seems Like Heaven Began on Earth,'" 268.

36. *Times and Seasons,* July 15, 1842, 855–58; see also *Teachings of the Prophet Joseph Smith,* comp. Joseph Fielding Smith (Salt Lake City: Deseret Book, 1938), 248–55.

37. Quoted in Smith, *Teachings,* 249.

38. Smith, *Teachings,* 252.

39. Smith, *Teachings,* 252.

40. Smith, *Teachings,* 322.

41. Joseph Smith Journal, September 28, 1843, in *An American Prophet's Record: The Diaries and Journals of Joseph Smith,* ed. Scott H. Faulring (Salt Lake City: Signature Books, 1989), 416; spelling modernized.

42. See Devery S. Anderson, "The Anointed Quorum in Nauvoo, 1842–45," *Journal of Mormon History* 29, no. 2 (Fall 2003): 137–57; Devery S. Anderson and Gary James Bergera, *Joseph Smith's Quorum of the Anointed, 1842–1845: A Documentary History* (Salt Lake City: Signature Books, 2005); and Andrew F. Ehat, "Joseph Smith's Introduction of Temple Ordinances and the 1844 Mormon Succession Question" (master's thesis, Brigham Young University, 1982).

43. *Words of Joseph Smith,* 4.

44. *Words of Joseph Smith*, 338–84.

45. 2 Maccabees 10:1–8.

46. Ehat, "'It Seems Like Heaven Began on Earth,'" 253–80.

47. Quoted in Joseph F. Smith, Minutes of the Council of Fifty, 21 April 1880, cited in Ehat, "'It Seems Like Heaven Began on Earth,'" 259.

48. Minutes, in Ehat, "'It Seems Like Heaven Began on Earth,'" 259.

49. Minutes, in Ehat, "'It Seems Like Heaven Began on Earth,'" 260.

50. Ehat, "'It Seems Like Heaven Began on Earth,'" 260–61.

51. Joel H. Johnson, "High on the Mountain Top," *Hymns* (Salt Lake City: The Church of Jesus Christ of Latter-day Saints, 1985), no. 5.

52. Lynne Watkins Jorgensen, "The Mantle of the Prophet Joseph Passes to Brother Brigham: One Hundred Twenty One Testimonies of a Collective Spiritual Witness," in *Opening the Heavens: Accounts of Divine Manifestations*, ed. John W. Welch (Provo, UT: Brigham Young University Press), 343–480.

53. *Words of Joseph Smith*, 367.

54. *Words of Joseph Smith*, 340.

55. See Lyndon W. Cook, "William Law, Nauvoo Dissident," *BYU Studies* 22, no. 1 (Winter 1982): 47–72.

56. William Clayton, cited in Ehat, "'It Seems Like Heaven Began on Earth,'" 267.

57. *Times and Seasons*, September 15, 1844, 651.

58. James R. Clark, comp., *Messages of the First Presidency of The Church of Jesus Christ of Latter-day Saints* (Salt Lake City: Bookcraft, 1966), 3:134; see Richard Neitzel Holzapfel and Steven C. Harper, "'This Is My Testimony, Spoken by Myself into a Talking Machine,'" *BYU Studies* 45, no. 2 (Spring 2006): 112–16.

59. Draft Declaration of the Twelve Apostles, ca. September 1844, reporting March 1844 meeting of Twelve, in Brigham Young Papers, Church History Library, Salt Lake City.

60. *Personal Writings of Joseph Smith*, ed. Dean C. Jessee, rev. ed. (Salt Lake City: Deseret Book, 2002), 11; spelling, capitalization, and punctuation standardized.

61. Bushman and Jessee, "Joseph Smith and His Papers," xxxix.

62. *Words of Joseph Smith*, 365.

63. William W. Phelps, "Praise to the Man," *Hymns*, no. 27.

Index

Page numbers in italics indicate images.

A

Abraham, Book of, 199
accusation, warning against, 423
Adam and Eve, 158–59, 304, 468
Adam-ondi-Ahman, 304, 378–79
Adam-ondi-Ahman Stake, 307–8
Adams, Charles Francis, 4, 500–501
Adams, George, 452
Adams, James, 405, 474–75
alcoholic beverages, 129–32, 134–35
Aldrich, Hazen, 292
Alexandria Gazette, 417–18
Alger, Fanny, 297
Allred, James, 169
altar, on Tower Hill, 305–7
Anderson, George Edward, 334n10
Anderson, Richard L., 438
angel Moroni, 29–35, 39–41, 48–49
Angell, Elizabeth, 377
Angell, Truman, 369
animal meat, 133–34
apostasy: Ezra Booth and, 98; members lost to, 330–31; in Nauvoo, 501–2, 513–14. *See also* Kirtland crisis

Apostles: office of, 211–12, 213; endowment of, 254–55; charge to, 514–15; testimony of, 516. *See also* Quorum of the Seventy; Quorum of the Twelve
arrests, in Far West, 316–23
Arthur, Michael, 173
Ashurst-McGee, Mark, 413
Atchison, David Rice, 153, 316
Avard, Sampson, 329, 330
Averett, Elijah, 338n39
Averett, Elisha, 308, 338n39

B

Backman, Milton V., 16
Baker, Edward D., 455–56
Baldwin, Caleb, 326–29, 346n79, 386n97
baptism, 210, 216
baptism for the dead, 225, 244, 245–46
Barker, Margaret, 236
Bartlett, Sylvester M., 447, 448
Battle at Crooked River, *290*
beer, 134–35
Bennett, James Arlington, 452
Bennett, John C., 442–47, 448
Bennett, Richard E., 370
Bennion, Samuel O., 91
Benson, Ezra Taft, 121–23

Bent, Lemuel, 344n74
Bible translation: process for, 55–56; purpose of, 57–58; changes made to, 58–63, 73n14, 75n33; scribes and schedule for, 63–65; manuscripts and publication of, 65–69; blessings of, 69–71; publication of, 74n29, 198
Bingham, Erastus, 382n32
Bird, Charles, 356, 382n32
bishops, 213
Bogart, Samuel, 323, 327–28
Boggs, Lilburn W.: extermination order of, 316, 340n55, 347, 348–49, 379; assassination attempt on, 442, 447–49
Bond, Christopher S., 379
Book of Commandments, *76*, 94–96, 196
Book of Mormon: New York and, 11–12; Martin Harris and, 35–41; translation of, 41–43, 45–48, 50n17; publication of, 51–54; priesthood and, 210; manuscript of, 423; Joseph Smith on, 424
Book of Mormon Critical Text Project, xvii–xviii
Booth, Ezra, 98, 157

Boynton, John F., 193n53, 283, 292, 311, 451
Brodie, Fawn, 25
Budge, Ernest Alfred Wallis, 45
Burch, Thomas, 324
Burgess, James, 472–73, 474, 480
Burkett, George, 171
Burnett, Peter H., 342n63
Bushman, Richard L., xxv, 9, 25, 217, 503–4
Butler, Caroline, 349, 353, 363–64
Butler, John Lowe: Missouri exodus and, 349–50, 351, 364; seeks redress, 353; in Quincy, Illinois, 369; callings of, 376–77; persecution of, 378, 389n123
Butler, Keziah, 363
Butterfield, Justin, 453–54, 456

𝒞

Cahoon, Reynolds, 307
Cahoon, William F., 353, 369
Calhoun, John C., 502
Calhoun, Patrick, 502
Call, Anson, 351, 359
calling and election, 479–81
Calvin, John, 208, 225

Campbell, Alexander, 163
Cannon, George Q., 25
Carlin, Thomas, 425, 440, 448–49, 453–54, 457–59
Carroll, James, 353
Carter, Phoebe, 275–76
Carthage Jail, 502–3
Catholicism, 206–9, 225
celestial kingdom, 120, 216, 242–44
Champollion, Jean-François, 43–44
Chandler, Michael, 199
Chase, Darwin, 325–26, 372, 386n97
Cheney, Elijah, 160
children, sealing covenant and, 481–90
cholera outbreak, 90, 106, 171–73, 192nn43–44, 196
Church of Jesus Christ of Latter-day Saints: prophecy on size of, 160–62; name for, 162–63, 190n26, 301, 336n23; printing operations of, 180–81; government of, 203–6; priesthood in early, 209–19; kingdom of God and, 505; Council of the Kingdom and, 511–12; leadership succession in, 512–14

Clark, John B., 316–17, 322–23, 344n69
Clay, Henry, 498
Clayton, William: eternal marriage and, 223, 479; John C. Bennett and, 445; extradition attempt and, 450; on return of Joseph Smith, 451; letter from Joseph to, 452; on Joseph Smith, 460; on Holy Ghost, 471–72; supports Joseph Smith, 514
Clemenson, John, 329
Cleveland, John, 367
Cleveland, Sarah, 367
coach, runaway, 397–99
coffee, 132
Colesville Branch, 85–87
colors, symbolism of, 509
Coltrin, Zebedee, 104, 157, 158–59
Commerce, Illinois. *See* Nauvoo, Illinois
Committee of Removal, 354–56, 370–71, 382n32
Community of Christ, 68, 69, 99n3
conferences, quarterly, 209–10
confession, 31
consecration, 83–84, 87–88, 102
Constitution, 472–73, 496
Coptic, 43–45
Coray, Howard, 483
Coray, Martha, 483
Corrill, John: washing and anointing of, 131; on redress for Saints, 153–54; Zion's Camp and, 171; Joseph travels with, 199; Richmond Court of Inquiry and, 329; apostasy of, 330
Council of Fifty. *See* Council of the Kingdom
Council of the Kingdom, 500, 506, 511–12
covenants, sealing and, 481–90
Cowdery, Marcellus, 296
Cowdery, Oliver: apostasy of, xii, 329, 330, 335n14; Book of Mormon and, 40, 41–43, 46–48; repentance and, 48; Jesus Christ forgives, 49n2; Bible translation and, 64, 65; Literary Firm and, 96; on washing with alcohol, 131–32; Medina conference and, 158–59; Church name and, 162; Zion's Camp and, 165; publication committee and, 181; as Assistant President, 182–84, 219, 421–22; patriarchal blessing and, 185; Egyptian papyri

and, 201; priesthood authority and, 209; baptism of, 210; as Apostle, 211, 212; on endowment, 221–22; revelation given to, 229n39; on washings and anointings, 241–42; on redemption of dead, 242; temple dedication and, 246; priesthood keys given to, 250–51; Kirtland crisis and, 268–69, 279; excommunication of, 297–98; leaves Kirtland, 333n5; leadership succession and, 513

Cowdery, Warren, 182, 266–67, 267–68

Crooked River. *See* Battle at Crooked River

crop failure, 9–10

Dana v. Brink lawsuit, 440–41

Daniel, 504–6

Darowski, Kay, 438

Daviess County, Missouri: expeditions into, 303–7; Mormon War and, 315–16; preemption claims and, 337n30; military occupation of, 351–54; Committee of Removal and, 354–56

Davis, Amos, 439

deacons, 213

dead, temple work for, 242–46

death(s): Missouri exodus and, 377–78; calling and election and, 486–87

decision making, 92

degrees of glory: Bible translation and, 70; vision of, 106–14, 216, 242–44, 470; requirements for, 120–21

Derby, Erastus H., 450

Dibble, Philo, 108–9

discernment, 470

dispensation heads, 468–69

Doctrine and Covenants: Bible translation and, 69–70; revisions to, 97–98; section 107, 97–98; Lectures on Faith and, 196; approval of, 199; section 124, 424–26

Doniphan, Alexander W., 153, 307, 318–19, 324, 342n63

Douglas, Stephen A., 453

Dunham, Jonathan, 344n74

Dunklin, Daniel, 153–54, 169–70

Dunn, Loren C., 387n113

529

E

Edwards, Jonathan, 245
Egyptian papyri, 43–45, 199, 201
elders, 211, 213
Elders' Journal, 313–14
Elias, 250
Elijah, 234–35, 250–51, 482–83
Elkin, William F., 454
endowment: early views on, 136–37; restoration of, 220–22; teachings on, 241; Apostles and, 254–55; fulness of priesthood and, 507
England: call to, 277–78, 311, 394; missionaries in, 300; departure for, 371–72
Enoch, 262–63
Esplin, Ronald K., xix, xx, xxv
eternal life, 479–81, 496–97
eternal marriage, 476–79. *See also* sealing
Evans, John Henry, 25
Evening and the Morning Star, 90, 111, 181
exaltation, 479–81, 496–97
excommunication(s): of Oliver Cowdery, 268; in Missouri, 296–99; of John C. Bennett, 444
exodus. *See* Missouri exodus
extermination order, 347, 348–49, 354, 379
extradition attempt, 447–59

F

family: during premodern period, 4; sealing, 481–90, 496–97
Far West, Missouri: Joseph arrives in, 294–95; revelations in, 295–96, 299–303; excommunications in, 296–99; arrests in, 316–23; Smith home in, 334n10; military occupation of, 351–54; Committee of Removal and, 354–56; desertion of, 378–79
Far West Temple: revelation on, 301–2; site dedication of, 308–10; dedication of, 338n37; construction of, 338n39; liberty pole and, 340n45; missionaries depart from, 371–72
Faulring, Scott H., xviii, 64
feet: dusting, 89; washing, 240
Fielding, Joseph, 113–14, 265, 278

INDEX

Fielding, Mary: letters from, 265; on Kirtland crisis, 268–69, 277, 280; on Joseph's illness, 278–79; marriage of, 283–84
Fielding, Mercy, 265, 269
First Presidency: in Church hierarchy, 218; reconstitution of, 283, 430; commanded to leave Kirtland, 333n5
First Vision, 120, 201
Fishing River revelation, 170–71, 179
Follett, King, 344n74, 372–73, 386n97, 500
Foote, Warren, 423
Ford, Thomas, 453–54, 502–3
foreordination, ix, xii–xiii, xxiii
Foster, Robert D., 396, 397–98, 439
friendship, 473, 474, 498
Fulton, Robert, 7

G

Galland, Isaac, 438
Garden of Eden, 304
Gates, Lydia, 7
gathering: to Ohio, 78–82; to Zion, 82–83, 88, 92–93; to Far West, 302–3; benefits of, 377; arguments against, 388n115; to Nauvoo, 426; temples and, 473
Gause, Jesse, 65, 102, 103, 104
general conferences, 209–10
Gibbs, Luman, 325–26, 386n97
Gilbert, Algernon Sidney, 85–87, 171, 172, 192n43
Gilbert, John H., 54
Gillet, John, 438
Godhead, 119, 502
Goforth, William G., 4–5, 500–501
Golligher, James, 378
Goodson, John, 114
gospel principle(s): introduction to, 25–27; repentance as, 27–35
Gould, John, 153, 292
"Government of God, The," 505
grace, 219–24, 225–26
grains, 134
Grandin, Egbert B., 11, 51, 54
Grandin Press building, *52*
Granger, Carlos, 450–51
Granger, Oliver, 310
Grayson, John, 292
Greene, John, 351, 354, 366, 367, 368
Grue, David, 438
Grund, Francis, 400–402

H

habeas corpus hearing, 455–57. *See also* writs of habeas corpus
Hagstrom, Vern, 387n113
Hale, Aroet Lucius, 353, 369
Hale, Jonathan H., 382n32
Hallett, Clark, 344n74
Hammer, Austin, 362
Hammer, John, 362–63
Hammer, Nancy, 362–63
Hancock, Amy, 358
Hancock, Francis Marion, 358
Hancock, Levi, 104–5, 308–9, 339n42, 357–58, 377
Hancock, Mosiah, 308–9, 339n42, 358, 378
Hancock, Solomon, 339n42
Hannay, James, xii
Harmony, Pennsylvania, 36
Harper, Steven C., 425, 432
Harris, George Washington, 295
Harris, Lucy, 36
Harris, Martin: apostasy of, xii, 329; Book of Mormon and, 35–41; repentance and, 48; consecration and, 87; Kirtland crisis and, 292; leadership succession and, 513
Harris, Martin Henderson, 450
Harrison, William Henry, 425
Haskins, Brother, 110
Haun's Mill Massacre, *290*, 315, 331, 362
health problems: of Joseph Smith, 278–79; in Caldwell County, 377–78
herbs, 133
Hibbard, Billy, 14
Hickman, William, 366
Higbee, Elias: Missouri exodus and, 351, 368; Washington mission and, 395, 398–400, 402–8; on Martin Van Buren, 410; funeral of, 482
High Council (Kirtland Stake), 152–53
"High on the Mountain Top" (hymn), 512
high priesthood, 101–2, 213–14, 221
Hill, Donna and Marvin, 25
Hinckle, George M., 317, 322, 329, 330
Hinckley, Gordon B., 18
history, periods of, 1–2
History of the Church of Jesus Christ of Latter-day Saints, xvii
Holbrook, Joseph, 338n41, 351, 357, 365, 383n39
Holbrook, Nancy, 351, 357

INDEX

Holbrook, Nancy Jane, 365
Hollister, Joseph, 451
Holy Order, 428
Holy Scriptures: Translated and Corrected by the Spirit of Revelation, The, 67–68
horses, runaway, 397–99
Hosanna Shout, 309, 339n44
Hotchkiss, Horace R., 438
hot drinks, 132
Howard, Luther, 54
Howe, Eber D., 157, 203
Hunter, Edward, 452
Hunter, Joseph, 344n74
Huntington, Dimick, 308, 338n39, 350–51, 373, 450
Huntington, William, 351, 355, 356, 370, 382n32
Hurlbut, Philastus, 157–58, 189n16
Hyde, Orson, *494*; degrees of glory and, 110, 111; Zion's Camp and, 153, 155, 156; Daniel Dunklin and, 169–70; mission of, 278, 300; apostasy of, 329, 330; solemn proclamation and, 435n31; correction of, 471–72

I

Illinois, impact of Saints on, 379
illness, of Joseph Smith, 278–79
Inspired Version, 56, 67–68. *See also* Bible translation
Isabella II (Queen of Spain), 426
Isaiah, 295–96

J

Jackson, Andrew, 393, 411
Jackson, Henry, 377–78
Jackson, Kent P., xviii
Jackson County, Missouri: as Zion, 83–84; foundation of Zion and, 85–87; temple property in, 99nn2–3. *See also* Zion
James, 211–12
Jefferson, Thomas, 7
jeremiad, 93–94
Jessee, Dean C., xxv, 438, 503–4
Jesus Christ: instruction and preparation of, 33; forgiveness of, 49n2; testimony of, 119–25; grace of, 219–24, 225–26; temples and, 237–42; appears in Kirtland Temple, 249–50;

Jesus Christ (*continued*):
prophet hierarchy and, 468;
eternal life and, 479–81;
reigning with, 508–10;
kingdom of God and,
512; Joseph as witness of,
516–18
Johnson, Benjamin, 223, 377
Johnson, Brenda, 64
Johnson, Joel, 110, 512
Johnson, John, 94
Johnson, Luke, 292, 311, 333n3
Johnson, Lyman E., 165, 292,
298, 311
Johnson, Seth, 110
John the Baptist, 470
John the Revelator, 211–12,
508–10
Joseph Smith Papers Project,
xviii–xxii, xxv, 391–92
*Joseph Smith: Rough Stone
Rolling*, xvii
justification, 225

𝒦

Kilbourne, David, 447, 448
Kimball, Heber C., *494*; Joseph
Smith and, viii, 104, 281;
degrees of glory and, 114;
on Zion's Camp, 166; on
Apostles, 212; mission
of, 252, 277–78, 300;
on Kirtland crisis, 266;
Committee of Removal
and, 354–55, 356, 370,
382n30; Missouri exodus
and, 359–60; extradition
attempt and, 452
Kimball, Hiram, 439
Kimball, Sarah M., 441
King, Austin A., 323, 325
King, Thomas, 449–50
kingdom of God, 503–6,
511–12
King Follett discourse, 500
Kingsbury, Caroline, 353
Kingsbury, Joseph C., 353
Kirtland crisis: effects of,
262; accounts of, 263–65;
beginning of, 266–67;
Cowdery brothers and,
267–69; Wilford Woodruff
and, 269–74; apostasy of
friends and, 274–77; Joseph
takes action in, 280–82;
leaving Kirtland and, 282–
85; Kirtland Safety Society
and, 291–92
Kirtland Safety Society, 291–92
Kirtland Stake High Council,
152–53
Kirtland Temperance Society,
128

Kirtland Temple, *232*; dedication of, 49n2, 246–49, 265–66, 274–75; construction of, 135–38, 179–80; endowment and, 222; revelation on, 235–37, 253–54; vision of Jesus Christ in, 237–42, 517; redemption of dead and, 242–46; priesthood keys and, 249–53; Wilford Woodruff and, 269–74; disputes in, 281; ordinances in, 426
Knight, Joseph Jr., 375
Knight, Joseph Sr., 348–49
Knight, Lydia, 201, 348–49, 360
Knight, Newel: wine and, 130; marriage of, 201; Missouri exodus and, 348–49, 351, 352–53, 360
Knight, Polly, 130

L

Lake, Dennis, 198
Lamborn, Josiah, 455, 456
Laney, Isaac, 370
Latter Day Saints' Messenger and Advocate, 181
Law, William: apostasy of, xii, 501, 513–14; Bible translation and, 426; John C. Bennett and, 443, 444; extradition attempt and, 450
Law, Wilson, 452, 454, 455, 456
law of consecration. *See* consecration
Lectures on Faith, 196
legal proceedings, 157–58
leg operation, 8
Leonid meteor shower, 144–45
letter(s): from Joseph to Church members, 140–43, 329, 345n77; from Joseph to Emma Smith, 165–66, 167–68, 319–20, 324–25, 327–28, 459; from Joseph to Almira Scobey, 198; from Elias Higbee to Hyrum Smith, 400; from Joseph to William Clayton, 452; of Emma Smith and Thomas Carlin, 457–59
Lewis, David, 351
Liberty Jail, 286–87, 326–29, 331–32, 386n97
Lightner, Mary Elizabeth, viii
Lincoln, Abraham, 139–40
Lisle, B. M., 340n55
Literary Firm, 96–97
Littlefield, Lyman, 326–27
loneliness, xii

Lott, Cornelius, 308, 338n39, 440
Louis Philippe (King of France), 426
love, 473, 474, 498
Lucas, Samuel D., 316–20, 322, 343n67
Luther, Martin, 207–8, 225
Lyman, Amasa M., 317–26, 452

M

MacArthur, John F. Jr., 477–78
Mace, Wandle, 366, 367, 374
Mack, Solomon, 7
Mackay, Charles, vii
Madison, James, 8
Major, William W., *494*
Markham, Stephen, 359, 382n32
Marks, William, 181, 310–11
marriage, 130–31, 223–24, 476–79. *See also* plural marriage; sealing
Marsh, Thomas B.: Zion's Camp and, 171, 193n53; Kirtland crisis and, 280–81; Far West excommunications and, 296; apostasy of, 329, 330; Far West Temple dedication and, 338n41; revelation for, 469
martyrdom, x, 502–3

Matthews, Robert ("prophet Matthias"), 200–201
Matthews, Robert J., xviii, 55–56, 64, 70, 71
Matthews, Timothy, 113–14
McCleary, Sophronia, 471
McConkie, Bruce R.: on testimony of Jesus Christ, 123–25; on prophet hierarchy, 468, 468–69; on calling and election, 486–87
McGee, Owen H., 338n37
McLellin, William, 95–96, 298–99, 311, 329, 330
McRae, Alexander, 326–29, 346n79, 386n97
meat, 133–34
Medina conference, 158–59
Melchizedek Priesthood, 211, 217–18, 427, 480, 507
"Memorial to Congress, A," 500
mercy, 486–88
Messiah ben Joseph, xiii
Miles, Joel S., 344n74
Millennium, 93, 503–4, 512
Miller, George, 450
Millet, Artemus, 179
missionaries: revelations for early, 88–89; swimming and, 91; callings for, 101–2, 252; degrees of glory and, 113–14; called to England, 277–78, 300

Missouri: commandment on, 82–83, 285, 293; as Zion, 83–84; Sabbath observance in, 84; foundation of Zion and, 85–87; temple property in, 99nn2–3; expulsion from, 138–48; Zion's Camp and, 153–57; second Zion's Camp and, 178–79; Joseph arrives in, 294–95; military occupation of, 351–54; Committee of Removal and, 354–56. *See also* Far West, Missouri; Missouri exodus; Zion

Missouri exodus: overview of, 347–49; of militiamen, 349–51; military occupation and, 351–54; beginning of, 356–57, 383n39; January accounts of, 357–58; February accounts of, 358–64; March accounts of, 364–66; arrivals in Quincy, 367–70; completion of, 370–73; petitions for redress and, 374–75; consequences of, 375–76; events following, 393–94

Missouri militia, 351–54

Missouri River, 89–90
Missouri Stake, 173
modern period, 1–2
Morgan, Lucinda, 295
Morley, Isaac, 171
Mormon, 29
Mormonism Unvailed, 157–58
Mormon Jubilee, 456–57
Mormon War, *290*; description of event, 315–16; arrests over, 316–23; Richmond Court of Inquiry and, 323–26; Liberty Jail and, 326–29; as trial, 331
Moroni, 29–35, 39–41, 48–49, 232, 233–35
Morris, George W., 344n74
Moses, 250, 251, 262–63, 272, 468
Mount Tambora, 9–10
Murdock, John, 129, 172, 298, 358–59
Murdock, Julia Clapp, 172
Murdock, Orrice, 358–59
Murdock, Phoebe, 172, 192n43
mysteries, 114–19

N

Nauvoo, Illinois: gathering in, 375; exodus from, 379–80; settlement of, 393–94;

Nauvoo (*continued*): Joseph's mission in, 432–33; land purchases in, 438; Joseph's responsibilities in, 439–41; difficulties in, 441–47, 501–2, 513–14; extradition attempt and, 447–59; writs of habeas corpus and, 462n31

Nauvoo City Council, 422

Nauvoo Expositor, 502

Nauvoo House, 432, 439

Nauvoo Legion, 440

Nauvoo Temple: events preceding construction of, 421–24; commandment to build, 427; priesthood and, 427–28, 430–31, 506–7; ordinances and, 428–30; completion of, 432; site for, 432–33; construction of, 439; revelation on, 499–500

Nelson, Russell M., 235

Nephi, 33

Nephite disease, 262

Newberry, James, 382n32

New Testament Manuscripts 1 and 2, 66–67

New Translation, 56. *See also* Bible translation

New York: Smith family moves to, 10–13; Second Great Awakening and, 13–17; commandment to leave, 79–80

New York Journal of Commerce, 415–16

Nibley, Hugh, 244

Noah, 468

Oaks, Dallin H., xii, 42

Ohio, gathering in, 78–82

Ohio Star, 98

Old Testament Manuscripts 1 and 2, 65–66

opposition, ix–xii

ordinances, 225–26, 428–30, 496–97

outer darkness, 121

Packer, Boyd K., 205, 485–86

Page, John E., 311, 330, 371–72

Palmer, Mrs., 13

palm fronds, 509–10

Panic of 1837, 264, 292, 393, 411

Papers of Joseph Smith, xvii

Park, Boyd, 192n44

Parrish, Betsy, 172

Parrish, Martha, 201

Parrish, Warren: marriage of, 201; attends temple, 270; Kirtland crisis and, 276–77, 279, 292

Partridge, Edward: buys land, 83; revelations for, 85–87; Sidney Gilbert and, 171; on priesthood authority, 204; Restoration and, 209; on redemption of dead, 242; Far West Temple dedication and, 338n41; Missouri exodus and, 364, 369; views on gathering, 377, 388n115; mentioned in revelation, 426

patriarchal blessings, 184–86

patriarchs, 214

Patten, David W.: Zion's Camp and, 193n53; Kirtland crisis and, 280–81; death of, 290; Far West excommunications and, 296; revelation on, 299–300, 426; Far West Temple dedication and, 338n41

Patton, John, 423

Paul, 33–34

Paulsen, David L., 245

Pearl of Great Price (Franklin D. Richards's work), 67, 68

Pearl of Great Price (scripture), 68–69, 199

Peck, Reed, 329, 330, 351

Perpetual Emigrating Fund, 380

persecution: of Joseph Smith, ix–xii, 102–3; of early Saints, 80, 138–48, 254–55, 316–17; Missouri militia and, 351–54; temples and, 426. *See also* Missouri exodus, redress

personal revelation, 114–19

Personal Writings of Joseph Smith, xvii

Peter, 211–12

Phelps, Morris, 344n74, 386n97

Phelps, William W.: calculates Second Coming, 93; on redress for Saints, 155; Zion's Camp and, 171; as Missouri Stake president, 173; buys land, 179; publication committee and, 181; Oliver Cowdery and, 183; on washings and anointings, 241; excommunication of, 296; on Far West Temple, 301; revelation for, 313; Richmond Court of Inquiry and, 329; apostasy of, 330, 338n41; solemn proclamation and, 435n31

Phelps, Morris, 325–26

Pike, Zebulon, 394

539

Pinegar, Rex D., 91
plural marriage, 441–42, 443–44, 513
Polk, James K., 498
Pope, Nathaniel, 454, 456
popery, 267–68
Pratt, Orson, *494*; *Pearl of Great Price* and, 68; Word of Wisdom and, 128; Zion's Camp and, 155, 156; attends temple, 270; Kirtland crisis and, 279; departs for England, 371–72; seeks redress, 500; on Church constitution, 511
Pratt, Parley P., *494*; Zion's Camp and, 154, 155, 156, 160, 164–65; meets with Daniel Dunklin, 169–70; Warren Cowdery and, 182; attends temple, 270; Kirtland crisis and, 279, 280; arrest and trial of, 317–21, 322–23, 343n68; Richmond Court of Inquiry and, 323–26; on Liberty Jail, 332; Hosanna Shout and, 339n44; imprisonment of, 386n97; solemn proclamation and, 435n31; discernment and, 470; on eternal marriage, 478–79
Pratt, Sarah, 442

prayer, 246–49, 431
preemption claims, 337n30
premodern period, 1–6
premortal existence, ix
presidential candidacy, 497–99, 501, 503–4
Price, Sterling G., 322
priesthood: interviews, 31–33; revelation on, 101–2, 105, 225–26; Church government and, 203–6; in Protestantism and Catholicism, 206–9; in early Church, 209–19; temples and, 219–24, 428–30; restoration of, 232–35, 253–56; Nauvoo Temple and, 427–28; reorganization of, 432; hierarchy of prophets and, 467–69; legal administrators and, 470; fulness of, 480, 506–7; leadership succession in, 512–14
priesthood keys, 217–18, 249–53, 254, 429–31
priests, 213
print media, 180–81
prodigal son, 488
prophecy/prophecies: on Joseph Smith, xii–xiv; on United States, 472–73; more sure word of, 479–81

prophets: instruction and preparation of, 33–34; hierarchy among, 467–69; characteristics of, 470; responsibilities of, 490; as witnesses of Jesus Christ, 516–17
prosperity, 262, 269–70
Protestantism, 206–9, 225
publishing, 180–81
Pulsipher, Zera, 160, 293, 365

Quincy, Illinois: exodus to, 347–51; reasons for choosing, 366–67; assistance in, 367–70; Joseph Smith arrives in, 373–74; appreciation for, 376, 387n113
Quincy, Josiah, 4–5, 500–501
Quorum of the Anointed, 428, 431–32
Quorum of the Seventy: organization of, 177–78, 214; callings to, 197; presidency and, 217–19; temple ordinances taught to, 239–40; Wilford Woodruff and, 272
Quorum of the Twelve: Zion's Camp and, 193n53; callings to, 197; establishment of, 214; presidency and, 217–18; temple ordinances taught to, 239–40; missions of, 266–67, 277–78, 394; revelation for, 311; Urim and Thummim shown to, 424; reconstitution of, 430; leadership succession in, 513; charge to, 514–15; testimony of, 516

ℛ

Ray County, Missouri, 322–23
redress, 147–48, 374–75, 500. *See also* Washington mission
Rees, Amos, 324
Relief Society, 428–29, 441, 507
religion: society and, 262–63, 267–69; freedom of, 473, 498
religious revivals, 13–17
reminiscences, on Joseph Smith, xiv–xv
Reorganized Church of Jesus Christ of Latter Day Saints, 67–68
repentance: Joseph Smith's instruction and, 27–35; lost manuscript pages and, 35–41; Book of Mormon translation and, 42–43, 46–48; conclusions on, 48–49

541

Restoration, of the gospel, 10–18

revelation(s): recording, xvi; canonized, 77–78, 99n1; received in 1831, 78–79, 99; to gather in Ohio, 79–82; on Zion, 82–84, 88, 92–93; on Sabbath observance, 84; on Colesville Branch, 85–87; on consecration, 87–88; for early missionaries, 88–89; on water travel, 89–91; on decision making, 92; of warning, 93–94; on Book of Commandments, 94–95; on Literary Firm, 96–97; revisions to, 97–98; on apostasy, 98; on high priesthood, 101–2; on United Firm, 102–3, 159, 189n20; on priesthood, 105, 214–16, 225–26; on degrees of glory, 106–14; Philo Dibble on, 108–9; mysteries and, 114–19; personal, 114–19; testimony of Jesus Christ and, 119–25; on Kirtland Temple, 135–38, 235–37, 253–54; on affliction, 146–47; on Zion's Camp, 170–71; for Warren Cowdery, 182; on Church organization, 204–6; on conferences, 209–10; on Peter, James, and John, 212; process for, 224; for Oliver Cowdery, 229n39; on redemption of dead, 242–46; to leave Kirtland, 285, 293, 333n5; on Isaiah, 295–96; received in Far West, 299–303; for Newel K. Whitney and William Marks, 310–11; for Quorum of the Twelve, 311; on tithing, 311–13; for Frederick G. Williams and William W. Phelps, 313; on seeking redress, 413–14; for Brigham Young, 422; on solemn proclamation, 424–26; taught in 1843, 469–76; on exaltation, 496–97; on Nauvoo Temple, 499–500

revivals, religious, 13–17

Reynolds, John, 405–6, 408–10, 414

Reynolds, Thomas, 410, 447, 448–49

Rich, Charles C., 350

Rich, Leonard, 292

Rich, Thomas, 345n74

Richards, Franklin D., 67, 68, 483

Richards, Jennetta, 431–32
Richards, Samuel A., xxiii
Richards, Willard, *494*; herbs and, 133; called as Apostle, 311; as scribe, 424, 441; attends Quorum meeting, 431–32; solemn proclamation and, 435n31; extradition attempt and, 452; on habeas corpus hearing, 455–56; Mormon Jubilee and, 456; on Joseph's teachings, 473; leadership succession and, 513
Richmond Court of Inquiry, 322–26
Rigdon, Sidney: as scribe, 65; degrees of glory and, 70, 107–9, 110; conversion of, 78–79; called to Missouri, 83; consecrates Zion, 85; apostasy and, 98; high priesthood and, 101; United Firm and, 102, 103; Missouri temple and, 137; as Kirtland Stake president, 152; Zion's Camp and, 155, 156; Medina conference and, 158; Church name and, 163, 190n26, 336n23; School of the Elders and, 180; publication committee and, 181; Oliver Cowdery and, 182–84; Lectures on Faith and, 196; preaches in temple, 272–73; supports Joseph Smith, 275, 279; prophesies on Church, 280; revelation given to, 285; leaves Kirtland, 292–94, 333n5; Far West Temple dedication and, 309; arrest and trial of, 317–23, 342n61, 346n79; Richmond Court of Inquiry and, 323–26; imprisoned in Liberty Jail, 326–29, 386n97; views on gathering, 377; as Church representative, 395–96; Washington mission and, 405; plural marriage and, 441
Ripley, Alanson, 298, 382nn30, 32
Roberts, B. H., xvii, 47, 305, 495–96
Robinson, Athalia R., 323
Robinson, Ebenezer, 357
Robinson, George W.: as scribe, 295, 304, 305; arrest and trial of, 317–23; Richmond Court of Inquiry and, 323–26; plural marriage and, 441

Rockwell, Orrin Porter, 394–96, 448, 449–50
Rockwood, Albert, 351, 357
Rogers, David, 370, 452
Rollins, James Henry, 345n74
Rosetta Stone, 43–45
Roundy, Shadrach, 382n32
Rowland, Moses, 325–26
Ryder, Symonds, 98

Sabbath observance, 84
sacrament(s): wine and, 129, 130–31; water and, 131; in Protestantism and Catholicism, 206–7; priesthood and, 216; grace and, 225–26
sacred experiences, 114–19
Salisbury, Wilkins Jenkins, 157, 165
salvation: Luther's views on, 207–8; priesthood and, 216–17; grace and, 225–26; of dead, 242–46; calling and election and, 479–81; exaltation and, 496–97
Samuel, 33
Satan, xi
Sayers, Edward, 450
Schaff, Philipp, 111

School of the Elders, 180, 200
Scobey, Almira, 198
Seager, Aurora, 14–15
sealing, 221, 222–24, 476–79, 481–90, 496–97
Second Coming, 93, 144–45, 503–4, 512
Second Great Awakening, 11, 13–17
seer stone. *See* Urim and Thummim
Sessions, Perrigrine, 374
Shearer, Daniel, 382n32
Shearer, Norman, 325–26, 372, 386n97
Sherwood, Henry G., 449–50
sin, 27–35
Skousen, Royal, xviii
slavery, 139
Sloan, James, 462n28
Smith, Alexander Hale, 307, 324
Smith, Alvin, 13, 216, 243–44, 245
Smith, Asael, xiv, 22n54
Smith, Bathsheba W., 431
Smith, Catherine, 8
Smith, Don Carlos (brother of Joseph Smith), 9, 361, 423
Smith, Don Carlos (son of Joseph Smith), 423
Smith, Elias, 382n32
Smith, Emma: on Book of Mormon translation,

50n17; as scribe, 64–65; preserves Bible manuscripts, 67; letters from Joseph to, 165–66, 167–68, 319–20, 324–25, 327–28; Far West home of, 295; visits Liberty Jail, 328; military occupation and, 353–54; Missouri exodus and, 359, 367; greets Joseph in Quincy, 373; moves to Nauvoo, 394; on Nauvoo businesses, 440; Relief Society and, 441; extradition attempt and, 450, 452, 457–59
Smith, Ephraim, 7
Smith, Frederick Granger, 307, 324
Smith, George A.: Zion's Camp and, 157, 164, 165–66, 166–67; ordained as Apostle, 371–72; on priesthood keys, 429; extradition attempt and, 452
Smith, Hyrum, *494*; mentioned, 13; on teaching mysteries, 117; Word of Wisdom and, 128; on hot drinks, 132; Zion's Camp and, 155, 156, 164, 169; cholera outbreak and, 172; as Assistant President, 184, 421–22, 430–31; patriarchal blessing of, 185; prophesies on Church, 279–80, 280; replaces Frederick G. Williams, 283; marriage of, 283–84; arrest and trial of, 317–23, 342n61, 346n79; Richmond Court of Inquiry and, 323–26; imprisoned in Liberty Jail, 326–29, 386n97; leaves Kirtland, 333n5; letter from Elias Higbee to, 400; John C. Bennett and, 443, 444, 445; extradition attempt and, 450; martyrdom of, 502–3; leadership succession and, 513
Smith, Jerusha, 185, 283
Smith, Jesse (uncle of Joseph Smith), 8
Smith, Jesse J. (cousin of Joseph Smith), 157, 165, 172
Smith, John (uncle of Joseph Smith): Adam-ondi-Ahman Stake and, 307; leaves Kirtland, 333n5; Committee of Removal and, 382n30; on seeking redress, 418; Joseph stays with, 450
Smith, John Murdock (son of Joseph Smith), 103

Smith, Joseph, *260*; history of, vii–viii, xiv–xviii; foreordination of, viii–ix; persecution of, ix–xii; prophecies on, xii–xiv; premodern period and, 2–6; childhood and early years of, 6–10; Second Great Awakening and, 13–17; as instrument in Lord's hands, 17–18

Smith, Joseph F., xiv, 135, 469

Smith, Joseph Fielding, xvii

Smith, Joseph III, 104, 151, 307, 324, 328, 346n85

Smith, Joseph, Sr.: death of, 7, 245–46; dreams of, 8; leg operation and, 8; moves family to New York, 10–13; Universalism and, 16, 22n54; as patriarch, 184–86, 422; illness of, 200; redemption of dead and, 242; arrest of, 281; leaves Kirtland, 333n5; Missouri exodus and, 360–61, 369; mentioned in revelation, 426

Smith, Julia Murdock, 151, 307, 324

Smith, Lucy Mack: history of, 6–7, 36; leg operation and, 8; on crop failure, 9–10; on move to New York, 12; on loss of manuscript pages, 37–39; on leaving Kirtland, 293; Missouri militia and, 352–53; Missouri exodus and, 359, 360–61, 369

Smith, Nathan, 8

Smith, Samuel Harrison: birth of, 7; degrees of glory and, 110–11; on temple revelation, 236; Missouri exodus and, 350, 361

Smith, Sylvester, 167, 175–78, 292

Smith, William: dispute with, xii, 200, 202; birth of, 7; Zion's Camp and, 157, 165; arrest of, 281

Smith family, 10–13, 16

Smith Improved Printing Press, *52*

Smoot, Abraham O., 363–64, 377

Smoot, Martha, 363–64

Snow, Eliza R., 264, 364–65

Snow, Lorenzo, 264, 489

society, religion and, 262–63, 267–69

solemn assembly, 246

solemn proclamation, 425–26, 435n31

soteriological problem of evil, 243–45

speculation, 266–67
Springfield, Illinois, 454–56
Spring Hill, Missouri, 304
Stockton, Benjamin, 243
Stoddard, Calvin W., 185
Stoddard, Sophronia, 185
Stowell, Josiah, 34
Swedenborg, Emanuel, 112
swimming, 91

Tambora (Mount), 9–10
Tanner, Nathan, 191n38
Taylor, James, 453
Taylor, John: called as Apostle, 311; departs for England, 371–72; Committee of Removal and, 382n30; solemn proclamation and, 435n31; on constitution of Church, 511; leadership succession and, 513
tea, 132
teachers, 213
Teachings of the Presidents of the Church: Joseph Smith, xvii
Teachings of the Prophet Joseph Smith, xvii
telestial kingdom, 121
temperance movement, 128, 132

temples: plans to construct, 83–84; property for, 99n2; priesthood authority and, 219–24; Moroni and, 232–35; revelation on, 235–37; presence of Jesus Christ and, 237–42; redemption of dead and, 242–46; persecution and, 426; gathering and, 473; last dispensation and, 508–10. *See also* specific temples
terrestrial kingdom, 120–21
testimony, of Jesus Christ, 119–25
Thomas, Daniel Stillwell, 361–62, 377
Thomas, Martha Payne Jones, 361–62, 377
Thomas, Morgan, 362
Thompson, Robert B., 423, 435n31
Tillery, Samuel, 326
Times and Seasons, xvi, 440, 446–47, 505
tithing, 311–13
Tower Hill, 305–7
translation: Oliver Cowdery and, 41–43, 46–48; Champollion and, 43–45; Emma Smith on, 50n17
treasure digging, 34

trials: revelation on, 146–47; refinement through, 286–87, 472; of Joseph Smith, 330–32; Missouri exodus as, 376–77
Turley, Theodore, 356, 371, 382nn30, 32
Turnham, Joel, 327
Tuttle, Smith, 438
typhoid epidemic, 8

U

Underwood, Grant, 111–12
United Firm, 102–3, 159, 189n20
United States: during premodern period, 5–6; Second Great Awakening and, 13–17; prophecy on, 472–73; presidency of, 497–99
Universalists, 16, 22n54
Urim and Thummim, 39–40, 46, 424

V

Van Buren, Martin: petitions to, 375; Panic of 1837 and, 393; meeting with, 403–8, 414–18; views on, 410–13

Victoria (Queen of Great Britain), 426
vision(s): of degrees of glory, 106–14, 216, 242–44, 470; of Adam and Eve, 158–59; during Zion's Camp, 191n38; of cholera victims, 196; in Kirtland Temple, 250–53; of last dispensation, 508; of Jesus Christ, 517
Vogel, Dan, 25

W

Washington mission: departure for Washington, 395–96; journey, 396–400; arrival in Washington, 400–403; meeting with Van Buren, 403–8; John Reynolds on, 408–10; motivation for, 413–14; accounts of, 414–18
water: traveling on, 89–91; in sacrament, 131; mild drinks and, 134–35
Wayne Sentinel, 54
weaknesses, 27–35
Weeks, William, 499
Wells, Daniel H., 445
Wells, R. W., 153
White, Hugh, 438

INDEX

White, William, 438
Whiting, Elisha, 365
Whitman, William, 345n74
Whitmer, David: apostasy of, xii, 329, 330, 338n41; as Book of Mormon witness, 40; on repentance and translation, 47; as Missouri Stake president, 173; on Church name, 190n26, 336n23; administers to Joseph Smith Sr., 200; as Apostle, 211, 212; rebukes Apostles, 273; Kirtland crisis and, 274; discipline of, 296; excommunication of, 297–98; leadership succession and, 513
Whitmer, Jacob, 298, 330
Whitmer, John: as scribe, 64, 65, 66; Literary Firm and, 96; documents persecution, 140; as Missouri Stake president, 173; buys land, 179; publication committee and, 181; as Apostle, 211; excommunication of, 296; apostasy of, 329, 330
Whitmer, Peter, 103
Whitney, Elizabeth Ann, 129
Whitney, Newel K.: United Firm and, 103; travels with Joseph Smith, 104; wine and, 130; name of Church and, 163; Sylvester Smith hearings and, 175; Missouri exodus and, 310–11; Relief Society and, 429–30; extradition attempt and, 450, 452
Whitney, Orson F., 484–85
Widtsoe, John A., 91
Wight, Lyman: Zion's Camp and, 154, 155, 156, 164, 169, 171; Daviess County and, 304; Adam-ondi-Ahman Stake and, 307; arrest and trial of, 317–21, 322–23, 343n68, 346n79; Richmond Court of Inquiry and, 323–26; imprisoned in Liberty Jail, 326–29, 386n97; on blessing of Joseph Smith III, 346n85
Williams, Frederick G.: as scribe, 65, 103; revelation for, 93, 313; United Firm and, 102; degrees of glory and, 110; herbs and, 133; Missouri temple and, 137; as Kirtland Stake president, 152; Zion's Camp and, 155, 156, 165; name of Church and, 162; publication committee and, 181; Oliver Cowdery and, 182–84;

Williams, Frederick G. (*continued*): performs Woodruff wedding, 276; Hyrum Smith replaces, 283; dissent of, 299; apostasy of, 330
Wilson, Moses, 319–20, 343n67
wine, 129–30
Winn, Kenneth H., 335n14
Wood, Gordson S., 11–12
Wood, William, 324
Woodruff, Azmon, 160
Woodruff, Wilford: diaries of, xix; on Joseph Smith, xxi, 491; on prophecy on Church size, 160–62; Zion's Camp and, 174, 190n23; Kirtland crisis and, 264–65, 269–71; on temple dedication, 275; marriage of, 275–76; called as Apostle, 311, 371–72; Missouri exodus and, 365; on return of Joseph Smith, 374; on calling and election, 480; leadership succession and, 513; on charge to Apostles, 514–15
Word of Wisdom, 127–35
Words of Joseph Smith, xvii
Works, Miriam, 300
writs of habeas corpus, 462n31

Y

York, Mary Jane, 366
Young, Brigham, *494*; on foreordination of Joseph Smith, xiii; Joseph Smith meets, 104–5; on degrees of glory, 113; on sharing revelation, 117–18; on sacramental wine, 129–30; Zion's Camp and, 156, 174; cholera outbreak and, 172–73, 196; on Apostles, 212; on prosperity, 262; Kirtland crisis and, 269, 284–85; supports Joseph Smith, 272, 281; revelation for, 299–301, 422; Far West Temple dedication and, 338n41; Committee of Removal and, 354–55, 356, 382n30; Missouri exodus and, 359, 360; departs for England, 371–72; supports gathering, 377; as president of Twelve, 430; extradition attempt and, 452; on families, 483; leadership succession and, 513
Young, Brigham Jr., 300
Young, Elizabeth, 300

INDEX

Young, Joseph A. (son of Brigham Young), 300
Young, Joseph (brother of Brigham Young), 104–5, 156, 172–73, 196
Young, Lorenzo Dow, 294, 350
Young, Mary, 300
Young, Mary Ann Angell, 284–85, 300–301
Young, Miriam Works, 300
Young, Phineas, 350
Young, S. Dilworth, 486
Young, Thomas, 44, 45
Young, Vilate, 300

effects of, 173–75; Sylvester Smith hearings and, 175–78; second, 178–79; visions received during, 191n38; Quorum of the Twelve and, 193n53

Z

Zelph, vision of, 191n38
Zion: revelation on, 79, 88, 92–93; gathering to, 82–83, 88; location of, 83–84; foundation of, 85–87; consecration and, 87–88; expulsion from, 138–48, 153
Zion's Camp: description of event, 153–57; begins journey, 163–66, 190n23; hardships of, 166–71; cholera outbreak and, 171–73, 192nn43–44, 196;

Acknowledgments

We appreciate our associates in the Religious Studies Center (RSC) at Brigham Young University for their tremendous efforts in bringing this project to a successful conclusion. We especially want to thank R. Devan Jensen, Brent R. Nordgren, and Joany O. Pinegar. Transforming oral presentations into polished chapters with notes could not have been done without the help of these three but particularly Devan's efforts.

Additionally, we are grateful for the RSC student editors, research assistants, and designers, including Kristin Call, Caitlin S. Channer, Jacob F. Frandsen, Amanda Kae Fronk, James D. Jensen, Christopher C. Jones, Rachael L. Moore, Kipp S. Muir, Jonathon R. Owen, Rosalind E. Ricks, Dayna K. Thomas, and Benjamin H. Tingey, for their various contributions to this project.

We are grateful for the cooperation of Gary L. Bauer, R. Neil Carlile, and H. Bruce Payne of Brigham Young

University's Continuing Education Adult Religion Classes program in allowing us to organize the "Joseph Smith's Prophetic Ministry" lecture series on which this book is based.

Cory H. Maxwell, our friend at Deseret Book, facilitated the taping of the lecture series to allow us to expand the audience well beyond the walls of the auditorium in the Conference Center on the BYU campus.

Finally, we appreciate the contribution of our colleagues Ronald O. Barney, Alexander L. Baugh, Ronald K. Esplin, J. Spencer Fluhman, William G. Hartley, Andrew H. Hedges, Robert L. Millet, Grant Underwood, and Robert J. Woodford. They took time from their busy research, writing, and teaching schedules to inspire those who heard their presentations at BYU or through the CD collection. The additional sacrifices in helping us turn their oral presentations into written essays are much appreciated. Without their thoughtful contributions, there would have been no lecture series, no CD collection, and no book.